NEST

ABOUT TRUCK
Making Things / Making the Store / TRUCK FURNITURE

THE PATH TO TRUCK
Tokuhiko Kise / Hiromi Karatsu

LONGING FOR A NEST

Searching for Land
Asahi Ward, Shinmori
Laying the Foundation

LONGING FOR TREES
Thinking about Trees / Tree Rescue / Planting Trees

Completing the House and Store
New Address
Opening TRUCK and Bird

— Bird Paper —

TRUCK NEST

City Trees, Fallen Leaves
Birds of the Garden
Living Here

窓からスズメが見える。小枝に止まって忙しそうに羽繕いしている。
庭に置いたベンチの上、ふわふわのクッションでジョンとジャックが気持ちよさそうに寝ている。
夢でも見ているのか時々前足がピクッと動く。ディンゴが意味もなく穴を掘る。
ジュニアがボールを投げろと持って来る。
Birdからはコーヒーのいい香り。微かに木を削る音。
ここに来て２年が経ち、以前からずっとそうだったかのように見える。

マギーに教えてもらった"NEST"という言葉とその意味。
そんな場所が欲しいと考え、形にしてきた日々。
すっかり馴染んでしまっているけど、ここでちょっと振り返ってみたいと思う。

I see a sparrow sitting on a nearby branch, busily preening its feathers.
Our dogs, John and Jack, lie sleeping on the bench.
They look like they're dreaming.
From time to time one of their legs twitches, then goes still.
Dingo is in another corner of the garden, digging a hole.
Not for any particular purpose, it seems, just to dig.
Junior is standing there, a baseball in his mouth, hoping for a game of fetch.
The pleasing aroma of coffee drifts over from Bird.
There is a dim sound of wood being worked.
It's only been here for two years, but it feels like it's been here much longer.

Margie had explained what she meant by the word "nest".
We thought that was the kind of place we wanted, and have been working continuously to bring it to actuality.
It feels like we have been here for ages, and that the place has been here longer.
Let's step back to where it started.

UNDER THE TREE

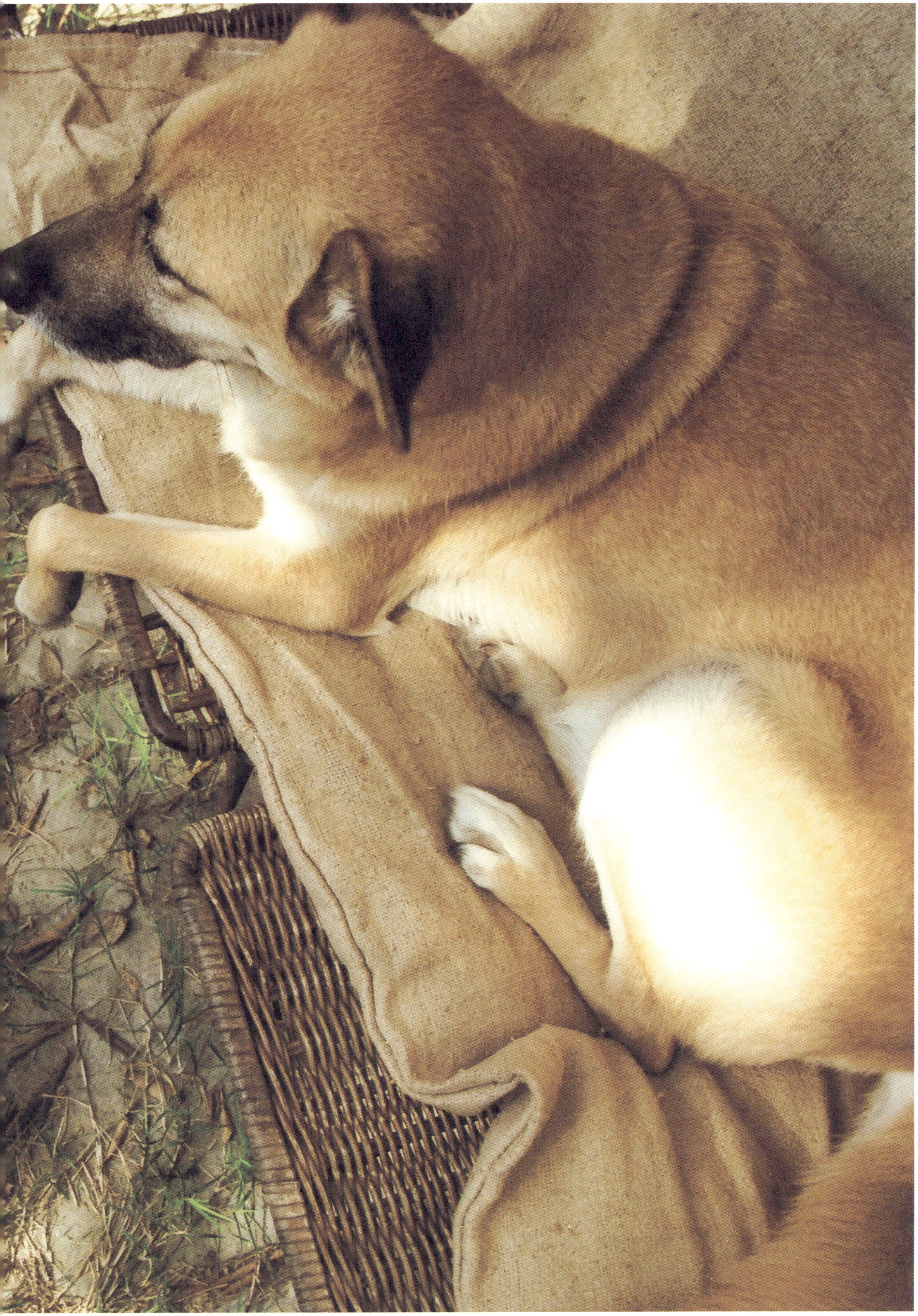

CONTENTS

8	To Noosa, Australia	オーストラリア・ヌーサへ
42	NEST	NEST
57	ABOUT TRUCK	ABOUT TRUCK
84	—About Me - Tokuhiko Kise	僕のこと
88	—About Me - Hiromi Karatsu	私のこと
100	Searching for Land	土地探し
108	Asahi Ward, Shinmori	旭区新森
118	Planning the House and Store	家と店を考える
136	Laying the Foundation	着工から上棟
166	Thinking about Trees	樹を考える
176	Tree Rescue	団地の樹、救出作戦
186	Planting Trees	樹を植える
204	Completing the House and Store	家と店を仕上げる
232	Moving House	家の引っ越し
268	Opening TRUCK and Bird	TRUCK、Bird オープン
	—Bird Paper— Photo by Keigo Saito	Bird Paper
321	TRUCK NEST	TRUCK NEST
340	City Trees, Fallen Leaves	街の樹、落ち葉
364	Birds of the Garden	庭の鳥たち
376	Living Here	住んでから
394	Afterword	あとがき

TRUCK nest

A RECORD: NINE YEARS IN THE MAKING

Approx. 385 PICTURES   21 STORIES   400 PAGES

Text and Photos by TRUCK

First Edition 2012

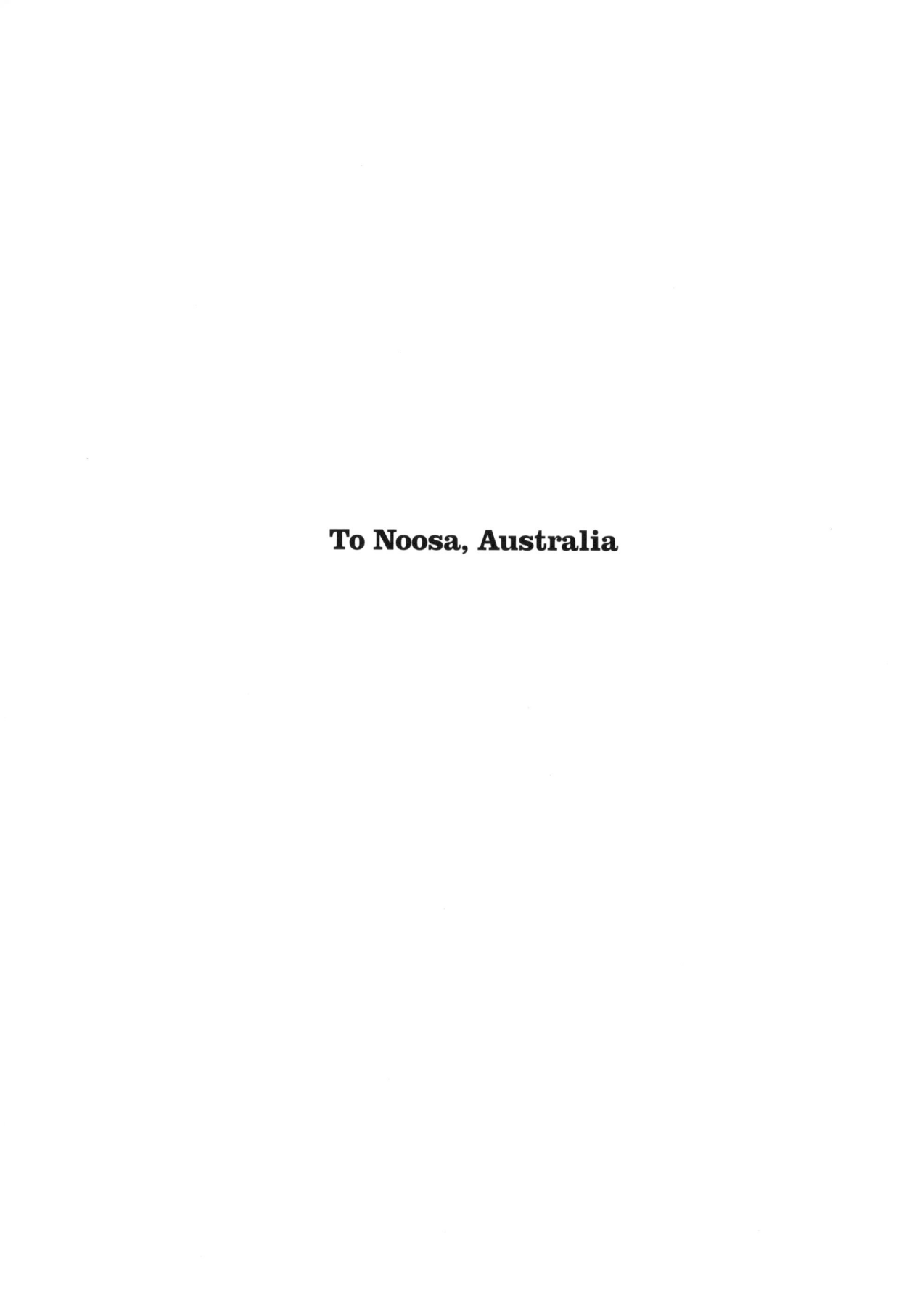

To Noosa, Australia

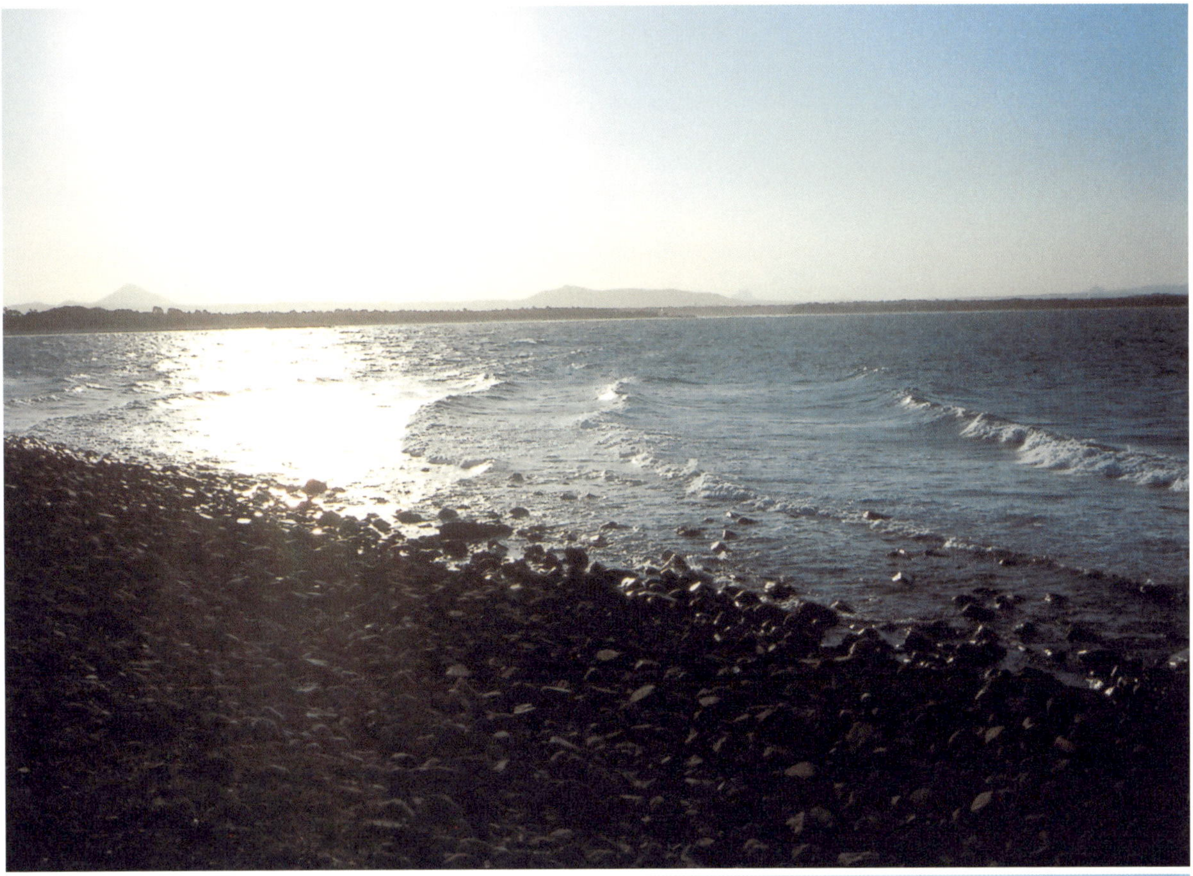

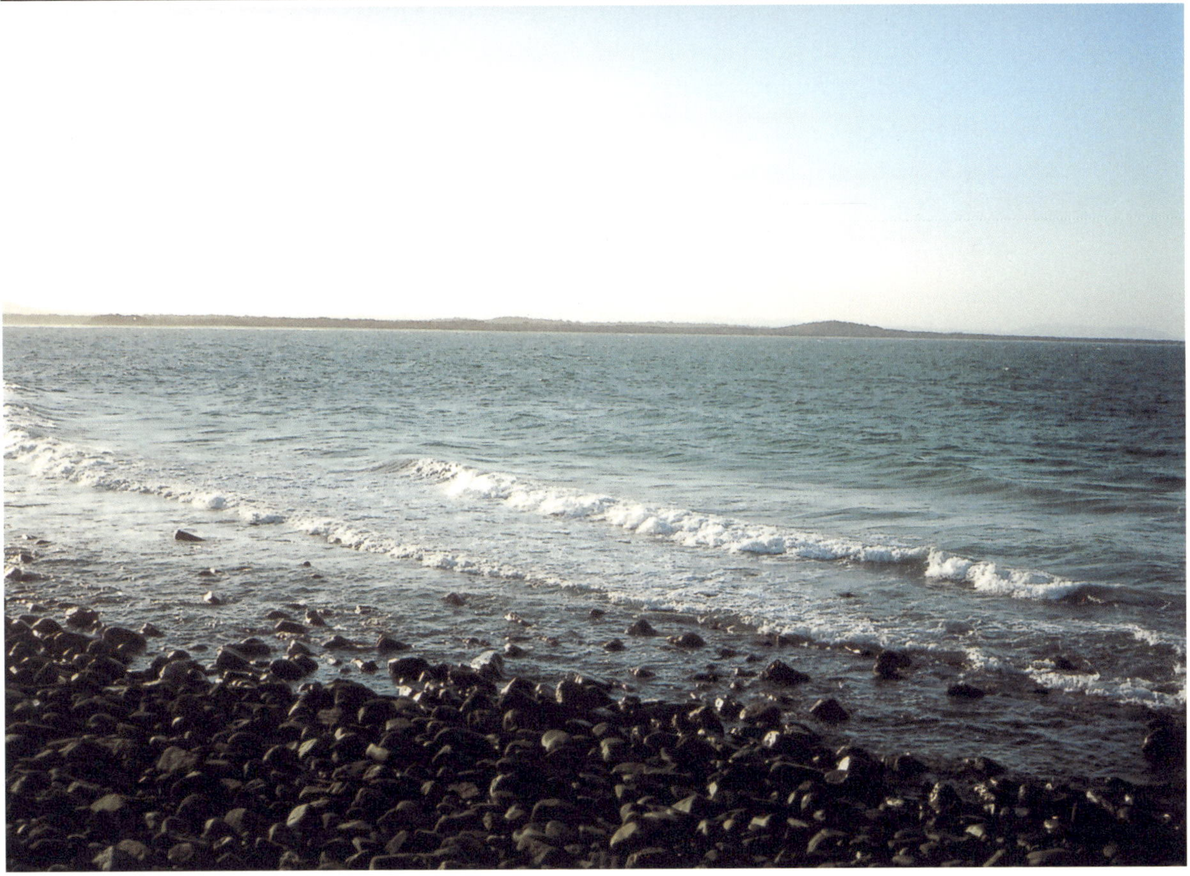

オーストラリア・ヌーサへ

「えっ？今日もフラット？マジで！」毎週のように大阪から伊勢まで、片道3時間運転して通っていた頃、4週連続で波がなかった。サーフィンを30代半ばを過ぎてから始めた。始めたのが遅い。早く上手くなりたかった。毎晩、イメトレのため、ビデオを見ながらバランスボードに乗る。毎日1kmクロールで泳ぐ。陸上でできることはいろいろ取り入れた。でも、サーフィンは波がないとどうしようもない。スキーならスキー場に行けば（もちろん雪があれば）、ボウリングもボウリング場に行けば練習できる。ちょっと勝手が違う。
面白くないから帰り道のコンビニで、おなかが減ったわけでもないのに、いろんなものを買い込んで半ばやけ食い？状態。全然サーフィンライフじゃない。こんなことしてたら40歳になってしまう。

そんな時、雑誌にオーストラリアのヌーサという所の記事があり、そこにカリフォルニアから移り住んだサーファーでありシェーパーのトム・ウェグナーのことが紹介されていた。トムの楽しそうな生活、そして何よりもそこに書かれていたのは、条件が揃えば2kmもの間、波に乗れるということ。脚がだるくなるくらい。歩いて戻るのもしんどいと。
えぇっ!! そんな所があるのか？ 行きたい！ 絶対行く。行くしかない。と心に決めた。そして上手くなって帰って来よう。

同時に考えたこと。それは、どうせ行くならこのトムに会いたい。それも行く前から知り合っておきたい。そこで、トムの作ったサーフボードを売っている店を鎌倉に見つけて買いに行った。
手に入れたサーフボードと愛犬バディ、ひりんこと一緒に写った自分の写真を自己紹介の文に添えて送った。
すると嬉しいことにトムから返事が来た。何回かやり取りをしているうちにトムは、僕が家具を作っているのを知って、日本の鉋とノコギリが欲しいと言ってきた。誰かにひとつもらったのを使っていて、すごく調子がいいんだと。その頃トムはフォームではなく木を削ってサーフボードを作り出していた。
そんなことならお易い御用と、トムが使っている木が桐であることを確認。そして金物屋に走って行き、やわらかい桐を削るのに適した鉋3つをカスタマイズした。そして出来上がった鉋、ノコギリ、砥石2種類を持ってひりんことケンタロウの3人で飛んだ。

2003年11月。冬の日本から真夏のオーストラリアへ。
このオーストラリア行きが、
後に僕とひりんこの生き方に大きく影響することとなる。

To Noosa, Australia

初めてのヌーサ。空港でレンタカーを借り、トムの家までブルースハイウェイを走る。2時間も行けば、雑誌で見てあこがれていたあの風景が目の前にあった。トムと奥さんのマギー、息子のフィンリー、そしてまだ赤ちゃんだったサンデーが迎えてくれた。懐かしい友達に会ったかのように、温かく。

広い敷地には家とサーフボードを作る作業場が隣接、庭にはハーブや野菜が育てられていた。

しばらくいろんなことをしゃべった。自分たちのこと、TRUCKのこと。
そしてケンタロウも自己紹介。「料理の鉄人」に出演した話になり、オーストラリアのTVでも「IRON CHEF」という番組名で放送され、トムたちも見ていたらしく話は盛り上がる。それから鉋とノコギリを渡し、鉋の研ぎ方を伝える。しばらくトムの家で過ごした後、これから一緒に海に行こう！となった。

To Noosa, Australia

トムのワーゲンにケンタロウが乗り、僕とひりんこは後ろからついて走る。ヌーサの海まで約30分、トムの車を追いながら、トムに会えたこと、話せたこと、感動興奮を噛み締めた。そして、今からトムと一緒にヌーサの海でサーフィン！まだまだ続く興奮と少しの緊張。丘を上りきった所で視界が開けた。海が見えた。初めて見るヌーサの海。遠く縞しまに波が見える。
トムは窓から腕を出しガッツポーズと共に「イェー!!」と叫んだ。少し驚いた。「え？ 毎日こんな波を見てるんちゃうん？ 毎日見てもあれだけ叫べるってこと？」海に着いてからも何度もトムは「ラッキー」と言う。少し不思議だった。期待通りのきれいな波。人も少ない。最高。（その後4回目のヌーサで初めて分かったこと。それは11月は普通、波のない時期で、本当に「ラッキー」だったのだ。トムも叫ぶほど）

3人がこの3週間滞在するのは、トムが「自分がビジターとしてヌーサに来るならここに泊まりたい」と教えてくれた、海から100mくらいの所にあるジャングルのような緑に埋もれるように建っている一軒家。
すぐそこの樹には1mほどもある大トカゲがいる。ターキー（七面鳥）がそこらへんをウロウロしている。ユーカリの樹ではコアラが昼寝、クッカブラ（ワライカワセミ）の声が響く。

毎日、朝5時にケンタロウと僕は起床。コーヒーでまだ眠たい頭を無理矢理起こし、少しでもパドルの足しになればと、エナジーを補充。バナナやシリアル、V8、ミロバー。冷蔵庫にある材料でケンタロウがサンドイッチを作る。2つは、腹ペコで海から上がった時の僕たちのパクつき用。そしてもう1つは、後で起きてくるひりんこの朝ご飯として、テーブルの上に置いて行く。ケンタロウが書いたメモを添えて。"ひりんこの分 HAVE FUN！"
男2人は昼過ぎまでサーフィン。

ひりんこは好きな時間に起きて、日本からどっさり持って来た画材道具とコーヒーとサンドイッチを、日射しが照りつけるベランダのテーブルに運び、生い茂った植物の匂いを嗅ぎながら、野鳥の声を聞きながら絵を描く。
TRUCKを始めてからバタバタとした毎日、絵を描く時間をなくしていたひりんこにとっても貴重な時間。
動物が好きなひりんこは、パン屑をベランダから点々と部屋の中まで並べて、ターキーをどんどん部屋の中に誘い込んでみたり、30cmはあるクッカブラを手なずけて触ってみたりも！

午後からは3人でランチに出かけ、スーパーで買い出し。調味料から食材、おやつ、歯ブラシに洗剤、ティッシュ…たくさん買い込む。どこにいてもこの3人、はしゃぎっぱなし。まるで小学生の兄弟みたい。夜中までずーっとたわいもない話で盛り上がる。
小さな町にはレストランもいくつかあるけど、晩ご飯はだいたい家で食べる。素晴らしいまかないシェフがいるんやから。みんなでわいわい買い出しに行ってキッチンで作って食べるのが楽しい。

ある日、トムからバーベキューに誘われた。
川沿いの公園、川から大きなペリカンが触れそうな距離まで近づいて来る。そこにさり気なくある作業台のようなもの。その天板にはグリルがある。そして、少し下にある丸い緑のボタン。それを押すと火がつく。衝撃的！
何の説明もない。もちろん無料。
もしこれが日本だったらどうだろう。
管理事務所に予め予約をし、時間制の料金を支払い、説明や注意書きの用紙を渡されたり、
「熱いので注意！」「ゴミはゴミ箱に」「後の人のためにきれいに使いましょう」「マナーを守って気持ちよく」
なんて看板に取り囲まれる。にもかかわらずゴミ箱からはゴミが溢れていたりする。多分。

嫌なものが1つもない気持ちのいい川沿いでバーベキュー。「友達のブッチャー（肉屋さん）からおいしいソーセージをもらってきた」とマギー。いいやん。いいやん。期待が膨らむ。ソーセージを焼く。焼いてない四角い食パンに包んで食べる。おいしい！最高！そして次、ソーセージを焼く。え？また？って思いつつ、種類が違うのかなと考える。食べる。うん。おいしい。違いはそんなに分からない。
さあ次。またまた見た目もそっくりなソーセージ。ちょっとびっくり。3回連続。それだけ!?
これが日本だったらどうだろう。いろんな種類の肉や野菜、魚介やら焼きそば、もちろんソーセージも。
でも、このシンプルさが潔くて気持ちいい。もちろんすごくおいしい。それとビール。じゅうぶん楽しい時間。
別にこれ以上必要ない。

夜、トムの家。みんなでくつろいでいたらマギーに「すごくいいものを見せてあげる！」と奥の部屋に案内された。「しーっ」静かにというジェスチャーをしながらドアを開ける。ベビーベッドに小さな金髪のサンデーが眠っている。「ね!!ビューティフルでしょ！」自分の子供の寝顔をこんなに嬉しそうに、キラキラした目で披露してくれるこの人は、最高にステキなお母さんだと、当時まだ子供がいない僕たちでさえそう思った。

トムの家の庭、広々とした敷地に大きな樹がたくさんある。樹の下でマギーと話していた時、上のほうに鳥の巣を見つけた。

マギーは教えてくれた。巣を英語でNESTということ。そして、オーストラリアでは、赤ちゃんを身ごもったお母さんの大きなおなかもNEST。生まれてくる赤ちゃんを心待ちに肌着などを用意するのもNEST。あったかい寝床からそっと抜け出した後のこんもりとした布団。さらに、家の中に心地いい場所を設えること、などの意味があるらしい。家具を作っている自分たちが考えていることにピッタリな言葉だ。
ひりんこと2人、この"NEST"という言葉がすごく心に残った。

To Noosa, Australia

Margie explaining the word "nest"

To Noosa, Australia

「簡単でおいしく、かつ洒落っ気があって現実的なもの」がモットーのイカした料理家ケンタロウ。どこで何を食べてもいつも楽しい。ムズカシイことぬき！
Kentaro is a chef whose motto is "Food that is practical, fun, delicious, and simple." He enjoys whatever he eats, wherever he eats it.

To Noosa, Australia

楽しく過ごした日々が過ぎ、ケンタロウがひと足先に日本に帰った。
ぽっかりと穴があいたような気持ちになった夕方、ひりんこと2人、何をするでもなく歩いて海を見に行った。海のそばに置いてあるテーブルとベンチ、そこでワインを飲んでいる年配の夫婦の姿があった。特別オシャレとかではない。短パンにTシャツ。でも、ちゃんとワイングラスとボトルワイン。すごく気になったけど横を通り過ぎ、少し離れた波打ち際まで下りて行って、しばらく海を見て過ごした。
さあ、そろそろ帰ろうと振り返ると、さっきの夫婦がまだそのまま座っていた。
僕は話しかけてみた。彼の名前はジョン。そして奥さんのキャッシー。
ジョン曰く、
「今日は朝5時から仕事を頑張ったので、ちょっと夕日を見ながらワインを飲みに来たんだ」
ぐっときた。なんてステキなんだろう。日常的な生活の中のこんな時間の過ごし方。

TRUCKを立ち上げ、これまで毎日おかげさまで忙しくしてきた。
朝から晩まで仕事。子供もいなかったから夜遅くなってもお構いなし。夕方なんて意識してなかった。忘れていた。以前は、細かく言えば、16歳で一眼レフのカメラを手に入れてからは、よく夕日を見ていたしオートバイで追いかけたりもしていたのに。
ちょっとしたこと、ジョンみたいな夕方の時間を持てること。これこそが豊かな生活だと思った。"豊か"なんて言葉、今まで使ったこともなかったけど。
ジョンと別れ、家に戻ったら無性にワインが飲みたくなった。ワインを買いに出たらジョンたちはまだそこにいた。お薦めのオーストラリアワインを聞いてみた。すごく親切にあれこれ教えてもらった。が、最後に「うちに来て一緒に飲む？」と言ってくれた。ジョンの家はなんと、僕たちの借りている家の並び2軒隣だった。

ジョンの家も僕たちの家と同じように樹々に覆われていた。
木造のさり気ない佇まいのその家は、周りの樹々に馴染んで、長年使い込んだ良さがあった。なんとも言えないいい雰囲気だった。
中に入ると、少し雑然としているところがかえって使いこなしている風にも見える。入り口（玄関のような構えたものはない）から入って突き当たり、右に曲がり左にキッチンを見て通り抜けると、そこには蚊帳に囲まれたポーチ。
外のような中のような場所。丸いテーブルといくつかの椅子がある。
座ってワインを飲んだ。いろんな話をした。ジョンも若い頃、オートバイでいろんな国を旅したそうだ。キャッシーを後ろに乗せて。古い写真を見せてくれる。また、家の話になると、その素朴で素敵な家を建てた時のことを、当時描いた図面を見せながら聞かせてくれる。ジョンが設計したという。
気がつくと、陽はほとんど沈み、だいぶん暗くなっていた。

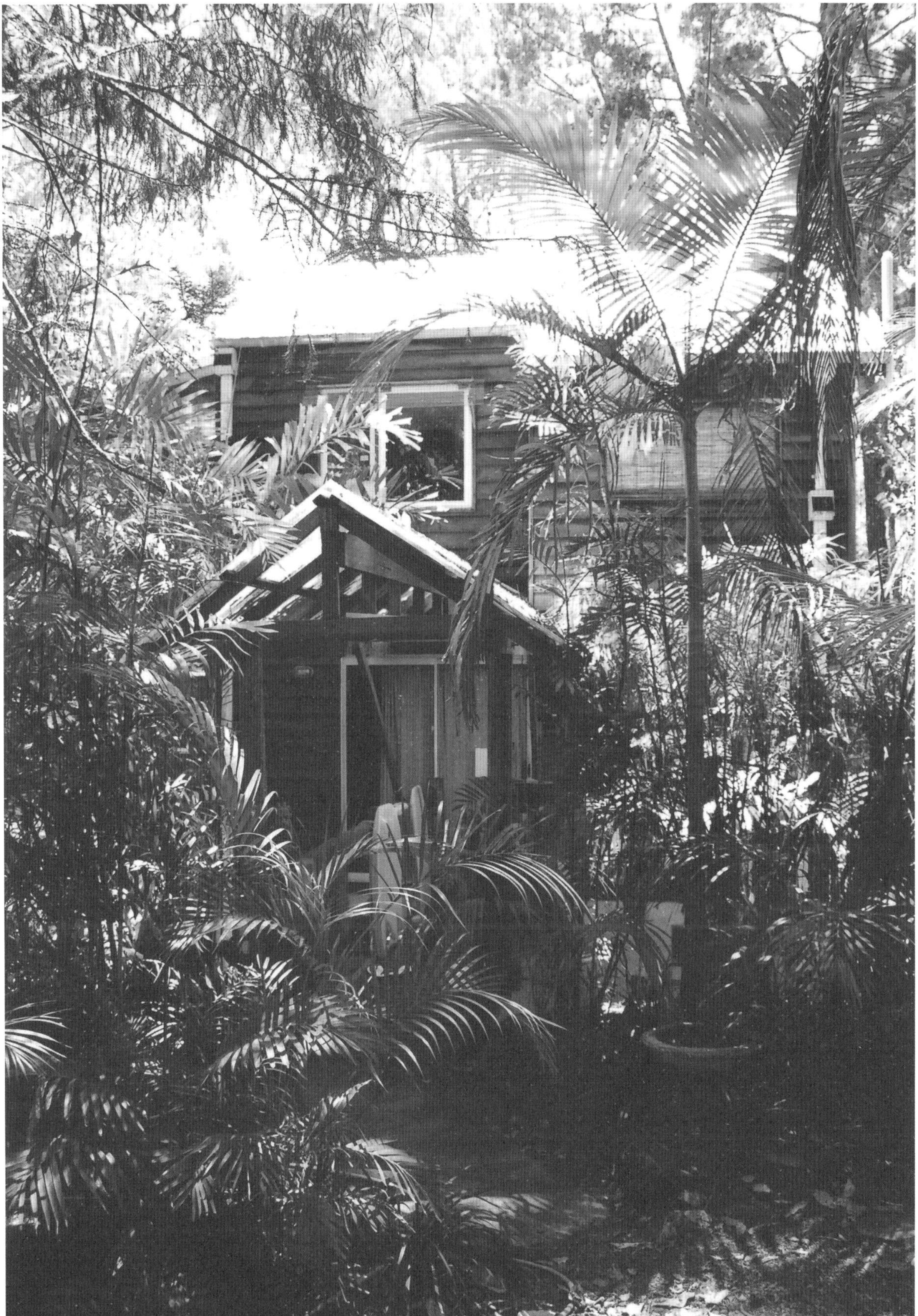

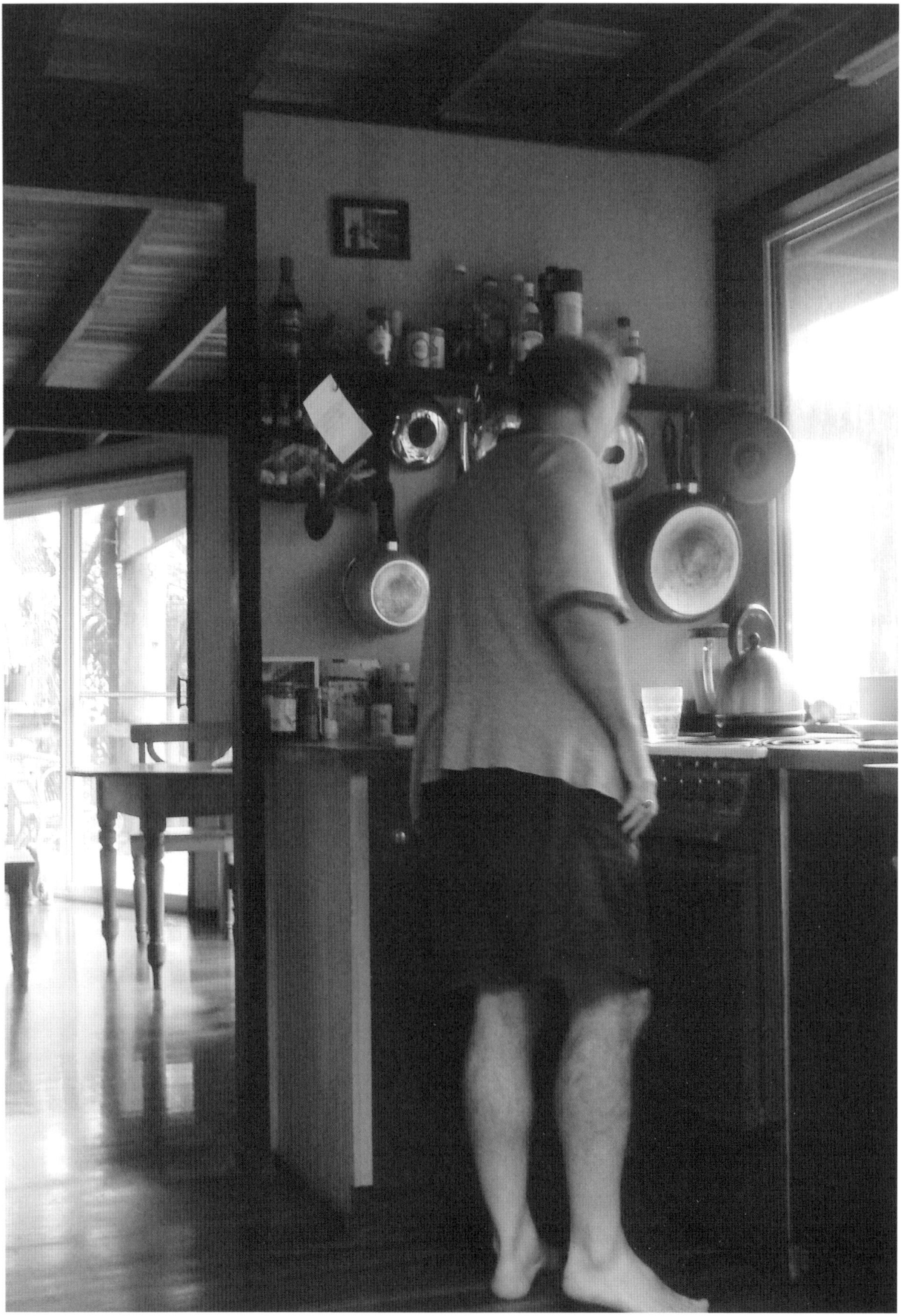

To Noosa, Australia

「ご飯、食べていく？」とジョン。そして1人キッチンに立った。冷蔵庫を開けたり、何かを洗ったりしながら、キャンドルを部屋のあちこちに灯し、照明の具合を調節したり、山積みされたCDから「うーん。どれがいいかな？」と音楽を選んだり、いろいろと忙しそうに家の中を行ったり来たりしている。
決してスマートではない。でも、全ての動きが見ていて楽しそう。
そんな間、キャシーはずっと僕たちの横に座ったままで、気にもせず話を続ける。「今日はジョンの番だから」と当たり前のように言う。それがまた良かった。慣れた感じ。
あっという間にジョンが作ってくれたご飯。ワンプレートに2、3種類何かが盛られていた。何だったかは思い出せない。特別な何かではなく、さり気ないもの。それが良かった。

朝から海でサーフィン。夕方は、ジョンに教えてもらった市民プール。その屋外にある50mプールで泳いだ。深さもしっかりある本気競技仕様。いくつかのレーンでは、イアン・ソープもいるかも、と思うぐらいの選手たちが練習している。かと思えば、そのすぐ横のレーンでは、子供たちが走り回ったり飛び込んだり。そう、飛び込んでる。
「走らないで！」とか「飛び込み禁止」なんて注意書きは1枚もない。ついでに、ロッカーもない。脱いだ服は壁のフックに掛けておく。

遠くに山のライン、周りは樹々に囲まれ、西日でピンクになった空。そんな中、クロールで10往復のノルマをこなした。1人で泳ぎ、心地いい気怠さを感じながら家までの道、車を走らせる。まだ空には、おおかた沈んだ太陽からの光が残っていて息を飲むほどきれい。
丘を上る道に差しかかった時、スピーカーから山崎まさよしの「未完成」が聞こえてきた。あまりにもピッタリで、その後、そこを通る度にその曲になるように仕込んだけど、なかなかタイミングが合わない。
それ以来、僕たちの中で、この曲が入ったアルバム「アトリエ」がヌーサの定番となった。

ヌーサには信号がほとんどない。大抵がランダバウト、時計回りに回るロータリー。ドライバーは自分で確認し、他の車が来ないタイミングで進む。信号機もいらないし、他の車がいないのに停まっていることもない。横断歩道は少し盛り上がっていて、車は自然に速度を落とす。歩行者がいれば、どの車も当たり前のように停まる。歩行者は「ありがとう」と渡って行く。
海から突き出たような半島がある。全体が森林公園になっていて、気持ちいい海沿いの道を、半島の先端に向かって森の中を進んで行くと、視界が開けて、アカプルコばりの切り立った断崖絶壁に出る。
そんな所でさえも、柵がない。看板や注意書きも何もない。あるのはそこにある風景だけ。公園のスイッチを押すだけで火がつくバーベキューもそうだし、全てが上手く機能している。そんなことをしみじみ考えると、こんな国なら税金も払いたいと思える。生かして使ってくれそう。
日本の国や自治体のエラい人たちは、税金を使って海外視察に出ていったい何を見ているのだろう。

To Noosa, Australia

日本に帰り、またいつもの仕事に追われる日々が始まった。
忙しく仕事ができること、それはとてもありがたいこと。店をオープンして1年目は、休んでる場合じゃないと無休で働いた。その後、定休日を作ったけど、実際に休む日は少ない。朝起きてから夜遅くまで仕事、あとは寝てまた朝が来て。でも、これでいいのか？こんな生活で魅力ある家具が作れるのか？

初めてのヌーサ体験ではいろんなことを考えさせられた。
たくさんの大きな樹々、シンプルなご飯、夕方の時間、よく機能した街。
ジョンが家で音楽をかけたり、キャンドルを灯したりして空間の演出を楽しんでいた姿。
マギーが教えてくれた"NEST"。
そんなことがすごく豊かに思えた。
今まで意識したことがなかった言葉"豊かさ"。
あのヌーサ以来、僕とひりんこは「豊かさとは？」と漠然と考えるようになった。
この時から、それまでとは何かが静かに、でも確かに変わり始めていた。

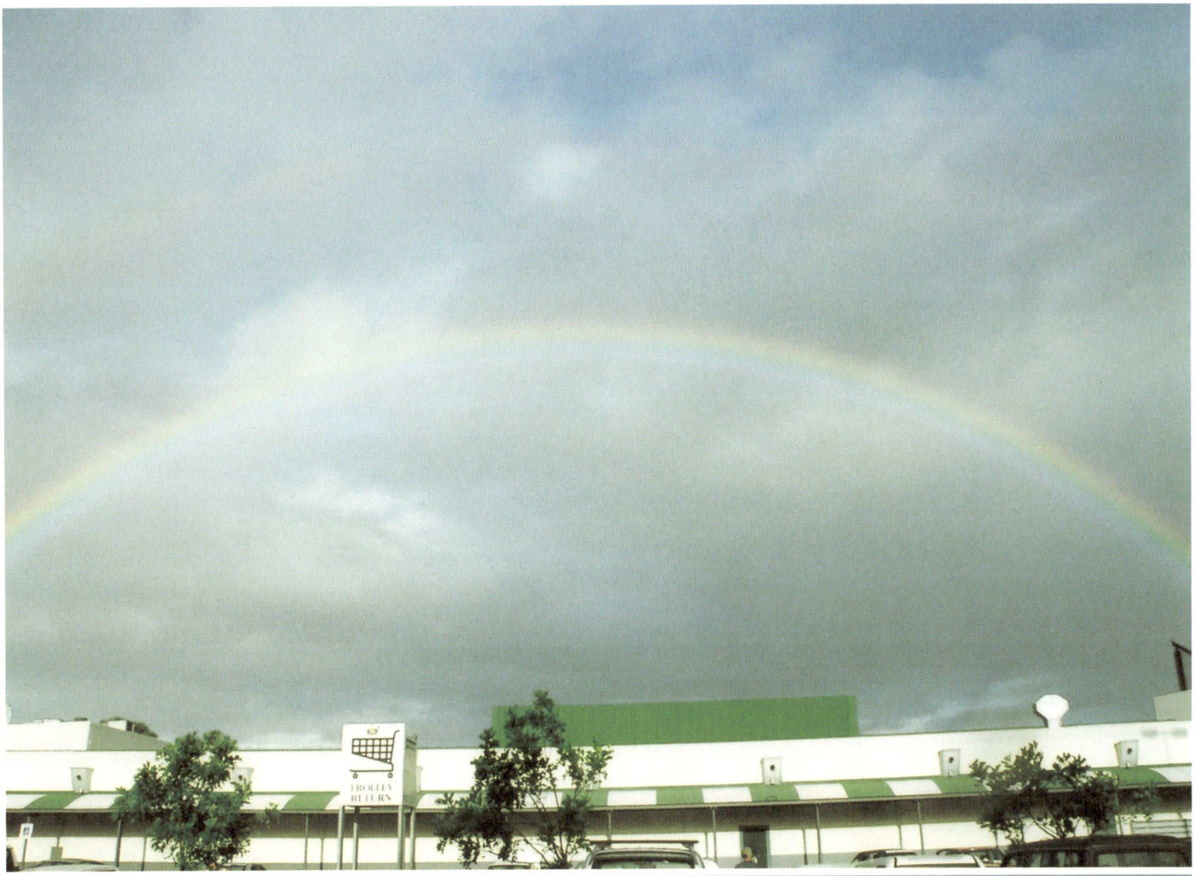
TROLLEY
RETURN

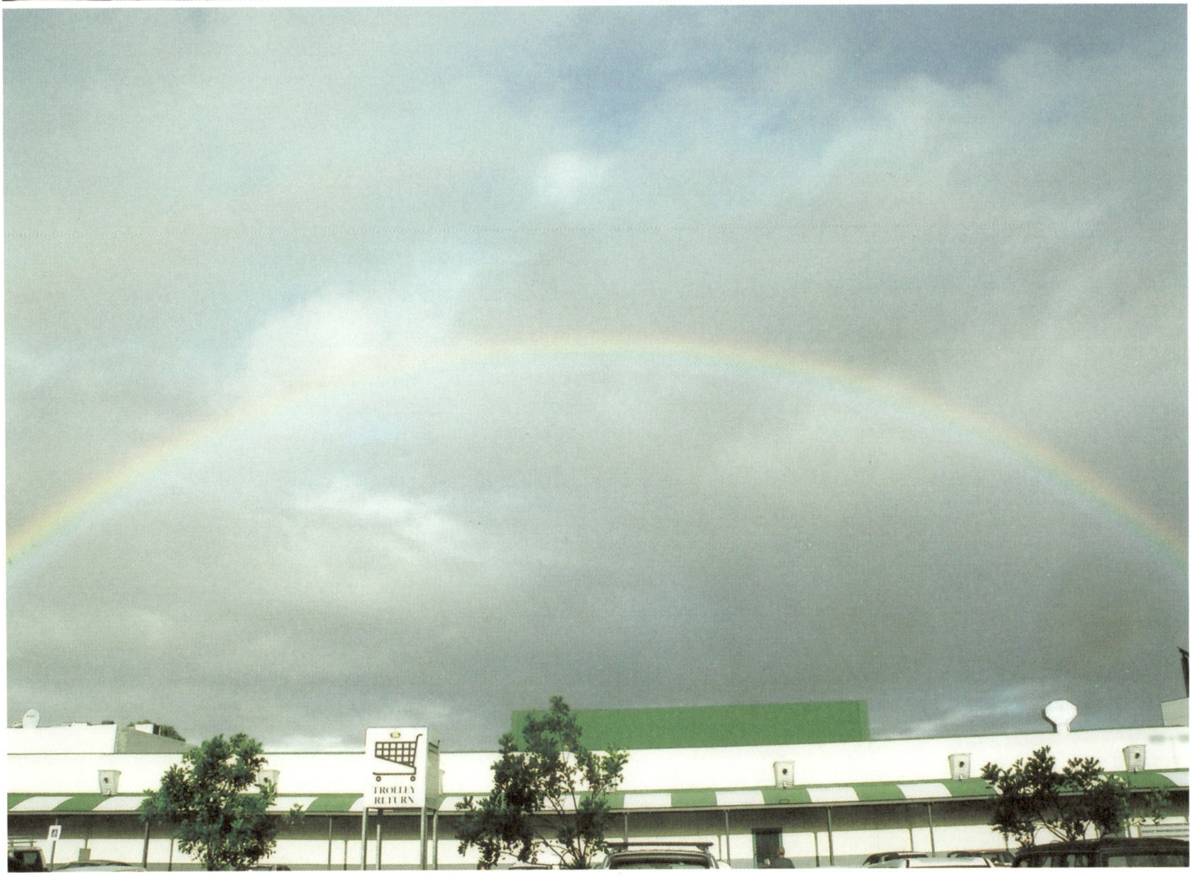
TROLLEY
RETURN

To Noosa, Australia

"What? Flat again today. Really?"

Back when I used to make the three hour drive from Osaka to Ise, there were four weeks in a row with no good waves. I had started surfing fairly late, in my mid-thirties, so I wanted to get up to speed as quickly as possible. I watched surfing videos every night while standing on a balance board, and swam about a kilometer every day, but I couldn't practice if there were no waves. If I'd wanted to learn skiing, I just had to go to a ski slope (if there was snow, of course). If it were bowling, I could just head to a bowling lane. It wasn't working out as I'd hoped. Before I knew it, I'd be forty, and still a beginning surfer.

It was around that time that I saw an article about Tom Wegener, a Californian surfer and surfboard shaper who had moved to Noosa, a town in Australia. He said that if conditions were good, you could ride a wave for two kilometers, long enough for your legs to go numb and make it tiring to walk back. If there really were such a place then I definitely wanted to go. I decided that I would.

If I went to Noosa, I thought I'd also like to meet Tom. I wanted to get in touch with him before I went, though. I tracked down a shop in Kamakura that had one of his boards in stock and took a photo of myself, Hiromi, and Buddy, with the board. I sent it off in an email and was very happy when he replied. We sent a few messages back and forth and when he heard that I was a furniture maker, he told me that he had been looking for a Japanese plane and handsaw. He'd been given one by a friend and really liked the feel. At that time, Tom was starting to make boards from wood rather than foam. I contacted a hardware store and had them custom-make three planes suitable for the soft paulownia wood Tom was using. When they were ready I packed them up with some handsaws, two kinds of whetstones and set off to Noosa with Hiromi and my friend Kentaro. This was in November 2003, winter in Japan, but summer in Australia. Our experiences on this trip would shape our lifestyle and thinking in the years to come.

When we arrived at Brisbane airport, we rented a car and set off along the Bruce Highway to Tom's place. After a two hour drive we ended up in a place with scenery that looked like something out of a magazine. We were welcomed by Tom, his wife Margie, his son Finley, and their newborn daughter Sunday. They gave us the kind of warm welcome you might expect from old friends. Their house shared the grounds with Tom's surfboard workshop and a garden full of herbs and vegetables.

We chatted for a while about ourselves and TRUCK. Kentaro introduced himself and we talked about Iron Chef, the Japanese cooking program he had once appeared on. Tom and his family had watched it when it had been broadcast in Australia and were excited to meet him. I showed Tom the tools I had brought with me and taught him the correct way to sharpen the plane. After a while we set off for the beach together.

Kentaro got a lift in Tom's wagon and Hiromi and I followed behind in our rental car. As we drove to the ocean I was very excited. We were in Noosa, had met Tom, and were about to go surfing with him. After about 30 minutes, we neared the ocean. We crested a hill and got our first glimpse of the Noosa waves. Tom punched the air through the window and shouted "Yeah!". I was a bit surprised. Didn't he see this kind of surf every day? Did he shout out like that every time? When we actually arrived at the beach he kept telling us that we were "lucky" which I also thought was a bit strange. The waves were as good as I had expected and there were very few people. It was great.

It wasn't until we had visited another three times that I understood why Tom had shouted. It turns out that November is usually a pretty bad time for surfing.

Tom had recommended a place for us to stay that was nestled amid jungle-like greenery about 100m from the ocean. "If I were to come to Noosa as a visitor," he said "this is where I'd want to stay." The forest was full of wildlife; lizards more than a meter long, wild turkeys wandering around, koalas sleeping in eucalyptus trees, and kookaburras sitting, laughing in the trees.

Every morning, Kentaro and I got up at five o'clock, forcing ourselves awake with coffee. To give us energy for the day's surfing, we gobbled down bananas, cereal, V8, and Milo Bars. Kentaro pulled all kinds of food from the fridge and made three sandwiches, two to keep us going while we surfed, and one for Hiromi, who would wake later. Kentaro attached a note to hers that said "For Hiromi, have fun!" Then we headed to the beach to surf until the early afternoon.

Hiromi woke when she wanted and took the sandwich, some coffee, and the painting supplies she'd brought from Japan out to the verandah. There, surrounded by the calls of wild birds she painted the morning away. For Hiromi, who'd been so busy since we started TRUCK that she'd had no free time to paint, this was a very important time. Sometimes she made a trail of bread crumbs from the verandah into the house and watched the wild turkeys follow it in. She also got to touch a kookaburra that had landed on the verandah.

In the afternoon, we headed out to have lunch and go shopping at the nearby supermarket. We bought food, condiments and other supplies. We went everywhere together, probably looking like three excited children. Every night we stayed up late, talking and laughing. Although it was a small town, there were quite a few restaurants. Usually, though, being lucky enough to have a wonderful chef with us, we ate at home, enjoying the fantastic things Kentaro made.

One day, Tom invited us for a barbecue. The park we went to was next to a river, from which came a pelican who wandered over to have a look at us, almost near enough for us to touch. In the park there was something that looked like a work bench. In the middle there was a grill, and underneath was a green button. If you pushed the button it lit the fire. I was quite surprised. It was free and so simple. There were no instructions anywhere.
"What would this be like if it were Japan?" I wondered. You'd first have to contact the park superintendent and make a reservation. There would be a time limit and you'd have to pay an hourly fee, as well. While you were eating you'd be surrounded by signs warning you that the hotplate was hot or reminding you to be sure to throw your rubbish away. The rubbish bins would probably be overflowing.

As we were getting set up Margie said "I got some delicious sausages from my friend's butcher." We looked forward eagerly to tasting them. Once the sausages were cooked we wrapped them in a slice of bread and ate them. They were really delicious. When we finished, they cooked some more sausages and we ate them in the same way. They tasted pretty good, too. They were apparently a different type but, to tell the truth, I couldn't tell the difference. I was surprised to see them start to cook another batch of sausages. "Is this all?" I wondered. "Sausages and bread?" If we had a barbecue in Japan we always had a wide variety of meat, seafood, and vegetables. We'd probably also cook some fried noodles as well. But there was something about this simple meal that I really liked. Just the simple sausages, with beer. It was quite enough. There was really no need for anything more.

One night at Tom's place Margie said "I'll show you something wonderful." She led us into the back of the house. Gesturing for us to be quiet, she gently opened the door. There, in the baby bed, her daughter Sunday was sleeping. "Isn't she beautiful?", she said. We didn't have children yet and to see a mother so happy looking at her daughter struck us deeply.

In Tom's garden there were many big trees. We were talking to Margie beneath one of them when she spotted a bird's nest in the branches above. She told us that it was called a nest in English and went on to explain that it had a deeper meaning. It could also describe the womb where an expecting mother's child grew. The phrase "building a nest" was used to talk about all the preparations done to get ready for a new baby, from buying the clothes, to preparing a comfortable bed and blankets. The word seemed to describe what we wanted to do as furniture makers. It left a deep impression on Hiromi and I.

We enjoyed many days together, but eventually Kentaro had to return to Japan. That evening, after we said goodbye, and missing him a little, we wandered down to the beach to look at the ocean. At a table near the beach was an older couple sitting, sipping wine. They were not particularly fashionable, wearing shorts and t-shirts, but I noticed that they were drinking from proper wine glasses. There was something about them that I really liked. We walked past them down to where the waves were breaking on the shore, and sat looking at the sunset. After a while, we decided to head back. The couple were still sitting there, so I decided to say something to them. The man's name was John. His wife was Cathy. He said "I've been working hard since five o'clock this morning, so I came to watch the sun set while drinking wine." His words struck me. "How great!" I thought, "to make time in your everyday life for such a thing."

I had been so busy since we started TRUCK. I worked every day from early in the morning till late at night. I had hardly ever paid attention to sunsets at all. When I was sixteen I had an SLR and used to ride around on my motorcycle looking for beautiful sunsets to photograph. It was something like John taking time to watch the sunset, something I had forgotten. I thought it was an example of a truly rich life. I'd never really thought about that before: what it means to live a rich life.

We returned to the house and soon began to feel like having some wine ourselves. I went out to buy some, and saw John again. I asked him if he could recommend an Australian wine for us to try. He named a few, but finally said "Why don't you come and have a drink at our place." It turned out that John lived on the same street, just two houses down from us.

Like ours, John's house was surrounded by trees. It was made of wood and fit in naturally with its surroundings. It had a warm, well lived-in atmosphere. As you came in the entrance you could see straight through to the other side of the house, where there was a kitchen leading out to a porch enclosed in a mosquito net. Sitting out there at the round table, it felt like being both inside and outside at the same time. We sat there for a while, drinking and talking. John told us that in his youth he had also been interested in motorcycles and had visited many countries to ride. He showed us some old pictures of him on a motorcycle with Cathy sitting behind him. The conversation turned to their simple, wonderful house. John had designed it himself and, as he talked, showed us the blueprints he'd drawn up. Before we knew it, the sun was almost gone and it was getting quite dark.

"Would you like to stay for dinner?" John asked. Then he started getting ready: opening the fridge, washing this and that, lighting candles, adjusting the brightness of the small lights scattered here and there, and choosing the right CD from a tall stack. He looked very busy, coming and going here and there, but seemed to be enjoying himself. Kathy sat with us on the porch. "It's John's turn to get dinner ready tonight," she said. It seemed like a very normal, natural thing for him to be preparing dinner while she sat out here. This helped us relax.

Soon, John finished preparing dinner and brought out the plates. I don't remember exactly what he had made, but I remember it wasn't anything special, just a couple of things on a plate. That he hadn't gone out of his way to make something special made it all the better.

John told me where I could find a public pool and I began to go there in the evenings. It was fifty meters long, of a decent depth, and split into a number of lanes, a true olympic-size pool. Some of the swimmers looked like proper athletes in training. I wouldn't have been surprised if Ian Thorpe had been among them. In the lane beside them were kids messing about. Here, too, I was impressed by the lack of signs saying "Don't run!" or "No Diving!" There weren't any lockers, either. People just hung their clothes on a hook.

The swimming pool was surrounded by trees. In the distance I could see a range of mountains. The sky was pink in the afternoon sun. Most days I swam about ten laps and, feeling nicely exhausted, drove back home. One evening, a little light lingered from the setting sun and the sky was breathtakingly beautiful. As I approached a hill, Masayoshi Yamazaki's song *Unfinished* came from the speakers. It was so fitting. I tried to have that song come on each time I came to that spot, but never again got the timing quite right. The album it came from, *Atelier*, became our favorite to listen to in Noosa.

There were hardly any traffic lights in Noosa. Instead there were roundabouts, so drivers could make their own decisions about when to stop or go. Nobody had to sit waiting at the lights even though there were no other cars around. The pedestrian crossings were raised a little from the rest of the road, so drivers naturally slowed as they approached them. If someone was on or approaching the crossing, they stopped and let them cross.

From Noosa, there's a peninsula covered in lush forest that juts out into the sea. If you follow the path along the sea's edge out to the apex of the peninsula you'll come to an abrupt cliff. What struck me was that there were no barriers and no danger signs to obstruct the view. In a way, it was like the simple green button to start the barbecue in the park. I noticed many things like this and remember them fondly. "If I lived in a country like this," I thought, "I'd be happy to pay taxes." I could actually see the money being used well. It made me wonder about Japanese politicians who use tax money to travel overseas on fact-finding trips. Why didn't they see things like this when they went abroad?

When we returned to Japan, our life quickly got back to its previous work-filled pace. We were grateful to be so busy, though, because we truly enjoyed our work. When we first opened the store we worked every day and were never closed. After a while, we closed once a week, but even then Hiromi and I rarely took a day off.

To Noosa, Australia

This trip made us wonder, though. Was this lifestyle, working from early in the morning till late at night, then waking up and starting again, a good one? Was this the kind of lifestyle that would enable us to make good furniture?

That first trip to Noosa made us think about many things. The many big trees, the simple food, the evening hours, the smoothly running city, listening to music at John's house, enjoying the candlelit ambiance, and Margie teaching us the word "nest".
Hiromi and I began to have a vague conception of something we had not previously considered, what it might mean to have *a rich life*.

Visiting Noosa, green and lush, where we met Tom, Margie, and John, sparked a change in us. A quiet change, but an important one.

Tom

トムのこと

2005年12月、3回目のヌーサ。

今回は、ひりんこが妊婦なので、男2人だけ。僕とケンタロウは、初めに比べると少しはましかもしれないけど、でもなかなか上手くならないサーフィンに挑んでいた。トムは木で作った、フィンもないペラペラのまな板のようなものに凝っていた。いつも海ではその板きれでボディボードのように腹這いになって波に乗っていた。僕とケンタロウにも「やってみろ」と何度も勧める。でも僕たちは1回でも多くサーフボードに乗って少しでも上手くなりたいと思っていたので、そんなに乗り気じゃなかった。

トムはビジネスマンのような顔つきで語った。そのアライヤという板きれで、世界中のボディボードの市場をごっそりいただく！なんて鼻の穴を少し膨らませていた。ケンタロウと僕は、そんなこと無理って心で思っていた。

それがある日、ジェイク（ヌーサに住むナイスガイ）が、その板きれに立って波に乗り、すごいスピードで横に走った。新しい扉が開いた。

日本にいて雑誌などでアライヤを頻繁に目にするようになっていった。正直、ケンタロウと2人、驚いた。そしてなんとトムが、2009年 シェーパー オブ ザ イヤーに選ばれた。すごい‼

その後、訪れたヌーサ。僕たちは勝手に想像していた。栄冠に輝き、アライヤも大ブレイク。トムとマギーの生活もリッチメンに変わり、マギーもメルセデスの奥様カーでショッピングかなと。でも、行ってみると、何も変わっていない。相変わらず、赤いトランクスにビーチサンダルのトムが出迎えてくれた。マギーに「メルセデスに乗ってると思ってた」と言うと、「何も変わってないよ」と笑い「メイビー、ネクストタイム」と。トムに聞くと「僕自身がたくさん作って売るってことには長けていないんだ。それより、みんなが作ったらいいと思うので、作り方のビデオを作ろうと考えている」前に見た、ビジネスマンのような顔は消えていた。なぜかほっとした。

In December 2005, we made our third trip to Noosa. Hiromi was pregnant with Hina, so she stayed at home. It was just Kentaro and I. We had improved a little from our first days of surfing, but we still had much to learn. At the time, Tom was really into finless wooden surfboards that looked like cutting boards. He always used them like body boards, surfing on his stomach. He asked us many times if we wanted to try it. We did, but it really wasn't our thing. We wanted to focus on riding proper surfboards.

Tom often talked about the board, called an Alaia, with his businessman face on. He thought that it would take over the world bodyboard market and was very passionate about it. Kentaro and I both thought it was unlikely. One day, Jake (a nice guy who lived in Noosa) tried riding one of the flat wooden boards while standing. He zoomed off at a terrific speed. It was like new door had opened.

To our surprise, the board soon gained in popularity and began to make frequent appearances even in Japanese magazines. In 2009 Tom was chosen as Shaper of the Year.

Before our next trip to Noosa we imagined all of the changes the success of the Alaia board might have brought to Tom and Margie's lifestyle. Would they have new clothes? A new house? Would Margie be doing her shopping in a Mercedes Benz?

When we got there, nothing had changed. Tom greeted us, as always, in his red swimming trunks and beach sandals. We told Margie we had thought she might be driving a Benz. "No," she said, laughing, "nothing has changed. Maybe next time." Tom said, "I have no talent for making and selling things myself. What I'd like is for everyone to make them. I'm thinking of making a video to show people how." The businessman face he'd previously worn had disappeared. It was something of a relief.

June 10, 2006
Hina

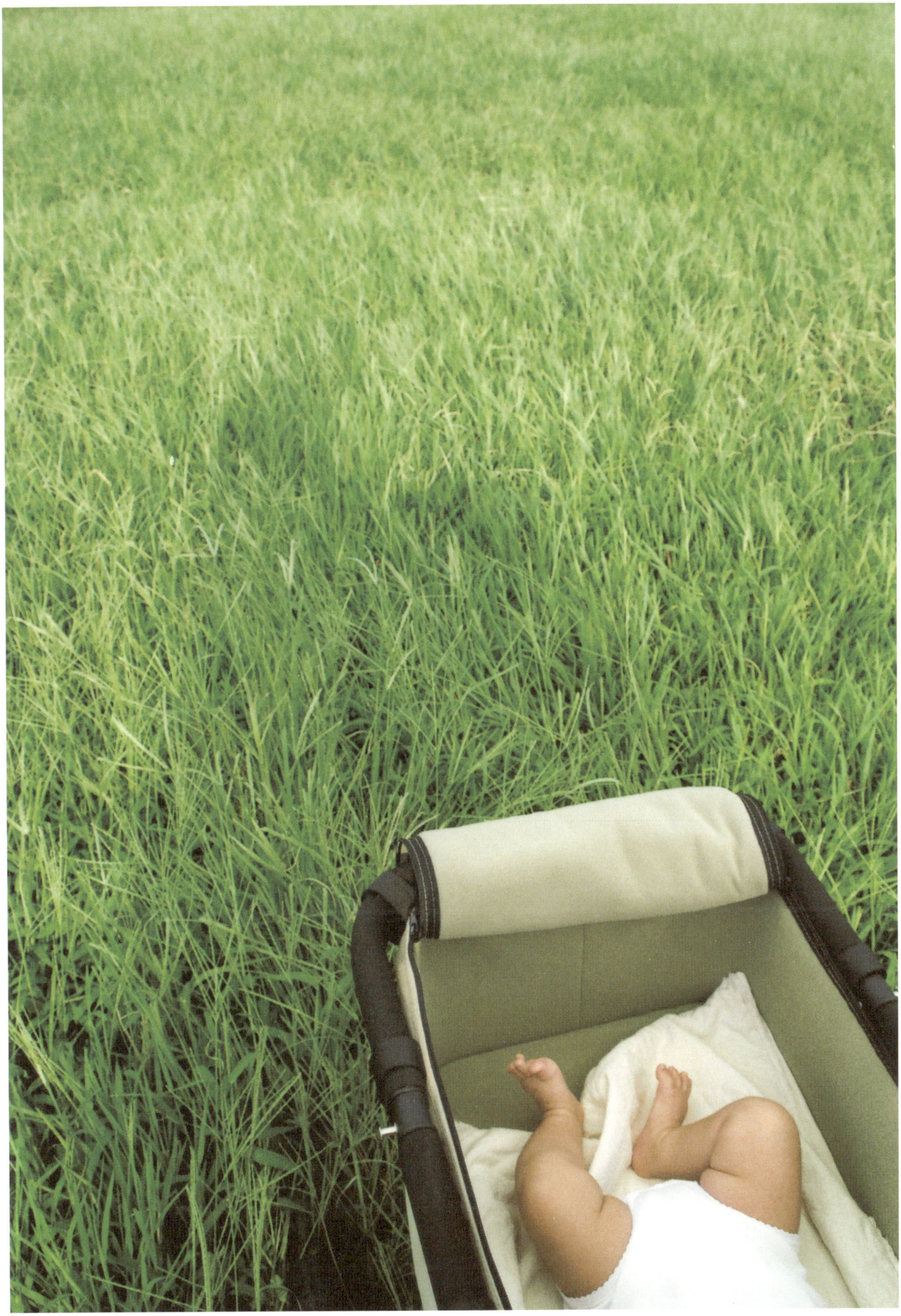

May 30, 2007
Buddy Jr.

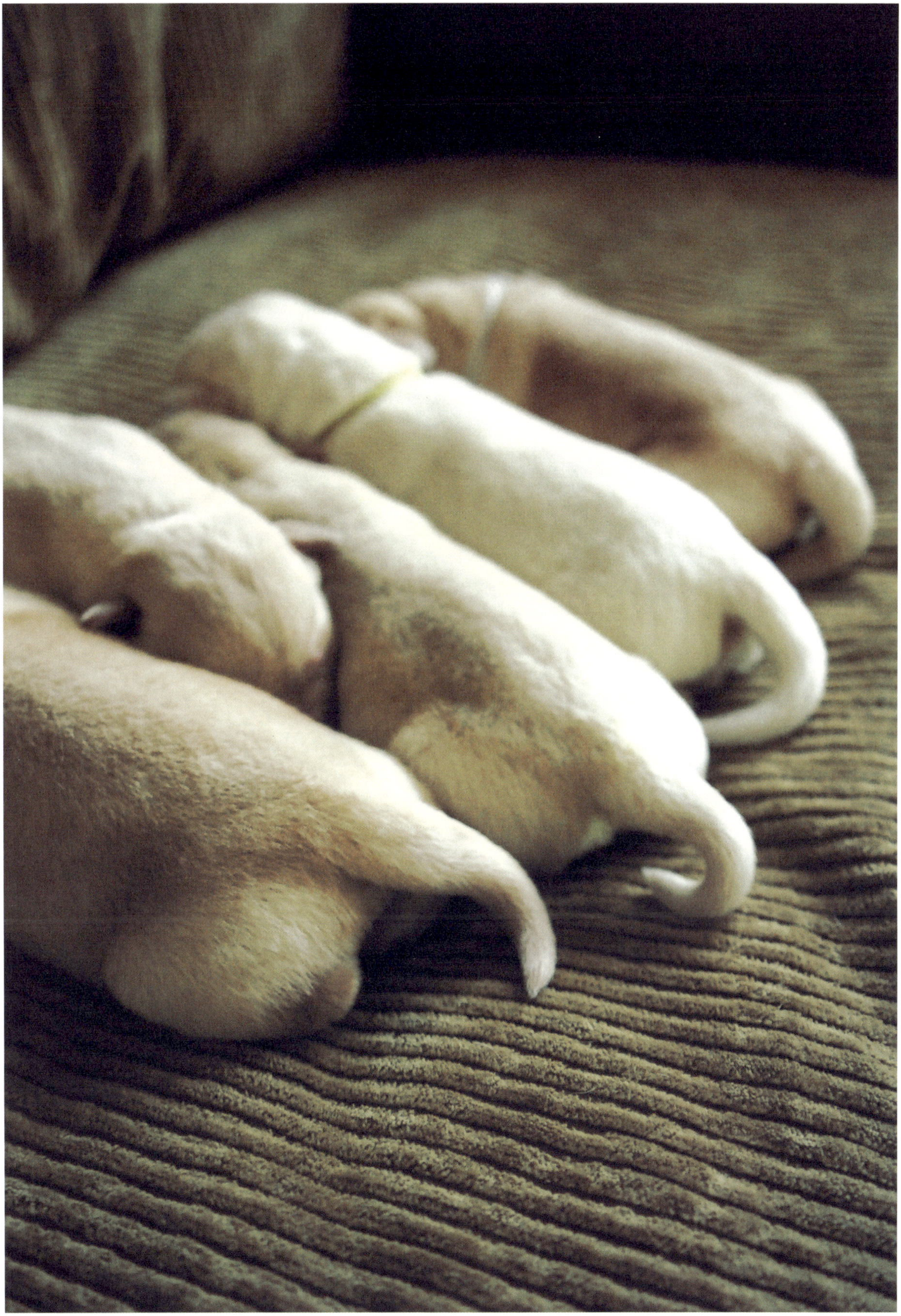

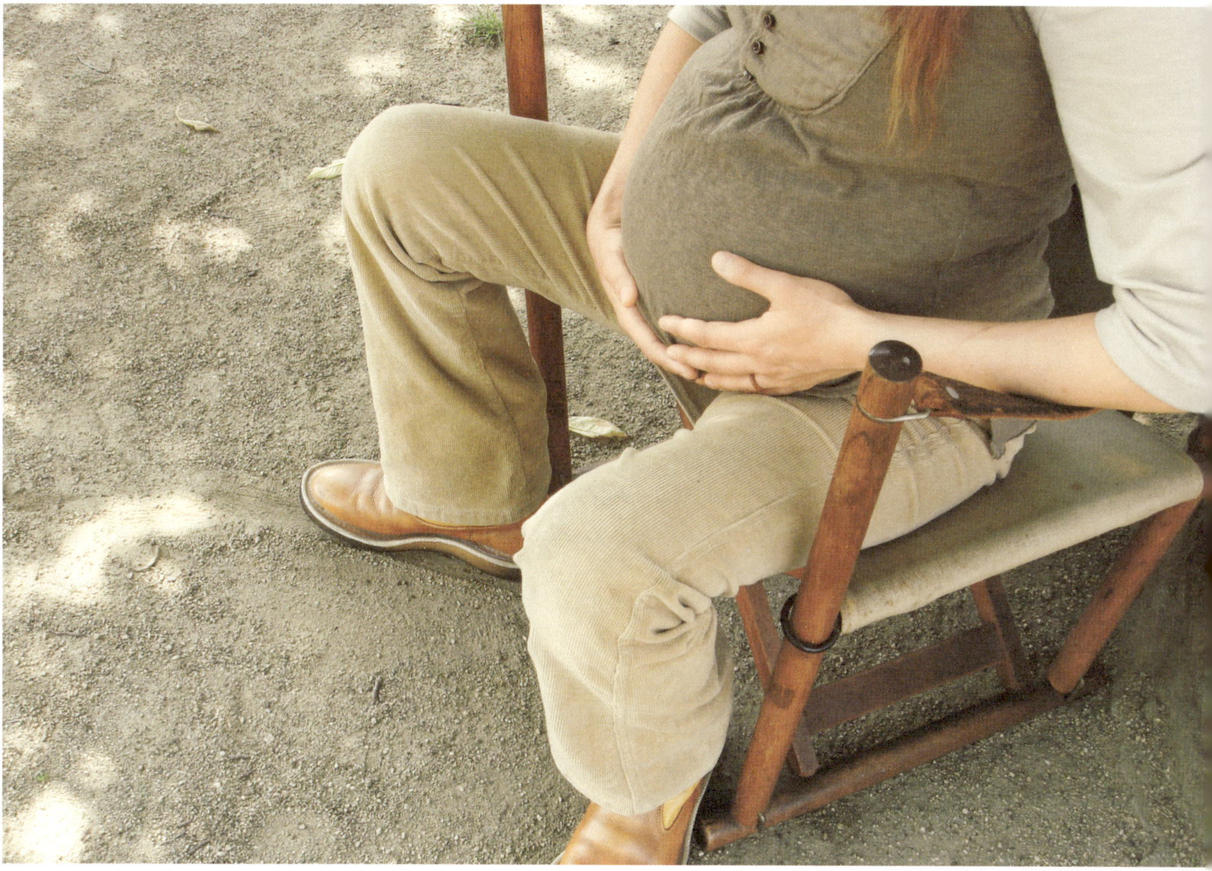

035

新入りジュニアがドキドキしながら先輩たちにご挨拶。努めて笑顔で、でも緊張を隠しきれずにソワソワとしっぽを振って。
貫禄のニャーが真正面からチェック。なぜかクマはそのニャーを嗅ぐ。

Junior, the new kid in town, nervously greets his seniors.
He's making an effort to smile, but his wagging tail gives him away.
Nya stands before him, making an inspection. For some reason, Kuma is sniffing Nya.

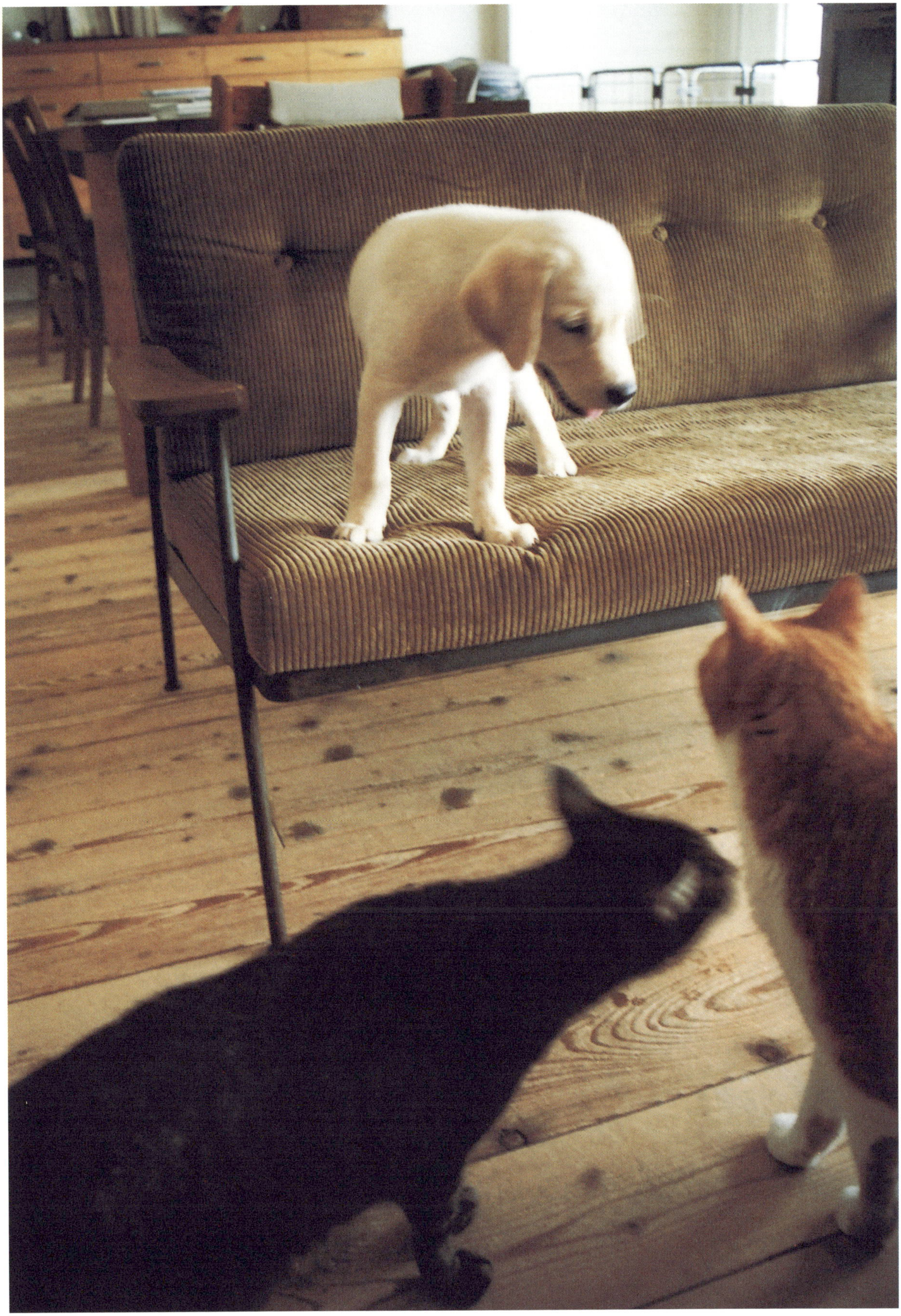

13匹と日菜

ワン4匹とニャン8匹が一緒に暮らすワンルームの家に新生児が仲間入り。
12匹のワンニャンに囲まれて日菜は育つ。それが良かったのかアレルギーの心配は全くなかった。
その後、さらにバディの息子のジュニアが加わった。
最初からいるバディは次々と増えたワンやニャン、そして人間の赤ちゃんをどう見ていたのだろう。
バブーしか言わなかったのに、だんだんと「おすわりっ!」とエラそうな口をきくようになった日菜を。

Hina with 13 cats and dogs

The family of four dogs and eight cats that lived together in one room were joined by Hina, our newborn baby. We raised her surrounded by 12 cats and dogs and have had no problems with allergies. They were soon joined by Buddy's son, Junior. I wonder what Buddy, who had been there from the start, thought as the number of cats and dogs continued to rise and be joined by a human child. Hina had only been able to say "Goo. Goo. Gaa. Gaa." at first, but was soon impertinently ordering even Buddy to sit.

Hina & Buddy

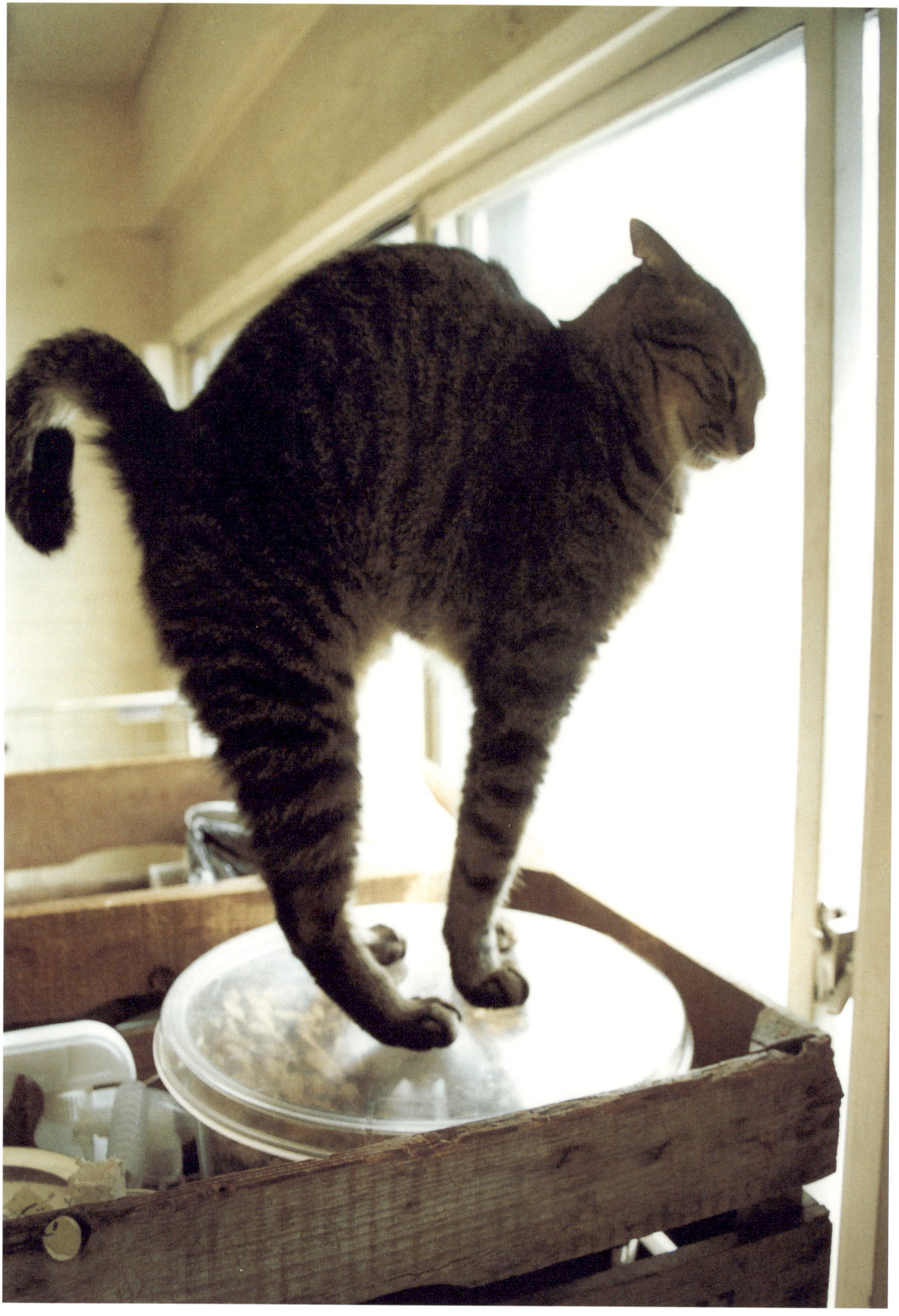

新入りが入ってもいつも通りマイペースのクマ。
みんな最初は「何? 誰や?」とざわついても数時間もすれば見慣れるのか、
あまり気にもしなくなる。馴染んでくる。このクマもやって来たその日は新入りだったのだから。

Newcomers didn't concern easygoing Kuma.
At first everyone makes a fuss over the new face, but after a few hours they become familiar.
Kuma, too, had once been a newcomer.

NEST

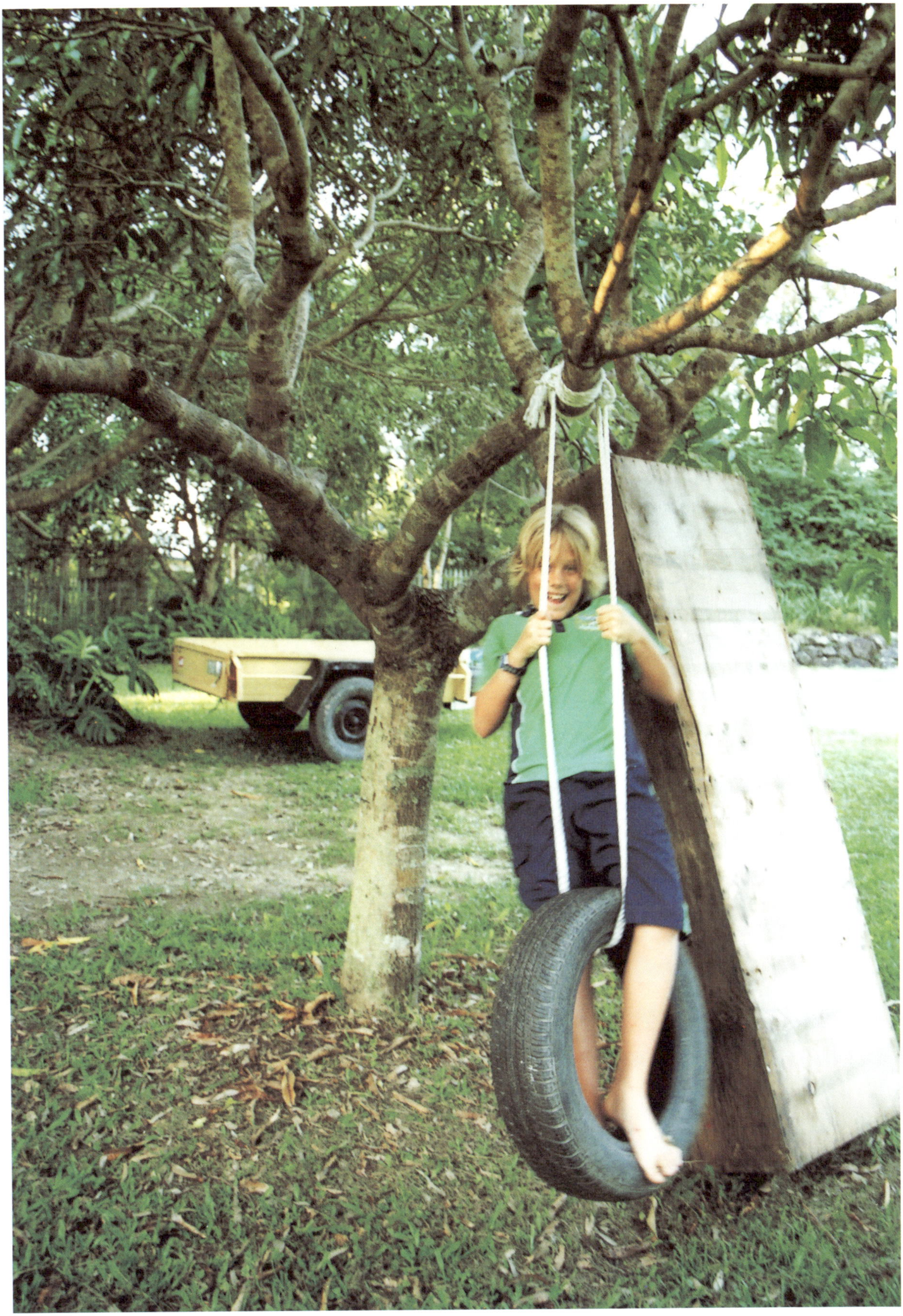

NEST

その後、すっかりヌーサ大好きになった3人は、毎年のように、あのジャングルの一軒家に滞在するようになった。日本に帰ってヌーサシックとも言える状態が続いた僕は、時にはヌーサの不動産屋に入ったりした。半分本気で「ここに住みたい」そう思った。「じゃあTRUCKはどうするのか？」と、ひりんこに言われて、ようやく思いとどまった。

その頃、シロクマ舎というひりんこのアトリエが増えて、中央区で店2軒、工場、自宅、倉庫、アトリエを借りていたことになる。全て徒歩1分の距離だが、次第にそれらをひとつにまとめたいと、ぼんやり考えるようになっていた。
自分たちのNESTをどうするのか？
いきなりTRUCKをひっさげてヌーサに移住ってのは現実的に難しい。でも、このままではどうも違う。どこかに新しい場所を見つけたい。でもそれはどこなんだろう？ あのヌーサ以来、ムズムズとした何かを日々体の中に感じ、じっとしてはいられない。ひりんこと2人、時間を見つけては大阪近辺の、できれば樹のありそうな場所へ車を走らせるようになった。どこかにあるかもしれない理想の場所を探して。

2007年、4回目のヌーサ。
いつもの気ままに過ごせる時間。そこに変化が訪れる。
日菜が生まれた。まだ9ヶ月の日菜を連れてのヌーサ暮らしは、以前とは全く違った。特にひりんこにとって。男2人が朝、海に行くのは変わらない。でも、ひりんこは以前のように、好きな時間に起き出してコーヒーを飲みながら、のんびり絵を描くなんて、全くできない。日本にいるのと同じ、赤ちゃんに従った時間があるだけだった。ひりんこは少し悶々としていた。

ひりんこによると、

いつものように、とりんことケンタロウは、朝から海へと繰り出して行く。
私はというと、日菜を抱っこしながらキッチンで離乳食を作る。部屋でおっぱいをあげる。オムツを替える。またおっぱいをあげて、オムツを替えて、離乳食を作る。（たまにはケンタロウも鶏のささみを煮込んだりして離乳食作りを手伝ってくれたが）
ヌーサに着いて何日か経った。が、始めにみんなと買い出しに行ったきり、どこにも行ってない。絵も描いてない。海もまだ1回も見てない。これじゃあ、自分だけ日本にいるのと全く一緒じゃないかと、ものすごくストレスが溜まってきた。夕方、楽しそうに海から帰ってくる野郎どもを見て、愚痴のひとつも言いたいところだったのだが、日菜がぐずるので、みんなのいるリビングでゆっくり話もできなかった。
ジャングルの家までトムやマギー、友達のルークが"TOKとHIROMIのベイビー"を見に来てくれても、日菜が大泣きするので、ほとんどしゃべれずじまい。みんながリビングで夜遅くまでビールを飲みながらおしゃべりしているのに、（私は授乳中なのでアルコールだめ）ベッドルームで日菜をあやしながら1人で赤ちゃんのお世話ばっかり。

ずっと今まで、大人だけの自由な旅だっただけに、この状況の変化は私にとってかなり不自由だった。
「来なければ良かった」なんて思ってしまった不完全燃焼な旅だった。
日菜がこの旅で唯一ご機嫌さんだったのは、
ファーストディップ（生まれて初めて海に入ることをそう言うらしい）が、ヌーサなんてカッコいいと、いつものポイントに連れて行った時、大きな海を初めて見て興奮したのか「あう—————!!」と叫んだ時くらいだったか。

…だそうだ。

そして翌年2008年、2度目の子連れヌーサ。
日菜1歳10ヶ月。
ひりんこは今回もやはり、子連れのストレスが否めない。行きの飛行機では大丈夫だったのに、日菜が急にケンタロウに対して人見知りを始めたので、またしても同じ部屋にいられなくなった。ひりんこと日菜は2階のベッドルームにひきこもり。今まであんなに楽しかった自炊の晩ご飯も、ひりんこと日菜の分だけベッドルームに運ぶ。そうこうしているうちに、ケンタロウが急用ですぐに帰国することになった。結局、一緒に来たのにほとんどしゃべれなかった。
空港にケンタロウを送って行き、その帰り道、トムの家に立ち寄った。
ひりんこは、またトムとマギーに会っても、赤ちゃん連れだとゆっくり話もできないし…なんてちょっと行くのが憂鬱だったらしい。人見知りが強く、他の人がいると殻に入り込んでしまう日菜。
が、マギーたちは「日本のビューティフルベイビー！」と大歓迎してくれる。
大きくなったフィンリーとすっかりお姉ちゃんになったサンデーがすごく優しく日菜に接してくれた。

Nest

The three of us (myself, Hiromi, and Kentaro) made it a habit to visit Noosa every year. We stayed in the same house in the jungle and always experienced the same sense of a rich life. When we came back to Japan, we always went through a period of withdrawal that we called being "Noosa-sick". I started to think, half-seriously, of moving there. I went so far as to visit a real estate agent, but when Hiromi asked me what would happen to TRUCK, I realized that it was unrealistic.

In 2003, we were renting space for two shops, our factory, our apartment, and our storeroom. To that we added an atelier for Hiromi. Although you could walk to each of them in under a minute, I began to think that it would be good to bring them all together.

How would we create our own nest? Since that first time in Noosa, I had started to feel restless. I wanted to find a new place that we could make our own. Whenever Hiromi and I found ourselves with some time on our hands, we hopped into the car and went driving around Osaka, hoping to find a place that matched our ideal.

Noosa, 2007

Our trip to Noosa in 2007 was quite different. It was our first visit with our daughter, Hina, who was just nine months old. It wasn't so different for me, I still went to the beach every morning with Kentaro, but it was for Hiromi. Previously she had been able to live at her own pace, rising late, sipping coffee outside and painting while surrounded by wildlife. This time, though, she had to follow the rhythms of life with a baby. It was rather stressful.

As Hiromi explains:
Things were much the same for Tokuhiko and Kentaro. They got up early in the morning and headed off to the beach. They were able to enjoy their trip much as before. I, however, had a baby to take care of. My mornings started in the kitchen, making baby food while holding Hina in my arms. Then I breastfed her, changed her nappy, fed her again, changed her again, then made more baby food. (Kentaro helped a little sometimes, making some baby food from boiled chicken breast.) That's how every day passed. Except for the supermarket, I didn't go anywhere. I didn't have time to paint. I didn't even see the sea once. I felt some resentment when I saw the boys return from their day of surfing. I couldn't even complain about it, though. As soon as we sat down in the living room Hina would start grumbling again and I'd have to go and see to her.

Even when Tom, Margie, and another friend, Luke, came to visit our house and see Hina, she cried so much that we didn't have a chance to talk. While everyone else was chatting and drinking in the living room, I stayed in the bedroom looking after Hina. Until then, I'd really been able to enjoy Noosa. I had total freedom to decide what I wanted to do. I knew that traveling with a child would impose some limitations on my actions, but it was harder than I had expected. I began to think it might have been better if I had not come.
The only time Hina enjoyed herself was when we took her to the ocean for her first dip. When she saw the ocean stretching out she screamed with excitement.

− Hiromi.

In 2008, we made our second trip with Hina. She was 1 year and 10 months old.

This trip was also a stressful one for Hiromi. Hina was great on the flight, but once we landed she suddenly became very shy and uncomfortable around Kentaro. It got so bad that she couldn't stand to be in the same room as him. So again, Hiromi got stuck upstairs with Hina. It was especially bad at mealtimes. We always looked forward to enjoying Kentaro's wonderful cooking together, but we found ourselves having to take Hina and Hiromi's portion up to their room. This went on for a few days when Kentaro suddenly had to return to Japan. We saw him off at the airport and on the way back, dropped in to visit Tom and Margie. Although she had met Tom and Margie, Hiromi hadn't had a chance to really talk to them. She was rather concerned about how Hina would go. When she was around other people she retreated into her shell. We were, however, very pleasantly surprised.

Margie and the kids gave her a big, friendly welcome, saying "Oh what a beautiful Japanese baby!" Finley and Sunday (who had grown a lot) treated her very gently.

Nest

トムの家の庭には、子供たちの遊び場がたくさん。
普通の家のキッチンくらいある子供キッチンには、おままごとセットがいつでも遊べるようにスタンバイ。
本気なサイズのトランポリン、サンデーとフィンリーが宙に舞う。
DIY好きのマギーのお父さんが作った子供のための小屋もある。
簡単に仕切られた畑にできたプチトマトをもぎって、フィンリーが日菜に持って来てくれた。
どれもすごく自然で、頑張った感がない。子供たちがテリア犬のハートと元気よく走り回っている。
どんどん日菜が打ち解けていく。
庭にいると、「いいものを見せてあげる」とマギーが両手でそっと包むように何かを持って来た。
覗き込むとそれは、小さな鳥の巣。そう、初めて来た時にマギーが教えてくれたNESTだ。
トムの家、ジョンの家、それぞれの使い込まれた、誰に見せるためではなく、自分たちが心地いい、そんなNEST。
自分たちもそんなNESTが欲しいと思った。

Tom's garden was full of things for the kids to play with.
There was a play kitchen that was as big as a regular kitchen,
and the toys for the kids to play house were always on standby.
There was a full-sized trampoline, and a clubhouse that Margie's father, a home handyman, had built.
Finley picked a cherry tomato from the vegetable patch and gave it to Hina.
It was all very natural, not at all as if they were making a special effort.
As Hina watched the kids play with Heart, their terrier puppy,
she gradually started to lose her shyness and come out of her shell.

When we were in the garden Margie said, "I'll show you something special."

She approached us with something gently cupped in her hands.
We peered into her hands and saw a small bird's nest.
It reminded me of the first time she had explained what the word nest meant to her.

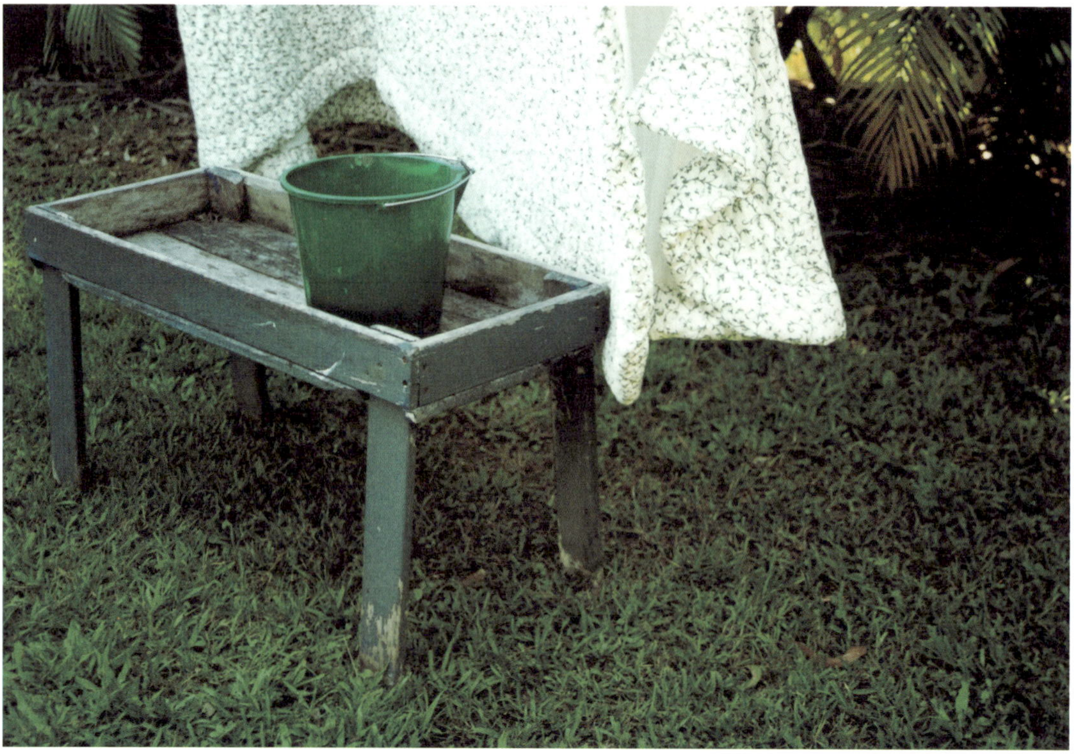

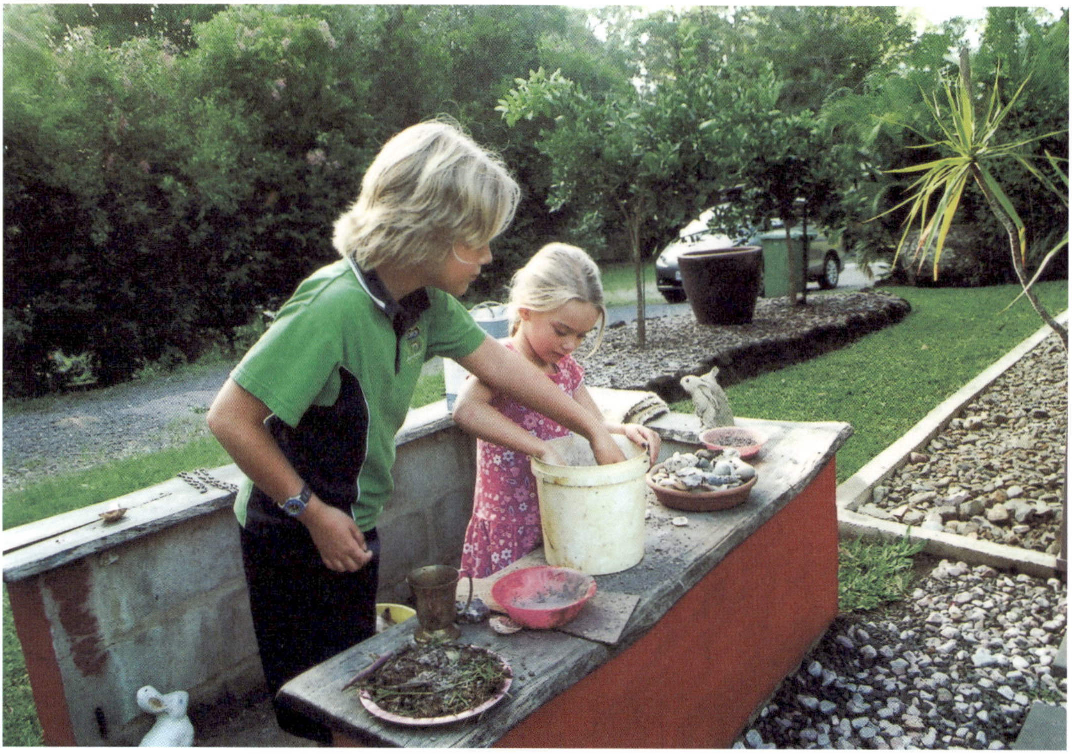

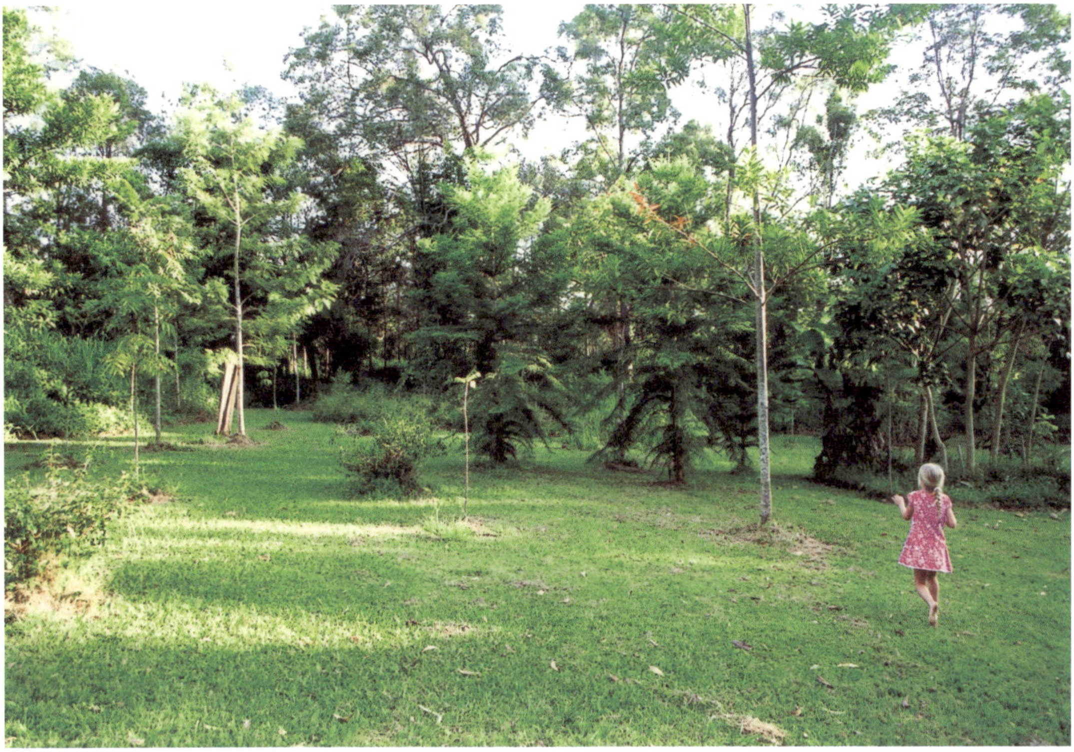

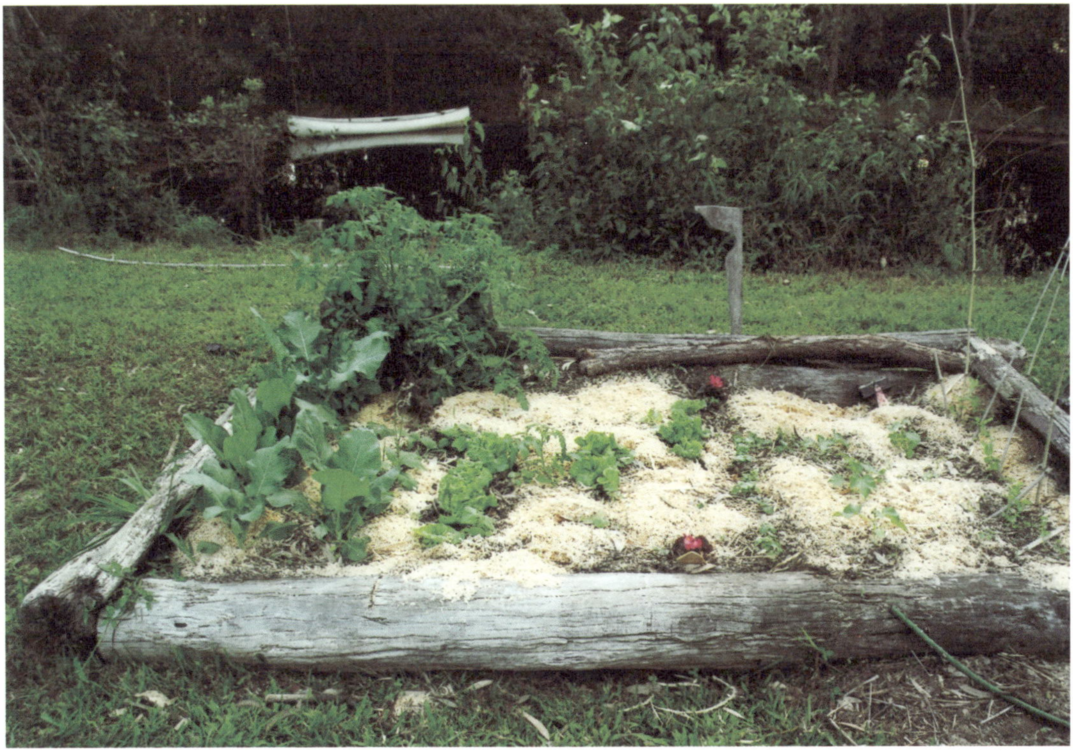

家の中では、マギーが大きな箱一杯、山盛りに入ったマジックや色鉛筆などを持って来て、「はーい。子供たちはこれでお絵描きよ！」とたくさんの紙と共に用意してくれた。子供3人とひりんこはお絵描きに没頭した。
日菜の、どこか凍っていたものが融けていった。同時にひりんこも子連れ旅の殻から解放された。一緒に「キラキラ星」を歌ったり。(もちろん日菜は日本語、マギーたちは英語で)子供には目や髪の色、言葉の違いなんて関係ないようだ。日菜も楽しそうに笑っていた。
その笑顔を見てひりんこは、ハッとしたらしい。いつもと勝手の違う旅にストレスを感じて悶々としていた、それは自分のことばっかり考えていたからだと。日菜だって遠い所まで連れてこられて大変だったんだ。「日菜、ゴメン」それと同時にひりんこの中で何かが吹っ切れた。自分が今まで通りに楽しもうとするんじゃなくて、子供と一緒にどう楽しむか、が大切なんだと。

その時、日菜がマジックでソファに線を描いてしまった。前までの花柄ソファから、新しくシンプルなベージュのソファに新調したところだったので、ヤバい！と思った。でも、マギーはこれっぽっちも気にするでもなく、「そんなこと、子供がいたら当たり前よ！」と笑って言ってくれた。先輩お母さんがかっこ良く見えた。

その晩は、トムの家で晩ご飯を食べることになった。マギーが「今日はイタリアンよ！」と発表。どんなイタリアンが繰り広げられるのかなと期待した。ところが、シンプルなパスタと簡単なサラダ。うん。まあ方向性はイタリアン。
でも、マギーは楽しそうにディナーっぽくテーブルセッティングをしている。それが見ていてすごく良かった。
じゅうぶんおいしかった。そこにあるテーブルや椅子も特別こだわったものではなさそう。でもしっかり機能している。じゅうぶんだ。これ以上はいらない。

正直に告白すると、今まで何回も訪れたトムの家、ロケーションは最高なんだけれど、ちょっとセンスが…。
オーストラリアだからって、そのケン・ドーン調のパステルカラーの花柄ソファはどうなん？初めて来た時にトムが乗っていた、ヤレたグリーンのいかしたフォルクスワーゲンも、2度目には、真っ黄色のワンボックスに買い替えられていた。トムは「調子よく走ってご機嫌！」と笑うが、絶対前の車のほうがかっこ良かったのに残念。なんて、ケンタロウと3人で、やいのやいの言っていた。でも、そんなことばっかり冷やかしていた自分たちが恥ずかしくなるほど、今、この家が、彼らがステキに見える。
家具屋である僕たちは、いつも頭の中で考えている。こんな椅子、あんなテーブル、細かいディテール、素材…。
でも、そんなこと、どうでもよく思えた。「椅子なんか座れたらそれでいい」とさえ思ってしまうほど。
そんなことより、いかに使うかが大事なんちゃうん。また衝撃が走った。

日本では、たくさんの雑誌にオシャレなモノの情報がたくさん溢れている。
○○スタイルが特集されればみんなが飛びつく。丁寧な生活が取り上げられれば、そうでなければいけないような風になる。どんどん新しいモノが作り上げられては消えていく。常に流行に振り回されている。

豊かなのはどっち？

日々の生活を心から楽しんでいる、彼らのほうが断然カッコいいと思った。
この感覚は、自分たちに子供ができたからこそ余計に心に響いた。
地に足ついた、豊かな生活。
緑がいっぱいあって、地べたがあって、もっと日々の暮らしを自分らしく楽しむこと。
そんな生活を、今こそしないといけないのでは？
それは決して、年を取ってご隠居さんになってからではなく、TRUCKとして現役で仕事をしている今。
いいものを作り、いい空間を作り出すためには、自分たちがそんな生活をしていないと魅力あるもの作りはできない。
そう確信した2008年、5回目のヌーサだった。

Both Tom and John's houses were well lived in. They weren't for people to look at. They were for the comfort of the people who lived there, like nests. We thought that we wanted a nest like that, too.

Back in the house, Margie brought out a huge box, full to overflowing with pens and crayons, and plunked it down on the table. By its side she put a mountainous pile of paper. "OK kids," she said, "let's do some drawing!" As Hiromi and the three children became absorbed in drawing, Hina's remaining shyness melted away.
She joined the other kids singing *Twinkle Twinkle Little Star*. Of course, Hina sang in Japanese and they sang in English, but to the children it didn't seem to matter that the words were different. Seeing Hina laugh so happily, Hiromi had an insight. She realized that the stress she had suffered was because she was thinking too much of herself. "Hina, I'm sorry," she thought, and the stress she'd been feeling suddenly dissipated. Instead of trying to use her time as she had before, she thought it was important to find ways to enjoy doing things with Hina.
While they were drawing, Hina accidentally drew a line on the sofa with a magic marker. Margie and Tom used to have an old flower-patterned sofa, but had recently replaced it with a much simpler beige one. But Margie seemed not to mind at all. "With kids around, these things are bound to happen," she said while laughing.
We were invited to stay for dinner and when Margie announced, "Tonight we're having Italian!" we looked forward to seeing what kind of Italian food would be served. It ended up being very simple pasta with an equally simple salad. It was kind of Italian, I guess, but the pleasure with which Margie got the table ready and laid out everyone's places made it something special. The chairs at the table were unremarkable, but they did their job, and that was enough. Anything else was unnecessary.

The location of Tom's house was fantastic, but the taste with which it had been decorated didn't really match ours. The flower-patterned sofa that looked like a Ken Done painting, for example. The first time we visited, Tom had been driving a cool old green Volkswagen. The second time, though, he had changed it for a bright yellow minivan. We thought the previous car was much cooler. Now that we could see how wonderful the house really was we felt embarrassed to have noticed such petty things.
Furniture makers are always thinking about small details of construction or material when they look at a chair or table. But I now thought that such things didn't really matter at all.
"If you can sit in a chair then it's all right," I thought. "How it is used is more important." It was another shock.
In Japan there are many magazines full of information about what's in fashion. If there is a special feature on this or that style then everyone tries to follow it. New things keep coming into fashion, replacing the old, and people are expected to run to keep up.

Which way leads to a truly rich life?
Seeing our friends in Noosa enjoying their everyday lives, the answer seemed clear. Now that we had a child, that perception struck us even more deeply. They were leading truly rich lives, with their feet planted firmly on the ground. Here, with the abundant trees and space they enjoyed their lives in their own way. "Isn't this the kind of lifestyle we should lead?" we thought. I didn't want to wait until I grew old and retired. I wanted to do this while we were still building and creating TRUCK. I became convinced that we had to change our own lifestyle so we could continue to make things that were good. That's what I took away from our fifth visit to Noosa.

Walking at Last

やっと歩いた

ちなみにこのヌーサは、歩くのがかなり遅かった日菜が1歳10ヶ月になってやっと1人で歩けるようになった記念すべき旅でもある。

2940gで生まれた日菜。1ヶ月健診の時にはすでに、平均よりずっと大きく育っていた。おっぱいが大好きで、お茶もリンゴジュースも嫌がる。粉ミルクを足すこともなく、おっぱい以外はほとんど飲まなかった。

1歳になる頃にはもう10kgになっていたが、いっこうに歩く気配がない。ハイハイもあんまりしない。ど──んと座ったまま。本当に抱っこが大変だった。

1歳半健診の時。ようやくつかまり歩きをしだした日菜。小児科の先生は、こんなに歩かない子は珍しい。筋肉か神経系、あるいは脳の発達の異常も考えられると言った。でも、日菜はその時すでに、数字やアルファベットも覚えていて、すらすら言うこともできた。この発達もまた珍しいと。なので、後者ではないと。とにかくあと2ヶ月経ってもまだ歩きそうになかったら、もう少しちゃんと検査したほうがいいと言われて焦った。

そんな中、ヌーサでの最後の日、帰りの荷物をまとめている横で、日菜がふらふらと歩き出したのだった。やっと。

Hina was comparatively slow to start walking. This trip to Noosa was especially memorable because it was the first time that she walked on her own.

Hina weighed 2,940g when she was born. At her one month checkup she was already heavier than average for her age. She loved breast milk and hated both tea and juice. She didn't like infant formula either. If it wasn't from a breast she generally didn't drink it. By the time she turned one year old, she weighed 10kg and showed no signs of trying to walk. She didn't crawl very much either. Carrying her took quite an effort. By her 18 month checkup she had finally started trying to walk, but could only shuffle along while holding something for support. The doctor said that it was unusual for children this age to walk so little. He said it was possible that she had some kind of muscle, nerve, or even brain problem. However, she had already learned numbers and the alphabet and could speak fluently. This was also rare. He told us to wait another couple of months and, if she was still not able to walk on her own, have some more comprehensive tests done.

On the last day we were in Noosa, while we were getting the luggage together, Hina took her first unsteady steps. Finally!

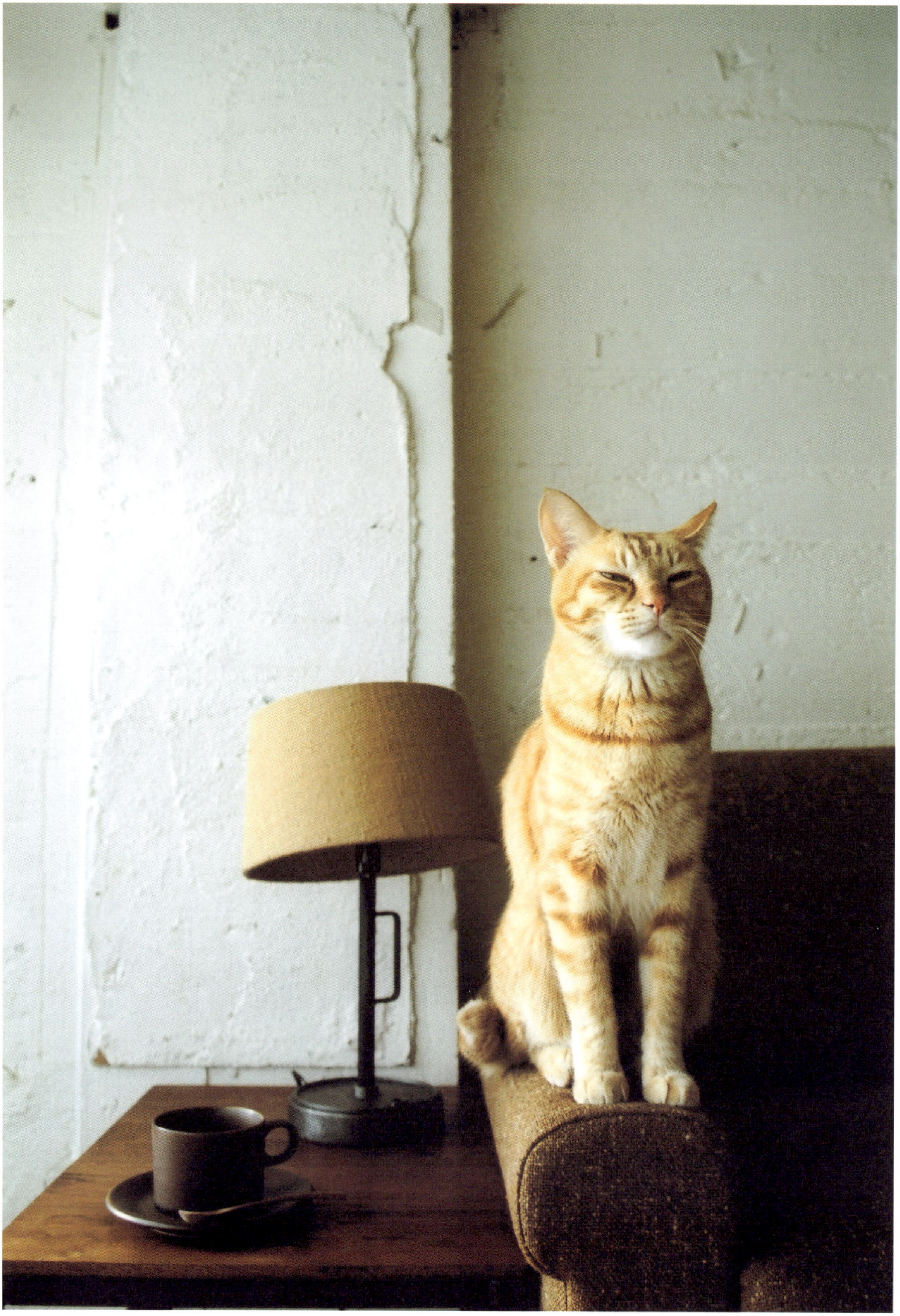

ABOUT TRUCK
since 1997

TRUCK was founded by Tokuhiko Kise and Hiromi Karatsu in 1997. We design the kind of furniture we want ourselves, regardless of fashion We respect the properties of the materials—wood, leather, steel—we use and never pursue novelty for its own sake. We create furniture that can be used for a long time.
We put a lot of care into the design and construction of every piece of furniture. Naturally we also care deeply about how it is presented to our customers.
We have designed our store from the ground up to create a certain kind of ambience, one that reflects our taste and values. This is why you won't find TRUCK furniture in other stores. Of course, some people can't make it to our shop in Osaka.
For them, we created TRUCK WORKS, a catalog of all except our most recent products. We did everything for the catalog, from styling to photography, ourselves. We shot it in the homes and shops where we live and work everyday, with our own things as props. Our own space in Osaka. Making it here, selling it here—that's always been our style.

This is the one: nothing but TRUCK.

TRUCK

Truck opened in January 1997.
We made furniture in the back and sold it in the front.
Hiromi and I lived upstairs with our dog Buddy.
Over the next 13 years, it became a home for our daughter
and twelve more cats and dogs.
It was also the setting for all the photos in our catalogs.

Jan. 1997 – Nov. 2009

Oct. 1999 – Nov. 2009

AREA2

AREA2 opened in October 1999 in a three-story building right behind TRUCK.
We moved our factory to the first floor,
made the second floor a stock room, and created a new store on the third.
As customers climbed the stairs they could see our staff
hard at work making furniture.

ABOUT TRUCK

もの作り

1997年、黄瀬徳彦（とりんこ）と唐津裕美（ひりんこ）が始めた家具屋「TRUCK」。注文を受けてから店の1階にある工場で、ひとつひとつ制作している。木、革、鉄など、それぞれの素材感を大切に、自分たちが欲しい、使いたいと思う家具を作る。張り地に使う生地や革もオリジナル。

基本的に家具は2人で考える。
普段の生活の中で、何気ない会話から、はたまた、たまたま見かけた何かからインスピレーションを受けて。
いつもの「なんでもノート」に書き込む。考える人と作る人が同じなので、ちゃんとした図面がいらない。簡単な落書きから始まり、そのまま形になっていく。
そう、とりんこが作る人。ひりんこは実際作るわけではない。作るのを手伝うわけでもない。作る作業にはノータッチ。あくまで、お客さん側の立場。あえて作り方は知らないでいる。知るとわがままが言えなくなるから。「こんなん欲しい」と言い放す。
非効率であったり、根本的にできない構造であったり、ひりんこは無茶を言う。とりんこはその都度頭を抱えて考える。そして新しいやり方が生まれる。つじつまの合わない断片的なイメージを、整えて形にしていく。作りながら考えていく。

こうして出来上がった試作品を、次は家に持ち込んで実際の生活の中で使ってみる。そこで自分たちが座ってみて、触れてみて初めて見えてくることがある。工場でちょっと座っただけでは分からないが、不思議と家で本でも読もうと座ってみると、もうちょっと背もたれがコケてるほうがいいかな？なんていろいろな所が気になって、本に集中できなくなる。FK SOFAのように試作を繰り返していくうちに1年かかることも平気。

机の上のデザイン画では終われない。
というか、自分たちが試してみないと分からない。
納得いくまで続けるので時間がかかる。
でも、いつまでにと誰かに新作発表の期限を決められるわけでもない。自分たちができたと思うまで細かい所も妥協せず、しつこく取り組む。それは家具だけでなく店、家、カタログ、この本作りも同じこと。

こんな思いで作った家具。
店でお客さんがソファに腰掛けた時にニヤッとなった顔を見ると、それだけで嬉しい。思わずにじり寄って、「いいでしょ？」と言ってしまう。セールストークなんてない。
それだけ言ったらあとは「じゃあ、ごゆっくり」

商品化してからも、さらによくできることを見つけたら迷わず改良していく。たとえ値段が決まった後でコストが上がろうとも。
自分たちには毎日繰り返し作っている家具でも、お客さんにとってはそのひとつがずっとの家具。だからちゃんと作らないと。
ちょっとでもいいものにして渡したい。裏側の見えない所でもウソのないものを正直に作りたい。

とりんこは自分はデザイナーではないと言う。でも職人でもないと言う。じゃあ何なのかと人に聞かれると、家具屋と答える。
木工所で働いていた時に「一生勉強や」と言う50年以上もの経験のある職人さんを見てきているので、ちょっと家具が作れるくらいでそんな簡単に自分のことを職人とはおいそれと名乗れないのだ。

もの作りにおいて、流行は意識しないし、売れ筋を狙うこともターゲットを設定することもない。
売上の予想とか計算もしたことがない。そっちのほうには全く興味がない。
自分たちが好きなものしか作ることができないので、○○スタイルっていうものにもあてはまらない。
そして、誰にプレゼンするわけでもないので、「コンセプトは○○でいってみよう」とか、「今度のテーマは○○スタイルでいこう」みたいな"ブランディング"という言葉とも無縁である。
「こんなのが今流行っている」「こんなのが次に流行るらしい」「普通、こうしないと売れない」「そんなやり方、常識では考えられない」人からこういった既成概念を押しつけられるのが一番キライ。普通ってなんだろう？ボリュームゾーンにウケることなのか？自分たちが最高‼︎って思えるもの、ずっと使いたいと思えるものを作りたい。

2人とも使い古された古いものが好き。
それは家具だけでなく職人さんが使っている道具だったり、工場で使われていた作業台だったり、生活の中の道具や文房具も。
有名な○○の椅子より、通りがかりの、とある会社のウインドー越しに見えた、なんてことない応接椅子に目を奪われたりする。

昔からある喫茶店のパーテーションなんかを見てカッコいいと思う。デザイナーの名前なんかない、使うために考えられた形。さらに人が使っていい味が出たもの。
家具を作っていて、常にそれらにはかなわないという思いがある。古いものの魅力にはかなわない。だからといって古材を使ってそれに似せたものを作るのではないし、必要以上にエイジングはしたくない。

TRUCKは新しい木を使って新しい家具を作っている。
それを買ってくれた人にずっと使ってもらい、それぞれの生活の中でいつしか古い道具のようになっていく。それが理想。
だから、長く使えるものを作らないと。

TRUCKの家具は、1点ものの作品というわけではなく、あくまで商品であると考えている。実用的な道具として毎日ちゃんと使える普通の家具。
ずっと使ってもらえるように無垢材を使い、奇をてらわず、飽きのこないシンプルなデザイン。手に触れたり、日に焼けたり、その人の使い方によって、家具も一緒に年を取り、風合いを増す。それを楽しんでもらえればと思う。

素材感を大切にしたいので、あまり表面のコーティングを施さないから、もちろん輪ジミや汚れがつくこともある。
「お父さんが置きっぱなしにしたビールの缶で輪ジミができてしまった！さらにうっかりこぼしてしまった醤油のシミも！せっかく一生モノとはりきって手に入れたのに！」
なんて、あまり神経質にならずに。
TRUCKでは特に念入りなお手入れは勧めていない。（もちろん、たまにオイルやワックスを塗ってもらってもいいけど）家具に気を使わずにガシガシ使ってほしい。
そして、その家での使いっぷりを味にしてほしいと思っている。

黄瀬家では、ホワイトオークのダイニングテーブルでたこ焼きも、すき焼きもガンガンする。もちろんテーブルクロスや新聞紙なんか敷かない。やっぱりものすごく油が飛んで、翌日天板にはたこ焼き器の四角い形がくっきりついていたりする。
が、不思議なことに、数日経つと気にならなくなるのである。天板全体の色が変わってくるとだんだん分からなくなっていく。
「これもある意味オイルフィニッシュや！」と言って笑っている。

TRUCKの家具。卸はしない。
自分たちの目の届く範囲で、自分たちで大事に売る。
家具だけでなく、そこにある空気感も大切だから。それは自分たちにしか作れない。

そして自分たちで作った場所。
ここで作って、ここで売るスタイルを、これからもずっと続けていきたいと思っている。
大阪で家具屋をやっているが、それは、たまたま2人が大阪生まれの大阪育ちだったから。特に大阪にこだわっているわけではない。かといって東京に行かないと、なんて全く思わない。いろいろお誘いがあっても離れた場所での出店は全く考えられない。
オイシイ話に乗って事業を拡大する。工場を大きくして店も増やし、スタッフも増える。それによって売上を作らないといけなくなって、売るための商品作りをする。数字が先にくるもの作りが一番コワイ。やりたくない。
ブレないで、自分たちの目の届く範囲で、好きなものを、納得いくものをずっと作っていたい。

こんな風にTRUCKでは自分たちの好きなものだけを作ってきた。それを分かってくれる人が手に取ってくれて、それを好きと言ってもらえる。まして買ってもらえるということは本当に幸せなことだと、いつも2人で話している。

Staff

スタッフのこと

スタッフを選ぶにもすごく時間がかかる。

人手が足りず、今、すぐに人員が欲しい時でも、とりあえずでは入れない。たとえ1年かかっても探し続ける。

職歴とか資格より、この人とずっと仕事をしていきたいか、どんないい笑顔をしているか、が一番大事。

TRUCKの一員となるからには、長いつき合いにしたいという思いでいる。将来その人の家族みんなが幸せに楽しく暮らせるようになってもらいたいと強く思う。

いったんお店に立つからには、お客さんには社長も正社員もバイトも関係ない。その時、接客して挨拶や言葉を交わした、その人の印象で店の印象が決まると思っている。

2人にとって商品がいいのは当たり前の基本の基本。飲食店なんか特にそうで、おいしいのは当たり前であってほしい。おいしくなかったらもちろんアゲインはしないのだが、さらに人がいいかどうかで2回目に行きたくなるか、もう2度と行かないかが決まると思っている。

TRUCKとBirdには自慢のスタッフが揃っている。男前でよく動く、男気のある奴ばかり。

「スタッフが気持ちいい。研修でもしてる?」とよく聞かれる。でも特に何もしていない。朝礼での挨拶の練習やスローガンなんてないし、数字の目標なんてゼロ。いい笑顔の人を選んでいるだけ。

Choosing the right staff takes time. They will wait until they find the right person, even if means the workshop is understaffed. In some cases the search has taken as long as a year. When they are looking for new employees, they choose people whose smiles they like, and who they think they'd like to work with for a long time. This is more important than qualifications or experience. If they choose the right person, the skills can always be learnt.

They want to have a long-term relationship with their staff. They want them, and their families, to be happy with where they work. One of the reasons for taking the time to hire the right staff is the impression it makes on people who visit the store. Customers don't know or care if the person they see is the head of the company, a full-time employee, or a part-time worker. The impression they make will be the impression they have of the store. That the furniture is good should be treated as a given. What will make people want to return is the staff. It's similar to a restaurant. The food may be excellent, but if the staff are unfriendly, people are unlikely to return.

Tokuhiko and Hiromi are proud of all the staff at Bird and TRUCK. They are sometimes asked if they have special training that makes their staff so good. They really don't. There are no special slogans, or greeting practice in the morning. The staff in the store don't have any sales targets either. They just choose people based on their smiles.

ABOUT TRUCK

Making Things

Furniture they want, regardless of fashion.

All the furniture is made, piece by piece, in the workshop below the store. They make furniture that they want to use themselves. They take care to bring out the individual character of the materials they use: wood, iron, and leather. All of the fabrics and leather are designed by them and made to their specifications.

Basically, they come up with their furniture together. Their ideas are occasionally inspired by something they see, but more often come from daily conversation. When they think of something, they write it or draw it in what they call their "Nandemo Notebook" (literally "anything notebook"). The designer and the maker are the same, so there is no need for rigid blueprints. A rough sketch usually suffices to for them to make a start.

The creator is Tokuhiko. Hiromi plays no part in the actual production. Her role is to take the side of the customer. She goes out of her way *not* to learn about how things are made. Knowing more about the process would lead her to judge her ideas and prevent her from suggesting things because they are difficult to do. Sometimes her suggestions are inefficient or even basically impossible to make. In trying to figure out how to make them possible, Tokuhiko can come up with new ways of doing things. Generally, Hiromi comes up with a vague concept and leaves it to Tokuhiko to fill in the details and decide how to make it.

Once they have a prototype, it goes to their house to be used in real life, to be sat on and used for real. Sitting on something for a few minutes in the workshop doesn't tell you much. To really understand something like a sofa, they believe you have to sit in it and do something like read a book. Whatever distracts you from the book (the cushioning, or the backrest, for example) is something that might need to be adjusted. It might take as long as a year of prototyping a sofa to make something that is really good. They have no problem spending that kind of time to get things right.

Design doesn't stop at the desk. They believe that without trying something, they can't truly understand it. They don't have a set release schedule, so they are comfortable working persistently until all the details are right. They apply the same philosophy to their store, their catalogs, and everything else do, including this book.

They put a lot of time into making furniture, so it always makes them happy when they see a customer in the store sit on a sofa and smile. Without thinking, they might say "It's good, isn't it?" It's not much of a sales pitch.

After they finish developing a product and start selling it, they don't hesitate to make changes if they find a way to improve it, even if it costs them more to produce. They will make the same piece of furniture many times, but their customers will only buy it once, and hopefully use it for a long time. They want to make it as good as it can be. It's important that even the parts of a piece of furniture that customers will never see should be made as well as possible. They want to make their furniture completely honestly.

TRUCK pays no attention to trends or notions of what is fashionable. They have no interest in trying to make a hot selling product. They don't do market research or try to make sales projections. They just make things as well as they can.

Tokuhiko and Hiromi both have a fondness for old, well-used, well-loved tools. This love extends beyond furniture, to woodworking tools, workbenches, everyday utensils and stationery.
Sometimes the most unexpected things catch their eyes. It might be a detail of a chair they see while walking past an office, or a kind of partition used in traditional Japanese coffee shops.

Nothing can compare to the charm of well used furniture. That's why they don't employ any tricks to make their furniture seem older than it really is.

TRUCK uses new materials to make new furniture.
It will become old naturally as their customers use it every day. That's why they make things that will last for a long time.

TRUCK furniture is made to be used like a tool for everyday life. They want it to be used for a long time, so the designs are simple, without superfluous touches, and made with solid wood. As the person who uses it ages, so does the furniture. As it is handled and exposed to sunlight its appearance and character deepens.

The furniture is not covered with a protective coating, so there are times that it will be stained through use. They don't want people to use it nervously. If someone's father leaves a beer can on the table that leaves a circular mark, then that's OK. If someone spills soy sauce on it, then that's OK, too.

They don't make any particular recommendations for how it should be used or cared for. They want it to gain character from how it is used.

In the Kise family house they often cook sukiyaki and takoyaki (balls of flour and octopus fried together) on their white oak table. They don't use a tablecloth or newspaper to catch the oil that splatters from the pan, so the rectangular silhouette of the pan is clearly visible the next day. Then, mysteriously, as the table is used more and more the color of the whole thing changes and what looked like stains or blemishes disappear.

"That's a real oil finish." Tokuhiko and Hiromi say, with a laugh.

TRUCK furniture is not sold through other stores. For them, the whole experience is important, not just the furniture. The only way they can ensure that everything is right is by doing it themselves.

They want to continue making and selling furniture in the same place. There's no special reason that their workshop and store is in Osaka, it just happens to be where they are from. That said, they've never felt the need to move the operation to Tokyo.

Many people have tried to talk them into opening shops in other areas of the country. This is something they are decidedly against. They are concerned that expansion would increase pressure on them to sell more, to make more and that gradually they would be forced to try to make things that will sell, whether they want to make them or not - it's the exact opposite of how they want to operate.

They are happy that there are enough people who appreciate their approach, and the furniture they make, for them to keep on doing it as they have so far.

TRUCK FURNITURE

First and foremost, TRUCK furniture is built to be used.
We want it to become a practical part of people's everyday lives,
a tool they can use without thinking.

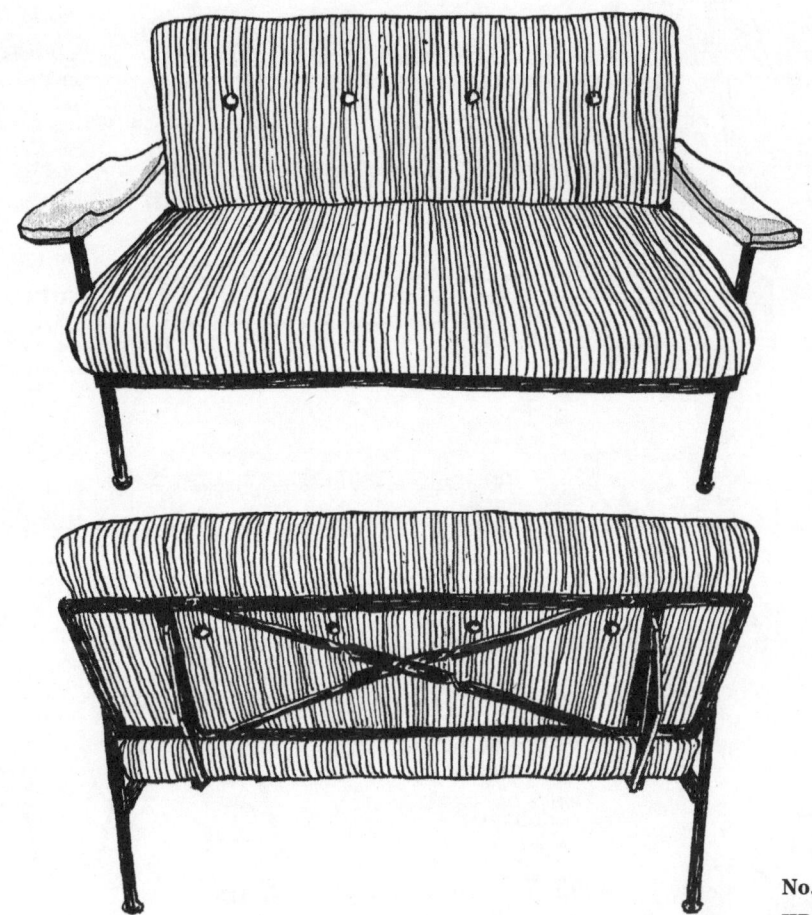

illustration_Hiromi Karatsu

No.130

HR SOFA

JAPANESE OAK, STEEL
seat_FABRIC, LEATHER

1-SEATER	2-SEATER
W 700	W 1250
D 710	D 710
H 720	H 720
SH 400	SH 400

CHAIRS

No.111
QUATTRO CHAIR
JAPANESE OAK
seat_FABRIC, LEATHER
W 430
D 520
H 795
SH 450

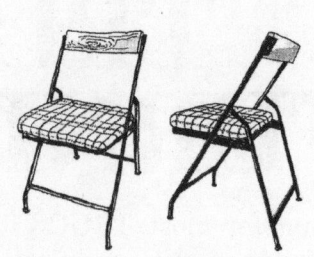

No.116
SUTTO CHAIR
JAPANESE OAK, STEEL
seat_FABRIC, LEATHER
W 435
D 540
H 780
SH 460

No.117
KT STOOL
JAPANESE OAK, CAST IRON
φ 280
H 405-480

No.112
TORCH CHAIR
JAPANESE OAK
seat_JAPANESE OAK

TORCH CHAIR: FABRIC SEAT
JAPANESE OAK
seat_FABRIC, LEATHER
W 415
D 510
H 755
SH 430

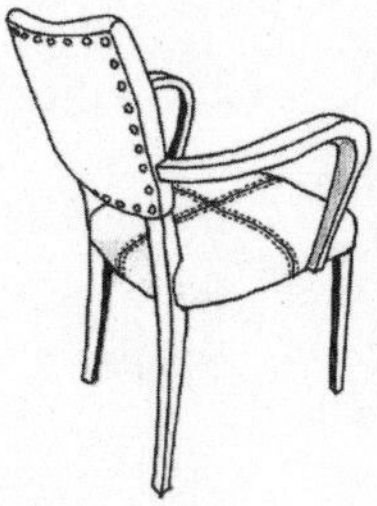

No.113
OAK SR ARM CHAIR
JAPANESE OAK
seat_FABRIC, LEATHER
W 530
D 540
H 770
SH 440

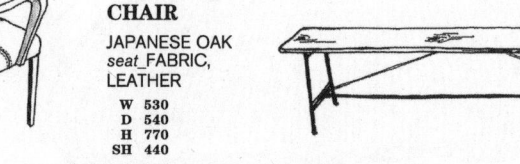

No.119
SUTTO BENCH
JAPANESE OAK, STEEL
seat_JAPANESE OAK
W 1750
D 320
H 430

No.1
DESKWORK CHAIR
STEEL
seat_LEATHER
W 490
D 560
H 780-850
SH 440-510

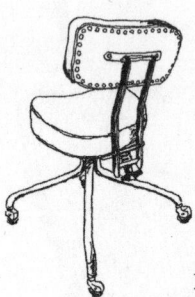

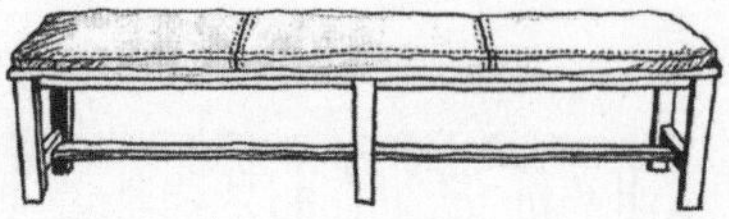

No.120
OAK SR BENCH
JAPANESE OAK
seat_FABRIC, LEATHER
W 1750
D 290
H 440

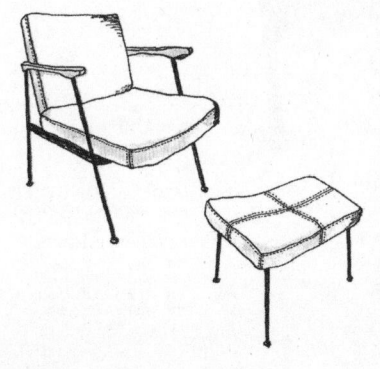

No.2
FURROWED-LEATHER ARM CHAIR
WHITE OAK, STEEL
seat_LEATHER
W 695
D 690
H 800
SH 410

FURROWED-LEATHER STOOL
STEEL
seat_LEATHER
W 590
D 450
H 410

No.115
BOOMERANG CHAIR
JAPANESE OAK, STEEL
seat_FABRIC, LEATHER
W 600
D 800
H 700
SH 390

BOOMERANG CHAIR OTTOMAN
JAPANESE OAK, STEEL
seat_FABRIC, LEATHER
W 600
D 390
H 380

TABLES

No.123
SUTTO TABLE
JAPANESE OAK, STEEL
W 1650
D 750
H 700

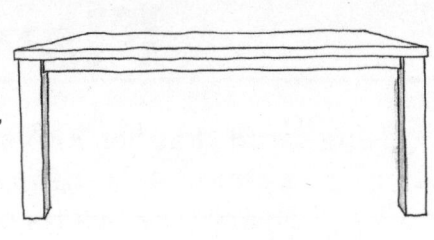

No.124
OAK SR TABLE
WHITE OAK
W 1300-2000
D 800-900
H 710

CUPBOARDS

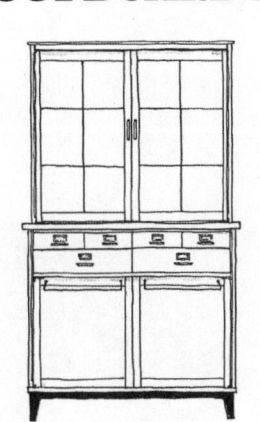

No.126
GATTO CUPBOARD
JAPANESE OAK, STEEL, GLASS
W 1200
D 465
H 2130

No.125
GATTO GLASS CABINET
JAPANESE OAK, GLASS
W 1110
D 400
H 920

SHELVES

No.146
AG SHELF
JAPANESE OAK, STEEL

S / W 930
D 365
H 970

L / W 930
D 365
H 1600

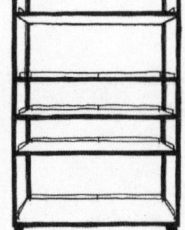

SOFAS

No.48
LEATHER SOFA
JAPANESE OAK
seat_FABRIC, LEATHER

	1-SEATER	2-SEATER	3-SEATER
W	860	1340	1870
D	830	830	830
H	810	810	810
SH	430	430	430

No.47
FURROWED-LEATHER OAK-FRAME SOFA
WHITE OAK
seat_LEATHER

	1-SEATER	2-SEATER	3-SEATER
W	760	1410	2050
D	830	830	830
H	750	750	750
SH	380	380	380

No.131
CS SOFA
JAPANESE OAK
seat_FABRIC, LEATHER
W 1800
D 800
H 780
SH 400

No.132
FK SOFA 3-SEATER
WALNUT, seat_FABRIC
W 2040
D 960
H 800
SH 430

FK SOFA 1.5-SEATER
WALNUT, seat_FABRIC
W 1190
D 960
H 800
SH 430

Flaws

Using wood that has knots and cracks requires
a completely different approach.
Every tree has its own character,
its own grain, knots, and coloring.
Making furniture that retains these elements really brings
out the true essence of the materials.

節、割れのある木

あるギャラリーでTRUCKの展示会をすることになった。家具の展示ではなく、TRUCKの世界観を違う形で見せるというもので、自分たちの好きな素材感のあるいろんなものを並べることにした。その時、それらを置く台が必要になった。定番で作っているTRUCKのテーブルにしても良かったのだが、何かもっと存在感のある台にしたいと思った。でも、古材を使うのも、どうも違う。

その頃、作っていた家具はメープル材やタモ材、アッシュ材が主で、ちょっとでも節や割れの部分があれば欠点として取り除いていた。でも見方を変えると、それこそが木の持つ力強さに思え、逆に魅力的にさえ感じた。———あえて節や割れ、荒木の部分を素材の味と考えて、そこがかっこ良く見える作りにしてみてはどうか。
しかし、その頃は世間一般でキレイな材木を使った家具が当たり前だった。それしかなかったと思う。特に日本では昔から節などのない材木が好まれていたので、欲しいと思った節がある木材なんて材木屋にもなかった。(今でこそ節や割れを使った家具が増えてきて、そのための材木が買えるようになったようだが)
探していくうちにアメリカにホワイトオークがあると聞き、それなら思っている感じの表情があるのではないかと、思い切って取り寄せることにした。展示会に間に合わせるため、どうしても早く入手したかったので、空輸した。材木代が10万円に対して運賃が50万円!!そこまでして思いを形にした。
こうして手に入れたホワイトオーク材。いかに節や割れをかっこ良く入れていくか、という今までとは全く逆の作業。木は、木目や節など、ひとつひとつ異なる。そのため出来上がったテーブルの表情も様々。節や割れ、荒木の部分を意図的に残すことで、さらに味が引き立った。他の素材とはまた違った存在感のある、無垢材らしい、力強さを感じさせるテーブルができた。展示会に置いていたノートに、「台として使われているテーブルの存在感がカッコいいです」って誰かが書いてくれた。嬉しかった。

その後、同じ仕様で大きなテーブルを作って店にも置いてみた。自分たちは大満足。でも、節や割れにフキンが引っかかってしまうようなテーブル、お客さんに買ってもらえるなんて思ってもなかった。そこにあるだけで喜んでいた。ところが意外にもそれを好きと言ってくれる人が増えていく。

1998年から始めた、今までなかったこの節や割れ、荒木を残したやり方はいつしかTRUCKの定番となっていった。

Soon after starting TRUCK, we decided to hold an exhibition in a gallery. It wasn't going to be a furniture exhibition. Instead it was an exhibition of miscellaneous objects (leaves, rocks we'd found, and the like) and materials reflecting TRUCK's outlook. We needed something to display them on. We could have used an existing TRUCK table, but I wanted something with a more powerful presence.

At the time we mainly used maple, ash, and Japanese ash to make our furniture. Even the smallest knots and rough areas were seen as faults and removed. Looking at the wood from a different perspective, though, I started to think that these things were a signs of a tree's strength and were very appealing. I wanted to make something that accentuated and made the knots, cracks, and roughness look good. At that time, in Japan especially, it was universally accepted that furniture should be made using only flawless wood. I began looking for rougher wood, but it proved impossible to find in any lumber yards.
During my search I heard about a kind of wood from America called white oak. I wasn't sure it would have the appearance I was looking for, but I went ahead and ordered some. For it to arrive in Japan in time for the exhibition it would have to be sent by air. The wood cost 100,000 yen, but the shipping was 500,000 yen, five times as much. That's how determined I was.

To bring out the beauty I saw in the knots and cracks, I had to adopt a completely different approach when designing and building the table. Every tree has its own grain, knots, and color, so each of the nine tables I made had its own unique look. The tables had a strength and solidity to them. At the exhibition there was a notebook for visitors to write their impressions. I was very happy when I saw that someone had written, "The display tables you used were very cool."

Soon after, I made a big table with the same kind of wood and put it in the store. We thought it was great, but we didn't expect anyone to buy a table that might snag their dish cloths. We were just happy to have it there. Gradually, the number of people who said they liked it increased. In 1998, we started making furniture with knots, cracks and visible roughness. It was unlike anything available at the time, and has since become a standard part of our furniture at TRUCK.

Furrowed Leather

TRUCK uses an original leather we call "furrowed leather."
Hides from Japanese cows are pretreated for a week.
Then they are tanned by soaking them in vats of vegetable tannins for about a month.
At first they are soaked in vats with a low concentration of tannins.
Gradually they are moved to vats of stronger and stronger concentrations.
To maintain the natural shape of the fibers within the hide, great care is taken when moving them.
After the hides are tanned, fish oil is spread across them to achieve the desired softness.
The tanned hide is hung to dry naturally over the course of about ten days.
We use it as is. We don't paint or coat it in any way.
Efficiency is not prioritized. It takes time and is labour intensive.
Leather that is tanned in this way has the depth of the skin on a face of a portrait of a old fisherman or farmer.
As it is used it develops its own patina.

ファロードレザー

TRUCKオリジナルの革"FURROWED LEATHER ファロードレザー"。FURROWとは車輪が通ってできた轍や顔の深いしわという意味。国産の原皮を1週間かけて下処理。そして濃度が徐々に濃くなるように調整された天然植物タンニンのピット槽で鞣されること約1ヶ月。じっくりとタンニンが皮に染み込み革となる。その間も皮自体に負担を掛けないようになるべく動かさず繊維の状態を自然な形で維持するように心掛ける。そしてたっぷり脂分を与える。強制乾燥はせず、自然乾燥させる。これにより風合いや腰感が維持される。塗装などのコーティングはせずに素の状態で仕上げる。効率を優先させるのではなく、手間暇をかけ徹底的に自然な手法で作られた革は経年変化による味わいの出方が違う。ポートレイトに収めたくなるような年季が入った漁師や農夫の顔の深いしわ。その奥行き、その渋さ。この革は使い込んで出てくるそんな味わいを楽しめる。

Atelier Shirokumasha

TRUCK uses furrowed leather to makes sofas and chairs.
There are many parts that can't be used, edges, offcuts, and the like.
These are often the pieces with the warmest, deepest colors.
Instead of throwing them away we kept them and had gradually amassed a large stock.
We decided to make something with them.
That's how Shirokumasha began making things with leather.
Yasuko sews each item by hand. Each item is the same shape but every piece of leather has
its own particular characteristics, so no two items are ever exactly the same.
The longer you use them, the deeper the colors become.

→ P. 252-
→ P. 321
→ P. 332-

シロクマ舎

TRUCKでファロードレザーを使ったソファや椅子を作る。家具には使いにくい部分、端の所などの切れっ端が残る。そこは味わいがより深くてカッコいい部分でもあるので、もったいなくて捨てられずに大切にとっておいた。それがシロクマ舎での革を使ったもの作りの始まりだった。様々な形状の革、そのひとつひとつが、そうなるために生まれてきたかのように使われて、全て手縫いで仕上げられていく。同じ形のアイテムでも、使う革の部分によってそれぞれ表情が全く異なるので、一点一点に存在感がある。使い込むほどに色が濃くなり、艶が出てさらにいい味になっていく。

Catalog

Published in 1998 / 2001 / 2005

TRUCK WORKS 3
57 SORTS OF FURNITURE
SIZE 27 x 21.2 x 2.1 cm   312 PAGES - 256 IN COLOR

This is the One. Nothing but TRUCK.
100 SORTS OF FURNITURE
SIZE 29.7 x 21 x 0.7 cm   100 PAGES - FULL COLOR

TRUCK WORKS 2
97 SORTS OF FURNITURE
SIZE 27 x 21.2 x 1.8 cm   264 PAGES - 188 IN COLOR

カタログ

自分たちで改造した店で、自分たちが考えて作った家具を、自分たちで売る。おまけにその上に住んでいる自宅も全て自分たちで改造した。このスタイルが新鮮だったのか、大阪の玉造という中心部から離れた場所にオープンした小さな家具屋に、その後、取材が来るようになった。(おかげさまでこの15年間、宣伝広告費は使っていない)全国誌に掲載してもらうのはいいが、今のようにインターネットも普及していなかったのでウェブサイトなんてない。雑誌を見た人から電話で「東京ではどこで商品を見ることができますか?」「大阪以外ではどこで取り扱っていますか?」との問い合わせが増えた。もちろん家具はこの玉造の店にしかない。なかなか大阪まで来ることができない人たちに、TRUCKの空気感を伝えることができる何かを作りたいと思うようになった。

カタログ。これもまたTRUCKらしい型破りなもの作りのひとつ。2人とも家具屋で働いた経験などない。
"カタログ"というものがどうやって作られるのかも知らない。そもそも、話の始まりは"カタログ"ではなかった。
"大阪のこの辺鄙な所にある小さな家具屋の自己紹介をするための何か"だった。家具を売るためではなくて、TRUCKの空気感がその1冊で伝わるような、何か。

それにはまず、家具の写真を撮らないと、ということになり、場所を作るために自宅を片付ける。家具だけ並べてもなんだかピンとこない時、当たり前に自宅で使っているものを持って来て家具の上に置いてみる。自分ではスタイリングをしているという意識はない。寂しいからちょっと何かをって感じ。

ひりんこが撮影を始めると、そこにいるワンニャンたちが割り込んでくる。ここに犬が欲しいから座らせて…とかではなく、実際に自宅でくつろいでいるところでこっちが撮影を始めるのだから。
写真を撮っている前を、バディが横切ったり、ニャーが上に乗ってきたり。どっちかというと、「ちょっとどいて下さい」ってほうが多い。バディは「どいて」というとあからさまに顔が曇る。カメラを向けると、気を取り直し元の笑顔に戻る。撮影のために借りてきたモデル犬や猫とは表情が全く違う。自然体なのである。
出来上がった写真を見ると、バディの表情がいいのでこれを使おうとなる。たとえ家具が半分、犬のお尻で隠れていても。

撮影は、ひりんこがイラストの作品を撮るために以前から持っていた、ご家庭用の一眼レフ。いつもの駅前スピード現像所へプリントに出す。ど素人なので曇りや雨の日は撮れない。晴れの日だけ。現像できたものを見ると、色が悪かったり、余計なものが写り込んでしまっていて使えないことも多々あり、また一から並べて撮り直し。その繰り返し。
カメラマンやスタイリストに依頼する、スタジオを借りる、スタイリングの小物をレンタルする、そんなこと知らなかったのである。全く、頭になかった。全て自分たちでプロデュースするといったそんなカッコいいものではなく。当時はただ単にそういう業界を知らなかっただけである。

それが良かった。らしい。
2人で家具を考え、試作して、使ってみて、修正して、また使って、完成形にして、それを自宅で写真に撮って、デザインして、家具の説明イラストも描いて、印刷に立ち会って…ものすごく時間をかけて作った。
自分たちの家具には、やはり強い思い入れがあるので、印刷の色はかなりこだわった。思い通りの家具の色が表現できるまで、さらにバディの顔色も妥協できないと、しつこく。印刷所に行って色のプロ相手に素人が「もう少し黄色を」「ちょっと赤みを抑えて」とお願いする。最初は「そんなことしたら、こっちも黄色くなるで」とか言われて

ギスギス感があった。ひりんこもプレッシャーで顔の筋肉がピクピク。それが、しばらくやり取りを重ねていくうちに、こちらの言っていることが理解してもらえるようになっていく。職人さんたちとの一体感が出てくる。最終的にはみんなで同じゴールを目指すチームとなり、全てのページが終わった時、全員で万歳！！と盛り上がった。職人さんたちは8時間交代制、2人は揃って24時間態勢の印刷機と共にノンストップ。納得がいく色が出るまで印刷所に何日もへばりついた。その間バディを家にひとり置いては行けないので、印刷所には内緒で控え室に連れて行った。すいません。

その頃の家具のカタログといえば、数百円あるいは店頭で無料で配るものがほとんどだった。そんな中、1800円で販売することに。だって自費出版でそれなりに印刷代も経費もかかったし、なんだかとてもいいものができたので、なにも無理して安く売らなくても、写真集を買うように、好きな人だけに選んでもらったらいいんじゃないかと、無知なだけに強気だった。

初めて刷ったカタログ VOL.1 は、2000冊。こんな小さな個人の家具屋がこんなもん作ったら、「こりゃあ、一生このカタログの上で寝なあかんな〜」と思った。2人でバッグにカタログを詰め込んで東京の本屋さんに行商に行った。
「僕たち大阪でこんな家具作ってます。TRUCKといいます」
なんやかんやで数軒に取り扱ってもらうことができた。2ヶ月後、在庫がなくなり、まさかの5000冊増刷。そしてさらに5000冊増刷。VOL.2は初版から10000冊刷った。VOL.3は初版から15000冊刷った。さらにそれぞれ増刷を重ね、累計68000部を超えたようだ。カタログの作り方は相変わらず、時間のかかるアナログなまま。

ところが、VOL.3を出版してから、新しい場所を作ることに集中していたので、気がつけばもう7年も経ってしまっていた。うっかりしていた。普通の店だったらありえないうっかりではないか？
最新号が7年前のって…。

2009年、中央区玉造から旭区の新しい場所に引っ越して、ようやく次のカタログが視野に入ってきた。この新しい空間で、今の気持ちで欲しいと思う新作家具を考えよう。（いい加減に次のカタログを作らないと。いや、作りたい）
ということで、ただ今新作を産み出しているところ。
おそろしくマイペースな店やなあと自分たちのことながら思う。

Catalog

When they opened, their style of doing things themselves was quite new. This got a lot of people interested in their story and brought a lot of magazines out to their little shop to do articles about them. Thanks to this attention, they have not had to spend any money on advertising over the last 15 years. They were happy that national magazines covered them, but there was no way for people to find out more about them. The internet was not as widespread as it is today, so they didn't even have a website. More and more people who had seen them in magazines called, wanting to know where they could buy their furniture in Tokyo or other cities, but they only sold it in their little shop in Osaka. They decided to make something to give people who were interested, but couldn't visit Osaka, a chance to experience the atmosphere they had created.

Just as neither of them had worked in a furniture store, they didn't know the first thing about how to make a catalog. It turned into a catalog, but their initial aim was much more modest. They weren't trying to make a sales tool. They just wanted something to communicate the atmosphere of TRUCK.

They used their home as the setting for the photos. They didn't want to just photograph lonely pieces of furniture, so they brought out things that they used in their everyday life and put in on the tables. They didn't consider what they were doing to be "styling", they just didn't want the tables to look so bare.

As Hiromi began to take photos, the dogs and cats made themselves at home resting on the furniture. Just before Hiromi pressed the shutter button, Buddy would wander into the frame or Nya would jump onto the sofa or table they were photographing. When they got the photos back from the developer they were happy to see how natural the animals' expressions were. They decided to use the photographs as is, even if it meant that the furniture was sometimes half hidden by Buddy's hind end.

Hiromi used a simple SLR camera she had bought a few years before to take pictures of her illustrations. They always got the photos developed at speed developing service near the local train station. They weren't professionals and really didn't know how to use the camera beyond the basic auto-mode. They could take pictures on sunny days, but not if it was rainy or cloudy. Once they got the pictures developed they looked them over to see if they were ok. If the color was bad, or there were unnecessary things in the picture, they scrapped them and took them again.

When they started, they had no idea that people making something like this would generally hire a photographer, rent a studio, hire a stylist, and the like. They just made it up as they went along. It wasn't that they were trying to be cool by doing things themselves. They just didn't know that whole world existed. It seems to have worked out OK.

Just as they had made their furniture, so they made their catalog. They took the photos, designed it, drew the illustrations, and attended the printing. It took a long time to get it all done. They felt a strong attachment to each piece of furniture, so they were very intent on the colors being right. They went to great lengths to ensure that the color of the wood or of Buddy's face matched what they wanted, overseeing the printing and checking each page as it came off the presses.

At first they felt uncomfortable as amateurs asking the professionals to boost the yellow in one picture or to lessen the red in another. The printing company staff were initially reluctant to make changes. "If we make the yellow stronger here, then this will be yellow, too." they protested. Hiromi found the pressure so taxing that her face began to twitch. However, as they persisted in asking for changes, the staff gradually began to appreciate their passion and they started working together as a team heading towards the same goal. When the final pages were printed they all cheered "Banzai!" together. The workers had eight-hour shifts, but Hiromi and Tokuhiko worked around the clock for days. They stayed until they were satisfied with all the colors in all the photos. While they stayed at the printing factory, there was nobody who could look after Buddy, so they secretly stashed him in an empty room. They apologize.

At the time, catalogs were usually given away in stores for free. They decided to sell theirs for 1800 yen. They had published it and paid for it to be printed themselves. What they had made, they thought, was very good, so they didn't want to set the price unreasonably low. They hoped people might buy it in the same way they might buy a photo book and set the price accordingly. Their lack of knowledge helped them take this strong stand.

They started off with a print run of 2,000. They were only a small furniture shop and worried that they'd be sleeping on catalogs for the rest of their lives. They packed a bunch of catalogs into a suitcase and headed to Tokyo to try to persuade some bookstores to carry it.

They introduced themselves, explained that they ran a furniture business in Osaka and were able to get quite a few booksellers to agree to sell it. Two months later they had sold their entire stock. They printed another 5,000, followed by another 5,000. Volume 2 started with a print run of 10,000 and Volume 3 with 15,000. So far, they've sold about 68,000 copies of their catalogs all together. They didn't change from the slow analog process they'd used for the first one.

After Vol. 3 was printed, Tokuhiko and Hiromi became absorbed in building their new place. Once that was completed they realized that seven years had passed since they had last printed a catalog. Such a long time without a new catalog would be unthinkable for a normal company.

Now that they have moved to their new place, making a new catalog has come back onto their radar. They are thinking about the kind of furniture they want to use here. It's not that they feel obliged to make a new catalog, it's something they really want to do. At the moment they are in the process of coming up with new items. Even they are somewhat surprised at the extent to which they are happy to move at their own pace.

130.
HR S
W12

123.
SUTTO TABLE
W1650 D750 H700   nara(light brown)   207,000 yen   _to 037, 051, 054, 057 page

116.
SUTTO CHAIR
W435 D540 H780 SH460   fabric: F-33(green)   back: nara(light brown)   48,000 yen   _to 045, 055, 057, 061 page

117.
KT STOOL
⌀ 280 H405-480   nara(light brown)   37,000 yen   _to 003, 053, 089, 097, 159 page

119.
SUTTO BENCH
W1750 D320 H430   seat: nara(light brown)   legs: steel   81,000 yen   _to 039, 051 page

146.
AG SHELF
S / W930 D365 H970   nara(light brown)   flame: steel   105,000 yen   _to 043, 058 page
L / W930 D365 H1600   nara(light brown)   flame: steel   128,000 yen   _to 041, 059, 061, 244, 247, page

147.
AG BOX
S / W146 D315 H142   nara(light brown)   8,500 yen   _to 042, 043, 058, 059, 061, 173, 247 page
L / W292 D315 H142   nara(light brown)   10,000 yen   _to 042, 043, 058, 059, 061, 173 page

TRUCK WORKS

LUCHA LIBRE
ARENA
COLISEO
PERU 77
CENTRO
DOMINGO 4 DE NOV DEL 2001 A LAS 5 PM
LUCHA EN RELEVOS 3 VS 4
GIGANTE SILVA
RAYO DE JALISCO
BLACK WARRIOR
TARZAN BOY
CIEN CARAS
BLUE PANTHER Y BLACK TIGER
TRES LUCHAS MAS
LUCHA LIBRE
ARENA
NEZA
AV CARMELO PEREZ 369
JUEVES 8 DE NOV DEL 2001 A LAS 8 PM
POR EL CAMPEONATO
MUNDIAL DE PESO SEMICOMPLETO
SHOCKER
VS EMILIO CHARLES
LOS 3 VILLANOS
VS TARZAN BOY
TRES LUCHAS MAS

This is the one: nothing but TRUCK.

93.
OAK TABLE
W2000 D900 H710   white oak(natural)   360,000 yen   _to 221 page

111.
QUATTRO CHAIR
W430 D520 H795 SH450   leather: L-4(black)   flame: nara(light brown)   57,000 yen
_to 079, 083, 085, 093, 221 page

Inhabitants

We share our home with many cats and dogs. Before TRUCK started, we were joined by Buddy. After TRUCK opened, Nya, a cat that hung around the front of the store, became a member of our family. Next was a kitten called Maru. Nya liked Maru and cared for her as if she were his own. We had only had her for a few months, though, before she became ill and passed away. Hiromi was very depressed. After about a month, she was feeling better and we were on the point of going to an animal shelter to find another kitten. But, over the next couple of months we came upon many stray cats that were in bad situations. It was like Maru was calling us to them. We now have eight cats.

One day, in a nearby park, Hiromi found a dog that couldn't move. We put up flyers around the neighborhood to try to find the owner, but had no success. We named her Dingo because she looked so much like the Australian wild dog. We took her to the vet when, after a few days, we noticed that her nipples were becoming larger, and discovered that she was pregnant with five puppies. We were told that it would be dangerous for her to have an abortion, so we let her give birth at our house and looked for people to take in her puppies. We decided to keep Dingo with us. She ended up giving birth to six pups. It was impressive to see how quickly they recognized their mother and how naturally she began to care for them without having to look at a textbook. After a lot of searching we were able to find good homes for four of the pups, and ended up keeping two, John and Jack, to live with us.

When Buddy's son, Junior, was born, we ended up with five dogs and eight cats living under the same roof. Over the years, we have picked up many other abandoned cats and dogs and found good homes for them. They are in many different places, living happily.

Buddy & Junior

Buddy on the Beach, 2002

Dingo's Family
John   Dingo   Jack

Nya   Nico   Coro

Savi   Kuma

San-Chan   O-Chan   Tig

1）サンちゃんとオーちゃんの毎晩恒例の姉弟ゲンカ。
　　真剣そうだけどどこか微笑ましい。
2）仲よく昼寝のジョンとニャー。

Every night, San-Chan and O-Chan engage in playful battle. 1

John and Nya take a peaceful nap. 2

黄瀬家に住んでるワンニャンたち。TRUCKを始める前からいたバディ。TRUCKがオープンした後、店の前にいたニャーが仲間入り。その後、マルと名付けた茶トラの子猫が増えた。ニャーとすごく仲よしでニャーは自分の子供のようにお世話をしていた。が、病気を持っていて他界してしまう。ひりんこはすごく落ち込んだ。ひと月ほど経つと、そろそろ気持ちの整理がつき、どこかの施設に子猫をもらいに行こうかと話し出した矢先、次々に死にそうな状態の子猫に出会った。まるでマルが呼び寄せているかのように。

ある日、ひりんこが近くの公園でバッタリと倒れて動けなくなっている雑種犬を見つけた。家に連れて帰り、ビラを作って電柱などに張り巡らして飼い主を探したが見つからない。オーストラリアのディンゴにそっくりなのでディンゴと呼ぶようになる。数日後、お乳が大きくなっているように見えたので、もしやと獣医さんに連れて行くと、おなかに５匹の子犬がいることが発覚。中絶は母犬も危険と言われた。かわいそうなので家でお産をさせて、もらい手が見つけやすいであろう子犬の里親を探し、母犬ディンゴは引き受けることに決めた。大安産で予想より１匹多い６匹が小１時間で生まれた。産んだ直後から母の顔に変わったディンゴがすごく印象に残っている。誰にも教えられないし、教科書もないのにディンゴは子犬の世話全てをこなしていた。

厳格に里親さんを探した結果、４匹はとても幸せに暮らしている。情が湧いて残した２匹、ジョンとジャックが家族の一員となる。その後、バディの息子ジュニアも加わって犬５匹、猫８匹が同じ屋根の下に暮らすことに。

その他にもたくさんの犬と猫を保護した。その度に安心できる里親さんを何人も見つけた。みんなそれぞれの場所で幸せに暮らしている。

Nandemo Notebook

なんでもノート

なんでも書くからなんでもノート。
家具の始まりは、なんとなくの会話の中から、なんとなくの落書きの中から。その落書きがどんな素晴らしい家具に発展するか分からないから、あなどれない。
初めの頃はバラバラのメモに書いていたが、たまたま3冊持っていたハードカバーで無地のA4サイズのノートを使ってみた。整理のへたくそな2人は、時系列に保存できるというこの方式が気に入った。3冊目が残り半分を過ぎた頃、次がないことが心配になり出した。同じようなノートを探したがどこにも売っていない。残りのページ数なんて気にしないでどんどん使えるように、TRUCKで商品化した。紙の色や質感を吟味して、欲しいサイズ、厚みのノートが出来上がる。これで安心。ずっと使っていける。

なんでもノートの1冊目。ちょっとページをめくってみると、どうやら初めは家具屋をするつもりではなかったようだ。出会った当時、ブルースにはまっていた2人は、ブルースバーをやりたくて、メニューやらなにやらいろいろ書き込んでいた。それがいつしか、本業の家具屋の想像図に変わっていく。その頃、2人がどんな話をした結果、ブルースバーではなく家具屋になったのかは今となっては思い出せない。
店の名前の候補もたくさん書いてある。辞書を片手に響きのいい単語をあれこれ探したりもしたが、2人とも、こじゃれた店やブランドの名前が全く覚えられないたちなので、シンプルな分かりやすい単語1つでいこうとなった。そこで、アメリカの農場などにありそうな、色褪せたピックアップトラックのイメージ（日本のトラック野郎のトラックではない）が頭に浮かんだ。ひりんこは「働き者で力持ち。ピカピカに磨くんじゃなくて、どろんこが似合う。まさにとりんこにピッタリ!!」と言った。そしてTRUCKに決まった。家具には全く関係ない。

まだ、TRUCKの"ト"の字もない頃、1996年1月。
ひりんこがなんでもノートに「りそう的」と書いた落書き。家と店と工場がひとつの敷地内にあって、犬と猫のいる暮らしがすでにそこにある。

All of Tokuhiko and Hiromi's furniture starts as rough sketches in what they call their *nandemo* notebook (*nandemo* means "anything" in Japanese). They are careful not to dismiss anything lightly. Who knows what great furniture might grow from the roughest of sketches?

At first they jotted down their ideas in all kinds of notebooks, but they had trouble keeping track of things. Hiromi had some big, hardcover, unlined notebooks she'd found. They really liked the idea of being able to keep a long-term record of their ideas, but they had only three of the notebooks they liked, and hadn't been able to find anything similar. They contacted a local paper company and had them make something similar. Since then they've used the same notebooks.

Flipping through the pages of the first *nandemo* notebook you'd see that they didn't initially intend to start a furniture store. They were both really into blues music at the time and were thinking of opening a blues bar, so there are quite a few ideas for menus and signage. Before long, though, these give way to their ideas for what a furniture shop might look like. Neither of them can now remember what led them to give up their idea for the blues bar.

There were countless candidates for a shop name. With a dictionary in hand, they searched for a name that had a good feel. Neither of them were any good at remembering brand or shop names, so they thought that a simple, easy to understand, one-word name would be best.

Then the image of a faded blue pickup truck like you might find on an American farm came to mind. Hiromi said it reminded her of Tokuhiko. It was powerful, and looked better covered in mud than shiny and clean. So they decided on the name TRUCK. It had absolutely nothing to do with furniture.

In January 1996, before they had taken the first step in making TRUCK, Hiromi wrote the word *risou* (meaning "ideal") in the *nandemo* notebook. Under it is a picture of their house, store and workshop all together, and them living with cats and dogs.

On Good Land
INSPIRATION
Father
OXFORD
PLATES
DISHES
Italian
大図典

THE PATH TO TRUCK
Tokuhiko Kise

僕のこと

text_Tokuhiko Kise

小学生の頃から大阪近辺の山によく行った。大げさな登山とかではなく、犬を連れた散歩の延長のような気軽さで。自転車を担いで山を駆け上がり、道なき道を下る。時には、7つ年上の兄の乗るHONDA XL250Sの後ろに乗せられ山の中を走り回った。タンデムステップに足が届くか届かないかで。

中学生になってからは、雑誌「BE-PAL」で紹介されていたマウンテンバイクを見て、これしかない！と、貯めていたお年玉をはたいて東京の店から取り寄せた。1980年、マウンテンバイクなんてほとんど誰も乗っていなかった頃。金剛山や信貴山。毎週のように担いで登り、乗って駆け下りる。登山者とすれ違う時は驚かさないように止まって挨拶をする。「そんなとこ走れるん？」と聞かれると「もちろん！」と言って下ってみせた。「すごいなぁ」と拍手をもらったりしてちょっと得意気だった。

初めてのキャンプ用のストーブ、登山用品店で「初めてやったら灯油のにしとき。ガソリンのは危ないから」と勧められてドキドキしながら手に入れた真鍮のマナスル。山の中で、ちょっと気持ちのいい場所を見つけてコーヒーを沸かし、クッキーを食べる。すごくませた中学生。でも気分に浸っていた。

16歳で免許を取ってからはオートバイで山に。
新緑の初々しい葉で覆われ、トンネルのようになった道に、降り注ぐキラキラとした木漏れ日。家を出た時とは明らかに季節が進んで寒く感じる初秋、山の奥のほうでは葉が色づいてる。遠くに見える山並みが赤く見える。冬に山里の川沿いの道、カーブを曲がりながら目に入る1本の柿の樹。ほとんど葉が落ちた枝に実がひとつ。通り過ぎる一瞬の風景なのに不思議とそんな記憶がいっぱい。橋をひとつ渡るだけで気温が変わる。車に乗っているのとは感じ方、見え方が違う。匂いや温度の変化まで敏感に感じる。その頃からか、落葉樹が好きと意識していたように思う。
あまり手入れされていない鬱蒼とした常緑針葉樹は走っていて暗い。落葉樹の多い山は明るい。明るい山、四季の変化を感じる山が好きだった。

18歳の夏。アウトドアの雑誌で長野県松本技術専門校が紹介されているのを見た。高校に入ってから進路を考え続けていた。

わりと進学校の高校だったので、周りのみんなは大学に行くのが目的のようだった。僕はなぜかそこに疑問を感じ、入学後、先生に進路を問われると「将来何をしたいのかを考えます。そのしたいことに大学が必要ならば行きます」と答えていた。かなり変わった奴に映っていたと思う。でも、やりたいことなんて簡単には見つからない。あっという間に3年になっていた。もういい加減に決めないとヤバい。そんな時にその記事はすごく輝いて見えた。「信州で家具作り。いいやん。爽やか信州！」

小学生の時から6月が嫌いだった。祝日が1日もない。そして梅雨。湿気で学校の階段の手摺がペタペタ。だから日本の中でも湿度が低いという信州に惹かれた。オートバイで走る気持ちいい道もいっぱいありそう。さらに工作は小さい時から大好き。「家具作って売ったらいいんちゃう」インテリア雑誌とかもあまりない時代、家具なんて気にしたこともなかったのに、そんな単純な理由で飛びついた。すぐに見学に行った。そして決めた。これだ。

1年間の松本生活。朝から午後3時まで実習。他に来ていた人たちは、地元の中卒、高卒の若者。それと、様々な地方から、失業保険をもらいながら技術を身につけ「これで食べていくぞ」とかなり真剣本気な年上の人たち。その人たちは放課後も夜中まで残って作業をし、卒業制作では婚礼セットなんて本格的なものまで作っていた。僕は不真面目ではないけど、授業が終わるとすぐに帰っていた。ある時はちゃぶ台の脚の仕組みが面白いと、ちゃぶ台を作ってみたり、先生に頼まれて、寮の各部屋の扉や学校の作業場の大きな引き戸なんかを作っていた。それはそれで楽しかった。でも、なぜか毎月のように19号線を突っ走って約400km離れた大阪に帰っていた。あれだけ山がいいと思っていたのに。
卒業後は先生の紹介で、大阪の実家から自転車で10分の木工所で働くことになった。やっぱり大阪が良かった。

松本で思ったこと。
田舎で作って都会で個展などをして売るというのではなく、自分は街でやりたい。街なかに昔からある自転車屋、畳屋。通りから見える所で作業をしていて、奥に住んでいる。近所の人が気軽に立ち寄って「兄ちゃん。ちょっと椅子頼むわ」「はい。じゃ明日の夕方には仕上げておきます！」的な軽やかさ。そんなのがいい。作品ではなく日常生活で道具として使う家具を作りたい。漠然とそう思った。

3年と少し、その木工所でお世話になった。5人の椅子作りのベテラン職人の仕事ぶりを見て働いてきた。かっこ良かった。でも、自分が将来そんな職人になるのはなぜか想像できない。まだまだひよっこなのに、今、自分が作れるものから作ってみようと退社。多分、誰もが3年目辺りってムズムズ考え出してしまう頃。

その数ヶ月後、1991年23歳。
20坪のプレハブを借りて独立。3年の間に貯めた貯金全部を、賃貸の保証金と中古の機械を買うのにあてる。あと、実家からもらった古いスチールの事務机と奮発して買った当時10万円もしたファックス1台。以上。家具を作る材料を買うお金すらなし。もちろん仕事をもらえるあてもない。でも自分の工場がある。それだけで楽しい。
目の前の空き地で拾った板きれを使ったりしてテーブルやスツールなんかを作っていた。そのスツールは今もTRUCKのボール盤の前、現役で使っている。
ある家具屋さんと話していると「こんなん作れる？もしちゃんと作れるんやったら買うで」と写真を見せられた。頑張って作った。無事、気に入ってもらい、祝、何十万円かの初売り上げ!! でも、喜んだのも束の間、材料代や外注でお願いした塗装代などを支払うと残りは意外と少なかった。現実が目の前に揺れて広がっていた。でも、何かが少し動き出したように思えた。

ある日メープル材で椅子を1脚作った。タウンページで調べて梅田ロフトに電話をする。「家具を作っています。見て下さい」と言った。すると「じゃあ写真を持って来て下さい」と言われた。写真ではダメと思った僕は、椅子を担ぎエスカレーターで売り場に見せに行った。それが良かったのか気に入ってもらい、「2週間、スペースをあげるから、やってみたら」と言ってもらえた。
すぐにアクセル全開でその椅子を軸としたシリーズを作った。テーブルにデスク、チェストに小振りのキャビネット。それらを工場の前に置いて写真を撮り、偶然隣にあった印刷屋さんでパンフレットに仕立ててもらう。家具と共にそのパンフレットを持って2週間に挑んだ。
驚いたことに評判が良く、2週間だけと言われていたのが1ヶ月に延び、それが3ヶ月、半年、気がつくとそのまま5年間もお世話になった。いつしか仕事っぽくなっていった。

その後、ひりんこと出会うことになる。

THE PATH TO TRUCK

From elementary school, I enjoyed going to the mountains around Osaka. I wasn't a serious mountain climber, though. It was more like I was just taking my dogs for a walk. I sometimes carried my bicycle up the mountains and rode down tracks through the trees. My brother was seven years older than me and had his own motorcycle, a Honda XL250S, whose rear footrests I could barely reach. We used to go on trips through the backroads of the mountains.

In Junior High School, I saw an article about mountain bikes in BE-PAL, a popular outdoor magazine. It was the first time I'd seen anything like it. I had to have one. I used all of my savings and ordered it from a shop in Tokyo. This was in the 1980s when almost nobody rode mountain bikes in Japan. Almost every week, I rode it down the nearby mountains: Mount Kongo and Mount Shigi. On my way down, whenever I came across a hiker, I stopped to say hello. They could hardly believe what I was doing. "Can you really ride down this slope?" they'd ask. "Sure." I'd say, riding off, often earning some applause or a few words of praise.

I remember when I bought my first camping stove. The camping store owner recommended that I get one that ran on kerosene rather than gasoline. I was only thirteen and he thought it would be safer for me. I took it along every time I went to the mountains. I'd find a nice place in the woods and heat up some coffee, which I drank while nibbling on cookies. I suppose I was a very precocious junior high school student.

When I turned sixteen I got a license, so I could ride my own motorcycle to the mountains. There's something about riding a motorcycle that makes you very aware of your surroundings. You are acutely aware of colors, scents, light, and temperature; much more so than when driving a car.

I remember riding over a bridge and feeling a sudden change in the temperature. I remember riding through a tunnel of fresh green leaves, and the sunbeams that streamed through them. I remember getting to the mountains and noticing how much cooler it was than the city. I could really feel that the season was starting to turn. I noticed here and there leaves starting to change color and the red haze of the mountains far off in the distance. I remember noticing a lone persimmon hanging onto an otherwise bare branch as I followed a curve on a road by a river.

I have many such memories, things I noticed in an instant as I passed by.

It was at this time that I began to appreciate deciduous trees. I felt that the neglected evergreen forests were very dark, but deciduous forests were bright and airy. In these bright mountains I came to appreciate and love the changes each season brought.

When I was 18, I saw an article for the Matsumoto Technical School in Nagano in an outdoor magazine. Since starting high school I had wondered what I'd do for a career. I was in a school where many people went on to university. That was the goal of everyone around me. For some reason, I wasn't so sure that it was the best path for me. When I entered high school, a teacher asked me what I intended to do after I graduated. I remember saying that I'd decide what I wanted to do in the future, and that if I needed to go to university to do it, then I'd go. He must have thought I was rather strange. It was difficult to decide. Before I knew it, it was my senior year. When I saw that article, something about it struck me. I knew that I had found a place to start.

Since elementary school, I had hated June. There were no public holidays and it was right in the middle of the hot, humid rainy season. I remember the handrails on the stairways at school being sticky with humidity. That's one of the reasons I felt drawn to Shinshu, one of the driest places in Japan. There were lots of roads that I could ride my motorcycle on, too.

text by Tokuhiko Kise

Since I was young I'd liked making things. Wouldn't it be nice, I thought, to make and sell furniture. At the time there were hardly any home interior magazines and I'd never paid much attention to furniture. However, something about the idea appealed to me. I soon took a trip to see the school and decided to enroll shortly after.

I lived and studied in Matsumoto for one year. Lessons went from early in the morning till three in the afternoon. Almost everyone else at the school had graduated from local schools. The rest were earnest older men who were doing training while collecting unemployment benefits. "This is how we can make a living," they said. They stayed long into the night working on their graduation projects. I took my study seriously, but I went home as soon as class finished. I used my free time in many ways. I found the leg mechanism of *chabudai* (a low Japanese table with folding legs) fascinating, so I tried to make one on my own. And, at my teacher's request I made new doors for the dormitory and a big sliding door for the workspace. I spent a lot of time riding, too.

I liked the mountains, but almost every month I made the 400km ride down Route 19 to visit Osaka. When I graduated, I got a job in a woodworking shop just 10 minutes from my family's home in Osaka. I was happy to be back.

When I was in Matsumoto, I decided that I didn't want to become the kind of furniture maker who built stuff in the country and came to sell it in the city at a personal exhibition. In the city there are many small businesses that have been there for years: bicycle shops, *tatami* mat shops, and the like. You can see the workspaces as you pass on foot. The owners live in the back or above the store. I imagined running that kind of furniture store. The locals would call out and tell me they needed a chair. "OK, come back tomorrow evening." I'd say in reply. It sounded good to me. I didn't want to make works of art, just things that people could use in their everyday lives.

I worked at the woodworking company for a little over three years. All of the other workers were true craftsmen who had worked for the same firm for over fifty years. I admired their skill, but I knew I didn't want to follow the path they had chosen. I was still relatively inexperienced, but I felt a strengthening desire to build my own things. In 1991, when I was 23 years old, I handed in my resignation and started up on my own.

I rented a 60m^2 workshop, using my entire savings to pay the deposit and buy the machinery - used, of course - that I'd need. I salvaged an old desk from my house and bought a fax machine. At the time, these were incredibly expensive. It cost more than 100,000 yen. I didn't have enough money to buy lumber, but I had my own workshop. That made me happy. I made tables and stools from bits of discarded wood from the vacant lot in front of the workshop. The first stool I made is still in active service. It sits in front of the drill in the TRUCK workshop.

At one furniture shop, I was shown a photograph and asked, "Can you make this? If you can, we'll buy it." I worked really hard and managed to make it. They were happy with the results and I got paid several hundred thousand yen. I was on top of the world, but my celebration was short-lived. Once I'd paid for the materials and paint, there was hardly any money left. It was a sharp taste of reality. I had taken my first step, though, and was moving forward.

After that, I made a chair from maple wood of which I was quite proud. I looked up the Umeda Loft (a popular department store in Osaka) in the phone book and gave them a call. I told them that I made furniture and would like to show it to them. They said they would take a look and asked me to bring some photos to show them. I didn't think photos alone would be enough to convince them, so I took one of my chairs along when I went to meet them. They were impressed by the quality and agreed to give me a space in their store for two weeks. I went to work making a series of furniture made from maple wood that included a table, a desk, a chest of drawers, and a small cabinet. I took photos of them in front of the workshop and had the printing shop next door make up some pamphlets. With these in hand I started my two weeks. My furniture turned out to be quite popular. Two weeks turned into one month then was extended to three months. I ended up selling my furniture through them for five years.

Before I knew it, it had become a job.

Soon after, I met Hiromi.

THE PATH TO TRUCK
Hiromi Karatsu

私のこと

text_Hiromi Karatsu

小さい頃から動物と植物と絵を描くことが好きだった。
芸大を出てからテキスタイルデザインの企画の仕事に就く。3年目に入った頃から、やっぱり自分でイラストを描きたいと次第に思うようになっていった。
毎日、満員の地下鉄に揺られながらオフィス街に通勤。駅から地下街を通って会社に着き、ビルの中で仕事をする。そして深夜、地下鉄で帰る。「今日、晴れてたっけ?」そういえば、空を見てない。こんな生活でいいのか? このままではいけない。
そして25歳、ぎゅうぎゅう詰めの電車の中で決断。

ドキドキしながら初めて自分のイラストを大阪の出版社に持ち込む。1人暮らしもスタートしたので、これからは家賃と食費も稼がなくてはならない。まだ、どことも仕事の話なんか決まっていなくて収入の予定はなし。貯金も約2ヶ月分の生活費くらいしかなかった。けど、これからは自分のやりたいことができるという喜びのほうが大きくて、今までのようなストレスは全くなし。いざとなれば、バイトのかけもちでもしながら、なんとかやっていけるさって感じでお気楽に考えていた。
ひとつ仕事が入り、その仕事を見てまた違う人から依頼があり、そのうち特に営業をするわけでもなく順調にイラストレーターとして回り出した。この時から、仕事をする上で大切なのはもちろん技術も必要だけど、人とのつながりが一番だと感じる。
気持ちよく仕事をこなせた相手とは、また次につながっていくということ。好きなイラストで自活でき、とても充実していた。思い切って飛び出して良かった。

昔から植木を育てるのが好きだった。皐月の盆栽をしていた父親の影響。でも決して、こじゃれたガーデニングではなく、おばちゃんが家の玄関先に並べるような、そこから歩道いっぱいまではみ出して侵略していってるような、もさっとした感じが好み。
電車に乗っている時、私は忙しい。ずっと、どんどん通り過ぎていく知らない街の家々のベランダと屋上ばっかり目で追っている。
ベランダや屋上。私にとって、そこは、その家独特の植木ワールドが展開されている魅力ある場所に他ならない。

時には、今すぐこの電車を降りてピンポンして見せてもらいたい!! という衝動にかられるくらい、すごい所もある。でも、その人たちはきっと"ガーデニング"しているつもりは絶対ないはずだ。もっと、ほったらかし感のある感じ。雨水だけでOK！みたいな。ほったらかしなようでいて、雪の日にはちゃんとおばちゃんにビニール袋をかぶせてもらえる多肉植物たち。王道はアロエ、金のなる木、ゴムの木、カポック、オリヅルラン、ユッカ、ソテツ、ゼラニウムといったところか。
たまに街で見かける、引っ越しの後の不要品の山や閉店した喫茶店など、まだ生きているのにゴミと共に平気で捨てられている鉢植えを見過ごせない。何度も持ち帰った。カリカリになった鉢でもちょっと横から出ている芽を摘んで、水にさしてやると根が出る。その強さが好き。TRUCKや自宅にはそうして仲間入りした植物がたくさんある。

小さい頃から好みは渋かった。中学生の時に自分で選んだ勉強机は、真剣なグレーの事務机だった。さらに気に入ったものは、しつこく持っている。小学生の時に300円くらいで買ったべっ甲もどきの手鏡や、中学生の時に買ったポーチは今も現役で使っている。（かなりヨレヨレ）
雑誌は切り抜いてこまめにスクラップしたが、高校生の時に大好きだった「Olive」だけは切らずに大事にとってある。ページを見ながら気になるものといえば、大抵クレジットのないスタイリングに使われている商品じゃないものばかりだった。

他人にとってはガラクタでも、大好きなもの。
それらのコレクションはいつしか"ヒリコレ"と呼ばれるようになった。
集まるジャンルはたくさんある。
ぶっさいくなぬいぐるみ、カゴ、ブラシ、鍋、がま口、箱もの、古い道具、猫のひげ、なぜか集まるゼンマイ仕掛けのクマ。
そう、クマもの。特にシロクマ好きなのが友人の間で知られているので、いろんな人がいろんな所から見つけては持って来てくれる。好きなものがはっきりしているのはお得である。
4Bの鉛筆が好きで（シャーペンは使わない）鉛筆削りではなくカッターで削る。鉛筆ホルダーを使って、使える所まで使い切ったチビた鉛筆たちもまた、捨てられない。お片付けが流行るこの頃だが、基本的に捨てたいものは家にはない。

私にとっては有名なものも、高価なものも、拾った石ころも、錆びたワイヤーのカゴも一緒。ブランド名、デザイナー名は興味ない。どうせすぐ忘れる。そもそも覚える気もない。コレクターではないので、年代とかブランドの価値で高価になるものとはちょっと違う。
好きかどうか。直感で選ぶので早い。ほとんど迷わない。
アンティークショップとか蚤の市だけではなく、なんだか怪しい古道具屋や外国に行った時にはスーパー、荒物屋、金物屋などを物色する。数ある中からほじくり出すのが大好き。
とりんこに言わせると「僕やったら10分も見たらもういいって思うような店で、何時間でも、ヘタしたら半日でもかけて、まるで鷹の目を持っているかのように獲物を見つけ出す。その獲物たちを並べてみるとすっかり唐津ワールドになっている。そのままステキな店になりそうなくらい」
TRUCKをしてからはカタログ撮影や店のディスプレイに使うという口実ができて嬉しい。

基本的にモノを選ぶ時は、素材、質感が決め手。革、木、鉄、籐などの味が出てヤレた感じが好き。だからアメリカ、イギリス、ドイツ、フランス、はたまたインドにタイにアフリカ、デンマークなどなどいろんな国と、古いもの、新しいもの、中途半端なものといった様々な年代が、ごちゃ混ぜになっていても不思議と統一感がある。
シロクマ舎には、特にすぐ使い道がないものでも、その存在に一目惚れして手元に来たものはずっと出番を待っている。スペースが許せば、できるだけしまい込んでしまうんでなく、見えるように置いておく。そして、それらはいつか店作り、カタログ作りに生かされる。何かの時に、膨大なコレクションの中から、あ！あれがピッタリ!! と思い出すのだ。それがまた、笑えるほどピッタリ！サイズなんかもミリ単位でピッタリ。これは私の得意技である。

いろんな所から縁あって家にやって来た、捨てられるはずだったもの。いつか出番が来るとずっと倉庫に置いておいた、日赤病院の昭和初期に建てられた小児病棟からもらった木製の窓やドアは、新しい店のイベントスペースにばっちりはまった。TRUCKの横にあったトヨタ自動車整備工場の取り壊しの時にもらった作業台は店のカウンターに。解体された古い団地のベランダの柵はレンガの外壁に溶接して取り付けた。廃業した革靴工場で使われていた革漉き機はシロクマ舎で今も現役で。どれも、新しい居場所で活躍している。

ニャーを筆頭に、うちの8匹の猫や雑種犬のディンゴだって、明日をも知れぬ野良だった。今ではみんなご機嫌さんで暮らしている。

THE PATH TO TRUCK

Since I was young, I have loved plants, animals, and painting. After finishing art school, I worked as a textile designer. Every morning I rode the crowded subway to work. All day I was stuck inside a building. Then at night I rode the subway back. *How was the weather today?* I wondered. I didn't know. I had not seen the sky at all. After three years, I became convinced that what I really wanted to do was draw my own pictures. At the age of 25 I decided to strike out on my own.

At first I took my illustrations to publishing companies in Osaka. At the time I had just started living by myself. I had to pay rent and buy food. My savings would see me through about two months. Beyond that, I would have to get work to earn money. It wasn't easy, but I was happy that from now on I'd be able to do what I wanted. The stress I'd felt before was gone. If I ran out of money, I would just get a part-time job and do that alongside illustration.

Happily, I was soon able to land my first illustration job. Someone else saw the work I'd done and from them I got my next job. In this way I continued to get work. I didn't have to go out and *sell* my stuff. I began to realize that while technique was important, it was just as important to build connections with people. Doing good work for one person led to getting work from others.

I have loved growing plants for a long time. My father kept bonsai trees and I think I was influenced by him. I wasn't interested in neat and tidy gardening, though. What I liked was the kind of garden an old woman might make with pot-plants in front of her house, so many that they spread out onto the the sidewalk.

I kept myself busy when I rode the train. As I passed through neighborhoods I didn't know, I saw a charming world of plants growing on the verandahs and roofs of many houses. Sometimes I was tempted to get off the train, go and ring their door bell, and ask to see it. But of course, the people raising these little gardens probably didn't see what they were doing as gardening. The plants looked somewhat neglected, as if rain was their only source of water. In winter, though, on snowy days, they were often covered with plastic sheeting to prevent them from freezing in the cold. Someone *was* caring for them, in a way. I saw the same plants again and again: Aloe, Jade Plants, Rubber Plants, Kabok, Spider Plants, Yucca, Cycads, and Geraniums.

When people move, or shops close, you often see plants left out in the trash. I can't just walk past them. If they have some life still left in them, I pick them up and take them home. Even a dried out plant that has even one fresh green bud on it can recover if given water and attention. I like that strength. There are many such plants in TRUCK and our home.

For as long as I can remember, I've had a strong sense of what I liked. In junior high school I chose my own study desk, a serious grey office desk, an unusual choice for a young girl. I keep the things I like for a long time, too. I still use the mock tortoise-shell hand mirror I bought for 300 yen in elementary school and a pouch I bought in junior high school (although it's very worn out).

I used to cut pictures from magazines and carefully keep them in scrapbooks. The one magazine I didn't touch with my scissors was *Olive* (a popular alternative fashion magazine). When I looked at those pages I found my eyes drawn most often to the items that were not the main products, the things in the background. Other people might see them as worthless knick-knacks, but I loved them.

I've collected a lot of things like that; ugly dolls, baskets, brushes, pots and pans, coin purses, old boxes, old tools, cat's whiskers, old notices, and wind-up bears. I especially like polar bears. Many of the polar bears I have, I've received from friends who found them here and there. There's value in people clearly knowing what you like.

I like 4B pencils, sharpening them with a utility knife rather than a pencil sharpener, and use them until there is just a little stub left. Even then, I don't throw it away. In my house there is nothing that I want to throw away.

I have no interest in brand names. For me, something famous or expensive is no better than a basket with rusted wire or an interesting stone. I'm not interested in designers'

text by Hiromi Karatsu

names; I soon forget them. I also don't try to collect things that might become valuable because of the brand or period they are from.

I choose things quickly, using intuition. I rarely hesitate. I gather things from many kinds of places: flea markets, dubious-looking old stationery stores, foreign supermarkets, and hardware stores. Tokuhiko has said, "Places that I would look at for ten minutes and think I've seen everything, she can look at for hours and find all kinds of treasures. She has the eye of an eagle hunting for prey. When she displays the things she's found, they always fit right into her world. Seeing them on display you could almost think you are in a cool little store."

Since TRUCK started, I've used many things from my collection in the store and in our catalog. It's nice to have an excuse for my gathering.

When I choose things, I'm generally making a decision based on the look and feel of the material. I like things that have been seasoned by the years, things made of leather, wood, iron, and cane. I gather things from many countries; America, the UK, Germany, France, India, Thailand, and Africa. I buy new things, old things, half-done things. They are all different, but there is something that unites them.

I like to keep my things close at hand in Shirokumasha, even if I don't have an immediate use for them. I don't pack them away. I prefer to keep them out where I can see them. Those things sometimes make an appearance in the store or the catalog. Almost without thinking, I can remember something that suits what we need down to the last millimeter. I'm quite proud of this skill.

There are many things that have come our way by chance that would otherwise have been thrown away. From an old 1950s Red Cross Hospital, we got some doors that we installed in the event space above the store. From an out-of-business car repair shop, we got a workbench that now functions as the main counter in our store. From the same old housing complex from which we rescued the trees, we got the fencing that sits upon our garden wall. From an old shoe factory we got a leather thinning machine that is now being used in Shirokumasha. Similarly, our eight cats and mixed-breed dog, Dingo, were all strays. They now live happily in our home.

ABOUT TRUCK

店作り

1996年、2人が出会って1年くらい経った頃、「せっかくいい家具を作ってるんやから、卸だけではもったいない。自分の家具をちゃんと見せる場所を持ったら？手伝うで」と、ひりんこが言い出した。とりんこの工場は畑の真ん中にあり、人通りの全くない所だった。迷うことなく次の日から物件探しがスタートした。

プレハブの工場、とりんこ、ひりんこがそれぞれ借りていた部屋。3ヶ所にかかる家賃がもったいない。ひとつにまとめよう。ロフトのような倉庫のような場所を見つけて、そこに住んでしまおう。風呂がなければキャンプ用の簡易シャワーでもいい。そこで家具を作って工場の前に出来上がった椅子でも並べて、通りがかった人に見てもらおう。そんな考えから始まった。住んで作ってちょっと見せて。そんな場所にしたかった。ちゃんとした店を構えるつもりはなかった。

大阪中、車に自転車を積んで、ポラロイドカメラを片手に物件を探し回った。車を停めて自転車に乗り換え、あらゆる通りを見て回る。空き家かどうか分からない物件は写真に撮り、持ち主を調べて直接話をしに行ったりもした。
そして大阪市中央区玉造にある古いビルを見つけた。ずっと前から誰も住んでいない幽霊ビルみたいな所だった。壁に掛かったままになっている10年以上前のカレンダーや、誰かが使っていた家財道具が置き去りになっていて、当時の空気もそのまま淀んでいた。息を吸うのも嫌な感じ。でも、1階を工場兼店にして2階に住んだらどうか。そんな想像ができた。
ワンルームを借りるのではない。年齢より若く見られる2人は相手にされない。ここに決めようと挑んでいるのに不動産屋のおっちゃんに、「家帰っておとうちゃんに聞いていで」と軽くあしらわれた。それから不動産屋へ行く時は、自分たちなりの大人っぽい服装に身を包むようになった。

約40坪の1、2階。コンクリート造りの建物の中に、床の間もあるしっかりとした純和風仕立ての部屋。天井も低く、全体に全てが遠い過去に取り残されたような状態。そのままでは住めるわけがない。自分たちで改造するしかなかった。
リノベーションという言葉も聞いたことがなかった当時、天井をめくりたいと持ち主に言っただけで絶対に駄目と即答された。若者がめちゃくちゃにして、結果、家賃も払えず出て行ってしまうのではといった想像をされていたみたい。でも諦めずに1ヶ月間かかって説得した。自分たちの思いを熱く伝えた。そしてなんとか改造の許可が出て賃貸契約に漕ぎ着けた。

まず、住む場所を作ろうと2階から取りかかる。
手始めに、ホームセンターで一番大きなバールをひとつ買った。何も分からず、そのバールを天井に食い込ませ、力任せにぐいっと引っ張ると、意外と簡単に天井が落ちた。落ちてしまった。びっくりした。もう引き返せない。やるしかない。
解体の粉塵で前も見えないような中、早朝から夜中までぶっとおしでぶち壊した。出たガラを捨てに行く用に軽トラックまで手に入れた。解体、ガラ捨て、ペンキ塗り、床張り、水道工事。電気とガス工事以外は全部2人でやった。知らないうちに電気の線が剥き出しになってしまって、あわや火事寸前？の危険な状態だったり、水道管から噴射して部屋中水浸しになったりと日々ハプニングの連続。素人恐るべし。ひりんこも初めて丸鋸を持った。床も張れるイラストレーター。

この玉造のビル、1ヶ月の家賃32万6千円！
今まで借りていたプレハブの工場、それに2人がそれぞれ借りている部屋の家賃が重なる。なんとかして早く仕上げないともたない。空家賃を払っている余裕はない。2人は仕事もそっちのけで、この改造だけに取り組んだ。そうして、なんとか気合いで1ヶ月間で2階に住むスペース、1階の奥に工場を完成させた。
引っ越し後、引き続き店になる部分を作るつもりだったのに、保証金やらペンキ、材木、その他材料費もかかり、軍資金が底をついてしまった。
店に着工するどころか、家賃が払えなくてはどうにもならない。「来月からは私が!!」とバトンタッチしたひりんこの貯金もなくなった。（なんといっても家賃、3ヶ月もすれば100万円！）
しばらくの間2人はそれぞれの仕事、とりんこは家具の卸、ひりんこはイラストで資金を貯めることにした。
並びにあった古い食堂で、毎日素うどん2つ。オプションのおかずを取るかどうかで喧嘩したことも。

でも、毎日楽しかった。誰に言われたわけでもない、自分たちのやりたいようにやっただけ。作業中も写真を撮ったり、ビデオで記録したり。寝不足で、全身ホコリだらけで、クタクタで、お金もなくて。でも面白くて面白くて仕方なかった。自分たちの場所を作っているのがとても楽しかった。

Making the Store

そうこうしながら、玉造に住み始めて数ヶ月経ったある日、ふらっと立ち寄ったアメリカ村のDEPT（1981年創業のカッコいい服屋さん）。そこで中古の椅子を見つけた。お金に余裕なんてないのに、もの作りの刺激をすごく感じ、どうしても手に入れたくて、店の人に相談した。すると奥からオーナーの松田さんが出てこられた。とりんこは自分が家具を作っていること、店も開こうと思っているけどまだできていないことなどを伝えた。
すると「えらい時間かかってんねんなぁ。やりたい奴なんかなんぼでもおるで。早よせえ。二番煎じになったらあかん」と言われた。スイッチが入った。ビリッときた。2人は少し安くしてもらった椅子と共に店を出てすぐに行動を開始した。
またまた工事の日々。火がついた2人は寝る間を惜しんで工事をすること2ヶ月半。ついに店ができた。
いっぱしの店になった。やってしまえば、なんとかなるものだ。

1997年1月18日 TRUCK オープン。
1階の奥で家具を作り、前半分のスペースを店にして家具を並べた。素人2人の手探りのスタート。そこで家具屋の経験のある中野ちゃんに店番を担当してもらうことにした。ひりんこは2階でイラストの仕事をしつつ、店のあれこれを手伝った。
オープンして1ヶ月目、「これ下さい」とお客さんに言われた。「えぇ？なんですって？」と驚いた。驚かれたほうも驚いた。おつりすら用意していなかったことに気づく。慌てて2階に駆け上がり財布を探しておつりを揃えた。店にはレジなんかなくて、タッパーに現金を入れていた。（実は、なんと2004年頃までタッパーのままだった‼）
それから少しずつお客さんも増えて注文も次第に増えていった。

1999年、TRUCKのすぐ裏手の通りに3階建てのビルを1棟借りることになった。AREA2と名付けた。

その頃、工場の前半分のスペースだけでは家具を展示する場所も狭い上に、出来上がった家具にオイルを塗ったり、梱包をしたりする場所も足りず、2階の自宅がほとんど占領されるようになっていた。
店に置ききれない家具は、2階の自宅で実際に使っているものを、お客さんに上がって見てもらう。1日中、ひっきりなしにお客さんが靴を脱いで「おじゃましま〜す」そんなプライベートなしの生活も限界になっていた。

そんな時にすぐ裏のビルが空くと聞き、見に行った。
60坪の3階建て。広い！「テニスできるなー！」とはしゃいだくらい。しかし、家賃84万‼ えぇっ!?そんなん払えるのか？でも、TRUCKから徒歩1分。こんないい物件、これを逃したら次はない。でも、家賃が払える保証も全くない。さあどうする？
悩みに悩んだあげく、ここを借りることにした。「頑張るしかない！なるようになる‼」こんな時の決断が勝負なんだと思う。
誰もが生活している中で、ちっぽけなことから時にはものすごくたいそうなことまで、大なり小なり常に決断しなければならないことの連続。ここぞという時に、巡ってきたチャンスをものにできるかどうか。よく運がいいとか言うが、その運は自分でつかみ取ってこそではないか。とは言いつつ、今、思い返してもあの時の決断は驚き。よく決めたと思う。かなりドキドキだった。

契約当初はこちらもまた、ちゃんとした店舗を構える気はなかった。まず、機械がいっぱいあるので当然1階が工場。そして、仕上げ、梱包の作業場が2階。残った3階は倉庫。その倉庫にTRUCKに置ききれない家具を置いておき、それを見たいというお客さんだけ裏へご案内しようと思っていた。

今度は前回と違う。TRUCKを営業しながらの改造。
閉店後の夜中、そして休日返上で解体、ガラ捨て、ペンキ塗り、フローリング張り、とまた全て自分たちでやったものだから、契約してからオープンするまで半年もかかってしまった。あまりに広いのでペンキを塗るだけでもものすごい量の一斗缶を使った。
そんな中、3階の倉庫はお客さんに見せることもあるのだから油断した内装にはできないと、こだわっていくうちになんだかかっこ良くなった。これまで2階の自宅に押し上げていたものや新作の家具を並べると、立派な空間になってしまった。
なので、じゃあここも店にしてしまおう。
でも、かなり急な階段を3階まで上がらないといけないし、作業している横の通路を通ることになる。こんなので大丈夫？普通、店って道路に面してるほうがいいよな。まあ、いいか。

店に立つスタッフは他に誰もいないので、AREA2の店番は愛犬バディとひりんこがすることになった。
とはいえ、ひりんこは家具のことは素人。だったら、見積などの伝票は元からあるTRUCKの店で中野ちゃんに書いてもらえばいい。そんなのんびりとしたAREA2のスタートだった。

ABOUT TRUCK

Making the Store

In 1996, Tokuhiko and Hiromi had been together for about a year when she first suggested that he create his own place to display and sell his furniture. Tokuhiko thought this was a good idea. At the time, almost all of his work was being sold through other stores. He had no control over how it was presented or sold. He was renting a small workshop surrounded by other factories and rice fields so, even if he had displayed furniture in the front, there would've been no people to see it. They began the search for a better place.

They were renting three places, Tokuhiko's workshop, his apartment, and Hiromi's apartment. Paying three rents was a waste of money, so they decided to simplify things by bringing them all together. They had in mind something like a loft or warehouse where they could both work and live. It wasn't important for them that it be especially comfortable. If there wasn't a shower, for instance, they would make do with a simple camping shower. Initially they didn't plan to make a proper store. It would be enough, they thought, just to have a place where passersby could see their furniture.

Over the next few months they searched around Osaka. They loaded their bicycles onto their car, drove to a suburb, then rode around, Polaroid camera in hand, looking for vacant buildings. Sometimes they found places that looked vacant, but didn't have a FOR RENT sign anywhere in sight. In those cases they looked up the owners and contacted them directly.
They finally found a suitable building in a suburb called Tamatsukuri, in Osaka's Chuo Ward. It wasn't much to look at, looking rather like a haunted house. The air was stale, musty, and quite unpleasant to breathe. A ten year old calendar had been left hanging on the wall and the floors were covered in old tatami mats. It had potential, they thought, they could live on the second floor and run the workshop with some display space on the first.

At first it was a struggle to get the real estate agent and the owner to take them seriously. Here were two young kids wanting to rent a whole building with a total floor space of about 260m². It would cost over 300,000 yen a month. "Go home and ask your father first." they remember being told. It didn't help matters that they wanted to strip the building back to its concrete framework. This was long before the renovation craze hit Japan, so the owner's reluctance was understandable. It took a month of visits (wearing their most adult-looking clothes), but they finally persuaded him to agree to their terms and sign a lease.

They started work immediately. They decided to make the second floor livable as soon as possible so that they could move in, and stop paying rent on their apartments. Tokuhiko bought the biggest crowbar he could find and gave it an experimental swing at the ceiling. He pulled down and was surprised as half the ceiling collapsed around him. There was no going back now. Together with Hiromi, he worked day and night in clouds of dust so dense that they could hardly see in front of them.

Aside from the gas and electric work, they did everything themselves: tore down the walls and the ceiling, disposed of the mountains of scrap, painted the walls, put in the floorboards, and installed the plumbing. Tokuhiko had experience working with wood, but a lot of this was new to him. Hiromi became one of the few illustrators who can lay floorboards and handle a buzz saw. Not everything went smoothly. Tokuhiko flooded the second floor a couple of times while he worked on the kitchen, and the electrician they got in was shocked to see the damage they'd done to some of the wiring. He said they were very lucky not to have caused a fire.

The work wasn't easy, but they enjoyed themselves every day. There was nobody to tell them what to do. As they worked, they took photos and shot video. They were exhausted, broke, and covered head to toe in dust, but the experience of building their own place was very rewarding.

They were able to get the second floor and the workshop ready in about a month. They had planned to continue working on the shop after they moved in, but their funds were running low. The rent for just three months cost them over one million yen! They had also had to pay for wood and paint. Their savings had almost run out, so they put their plans on hold. Tokuhiko started making furniture for wholesale again, and Hiromi took on some illustration work. For months they could only afford to eat at the cheap Japanese diner nearby. They bought a bowl of udon noodles each and argued about whether they could afford even the cheapest side dishes.

One day, after they'd been in Tamatsukuri for a few months, Tokuhiko and Hiromi were looking around a clothing/lifestyle store in Osaka called DEPT. There they

found a couple of cool old chairs that were unlike anything they'd seen before. They didn't have much money, but the chairs were so stimulating that they knew they had to have them. While Tokuhiko was trying to talk the shopkeeper into giving them a discount, the owner, Mr. Matsuda, came out from the back of the store. Tokuhiko introduced himself, telling him that he was making his own furniture and was working on opening his own store. "It's taking you a long time, isn't it? There are lots of people out there looking to do something similar." Mr. Matsuda said, "If you don't want it to look like you are just copying someone else, you'd better make a move soon."
Mr. Matsuda's words were a wake-up call. As soon as they left the store (chairs in hand) they set about setting up the store in earnest.

Tokuhiko and Hiromi started construction work once again. They worked around the clock and got everything set up in about two and a half months. Their lack of funds forced them to find different ways around various problems, but it all worked out in the end. They felt they had made a pretty good store.

On January 18th, 1997, TRUCK opened.

The furniture was made in the rear half of the first floor, and displayed in the front. Neither Tokuhiko or Hiromi had had any experience working in any kind of store at all so, to help run the store, they enlisted Ms. Nakano, a woman who had previously worked in a furniture store in Kyoto that had sold Tokuhiko's furniture. Tokuhiko worked in the back and Hiromi continued her illustration work and helped around the store.

It took some time for TRUCK to start selling. A few people came in to look around each day, but it was a month before they made their first sale. They were such amateurs that they didn't even have change ready. Tokuhiko had to hurriedly run upstairs to find his wallet. The number of customers gradually grew and they began to get some orders.

After a couple of years, they were running low on space. Tokuhiko had hired another two people to work with him in the workshop so it had become rather cramped. When each piece of furniture was finished, it needed to be oiled then packed up. With two other people working there, that work often happened on the second floor, in their home, which was also used as an overflow display space for furniture that didn't fit in the store. There was a constant stream of people, both customers and workers, coming in and out. The lack of privacy became rather restricting.

A building directly behind TRUCK had recently become vacant. Tokuhiko and Hiromi went to see it, and were amazed at its size. It was three stories high and had a floor space of 180m². "There's enough space to play tennis!" they remember thinking. It seemed like the perfect opportunity. It was just a minute away from TRUCK and it seemed unlikely that an equally good place would become available in the future.

There was a problem, though. The rent was very high. At 840,000 yen per month it was more than twice as much as they were paying for their current building. They worried that they might not be able to pay it. They believed, though, that when you are given a good opportunity, you have to take it. They finally decided to sign the lease. Looking back now, Tokuhiko says he is surprised that he was able to make such a decision.

They hadn't initially intended to turn it into a proper store. The original plan was to move the factory to the first floor and use the second for packing and finishing work. The remaining third floor was to be a storeroom. If customers wanted to see the furniture there, they could, but it wasn't intended for that purpose.

Once again, Tokuhiko and Hiromi did the remodeling of the new building themselves. The TRUCK store and workshop continued running while they worked on it. They spent all of their spare time preparing the new place. It took six months until they were ready. Customers were going to visit the third floor, so they tried to make it look as good as possible. When they saw it with furniture set up, they really liked how it had turned out and began to think of turning it into a proper shop. They had a few concerns; the stairs leading up to the 3rd floor were very steep, and to get to the shop customers would have to walk past the factory. It'd be unusual, but they decided it would be OK.

There were no staff to spare for the the new place, so they decided that Buddy and Hiromi would work there. Hiromi wasn't an expert in furniture so, if people wanted to make orders they went to the main TRUCK store to fill out an order form with Ms. Nakano. AREA2 opened in October 1999.

Making the Store

AREA2でのバディは、いつも展示品のベッドで気持ちよさそうに寝ていた。
時にはお客さんと一緒にソファに座ってくつろいだり、遊んでもらったりした。
倉庫の延長くらいの気持ちで作ったAREA2、結果的には、見せる家具もぐっと増えて、いい店になった。
その後、思いがけず「作り手の姿が見える家具屋」なんて取材されるようになり、バディも取材慣れしていく。
撮影が始まると、自らソファに座っていつしかカメラ目線を意識するようになっていた。

Buddy always made himself at home in AREA2.
He could often be found sleeping on the beds or sofas on display.
Customers often found themselves sharing a sofa with him. They didn't seem to mind, and neither did he.
AREA2, which had started out as just a storeroom, became a good shop in its own right.
It hadn't been planned, but magazines often pointed out that you could see the furniture being made in the workshop on your way to the store.
Buddy was also popular, and always seemed to be right where the camera was pointing.

TRUCKの家具にそっくりな模倣品を雑誌の中で見かけたり、知り合いやお客さんから「あまりにそっくりでひどすぎる！」「TRUCKが卸しているのかと思った」などと、教えられたりすることが多くなってきた。
TRUCKのソファをサンプルにひとつ買って、それをそのまま中国に送ってズバリ作りました、みたいなものから、中には内装、外装も含めて店まるごと１軒TRUCKそっくり！ おまけにシロクマ舎の革製品もどきまであったり。カタログも、写真だけでなくイラストや文章までそのまま使わせていただきました、みたいな悪質なケースもある。
発見した時はとても腹が立つ。だって、自分たちが時間をかけて産み出したもの、考えて考えてやっと形にしたものを、こうも簡単に表面の見た目だけ真似されるなんて、信じられない。オリジナルには、全てにストーリーがある。例えば、このソファの肘の形、どういった流れでこの形に行き着いたか。この張り地の素材が、なんでこのコーデュロイでないといけないのか。店の内装にしても同じ。このタイルを、この床材を決定するまでに、どれだけの時間をかけて、他にどれだけのものを見てきた中でそれにいたったか。どんな思いがあるか。その仕様にするためにいろいろと試作をし、素材を探し回り、紆余曲折を経て、全てがまとまるべくして、やっと、ひとつが完成するのである。
TRUCKの模倣品をいくつも作っている、東京のある家具屋と話し合いをした時、２人は言った。「僕たちは、この家具ひとつひとつに対して何時間でも話すことができる。あなたたちが何も考えずに安易に真似して作ったそれらに、どれだけの思い入れがあるかを、僕たちの前で語ることができるのか」と。そして、面白いことに確信犯はたいてい口を揃えてこう言う。「TRUCKの家具なんて見たこともない」と。
最近では家具だけでなく、内装も参考にされることが多いのか、見るからに内装業者です、といった人たちが図面を片手に店の床や壁などの写真を撮ったりしにくる。ひどい時には、オリジナルで作った店の鉄製の窓のサイズを、レーザーで測っている建築業者まで出る始末である。よその窓を測って、何がしたいのか？ もちろん、そんな非常識な現場を見つけたら、お断りして帰ってもらう。
もの作りをしていく中で、いろんなものを見て、そこからインスパイアされることはもちろんある。でも、それをそのまま真似するのではなく、いったん自分の頭の引き出しに入れて、自分の中で昇華して、それから自分らしい形で産み出していくものだと思うのに。モラルもなく安易に真似たものに奥行きはない。

Over the last ten years they have received a number of reports from friends or customers that they had seen something that looked just like TRUCK furniture in another store, or in a magazine under a different brand.
Sometimes they find sofas that are exact copies of theirs, as if one real one had been bought and sent somewhere to be copied. They even found a shop that was, both inside and outside almost exactly like their own. The photos and illustrations in the store's catalog were very similar, and the text, in many places, was *exactly* the same. It is extremely annoying.
They spend so much time and energy coming up with their furniture, they can't believe that someone would just copy the way it looks.
Everything they make is original. There is a story behind every decision. They can explain the process they took to decide on even small details like the shape of an armrest on a sofa. It's the same with the interior of the shop. They can tell you why they chose the particular tiles or floorboards they use. It's a long road to the final product, full of missteps and backtracking. They make many different versions of something before they come to a final decision.
Hiromi and Tokuhiko once met with representatives of a big company that was making imitations of their work. "You just made these copies without thinking." they said, "We could talk for hours about how we made each of these things. Can you do that? Can you tell us to our faces how emotionally attached you are to them?"
They always got the same answer:
"We've never even seen any TRUCK furniture."
Recently people have started trying to copy their buildings, too. They've had people who obviously work for interior decoration companies come to their store and blatantly, blueprint in hand, take pictures of their floorboards and walls. In one of the worst cases they found someone from an architecture company using a laser measuring tool to measure the metal frames they designed for the windows in Bird.
Of course, they see and get inspiration from many different things, but they never copy them or try to make something exactly the same. They absorb what they see and develop work in their own style, that is their own. Things that have been copied have no depth.

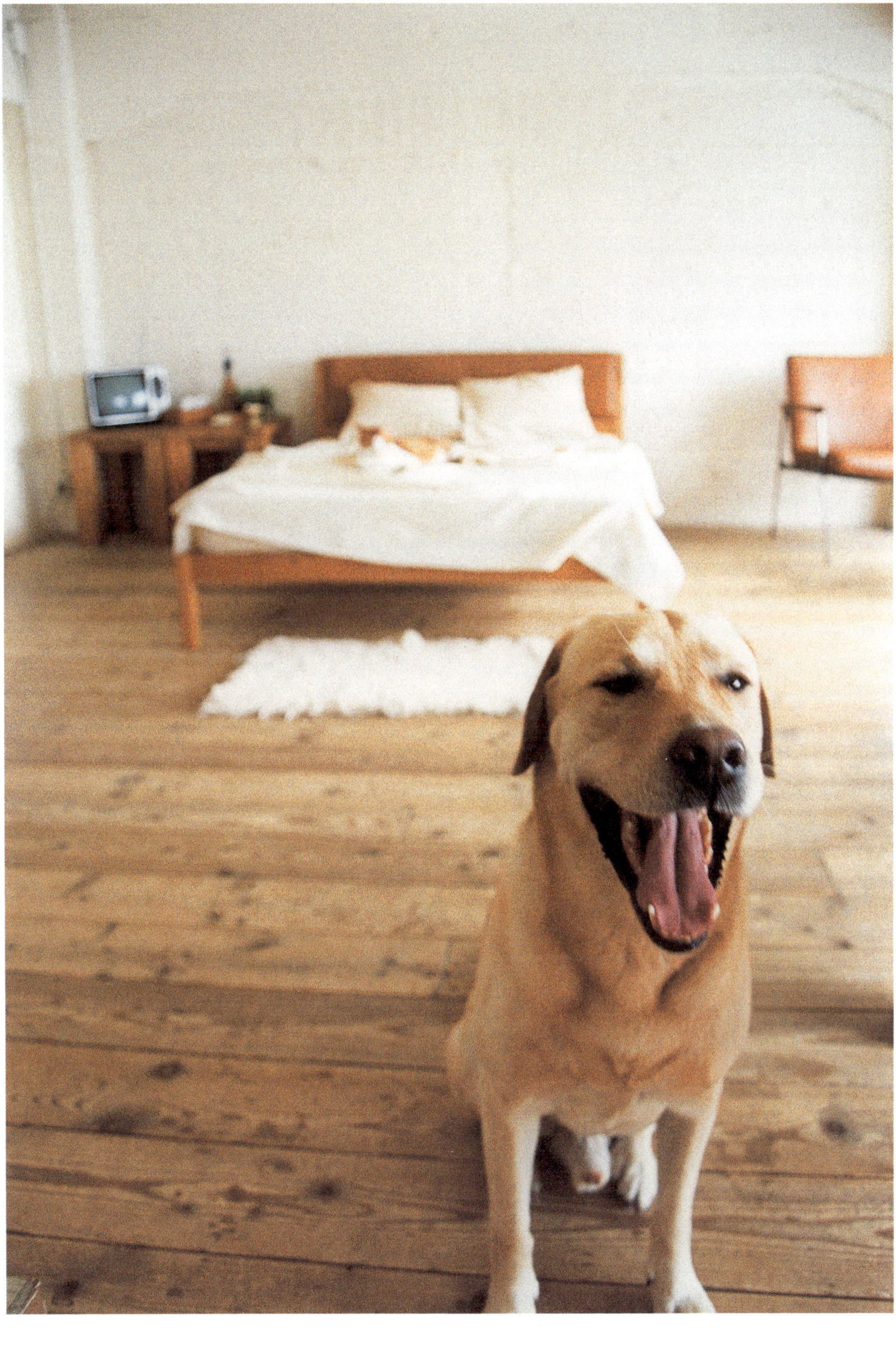

LONGING FOR A NEST

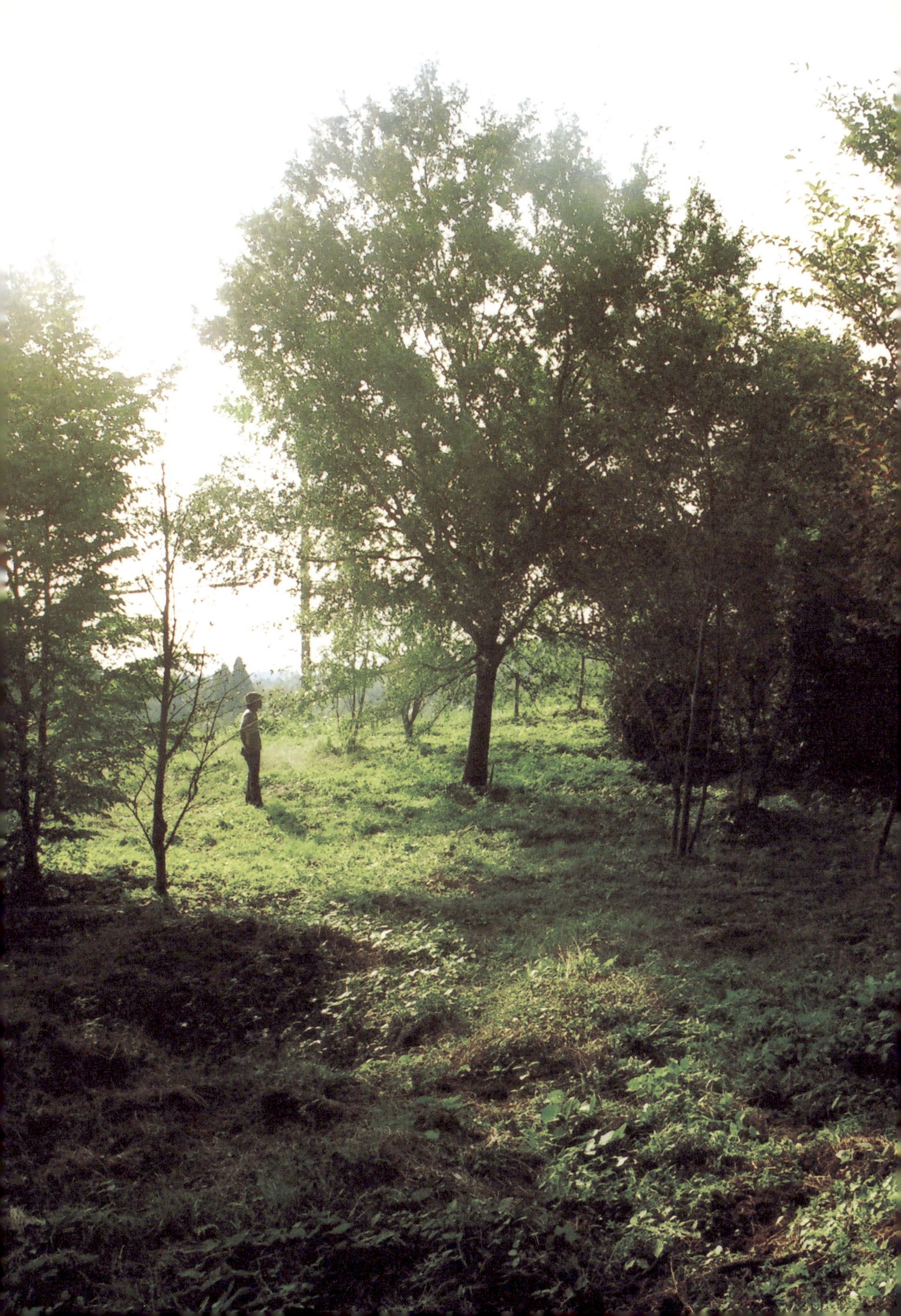

土地探し

今までいろいろな国、街に行ってみて印象に残ったこと。いいなぁと感じたこと。それは街の中でも大きな樹がたくさんあるところ。公園に限らず街路樹や個人の家にも。1人では抱えきれないような幹周りのオークやメープル。映画の中のアメリカの住宅地、道路と家の前の芝生の間にも大きな樹が当たり前にある光景。実際、行ってみると本当にそんなのはどこにでも見かけることができる。特別ではない。街に暮らしていて日々大きな樹が見られること。樹の姿で季節の移り変わりを感じること。それがいい。そんな毎日が欲しい。

玉造にTRUCKをオープンして数年。
店や住まい、アトリエの内装は、全て自分たちで改造したので、それぞれに思い入れもあったし気に入っていた。
でもドアを開けて1歩外に出れば、近隣がひしめく街の中。車がビュンビュン通る大きな道路、たくさんの路上駐車。
隣接したビルの会社の営業車も店のすぐ横を常に出入りしている。目に飛び込んでくる、たくさんの派手な看板類。
道路を挟んだ向かいに高層マンションが建ち10時から2時までの間、日当たりもなくなってしまった。
決して気分は良くない。でも、それが現実の毎日。
何年かずっと心の片隅で、もやもやとこんなことを考えながら、どこかにいい場所はないかと探し続けてきた。

「住まい、店、工場、倉庫、アトリエ。これらをひとつに集めたい」
そしてさらに、毎年訪れるヌーサでのこともあり、
日に日にもっと豊かな毎日を過ごしたいと思う気持ちは強くなっていった。
「地べたのある、樹に囲まれた気持ちのいい場所に」
思い浮かべるのは簡単。
でも、それってどこ？ そう、ここは大阪。ヌーサでもトスカーナでもない。
そんな簡単にステキな環境が見つかるわけではなかった。
家と店と工場。今までずっと肩を並べてやってきた。自分たちはやっぱりそれでしかない。切り離せない。
それら全てをとなると、どうしてもある程度まとまった敷地がいる。そして樹がある所となると必然的に郊外へと足は向いた。まずは大阪近隣の山近くをいろいろ見て回った。いろんな不動産屋にも声をかけて、土地や物件の情報があればファックスをもらい、チェックしに行く。自分たちでも時間を見つけては地図を見ながら車を走らせ、知らない土地を手当たり次第探す。

結構見た。
でも2人はどうもピンとこない。何がピンとこないのだろう？
山まで来た。確かに樹はたくさんある。あるけど何かが違う。
針葉樹林が多いせいか、暗く感じる所が多い。落葉樹が多い、明るい雑木林のほうが好きなのに。
そして街から離れて郊外へ行っても、やはり大きな看板やのぼりはいっぱいある。産業廃棄物が山積みだったり、民家の軒先をダンプがかすめてぶっ飛ばして行く。周りに樹はあっても、村では住宅が密集している。

Searching for Land

これが、信州や北海道まで行けば話は違うのだろうが、なかなか思い描いているようなロケーションが見当たらない。

2人が思い描いていたこと。

以前イタリアのトスカーナで見たような、国道から逸れた地道に入り、そのまま少し走っていくと広がる敷地に、家と店と工場、アトリエが点在している。周りには大きな樹がたくさんあって、隣接する建物もない。そこを自由に走り回る犬たち…。

2003年4月。
イタリア、トスカーナの小さな街、モンテプルチアーノに行った時のこと。アグリツーリズモといってホテルではなく農家に滞在する。そのオーナーであるカリーンのセンスの良さときたら、まるでインテリア雑誌の中に入り込んだようなステキ具合。古い石造りの建物、部屋のしつらえ。朝食のセッティングひとつとっても洗練されている。ひりんこはウハウハになって写真を撮りまくった。食べるまでにフィルム1本は使った。
それもそのはず。話を聞けば彼女はミラノのファッション業界の最前線で活躍した人だった。都会ミラノでの生活に疲れて、夫婦で何もない田舎のキャンティに移って農家を始めた。そして子供が生まれてから、今のモンテプルチアーノへ移って来たそうだ。ここには学校や病院、大きなスーパーマーケットも歩いて行ける距離にある。すぐ近くに見える古い城壁の中が街になっているのだ。
そして窓の外には見渡す限り、いわゆるあのトスカーナのオリーブ畑が延々と続くステキな風景。
「ずるい。日本ではありえない。こんなの見てしまったら日本に住まれへん」

MONTEPULCIANO, ITALY
APRIL 2003

Searching for Land

MONTEPULCIANO, ITALY
APRIL 2003

Searching for Land

ちょうどひりんこが妊婦の頃のこと。
「10年の契約の終わりが近づいています。こちらは更新するつもりはないので立ち退いて下さい」と家主さんから電話があった。びっくりした。もちろん期限があるとは分かっていたけど、そのまま継続していられると勝手に思っていた。急に足元が崩れていく思いがした。借りてるってこういうことなんだと。
大事な妊娠中に不安な気持ちなんて大敵。まして、「分かりました。すぐに引っ越します」なんて絶対できない。
この場所で10年、築き上げたTRUCK。急に出て行けと言われてもそう簡単にはいかない。
家と2つの店と工場、倉庫、シロクマ舎、そして5匹の犬、8匹の猫がいるのだから。
取り急ぎ話し合って状況を説明し、新しい場所を見つけるまではいられることにはなった。でもずっとではない。
見た目は変わらない毎日だけど、ゴソッと何かが滑落したような不安な気持ち。

TRUCKを始めて数年後、会計士さんから「中央区でこれだけ賃貸の家賃払ってるんやったら、土地、買ったほうがいいんじゃないか」と何度か言われていた。でも、土地や建物を買うなんて大人なこと、全くの圏外と思っていた。興味がなかった。身軽なのがいいと思っていた。
でも、気持ちが変わった。しっかりと地に足をつけようと。なんとなくだった土地探しに火がついた。人に言われて急遽間に合わせの場所で、間に合わせの店なんか絶対にできない。一刻も早く自分たちでいい場所を見つけないと！

待っていたって見つからない。
情報なんかなくてもありとあらゆる所を見て回った。が、探しても探してもない。理想を求め車を走らす日々。
2人とも特に大阪にはこだわっていなかったので、どんどん足をのばし、ずいぶん遠い所までやって来た。
うん、ここなら周りに民家も隣接してないし、この山林を切り開いて開拓すれば…でも、待てよ。家具屋をやめるわけではないのに、こんな奥地に引っ込んでしまって、はたしてお客さんは来てくれるのだろうか？いや、スタッフもどうやって通うのか？
ここでもないあそこでもないと走り回っているうちに、月日は流れ、日菜という家族が増えた。

樹を、自然を求めて山の奥へ奥へと探しながらも、ふと、子供がいるのに保育園、学校は？子供の毎日の送り迎えに車で片道30分以上かかるなんて不便すぎる。病院は？買い物は？なんて考え出すと、現実的じゃないかも、とまた暗礁に乗り上げる。探しに出かけては行き詰まる。その繰り返し。
自分たちが思い描くイメージと、お店を経営、そして生活をするということは矛盾しているのか？

そして気づいたこと。2人とも、別に田舎暮らしがしたいのではない。
自給自足を目指しているわけでもない。
どちらかというと、近くにコンビニがあったらあったでそれは便利、と思えるタイプだったりする。
今までのように街に住み、仕事をしている日常に樹が欲しいだけ。そう、いろんな国の街で見てきた普通なこと。

どうも、安易に樹があるという理由だけで山に行けばいいってもんじゃないみたいだ。
なんとなく2人の間にそんな空気が漂ってきた。ここらで方向を切り替えて、街で探してみるか？
樹は？樹に囲まれて暮らしたいんじゃないのか？
なければ自分たちで植えればいい！
数年かかって、とうとう2人はこういう決断にいたった。

旅する度に、毎回つくづく思っていたこと。
街の中に大きな樹がたくさんあり、都会なのに公園も広くて、緑が多い。地べたのある、当たり前に樹のある生活。
羨ましい。それに比べて2人の住んでいる大阪は本当に緑が少ない。少なすぎる。東京のほうがたくさん大きな樹がある。「なければ植えよう」と思ったのもそんな悔しさがあったからかもしれない。

作戦変更。「街で探そう」
街の中で、できれば近くに樹のありそうな場所。公園の周りなど。

工場、店、倉庫、自宅、アトリエをひとつにする。
今現在、実際に使っている床面積を足してみる。さらに地べたに樹をいっぱい植えたい。できるだけ大きな樹を。
そうなると、やっぱり300坪は必要。
手当たり次第に不動産屋に入って聞いてみる。
でも探していた約300坪というサイズの土地なんてなかなかない。不動産屋に入って「300坪の土地を探しています」と言っても、「この兄ちゃんたち、何言うてるん？桁、間違えてるんとちゃう？」と相手にもされない。
軽くあしらわれる。まともに請け合ってくれない。10年前、玉造の物件を決めようとしていた時の状況と一緒。

そして、ちょうどその頃はマンション建設ラッシュ。大阪では大きなマンションがニョキニョキ建てられている時期だった。だから、300坪なんてまとまった土地は、一般に出回る前に業者間で取引されてしまう。素人の僕たちには情報すら入らないと聞かされた。そんな中でも、数少ない情報を入手しては見に走る。
樹を植えるといっても限界があるので、できれば隣や前が公園で初めから樹があるほうが借景できて嬉しい。
そんな条件に合った大きめな土地。

それが街は街でまた、なかなか思うようにはいかなかった。見に行っても一瞬で終わることのほうがほとんどだった。
例えば、確かに隣は公園。でも反対側は目が潰れんばかりに蛍光灯がまばゆいクリーニング屋だったり。
向かいに大きなコインパーキング。これは要注意である。いずれ高層マンションが建つかもしれない。あるいは、閑静な住宅地。住むにはいいかもしれないが、そんな中で店を営業するのは難しそう。たくさんの人が来ると近隣とトラブルになるのは目に見えている。はたまた、騒がしい商業地域や完全工場地帯。店はできても、そんな所には住みたくない。

店と工場と家。
それぞれが近くで当たり前のようにやってきたことが、新しくまとめてとなると、なかなか難しい。

土地を気にし始めてからかれこれ4〜5年。かなりな所を見て回ったので、地名を聞くだけで、ああ、あの感じの辺り、とその街や山道の景色が浮かぶほどになっていた。

手当たり次第見に行く中には、ここやったら、と思う時もあった。その土地をどう使えるかを真剣に考えたが、よし決めようと思っても、上手く話が進まず、流れていった。
ある時、堺に700坪の物件の情報を得た。見に行くと、広い！700坪。でも工場跡ということで、土壌汚染の心配があった。そんなわけで坪単価が安い。この問題は土壌改良すればクリアできるのでは？倉庫にそのまま使えそうな建物もあるし、なんといっても広さが魅力だった。結構本気になって契約寸前までいった。
敷地内でのレイアウトなんかも考え始めたりもした。でも、やっぱりどんなに、ここだ!!と思っても縁のない所は不思議と決まらないようになっている。土壌汚染に関する堺市からの資料がなかなか出てこないので、契約がズルズルと延びてしまった。この期間に、盛り上がっていた頭が少し冷静になれた。

その2ヶ月後、今の旭区の物件と出会うことになる。
やっぱり、なるようになっていくのである。

旭区新森

ある日1枚のファックスが届く。"大阪市旭区、300坪"
2人とも旭区がどこかもはっきりとは知らなかった。いつも情報が入って実際に見に行っても、一目見たら一瞬で終わりだった。どうせまた空振りだろうから、ひりんこに「ちょっと見てくる」と、まだ数ヶ月の日菜を初めてのチャイルドシートに乗せて出かけた。買ったばかりのチャイルドシートを使ってみたかったのがメイン。

着いてみると、古いタクシー会社の事務所と車庫、立体駐車場が敷地いっぱいに建っていた。
樹なんて1本もない。建物にも魅力はなし。でも周りを見ると東、西、北と3つの学校に囲まれている。空が広い。
家に戻り、ひりんこに「学校に囲まれていて空が広い」と言った。
悪くない、と言える物件は貴重なので、すぐその足でUターンして今度は3人で見に行った。
やっぱり印象がいい。
細長い土地で三方が学校。しかも、校舎側ではなく、グラウンドや裏庭に面しているのでヌケがよく空が広く感じられる。前の細い道は行き止まりになっているから車の通り抜けがない。東西に長い南向き。
「うん。いい」ひりんこもすぐ感じた。
隣接する建物がない。公園ではないが、学校。そう、不変である。近隣に悩むことはない。街の中にあってこれは奇跡に近い。ここ4〜5年ほど探し続けてきた2人は、すぐにそう感じた。

でも、大きな道に面しているほうが短いので、店をするには間口が狭いと思った。ふと見ると向かい側の一角が宅地として分譲されていた。そこにいた営業マンに「土地だけでも買える？」とチョコレートでも買うように聞いてみたら「売ります」と。そこでタクシー会社に面した40坪を欲しいと話を進めた。
土地なんて買ったことないのに感覚が麻痺していたのかもしれない。
ついでに40坪って。でも、そこがなかったらこの場所は決めていなかったと思う。前にある300坪の土地に新しい場所を作るには、向かいに面しているこの土地があってこそだと、2人とも同時に考えていた。

こうしてやっと、新しい場所を見つけた。
ここだ！と思うのは早かった。
早かったけど、契約にいたるまでの約1ヶ月半の間、僕は今まで経験したことのない大きな決断を前に、何度も夜中にガバッと起きた。目が覚めた。「やっぱり無理！そんな大きな買いもん!!」頭の中でもう1人の自分が叫ぶ。
ひりんこは赤ちゃん日菜のおっぱいやオムツのことで忙しくてそれどころではなかったらしい。
よく寝ていた。それが良かった。2人とも飛び起きてたら決断できなかったと思う。

ひりんこと僕は決してイケイケには（特に数字的なことでは）考えない。常にどちらかといえば控えめにしか考えない。
右肩上がりの商売なんて計算しない。
そんな控えめな2人がとんでもないことをしようとしてる。

初めての子育ての最中でもひりんこは「子供ができたとこやのに、そんな不安定なこと無理。やめとこ」なんて決して言わない。決める時は決める。そう、また1歩前に。

いよいよ契約の日、体の中にはまだもう1人の自分（弱気なほう）がいるのが分かる。「ほんまに契約するん？」なんて囁く。でも足は昔から決まっていたことのように約束の場所、銀行に向かっている。
到着して入ったこともない銀行の2階の応接室。（銀行に2階があるなんて知らなかった）たくさんの大人に囲まれる2人。（ほんというと自分たちもじゅうぶんおとななんだけど）よく分からない書類がいっぱい。それらに次から次とハンコを押す。言われるがままに押していく。（黄瀬家、唐津家どちらも商売人の家で育った。物心ついた頃から「ハンコだけはついたらあかん」意味も分からなかったが言われ続けてきた。なのに‼）

契約してしまった。

こうして長い時間をかけた土地探しは、ある日突然ピリオドを打った。

Searching for Land

Of the many places I've traveled overseas, the cities that impressed me the most were those where trees of all kinds were a common and accepted part of the landscape. Where they can be seen all over the place, not just in parks, but in people's yards and running along the streets. Not just small trees, either, big oaks and maples with trunks so thick you could not put your arms all the way around them.

I'd seen the tree-lined streets of American suburbs in movies and, until I went to see them myself, could only half believe that they really existed. Not only did they exist, they were taken for granted as a normal part of everyday life. In such places, people could truly understand the passing of the seasons. I wanted the same thing in my own daily life.

We loved our home and shop in Tamatsukuri. We had done all of the work on the interiors of the store and our house ourselves and turned them into places that reflected our sense and taste. When we stepped outside the door, though, it was a different story; we were in the middle of a busy, bustling city. There were cars everywhere, racing along the street, parked here and there, and coming and going from the neighboring businesses. Everywhere we looked there were gaudy signs and flags. The high-rise apartment building across the road blocked the sunshine from 10 am to 2 pm. It was far from perfect, and the idea that we should find a different, better, place had been in the back of my mind for a number of years.

I wanted to find a place where we could live a more comfortable, richer life. I also wanted to bring together the store, our home, the workshop, and the atelier. My idea of a good place was simple: somewhere with some space, surrounded by trees. Simple though it was, I knew it wouldn't be easy to find, this was Osaka, not Toscana or Noosa.

I knew that to bring everything together we'd need a very large plot of land. We wanted to be surrounded by trees, so we directed our search to the outskirts of the city and the mountains near Osaka. We contacted many real estate agents and explained the kind of place we were looking for. Whenever they found something that they thought was a good match, we hopped in the car and went to see it. Sometimes, when we had some spare time, we'd just pick up a map and go off exploring places we didn't know to see what they were like.

We looked at a lot of places, but nothing met our needs. There were certainly trees in the mountains, but they weren't what we wanted. The forests were dominated by large evergreen trees that formed a dense, dark canopy. I far preferred the brighter forests of deciduous trees. Outside of the forests things weren't much better. Even in the countryside, there were big signs wherever you looked and small mountains of garbage piled up here and there. The houses, too, were odd. Although there was more space out here, they were all clustered together in a cramped formation, with no more space between them than there would have been in the city. It might have been different if we had looked in Shinshu or Hokkaido, but around Osaka there was nothing that suited us.

The kind of place we were looking for was something like we had seen in Toscana, Italy. If you take a turn off the national road and drive for a while, you'll come to a wide open space surrounded by trees. The houses sit alone rather than jammed up against one another. There is space for dogs to run around as they please.

In April 2003, Hiromi and I stayed on a farm in Montepulciano, a small town in the Toscana region of Italy. The owner, a woman named Karine, had wonderful taste. Walking into her house was like walking into the pages of a stylish interior design magazine. Hiromi was captivated. Before she knew it she had used a whole roll of film taking pictures of the wonderful breakfast and refined table setting.

Karine had previously worked in the fashion industry in Milan. Some years ago, she and her husband had got tired of the bustle of city life and set off to live on a farm in Chianti. After they had their first child, they moved to Montepulciano, where there was a hospital, a school, and a big supermarket within walking distance. From where we were I could see the town, surrounded by an old castle wall. On every side there were olive trees stretching out as far as the eye could see. Having seen this place, I wondered how I could go back and live in cramped, noisy Japan.

Soon after Hiromi became pregnant, we received a phone call from our landlord that came as quite a shock. He told us that our lease was about to end and that he didn't intend to let us renew it. He asked us to make arrangements to leave. Leave? I felt as if the ground was crumbling beneath my feet. We had ten years of work invested in the place. I had known that the lease would end soon, but had assumed that it'd be renewed. It was just the kind of uncertainty that we didn't need just as we were about to start a family. I rushed to explain the situation. Here we had our home, two stores, our workshop, and the atelier. Not to mention the five dogs and eight cats. Thankfully I was able to persuade him into letting us stay on until we found a new place. Our life and work went on as normal, but we knew the foundations were shaky.

Once we had gotten TRUCK up and running, my accountant had often recommended that we stop renting and buy some land. At the time, though, I wasn't interested. I only wanted to think about furniture. The idea of buying land and building something seemed dauntingly adult and somewhat out of my league. Now the situation had changed. I knew, though, that I didn't want to rush to find a temporary place to set up as a stopgap measure. I wanted to find a place that would be right for us.

Our search gradually took us further and further from Osaka. There were some places we found that had plenty of trees and no houses nearby, but the remoteness brought up other concerns. We certainly weren't planning on stopping the business. I wondered if customers would come so far, and what would happen with our staff.

A few months into our search, Hina was born. We needed to make sure that the place we chose was near a kindergarten and school. It also needed to be accessible to a hospital and supermarket.

I began to wonder if it were even possible to find the kind of place we wanted that would also be good for running a business and raising a family. Neither of us really wanted a country life. We weren't trying to break from the city and live self sufficiently off the land. We wanted the convenience of living in the city, but also to be able to have trees nearby. I'd seen that kind of lifestyle overseas and was rather envious of the people who lived there, going about their everyday life surrounded by so many trees and greenery. Compared to those places, Osaka was a gray, concrete city. Even Tokyo had more greenery.

Searching for Land

We searched in the mountains because we thought that if we wanted to be near trees, then that's where we should go. We gradually came to think that we were mistaken. Having searched for a few years we decided to look again at the city. We were still determined to live surrounded by trees. We decided that we would have to plant them ourselves.

To get an idea of just how much space we'd need, I added up the area of all the places we were currently renting, our home, our stores, the workshop, and the atelier. In addition we wanted space to plant trees, large ones if possible. It came to a total area of 1,000m².

I visited every real estate agent I could find and explained what we were looking for. Many of them didn't take me seriously. It was just like 10 years before when we had tried to rent our first building in Tamatsukuri. They asked if I was sure about my calculations and explained how rare it was to find such large lots in the city. There were many big apartment buildings being built all over Osaka. If a 1,000m² plot became available, it was snatched up by developers before even going on the market. We were told that information about such opportunities rarely made it to people outside the industry.

When we got word of a place, we rushed to see it. If possible, we wanted to find a place that was next to a park or some other place with trees, but none of the places we looked at were right. We were usually able to see right away that they wouldn't work for us. One place was next to a park, but right in front of it was a big, brightly lit, dry cleaning shop. We were wary of places that had big parking lots nearby, as it was common for them to be bought up and developed into apartments. Some places we saw were nice and quiet. They might be good to live in, but we also wanted to run a store and a workshop. We thought that doing business in such a place would be difficult. With so many people coming and going I could see many opportunities for trouble with the neighbors. It seemed like we had a choice between a noisy shopping area or a completely industrial area. Places where we might be able to run a shop, but certainly wouldn't want to live.

We'd been searching for a new place for four or five years. Just by hearing the name we had a good idea of what kind of area it was.

There were some places that we seriously considered. One was a massive plot in Sakai city. It met our criteria and at 2,300m² was even larger than what we had hoped to find. The price was very reasonable, too. As soon as I saw it I was overwhelmed by the size. My brain immediately started racing with ideas of how we could use the space. It had one big drawback, though. It had previously housed a factory and it seemed that the soil had been polluted. We were told, though, that there were processes that could rehabilitate the soil. I was so tempted by the size that I was convinced that this was the place I wanted. I was almost ready to sign a contract but, before we could sign, we needed to get some information on the state of the soil from the city government. As we waited for the information to come through, I began to think about it with a cooler head. After two months of waiting and thinking, we got word of a place in Asahi Ward.

Asahi Ward, Shinmori

One day we got a fax that read; *Osaka, Asahi Ward — 1,000m².*

Neither of us had a very clear idea of where Asahi Ward was, and we had seen so many places that were obviously wrong that we no longer got our hopes very high whenever a new lead came in. I thought it'd be a nice chance to try Hina's new car child seat out, so I got her strapped in and headed off to take a look. I was much more excited about driving with Hina than seeing the land.

What I found when I got there was an old taxi company, with an office and a big multilevel car park. The whole lot was paved over, with not even one tree in sight. It had one important advantage, its location. It was bordered on the east, west, and north by schools. The sky seemed wide and open. I headed home and picked up Hiromi so we could take a closer look at it together.

My initial good impression was confirmed. It was a long thin plot of land surrounded by schools, but it was the school grounds rather than the school buildings that were close to the plot. This made it seem very spacious and not at all cramped. An added benefit of the nearness of the schools was that they were unlikely to be developed into apartment buildings that would block out the sky. It bordered two streets, one a quiet cul-de-sac and the other a wider two-lane road. To find something so close to what we wanted in the city was close to a miracle. We felt that our five year search might be nearing an end.

One drawback was that the side of the plot that faced the main street was very narrow. I thought it might make the entrance too small. We were incredibly lucky that there was vacant land for sale on the opposite corner. I rushed across and talked to the salesman there, telling him that I wanted to buy some land, about 120m². It seems ridiculous in hindsight, casually talking about buying land as if I were talking about buying a bar of chocolate. Fortunately, the land was available. Having space on both sides of the cul-de-sac would give us much more flexibility in the future. If we hadn't been able to buy that smaller plot, I doubt we would have been able to decide so easily.

It was relatively easy to make the initial decision to buy the land, but in the month and a half before we signed the contract I was wracked with doubt. Many nights I woke up in a panic, sure that I was making an expensive mistake. It seemed like too big a purchase that would expose us to too much risk. It was like I had another voice inside my head, warning me not to go through with it. Hiromi had her hands full looking after Hina, so she had little time to join me in my worry. This was a good thing. If we had both been panicked, we probably couldn't have decided. Neither Hiromi or I had much of a head for figures. We weren't interested in expanding our business. For such a simple couple, it felt like we might be making a mistake. Hiromi never said anything like, "Doing this while we raise our child is too uncertain. Don't do it." When it came time to decide, I was able to take the step.

On the day we signed the contract there was still a nagging voice inside me telling me it was a mistake. "Am I really going to sign this?" I wondered. However, as if I had long ago decided, my feet took me to the right place. We went to the bank and were ushered up to a reception room on the second floor. (I didn't even know that there was a second floor in the bank.) We were surrounded by adults (of course, we were adults ourselves) and went through a mountain of papers. I stamped each of them with my personal seal, just as I was told. Of course, what each one meant was explained, but it soon became a blur.

Before I knew it, I had gone and signed the contract, for better or worse.

Our long search had come to an end.

2つの土地を決めてから知ったこと。
間にある細い道を隔てて区が違うと。
しかも、旭区新森6丁目と鶴見区緑4丁目。
偶然にも、この2つの住所はこれから樹を植えようとする場所にピッタリ!!
ひりんこは何度も嬉しそうにそのことを話していた。
さらにラッキーなこと。
うちの物件選びは常に自分たちの直感だけで進むので、探し始める条件の中に、
お客さんが来やすい交通の便がいい所とか、人通りの多い流行りの何々エリアにしよう、
なんてことは考えて探したことがなかった。
なのに、玉造の店の時はオープン後すぐに、徒歩5分以内の所に地下鉄が開通したし、
偶然にも旭区のほうも、土地を決める直前に地下鉄が近くに通ったとこだった。

After we decided to buy the land in Asahi Ward,
we found out that the narrow cul-de-sac between our two lots marked the boundary between two wards.
The address on one side is Asahi Ward, Shinmori.
The other is Tsurumi Ward, Midori. *Shinmori* means "new forest" in Japanese and *midori* means "green".
By chance, it was along this road that we intended to plant our trees.
Hiromi often said how happy this made her. It seemed like a good omen.
When we were first looking for land we hadn't really worried much if it was easy to get to or in a shopping area.
We've been lucky, though.
Soon after we opened in Tamatsukuri, a subway station opened a few minutes away.
We had similar luck in Asahi Ward.
Just before we decided on the property, a new subway station opened nearby.

Asahi Ward, Shinmori

そこにあった建物の解体が終わり、目の前に広がった300坪の更地。右手、奥に見えるのは先行して植えた9mのアキニレ。
The old buildings demolished, 1,000m² of empty space stretches out in front of us.
The 9m tall Chinese elm we planted is visible on the right.

1年間かかって新しい場所を考えた。その軌跡。膨大な量のスケッチ。
It took over a year to plan the new place. These are the footsteps. An enormous number of sketches.

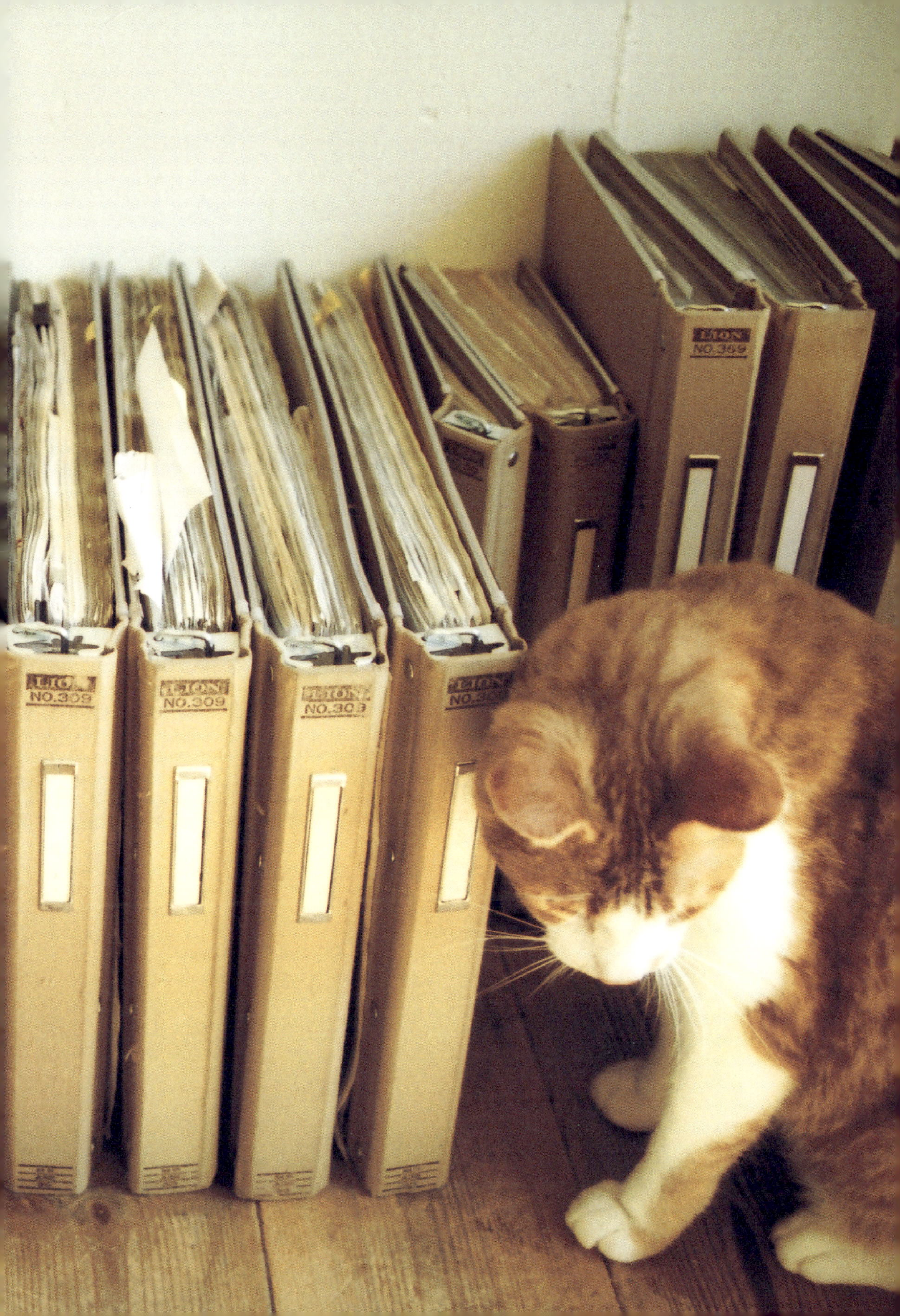
LION
NO.309
LION
NO.309

家と店を考える（1）

旭区に土地を決めたはいいが、建物を考えるのに、1年かかった。プランだけで丸1年間。素人2人で考えまくった。
「新築ってどうなんやろ？」
ニューヨークのロフトのように、元々雰囲気のある建物があるわけではない。
今までの店TRUCK、AREA2や家、アトリエであるシロクマ舎も、古いコンクリートのビルを改造して作ったので、天井や床をめくってペンキを塗れば、それだけでいい雰囲気だった。
それが今回、一から全て建てる。新築である。

新築って響きは、僕にはなんともピカピカして、少し恥ずかしいようにも聞こえる。子供の頃、新品の白いスニーカーが照れくさくて右足で左足、左足で右足を踏んで汚した。2人とも、使い古されたもの、使い込まれたもの、長い年月で雨風にさらされてきたもの。そんなものが大好き。でも、今まで家具を作ってきて、古いものに見せるようなエイジングはしてこなかった。新しく作っていきなり「僕は古いものです」っていう顔をするのはウソだし、どうも恥ずかしい。経年変化した素材感にはかなわない。ただ、好きで持っている古いものたちと、同じ部屋にあってよそよそしいのは嬉しくない。だから、先輩には「よろしくお願いします」と挨拶しつつ、気がつくとすっかり馴染んで一緒に暮らせる。そんな家具が作りたい。そう思ってやってきた。
店も然り。
ファッションビルの中にある店舗の内装のように、過剰なエイジングはしたくない。
はたして、新築で思い通り雰囲気のある店なんかできるのだろうか？

ある日、DEPTの創設者である永井さんに電話で、そんな新築に対しての不安感を話すと、
「黄瀬くんは新しい家具を作ってきたんやから大丈夫」と言ってもらった。
永井さんがさらりと話す言葉はぐっとくる。古くてカッコいいモノを、さんざん見てきた大先輩が言うのである。
新築でも、TRUCKらしい店ができるはず!! と吹っ切れた。
ありがとう。永井さん。

ウソみたいだけど本当に土地を手に入れた。手に入れてしまった。
今建っているタクシー会社の古い建物は、残念ながら生かせるものでは全然ない。とりあえず、
まず目の前にあるもの全てを解体して、いったん更地にするところから始めないといけない。
そして目の前に広がった340坪。
建築家でもないのにいきなり（自分でしたことだけど）この更地どうするん？
2人とも頭の中は真っ白。
まず、今使っている4つの建物それぞれに分かれたTRUCKとAREA2、工場、仕上げ場、倉庫、シロクマ舎、そして家。
それらの面積をパズルのように敷地の中に置いてみる。

Planning the House and Store (1)

意外と狭い。そう、足し算をしていくと思ったほど余裕がない。店も工場も倉庫も少しは広くなればと期待していたのに、同じどころか、いや、ちょっと狭い？　駐車場はどうする？　でも欲しかったのは、たくさんの大きな樹。そう、それが一番大事。そこは譲れない。

旭区に土地を決める時、会計士さんに
「新しく移って売り場面積が広くなるのか？」「工場が広くなって製造効率が上がるのか？」そんな風に聞かれた。
「何も変わりません」と答えた。
「別に商いを広げようとしているのではなくって」
「えっ？？」
「気持ちがいいからです」
普通はそういった計算に基づいて投資をするらしい。なるほど。そうかもしれない。そんなこと、考えてもみなかった。でも、そんな捕らぬ狸を数えてもしょうがないと思うし、そんな計算は今まですることなくやってきた。
別に事業拡大したいわけではないので、工場も売り場もスタッフの数も変わらない。(実際、売り場面積は TRUCK と AREA2 を足した分より少し狭くなってしまった) これは、かなり大バカ野郎なことらしい。
というか、会計士さんに言わせると「それだけの投資をするのに、ありえない」
常に自分たちのやりたいことに直感だけで突き進んでいる2人。

毎日、樹を見て暮らす。仕事をする。
樹の横を通り過ぎる時、「新芽出てきたなあ」「葉っぱ、黄色くなってきたなあ」と
季節の移り変わりを日々身近に感じること。それがやりたいこと。
まず、自分が嬉しい。そしてそこで働くスタッフも気持ちいいと思う。そんな店はお客さんもきっと気持ちいいはず。
家具を作る時、いつも考えてきたこと。自分が嬉しいもの。欲しいもの。使いたいもの。なんてことないもの。
奇をてらうのでなく普通に使えるもの。元々そこにあったように思えるもの。
作るものが大きな建物になっても多分同じこと。そうとしか思えない。

紙の上で敷地の形を描き、そこに店と工場がある建物、家、ひりんこの基地であり、妹のやーちゃんの仕事場であるシロクマ舎、そして倉庫、これらを配置してみる。4つの建物を建てる。建築なんか勉強もしたことないし、今まで建物をゼロからなんて考えたことすらもちろんないのに、いきなり4つを同時に！　でもやるしかない。自分で欲しいものは自分が一番知っているし、他の人では多分無理。と思う。
ひりんこと2人、毎日、明けても暮れても建物のレイアウトに挑む。
その頃、まだ日菜は1歳にもなってない。初めての子育てにワタワタしながら、おんぶしたり、あやしたりしながら、時にはやーちゃんにベビーシッターしてもらい、なんとか打ち合わせを続けた。
考えることはきりがない。いろんな動線、想像できる限りの起こりうること。

4棟の配置を決めるだけでも何十通りも考えた。結構いいやんって思えるのができても、次の日に眺めてみると、また問題点が見えてくる。2人でああでもない、こうでもないと何度も繰り返していくうちにだんだん精度が高まってくる。配置を考えるにはある程度、建物の形がないと置きようがない。じゃあ形を考えようとすると中身を考えないと形が見えない。ただの四角い箱のような建物でいいと思っていたが、いざ考えると要素が山盛り。
どんどん枝道に入って行ってしまう。
山頂を目指し歩き出したのに、裾野の小道に団子屋を見つけ、団子を食べていたら店のおばちゃんと話が弾み団子作り体験。もっとおいしいのを作るためにヨモギ摘みに行く約束をして…。

まさに、今、この文章を書いているのと同じ。
文章を書くのも初めて。
建築の話を書こうと思ってもなぜかどんどん枝道ばかりに進み中心に入っていけない。
でも、面白い。なんでもやってみると面白い。
体験してみると、今まで気にもしたことなかったものが急に身近なことになってくる。それが嬉しい。

話は建築に戻ります。戻します。
目一杯、できる限りのシミュレーションを繰り返し、何回も行ったり来たり。たくさんの脇道、枝道。
それらを全て盛り込んで何とか輪郭が見えてきた。

家を考える。
今の家は、古いビルに無理矢理住んでいるので不便に感じることが多い。
これらを改善したレイアウトを一から考えられる。これは新築の醍醐味。
まずは、思いついたものをどんどん挙げていく。

朝日が差し込む明るい寝室。
（今までは、ベッドを置いている部屋は北側にあり、すぐ裏にビルが建っていたので朝が来たのも分からないくらい暗かった）

風通しのいい明るい風呂。
（同じく北側にあった）

寝室から直結でバルコニーに布団を干したい。
（キッチンの横にあるベランダに出るドアが狭すぎて、布団を抱えて出るのが大変だった）

ご飯の用意が楽しくなる、緑がいっぱい見える窓があるキッチンは、2人並んで立てる広さが欲しい。
（北側で狭かった）

猫たちの世話がしやすいように。猫トイレに換気扇を。
（ワンルームに、ワンニャン総勢13匹と大人2人、赤ちゃん1人が同居していた）

快適な空間。
（ボロいビルは隙間風だらけで冷暖房が全く効かなかった。それに、前の通りの車の騒音もひどかった）

次。今はないけどぜひ欲しいもの。

- 洗面のシンクは2つ。
- 洗面所に窓。毎朝、歯を磨きながら好きな樹を見たい。
- 土間的な場所が欲しい。その土間は裏側の庭に突き抜けている。
- どの部屋からも樹が見えるように大きな窓。
- TRUCKの工場で今まで捨てるしかなかった、たくさんの木っ端を燃料として使える薪ストーブ。
- 日菜が娘さんになった時の部屋。ひょっとして将来もう1人いるかもしれない子供の部屋。
- ゲストルームとゲストが気にせず使えるシャワーやトイレ。
- ワンたちもご機嫌。広いサンルーム。
- 外のような中のような場所。
- 家のぐるりに回った広いバルコニー。
- 屋上。
- 日常的にお茶をしたりご飯を食べたりできるポーチ。そのポーチにいる人に料理を手渡せるキッチンから近い窓。
- 僕の基地。
- 庭にピザ窯とBBQコンロ。
- ひりんこの小さな畑。

どんどん出てくる。考えただけでワクワクする。

Planning the House and Store (1)

It took us a full year to plan the buildings.

"How do you build a house?" we wondered.
It wasn't like a loft in New York, where you already had something on which to base your plans. When we'd remodeled our other places, we had the basic concrete building to work with. We'd stripped the walls and the ceiling and had been able to reveal the atmosphere already present in the space. This time, though, we were starting from scratch. Having nothing to base our plans on was quite daunting. There's something about newness that makes me uncomfortable. When I was a kid and got new sneakers, I always used to stand on each in turn to scuff them up a bit before wearing them.

Hiromi and I both have a fondness for things that have been used for many years and look somewhat worn, things that have seen some wear and tear. When we make furniture, though, we don't do anything to make it seem older than it is. There's something dishonest about a new thing trying to pass itself off as old. Nobody knows how the years will affect a piece of furniture. When you see something that has been artificially aged, in a room with things that have aged naturally, it always looks out of place. I want to make furniture that will come into a room, greet it's elders politely and gradually find a place among them.

I feel the same way about buildings. I didn't want to create the kind of artificially aged interior you can see in stores in fashionable shopping areas. I wondered if I would be able to create a place with the atmosphere I wanted.

One day on the phone I discussed my doubts about planning the house with Mr. Nagai, the owner of DEPT., a Japanese clothing store. He had a lot of experience dealing with all kinds of cool things and I respected his opinion a great deal. He told me that it would be okay, that I had been able to make new furniture and I'd be able to do this, too. His words gave me a little more confidence in my ability to face the task ahead.

There was nothing that we could use from the old buildings of the taxi company. We had to knock them all down and start from bare earth. Seeing that massive expanse of over 1,000m², both Hiromi and I felt our minds go completely blank. Neither of us were architects. What would we do with all this space?

To give myself somewhere to start, I took the floorspace of the existing buildings we used in Tamatsukuri and played a puzzle game with them, laying them out in our new space. It was a very, very tight fit. I saw that I didn't have quite as much land to use as I'd thought. I had hoped to make the store, workshop, and storeroom a little larger than before but, even at the same size, it was very cramped. "What about the parking lot?" I wondered. The most important thing for me, though, was to make space for trees.

When we were deciding whether to buy the land, I had this conversation with my accountant.
"So when you move, are you going to expand your shop?" he asked, "Are you going to expand the workshop so you can increase production?"
"I don't know." I said, "I'm not doing this to increase sales."
"What?" he asked, somewhat surprised.
"I just want to make a place that is comfortable."

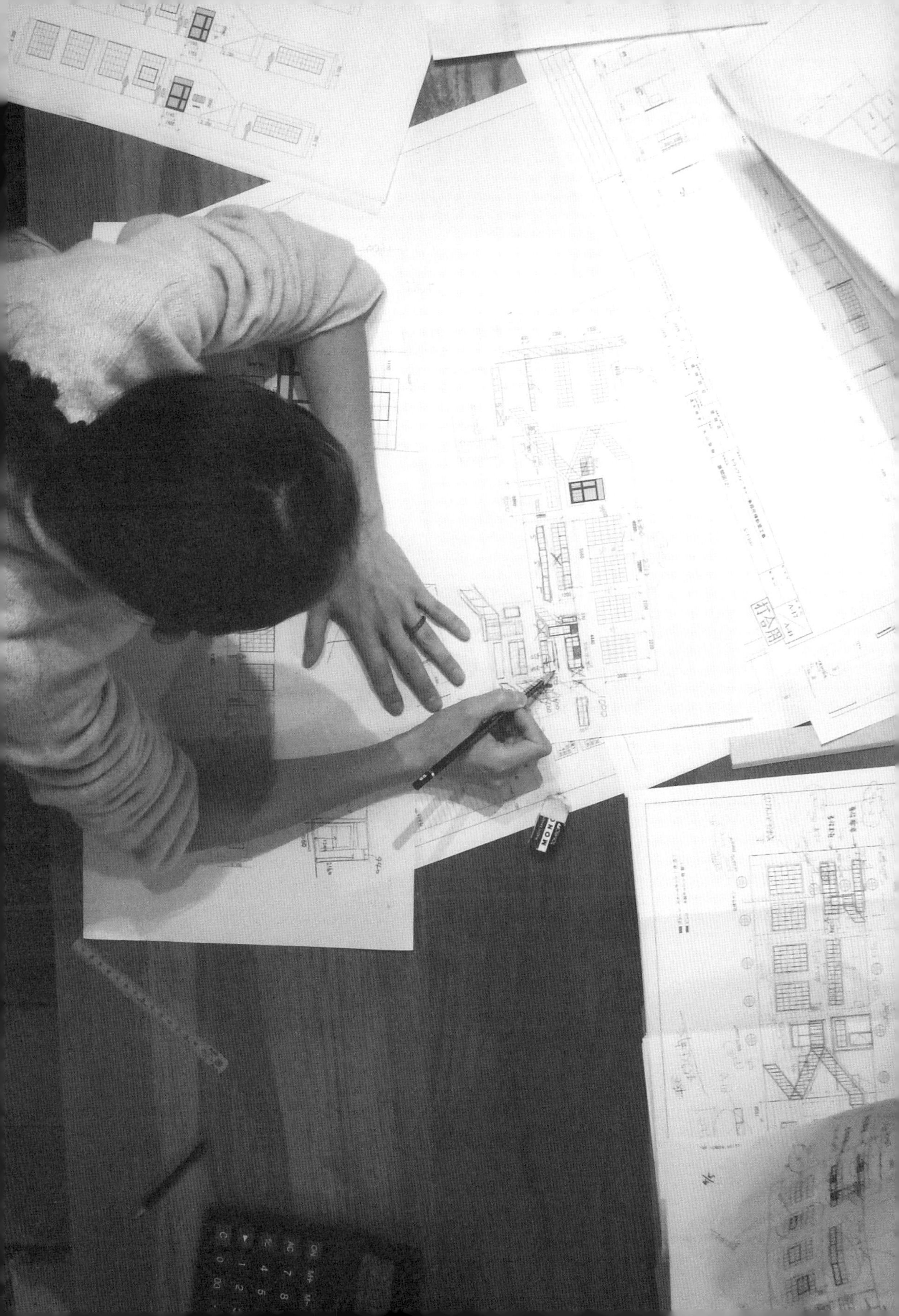
MONO

For him it seemed obvious that we would want to expand the store, but I had never really considered it. I intended to keep the store, the workshop, and the number of staff the same. In fact, the shop would be a little smaller than the TRUCK and AREA2 stores in Tamatsukuri combined. The accountant seemed to think I was a fool.

"You're paying so much money!" he exclaimed, "and you aren't going to expand? It's unbelievable."

What I wanted was not to make more money or build a bigger business. I wanted to take the business I had and make it a better place for both me and my staff to work. We would be surrounded by trees and nature all the time. We would be able to feel the change of the seasons. Wouldn't that be the kind of place people would like to work? And wouldn't that in turn make it a place that customers would want to visit?

When I make furniture, I always make things that I want to use. I'm not interested in making spectacular things that stand out. I want them to be used normally until they become part of people's everyday life. Over time, I came to realize that designing a building was not that different from designing furniture.

From the start, I knew I didn't want to hire an architect to design it for us. I thought it would be too difficult to explain, seeing as I didn't have a clear idea of what I wanted myself. By doing the planning I would find that out. I started with a blank piece of paper. I just tried drawing what I wanted and went from there.

Every day, from morning to night, Hiromi and I worked on our plans. At the time, Hina was not yet one year old. As this was our first time raising a child there was lots of fussing about. Occasionally, Hiromi's sister Yasuko looked after her. Somehow we managed to get things sorted out.

At first our ideas were unclear. I had a vague idea of how I wanted things laid out, but even just working out how to arrange the four buildings took many attempts. I didn't know the shape of the buildings so I didn't know how to place them. When I came to plan the shape, I realized I didn't know what was going to be inside them. There were so many elements to consider. Even when I thought I'd come up with something good, I'd look at it the next day and see all its weaknesses. We drew things over and over again until they became more precise.

When we were planning, I often found myself getting sidetracked. The experience was similar to writing this book. This is the first time I've tried to write and I find, when I try to write about the planning, for example, somehow I get off track and start writing about something else. When you do something for the first time you make many mistakes and go down many dead ends, but the whole time you're learning. You start to care about things you've never thought about before and your world gets wider.

Planning the House and Store (1)

There were many things we didn't like about our current home that we wanted to improve in our new one. Some things we wanted were:

— A bedroom that would be flooded by the morning light.
 (Until then our bedroom had been on the north side of our building. There was a building right outside that blocked the morning sun. It was so dark it was difficult to tell that it was morning.)
— A bright bathroom with good ventilation.
 (As before, facing north.)
— A balcony we could go to directly to air our futons.
 (Our verandah at the time was reached through a door by the kitchen that was too small to fit a futon through easily.)
— A kitchen big enough for two, with trees visible through the windows.
— A better setup for looking after the cats.
— A comfortable living space.
 (Our old building was drafty and continually assaulted by the noise of passing cars.)

Making improvements to things that had been less than ideal about our old place was one of the great pleasures of planning the house.

In addition to things that we wanted to improve there were things that we really wanted.

- Two washbasins.
- A window in the bathroom. Every morning, while brushing our teeth, we could look at the trees.
- An entrance with an earthen floor that looks straight through to the back garden.
- Windows, so we could see trees from any room.
- A wood-burning stove where we could burn the piles of scrap wood from the workshop.
- A room for Hina when she gets older.
- A guest room, a guest shower and toilet.
- A room for the dogs.
- A kind of place that was both outside and inside at the same time.
- A wide balcony that goes around the whole house.
- A rooftop.
- A porch where people could drink tea and eat.
 It would be near the kitchen, so food could be passed through a nearby window.
- My personal workshop and shed.
- In the garden: a pizza oven and BBQ.
- A small vegetable patch for Hiromi.

The ideas kept on coming. It was exciting just to think of them.

家と店を考える（2）

そんなこんな考える中、家や建築に関する何十冊もの本を読んだ。手当たり次第読んだ。そこには、いろんな考え方が渦巻いていた。そしてひとつ知ったこと。それは家の性能。性能？

日本では昔から「家のつくりようは、夏をむねとすべし」と考えて家は建てられてきたという歴史があるらしい。夏の風通しがいい。それはいい。気持ちよさそう。では冬は？
火鉢で手元を暖めたり、こたつで足を暖めたり、石油ストーブやエアコンで部屋を暖めたり。そこだけ、その部屋だけ、人がいる時だけ暖める。それも風通しのいい隙間だらけの部屋で。外から帰って来て冷えきった（夏なら暑くなった）部屋を急いで暖める。（冷やす）
それが欧米諸国では、建物全体の温度を調整する考えが昔からあったらしい。
よく映画や雑誌で見かける窓のそばにあるオイルヒーター。あれはオシャレであるのではなく、窓ガラスから入ってくる冷気から部屋を守るため。つけたり消したりするのではなくずっとつけたままにしておく。
セントラルヒーティングという響きには何か贅沢で高級なイメージがあり、自分たちとはあまり関係のないことのように思っていた。でも、冷えきった部屋を急激にフルパワーで暖めたり、熱々になった部屋を全開で冷やしたりするにはすごいエネルギーが必要。だから緩く継続的に温度を保っておく。すると最強とかパワフルのボタンを押さなくていい。

さらにすごく大事なこと。それは断熱材や気密性。
断熱材を必要な所にしっかり施し、気密性の高いサッシやドアにする。素材はできれば木製または樹脂がいい。なぜかというと、木や樹脂は熱をあまり伝えない。だから外気温がすごく暑くても寒くても、部屋の中に伝えない。アルミは逆にすごく熱を伝えやすい。

もうひとつ大事なのがガラス。薄い1枚ガラスの窓からは冷気がダイレクトに入ってくる。また暖まった部屋の空気を逃がしてしまう。そこを守ってくれるのがペアガラス。これで冬の風物詩的？な結露も起こらない。そしてカビも発生しない。気密性が高いということは、隙間風がない。だから外気に影響されにくい。気密性が高いと聞くと何か息苦しい？と思いがち。でも違うらしい。必要な所に換気扇をつけて必要な所に吸気口をつける。出る所と入る所を管理した換気をして空気の流れをコントロールする。隙間だらけの家だとコントロールできない。
などなど。今まで全く知らなかった世界。興味津々。面白い。

こういったことをしっかり考えて建てた家を性能が高い家と呼ぶらしい。
オートバイとか車の性能は気にしたことがあったけど、家にも性能！ いずれにしても性能が高いのはカッコいい。

性能が高いと、ちょっとのエネルギーで冷暖房ができる。なるほど！ だから人がいてもいなくてもスイッチは入れたまま。寒い冬や灼熱の夏に帰ってきても家の中は常に快適。家中どの部屋に行っても快適。これはぜひ取り入れなければと思った。

Planning the House and Store (2)

では、どうやって家中を暖めるのか。いろんな本が出ていて、いろんな考え方があった。気になったものは実際に施工された建物を見せてもらいにも行った。その中でこれにしようと思ったのが、太陽熱を利用してお湯を沸かし、床の下に設けた厚み10㎝くらいのコンクリートの中を通すという考え方。コンクリートは蓄熱といって熱を溜めることができる。そしてじわっと床下から家を暖める。このじわっとが良さそう。

よくある床暖房は床材のすぐ下に熱源がある。そして人がいる部屋、または人がいる部分だけを、必要な時だけスイッチを入れる。ホットカーペットのように。

でも、コンクリートに熱を溜める方法だと一度暖まると冷めにくい。だから24時間そのまま。さらに、いいなぁと思ったのは、寒くないくらいの温度にするという考え方。朝起きてぬくぬくの布団から出る時や、夜中にトイレに立つ時に急いで何かを羽織ったりしなくていいくらい。でも、Tシャツ1枚で過ごすような温度ではない。家中、温度差が少ない。エアコンからのむっとした暑い風もない。すごく気持ちよさそう。そしてそれを太陽の力でできるなんてカッコいい。これでいこう。

Thoughts on Home Efficiency

節電を要請されて、暑すぎる夏にエアコンを止め、家の中で熱中症になるなんて異常なこと。断熱やガラスの性能を高めた家を作るにはコストが増す。そこで税金を生かして、みんなが当たり前のこととして、ペアガラスなどを使えるようにすれば、もっと一般化すれば、エアコンの使い方が変わるはず。室外機からの熱風も減り、都会の暑さもましになるはず。遅れている日本の省エネルギー基準。かっこ悪い。お隣の韓国では新築住宅のほぼ100%がペアガラスを使っているというのに。

Recently, Japanese people have been asked by the government to use less electricity. This was a problem last summer. People tried to use their air conditioners less and there was an increase in cases of heatstroke.

Building a house with good insulation and double glazed glass is expensive compared to less energy efficient methods. If the government subsidized double glazing, it would become more common. Living in efficient houses, people would have less need to use their air conditioners. Fewer air conditioners blasting hot air out would make the cities cooler, too. It would cost more over the next few years, but would be cheaper over the long term.

Japan is lagging behind the world when it comes to energy efficiency. Even in nearby Korea, almost 100 percent of new homes have double glazed windows.

Planning the House and Store (2)

To help us with our planning, we read as many books about building and architecture as we could get our hands on. One of the things that we learned about in our reading played a very important role in our planning — the concept of home efficiency. I'd been aware of efficiency when it came to motorcycles, but hadn't really considered it when it came to buildings.

Japanese houses had long since been designed for the air to flow through them easily and make the summer livable. It's works well for summer, but is less desirable in winter. In older times, people warmed their hands around the *hibachi*, a kind of charcoal brazier. They warmed their legs with a *kotatsu*, a low table with a heater beneath it. Nowadays, they use a kerosene stove or air conditioner to warm the room. The traditional Japanese approach to heating has been focused on temporarily heating one place just for as long as needed, while people are there. Anything done to heat a room is undercut by the cold drafts that blow through. Another drawback is that when you come home, the house is freezing cold and you have to heat it quickly. It seems that in Europe people have given more thought to ways of warming the whole house. In movies and magazines I had seen oil heaters placed beneath the windows. They're not there because they look fashionable. They're to warm the air coming through the windows. And they are left on all the time, not turned off and on.
To most Japanese, the idea of central heating sounds rather expensive and perhaps wasteful. However, the normal Japanese way of heating or cooling a house (or more often, just a room) by turning the air conditioner on full power, uses more power than maintaing a low heat.

To make this work, though, two things are essential: proper insulation and airtightness.
When it comes to materials for door and window frames, it is better to choose things like wood, that don't conduct heat. If you use wood, the outside temperature has little influence on the temperature inside. Aluminum, on the other hand is very conductive. It brings external heat or cold into the house.

Another important thing is glass. The cold comes right through a single pane of thin glass, making it much harder to keep a room warm. The way to keep that heat in is to use double glazed windows. Even in winter there is no condensation, which means there is virtually no mold. It eliminates drafts, too. An airtight room might sound stuffy. Of course, there has to be some air flow through the house. The careful placement of ventilation fans and air inlets lets you control the flow of air in a room. You can't control that in a room with lots of drafts. This was all new to me and I found it fascinating.
In an efficient house you can cool your house using less energy. That's why you can leave the system running even when nobody's there and come home to a comfortable house in either summer or winter. It doesn't matter which room you go to, either. I knew I definitely wanted this kind of house.
Another problem we considered was the best way to heat the house. I read many ideas in books, and wanted to see the things I read about in action, so I always tried to find buildings that already used the methods I was interested in. The method I most liked used water heated using solar energy. The water flows through a pipe in the middle of a ten centimeter layer of concrete that lays beneath the floors. The concrete absorbs and stores the heat, so the house can be heated by the floors. There are lots of floor heating systems, but many just heat the actual floor and are designed to be turned on and off depending on whether people are there or not.

（写真・右）家具を作る時に出る木っ端を燃料に使えるのが嬉しくて家とBirdに薪ストーブを設置。
ところが家のほうは、断熱や気密、ソーラーでの床暖の効果が素晴らしすぎて、出番がなかった。ちょっと残念。(Birdの薪ストーブは大活躍)

Concrete, though, is great at absorbing and retaining heat. Once it warms up it takes a long time to cool down, so it can be left on 24 hours a day. With a house that was always warm, it'd be easy to get out of bed in the morning or to head to the bathroom in the middle of the night. It wouldn't be the kind of warmth where you could walk around in just a t-shirt, though. The temperature would be the same throughout most of the house and there would be no hot wind from an air conditioner. It sounded very comfortable, and the fact that it was powered by solar energy made it all the more attractive.

In both our house and Bird, we installed wood-burning stoves that could be fueled by the copious scraps of wood left over from building furniture. The efforts we took to insulate and make our home airtight, coupled with the solar-powered floor heating, have been so successful that we have yet to light the stove in our home. The stove in Bird, though, is kept very busy.

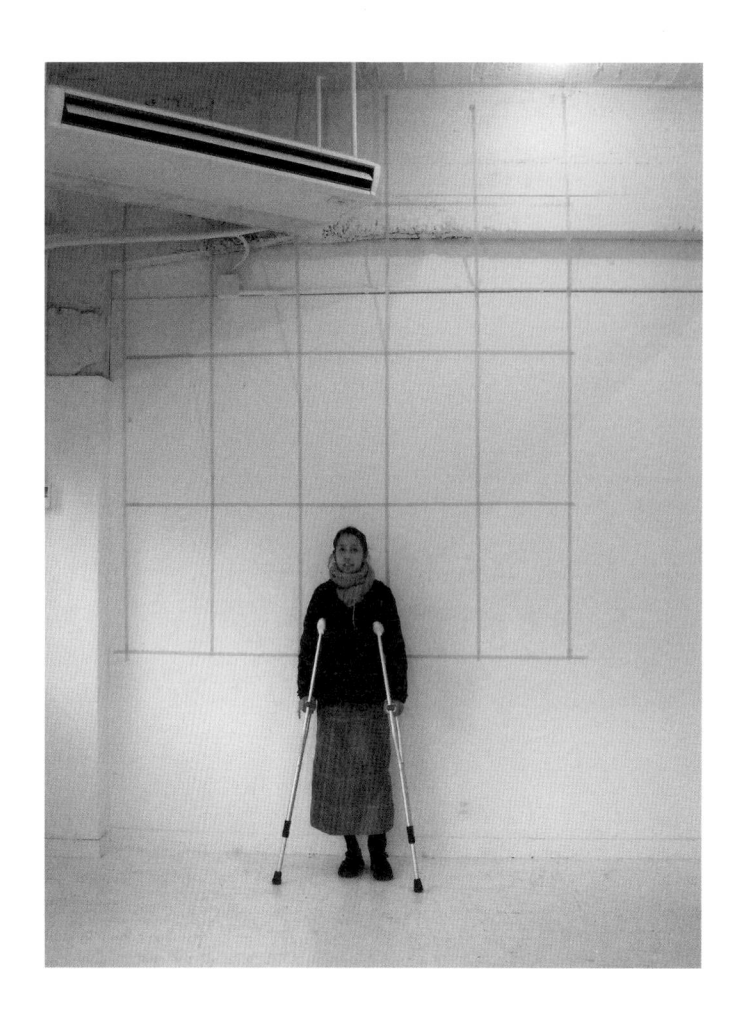

家と店。この2つをまずメインに考えていく。(でもシロクマ舎、倉庫も考えつつ) 毎日毎日、ひりんこと2人、朝から晩まで。寝ても覚めても。建築家みたいにパキパキの図面は描けないけど、簡単なお絵描き程度で2人にはじゅうぶん。ただ、実際のサイズはちゃんと入れつつ描いてみる。何度も、建物の形を、そして建物の中を目一杯想像して描いてみる。でも、いくら描いても小さな紙の上では全然分からない。だからマスキングテープを床や壁に貼り、椅子とかいろんなものを並べて距離感を実感する実験を繰り返す。
窓のサイズ、窓の始まる高さ、大きさ。洗面所の広さ。通路の幅。天井の高さ。キッチンの広さ、レイアウト。トイレの大きさ。階段の踏みしろの奥行き、高さ、手摺の太さ。工場の広さ…全て実寸で確認していく。
店の窓のサイズは大きすぎてあまりに想像ができないので、知り合いのフォトスタジオを借りて天井高いっぱいまで使って、壁に等倍でマスキングテープを貼ってみた。

ついには、家と店、そしてシロクマ舎の建物の大きさや建物間の距離を見ようと、隣の学校（ちょうどいいことに隣に学校がある）で白線引きを借りてきて、実際の寸法で地面に描いてみた。コロコロと運動場に線を引く道具。懐かしい。実際にその場に立つと、体感としていろいろと見えてくる。

そうこうしながら、ほぼ1年かかってようやくまとまってきた。設計士にプランをお願いしたわけではないので、よくある模型はその間、一度も見ることがなかった。それでも、その頃には2人とも頭の中では3Dの動画で建物の中、外を理解できていた。それも多分同じ映像で。その証拠に、最終的に図面への落とし込みをお願いした設計事務所に作ってもらった簡単な模型を見た2人は、「わー！こんな風になるのか！」ではなく「そうやんな。こうなるよな」と、まるで答え合わせをしているような感覚だった。

The house and the store were the two things we focused on first. Hiromi and I spent all of our time working on the plans. We weren't architects, of course, so we couldn't draw the kind of detailed plans they would. We made rough sketches, but made sure to include exact measurements for everything. Over and over we drew out our ideas of what the house should look like, both inside and out. Sometimes it was difficult to visualize things just by drawing them on paper, so we used masking tape on the walls and floors and arranged chairs and the like to get a better sense of distance.

We tried to check everything — the size and height of windows, the size of the bathroom, the width of the hall, the height of the ceiling, the size and layout of the kitchen, the size of the toilet, the depth and height of the stairs, and even the circumference of the handrail.
We wanted to make sure that what we drew on paper would actually be useful in real life.

The storefront window was too big to imagine, so I rented my friend's photo studio and used masking tape on the wall to get an idea of the size we were dealing with.

Finally, to get an idea of the size of the buildings we borrowed a white line marker from the school next door and marked it out in our lot. Seeing it laid out we could really get a sense of how it would fit together.

A year passed in this way. We had not passed the job on to an architect, so had never seen a model of the buildings. What we had instead was a clear three-dimensional image in both our minds. My feeling that this image was the same was proved correct when we finally got an architect to draw up the plans and make a model. When we saw it, we didn't say, "Oh, is that what it will look like?"
Our response was more of a confirmation.
"Yes, that's right. That how it should look."

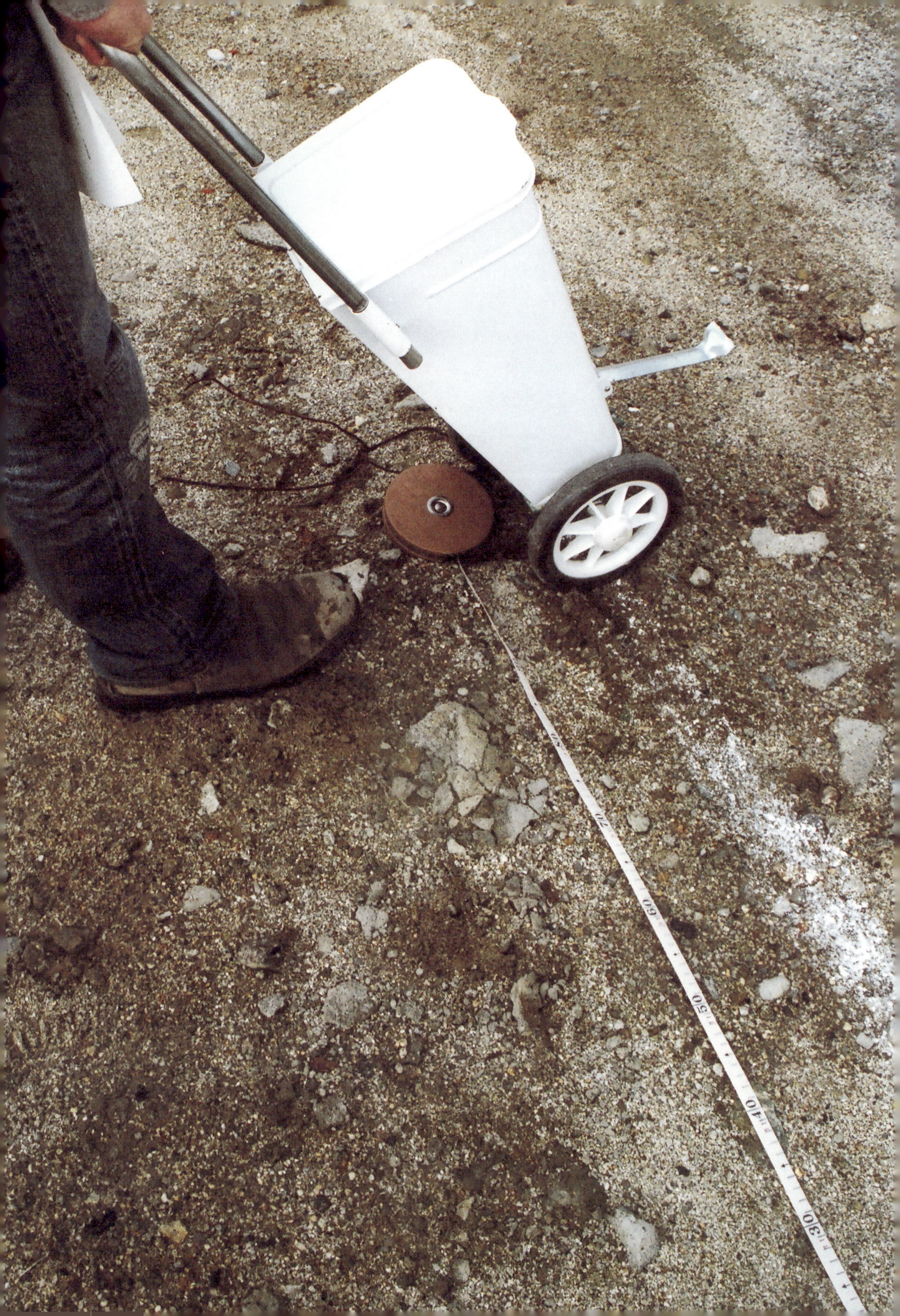

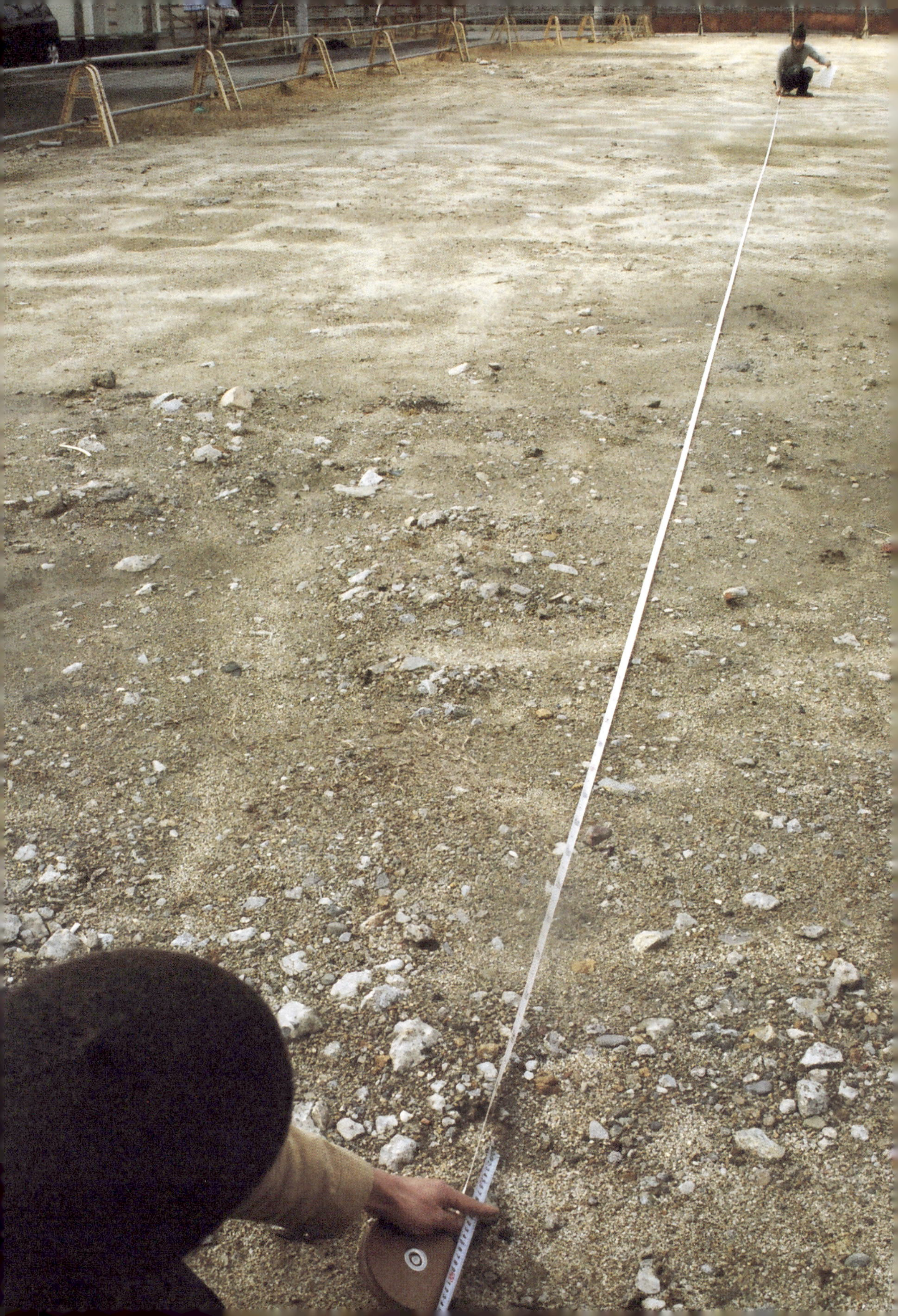

Framework Construction

From Commencement to Completion

May 2008 – Dec. 2008

Planting Trees

Thinking about Trees / Tree Rescue / Planting Trees

Jun. 2007 –

Completing the House and Store

From an Empty Shell to a Warm Nest

Dec. 2008 – Dec. 2009 –

着工から上棟（1）

いよいよ工事が始まった。
家と店、この2棟から。いきなりいっぺんに2つ。どちらも鉄筋コンクリート造2階建て。まずは杭打ちから。長さ15m太さ70cmもあるコンクリート製の杭。地べたに横倒しで待機している山積みの杭たち。それらが1本ずつ垂直にクレーンで吊り上げられ打ち込まれていく。その杭が15m下の支持層（固い丈夫な地盤）に到達して建物を支える。
2棟合わせて約40本が次々に地面の中に消えていく。ド迫力。
たくさんの作業員が関わって進められていく。家具を作るのと違ってスケールが大きい。そんな中、「うわぁーすごい！」とか言いながらひりんこと2人、まるで社会見学に来た小学生みたいに。誰が見てもこの2人が施主とは思わない。

杭が終わると次は基礎の地中梁。たくさんの細い鉄筋を縦に横に組み上げていく。その周りを型枠で囲み、そこにコンクリートを流し込む。毎日その作業を見ていてつくづく思った。「すごい手作業なんやなぁ。こんな風に作られてるんや」初めて知ったことに純粋に感動していた。コンクリートの建物がこんなに手作りだったとは。

September 5, 2007 Breaking Ground

1) 樹を植える前に、土の状態を見てみようと穴を掘った。記念すべき初穴掘り。なんでもやってみたい僕はショベルカーを運転させてもらって大はしゃぎ。　2) ひりんこが骨折した。日菜を抱っこして公園からの帰り道、自転車が後ろから来た。それを避けようとした僕の足につまずいたのだ。ひりんこはとっさに日菜にケガをさせまいと、両手を上に伸ばして膝からコケた。自分と日菜の体重を左膝で受け止めてしまった。松葉杖をつきながら、日菜をおんぶして打ち合わせの日々。

1) We dug a hole to check the soil condition for the trees to come, breaking the ground for the first time. I jumped at the chance to operate the hydraulic shovel. 2) One day while we were planning the new buildings, we took a break and took Hina to the park. On the way home we were walking side by side with Hiromi carrying Hina. I stepped out of the way of a passing bicycle and Hiromi tripped over my foot. To prevent Hina from being injured, Hiromi lifted her into the air, falling straight onto her knee with no hands to help break the fall.

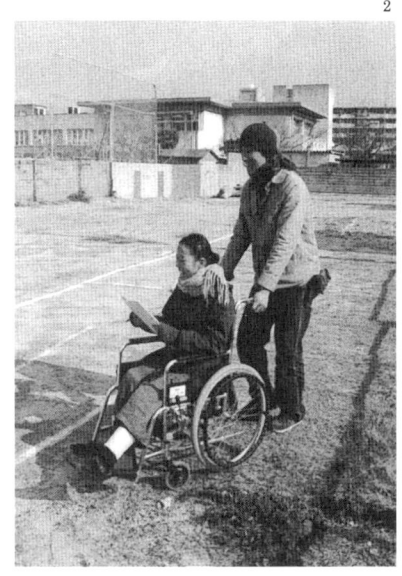

ところがある日、事態は一変する。
型枠が外され地中梁が完成。掘り下げていた地面に土を戻し1階の壁作りに進んでいく直前。
毎日作業を見ていて、「すごいなあ」と思いながらもちょっと気になっていた。組み上がった鉄筋がなんとなくぐにゃついている。シュッとしていない。でも、こんな建築現場を見るのなんて初めてだったので、そんなに気にしていなかった。というより、そんなものだと思い込もうとしていた。
型枠が外れた地中梁。コンクリートの幅の中から鉄筋が突き出て並んでいる。でも、それらがどこもかしこも、すごくぐにゃぐにゃ。右に左に、まるで蛇のよう。嫌な予感がした。

慌てて家に帰り、たくさん買っていた建築関係の本を探した。ひりんこがその中にあったコンクリートの本をひも解くと、そこには、こんな説明があった。
"かぶり量：コンクリートの端から鉄筋までの距離が最低40mm"
理由はその数値が少ないと（土に近いと）万が一水分が浸入した場合、鉄が錆びて膨張する。そしてコンクリートが割れる!!
えぇっ？40mm!? 全然ない。10mmもない所がいっぱいあった！慌てていろんな人に電話して聞いてみる。すると誰もが口を揃えて「40mm以上が当たり前」と言う。愕然とした。
急いで現場に戻り、現場監督、設計者に聞いてみる。「どういうことなん？」
みんなはっきりしない。何かモゴモゴしている。おかしい。

7月のギラギラ照りつける太陽の下。僕はさしとデジカメ、紙とペン、図面を持って片っ端からかぶり量を測って回った。2棟分の全ての地中梁30通り以上。鉄筋からコンクリートの端までの距離をさしで測り、基準の数値に達していない所、それぞれに番号をつけ写真を撮り、図面に書き込んでいく。
ひどすぎる。店側は数字で1、2、3と番号をつけると17番まで。家側はA、B、Cで結果Zまで。ほとんどができていない。40mmなんてどこもない！
その間、設計、工務店それぞれの偉いさんたちが次々と集まって来て、無言で作業する僕を、固唾を飲んで取り囲みついてくる。10人くらいに囲まれたまま1時間以上あっちこっちと移動して記録していく。炎天下、暑さと、突然氷河期に立たされたような緊張感、そのどちらからか分からない汗が体中を流れる。
誰も何も言わない。何も言えない。

持っていた本の中に「ひび割れのないコンクリートのつくり方」というのがあった。そんな本まで買っていたことに自分で少し驚きつつ開いてみる。やはりそこにもあった。かぶり量。すぐにその本の著者に電話をした。今現場で起こっていることを熱く説明した。すると何の面識もないのに「明日見に行きます」と言ってもらえた。はるばる東京からそのコンクリートの先生がやって来た。そして現場を見て言った。
「これはひどい」やっぱり。

Laying the Foundation (1)

この日以来、現場の空気は急変。真夏の抜けるような青空の下なのに、目に映るのはどんよりと曇った冬空の風景のようになった。楽しく通っていた希望に満ちた場所。それが、行くのも嫌と思ってしまうようになる。

何度も設計者と工務店に説明を求めた。これまでいろんな建築のプロが関わって進められていたはず。その都度、管理されてきたはず。なのにどうしてここまで２棟の全ての箇所が駄目なのか。理解ができない。すごく単純に40mmあればいいだけ、その常識が満たされていないのはなぜか。
プロ側の態度は、なぜそうなったかの説明は一切なく、最悪の状況を目の前にしても、ただ是正をしたいとの一点張り。是正？ 聞き慣れない言葉。それが何かと問うと、足りない所にコンクリートをつけ足すことらしい。なるほど。そうか。でも、ちょっと待て。１ヶ所ちゃうで。いたる所全部やで。百歩譲って、たまたま１ヶ所上手くいかなかった、一生懸命注意してやっていたのに。というのならまだ分かるし、それなら是正でもいい。
でも２棟の全て、40ヶ所以上も。みんな目瞑って仕事してたんか!? というありさま。これでは到底納得できない。

建築が正しく規定通り進んでいるかをチェックする第三者機関、そこにも連絡をして見てもらった。すると一言。
「是正して下さい」さらりと。
「えっ？」耳を疑った。その機関がチェックする箇所。それは鉄筋の数、太さ、コンクリート自体の厚みなど法律で定められている数値であって、かぶり量は守るのが当たり前。当たり前すぎて、チェック項目に入ってない。だからそれを守っていないということに対しての法的な罰則はないと。
びっくりした。誰も守ってくれない。素人１人。一世一代の大きなことをしているのに、誰も味方がいない。これだけプロがいて。国の機関でさえも。
武装した悪者（その中には味方だと思っていた人までいる）に囲まれた真ん中に急に１人丸腰で立たされる。
このかぶり量事件発覚から今まで味わったことのない、眠れない、笑うことが一切ない、どん底の日々が続く。

こちらが求めたことは、きちんとした経緯の説明。一から作り直すこと。

これから先ずっと暮らしていく場所。子供も育っていく場所。そして何より、もの作りをしていく場所。裏の裏まで言い訳やウソのない家具を作ってきた。これからもそこが一番大事と思っている。その全ての基盤になる建物の基礎。それが、いい加減に作られた、またはウソで固められたようなものの上では絶対にやっていけない。強くそう思った。そんな上ではこれからの将来は考えられない。譲れない。

何度も設計、施工の２社と話し合う。が、口裏を合わせてくるので話す度に先方の言うことが変わる。
最初、少しは残されたプライドがあったのか、現場では「恥ずかしいことをした。責任を持ってやり直す」と言っていたのが、翌日になると是正の話に変わり、ついには逆切れで怒鳴り散らされた。「お前ら素人に何が分かる！」びっくりして開いた口の顎が外れそうだった。

Laying the Foundation (1)

業者を変えたくても、前金はもう支払い済み。裁判にもっていくと10年は現場が止まると言われた。どうしようもなかった。業種は違っても、同じように自分たちももの作りをしてきた。常にお客さんにいいものを、と思うのが当たり前だと思っていた。今、相手にしている人たちには誠意というものがかけらもない。こんな人種がいるということを初めて目の当たりにした。

そんな中、「ひび割れのないコンクリートのつくり方」を熟読した。面白い。著者の考え方がダイレクトに伝わってきて、やり直すならばこの方法しかないと心に決めた。

それがどういう考え方か少し説明。

近年は作業性が優先され水分の多いコンクリートを、打ち込むというより流し入れているに近い。そうすると乾燥の過程で蒸発する水の量も多くなり、ひび割れが生じやすい。そこで水分を少なくした生コンを使い、打設後に再び振動を与え、無駄な水を追い出す。その後、水を撒いたり養生シートで覆ったりして水分が急になくなるのを防ぎ、コンクリートがしっかり固まるのを助ける。

実際、この手法を取り入れると工期は長くなるし、作業員も多く必要になる。いろんな手間暇がかかり結果、コストも上がる。でも、いいものが作りたい。もう他人任せにはできない。

約1ヶ月間押し問答が続いた。その中で何度かこの本の話を出した。でも全然相手にされなかった。

それがある日どういうわけか、設計会社側が本を手に取った。パラパラと見て、「理解できることが書いてある」と言った。風向きが変わった。

話は急転、やり直すことになった。初めて少し眠れた。

MAKING UNCRACKABLE CONCRETE

**CONCRETE OF DRY CONSISTENCY FOUNDATION,
SLAB : SLUMP 10   BEAM, POST
WALL : SLUMP 12   VIBRATOR : 50Φ
TIE REBAR ALL CROSS POINT   WATER CEMENT RATIO : LESS THAN 50%
UNIT CONTENT OF WATER : LESS THAN 170KG/M3
CLEAR OFF THE LAITANCE   TAMPING AND STAMP FOR SLAB**

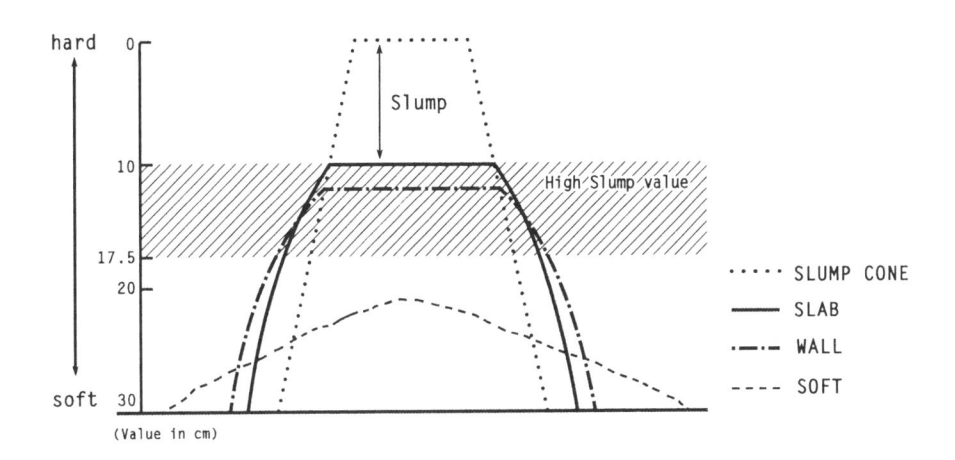

SLUMP TEST

スランプ(SLUMP):スポーツ選手の調子が崩れたり、株価が暴落など、下がるという意味がある言葉。それが生コンクリートのやわらかさを表す数値として使われる。
現場に到着したミキサー車からのコンクリートを、バケツをひっくり返したような形の容器に入れ、棒で突き込んだ後、容器を垂直にそっと持ち上げる。コンクリートの高さがどのくらい下がったかをスランプ値として用いる。スランプ値が小さいほうが固い(水分が少ない)コンクリートとなる。20cm前後が通常よく使われている。この現場では10〜12cmという固いコンクリートを使った。

Slump: the word "slump" is usually used to describe the poor performance of an athlete or a fall in stock prices. It is also used to describe a test performed on concrete to gauge its level of softness. When a concrete mixer arrives at a site, a bucket is filled with concrete and turned upside down on the ground. The bucket is removed and the distance the concrete falls is measured, producing a slump value. If the slump value is low, then the concrete will be hard.
Concrete that slumps about 20cm is commonly used these days. At our site we were making hard concrete, so we aimed for a slump of between 10cm and 12cm.

Laying the Foundation (1)

Finally, construction got underway. We started with the house and the store, both two-story buildings made of steel reinforced concrete. The first step in laying the foundation involved driving concrete posts into the earth. These posts have a diameter of 70cm and are 15m long. The house and the store required forty of these. The work required a small army of workers. Compared to building furniture, the scale was much larger. It was impressive to see each post disappear into the earth. While we watched, we couldn't help but gasp at some of the things we saw. We were like two elementary school kids on a field trip. No one seeing us would have thought we were the owners.

Next, the foundation needed to be laid. A framework of thin steel rods was laid out in a wooden mold which was then filled with concrete. As I watched them work everyday, I was struck by how much manual labor it required. I previously hadn't thought of concrete buildings as being handmade.

Then one day things changed. The molds were removed from the girders that formed the foundation, and as I watched the construction, my sense of wonder gradually gave way to a feeling of concern. When the wooden mold was removed from the concrete, many of the steel rods were twisted and crooked. At first I wasn't too worried. The work was being done by professionals, after all. I had a feeling, though, that something wasn't right.

I rushed home and rifled through the stack of architecture books I had bought. Among them was a book about concrete in which Hiromi found an explanation of how the steel rods should look. It said that the minimum width from the reinforcing rods to the edge of the concrete was 40mm. "40mm?" I wondered. There was nothing like that. In some places it was less than 10mm. I called around to some friends in the construction industry and they all agreed that it should be at least 40mm thick. I rushed back to the site and asked the foreman and the architect what was going on. They didn't give me an answer. They didn't say not to worry or that everything was fine. They just stayed silent. I told them to stop work.

That day, beneath the hot July sun, carrying a ruler, a digital camera, pen, paper, and a map in hand I went around measuring the concrete from point to point. For the two buildings there were more than 30 beams. I measured the distance from the steel rod to the tip of the concrete. Any place that didn't meet the standard I marked on the map and took a picture of. The results were terrible.

I tracked the bad points for the store with numbers, coming to a total of 17. I tracked the house using letters. I got all the way from A to Z. There were very few points that measured 40mm. While I was doing this some of the higher-ups from the construction and architecture companies came and watched me in silence. With bated breath they gradually encircled me. Surrounded by these ten people I moved here and there taking measurements, dripping with sweat from head to toe. Whether it was from the blazing sun or being dropped unexpectedly into this situation, I don't know. Nobody said anything. There was nothing they could say.

Among the books I had was one by an expert on concrete, Mr. Iwase, called "Making Concrete That Won't Crack". As I opened it I was a little surprised that I had gone so far as to buy such a book. As expected, it said the same thing as the other book, that the distance should be 40mm. I decided at once to call the author. Once I got him on the line, I explained what had happened so far. Although we were entirely unacquainted, he offered to come to Osaka from his home in Tokyo and see it the next day. After he had inspected the site he said, "This is awful." From that day, the mood at the site changed. Although it was still bright summer, it felt more like an overcast winter day.

I made repeated demands for an explanation from the architecture and construction companies. The people in charge were professionals with all kinds of experience. I couldn't understand how there could be so many bad points in both the buildings. Why couldn't they meet the simple standard of 40mm?

They didn't even try to explain how it had happened. The terrible situation was there in front of their eyes, but they never once offered to do it over. They persisted in saying that they wanted merely to "correct" it. The Japanese term they used for "correct" is an unusual one, only used in the building industry. I'd never heard it before. Basically, they suggested adding concrete to the parts that were lacking. I didn't think this was appropriate for the scale of the problem. If they had tried as hard as they could and, in spite of their best efforts, one place were unsatisfactory then I would accept their idea of "correcting" it. But that was not the case. There were almost 40 points that were bad. It seemed like they had been working with their eyes closed. There was no way I could possibly accept their "correction".

To see if the construction company had followed correct procedures, I asked a government building inspection organization to come and check it. I was stunned by their verdict: It should be "corrected." The organization checked many things, the number and thickness of the steel rods, the overall width of the concrete, but not such an obvious thing as the distance from the rod to the outside of the concrete. There were no legal regulations governing the width.

I was surprised. No one could support me. Here I was, doing a once-in-a-lifetime thing, and I had no one on my side, neither the professionals or the government organizations. Since the discovery of the problem with the concrete, I've never experienced anything so bad. It was a real low point. For days I was very low. I couldn't sleep or even smile.

This is where we intended to live for the rest of our lives, where we were going to raise our children. We wanted above all for it to be built properly. I make furniture that is honest and uncompromised down to the smallest unseen details. I think that is the most important thing. You must not build on a foundation that is based on lies. That was my strong conviction. I couldn't imagine a future based on such a thing. It was non-negotiable.

I spoke many times with the construction and architecture companies. At first, maybe they had some pride left. At the site they said "We're embarrassed by what we did. We will take responsibility and redo it." The next day, though, they said that it would be fine to just correct it. Then finally, during one meeting, one of the presidents turned on me and shouted, "You're just amateurs. What the hell do you know?" My jaw dropped in astonishment. I wanted to change companies, but I'd already paid one third of the total fee as an advance. I was told that if it went to court, construction might be stalled for up to ten years.

Although it is a different business, they are also making something for their customers. It seems obvious to me that they would want to make something good. I had no trust in the people we were dealing with. It was the first time I'd dealt with such people.

Laying the Foundation (1)

During that time I devoured the book, "Making Concrete That Won't Crack". It was very interesting. I decided that when we were finally able to start over, we would do it as described in the book.

Let me briefly describe the approach outlined in the book. In recent years, very wet concrete has gained in popularity because it is easier to work with and to pour. One problem with this is that when the concrete starts to dry, a lot of water evaporates, which can make it easy for cracks to appear. The method described in the book uses relatively little water. After it is poured it is tamped with a vibrator to push out the excess water. Then a curing sheet sprinkled with water is laid over it to prevent water from escaping. This helps the concrete harden better.

This method is more time consuming and requires more work so it is more expensive. I decided that I wanted to build the best building I could. I couldn't just leave it in someone else's hands.

The dispute continued for about a month. During that time I often tried to discuss the method described in the book, but they didn't want to hear about it. They didn't take me seriously at all. Then a day came that, for some reason, they changed their minds. While I was talking to the architect he picked up the book, flipped through it, and said, "This makes sense. I can understand this."

They soon agreed to tear up the work they had done and start over. I didn't know what had prompted them to change, but I was happy that I could finally get some sleep again.

出来上がっていた基礎を全て解体。無惨な鉄筋とコンクリートの山。
The mountain of broken concrete and twisted metal left after the demolition of the unsatisfactory original foundations.

December 13, 2008 TRUCK 2nd Floor

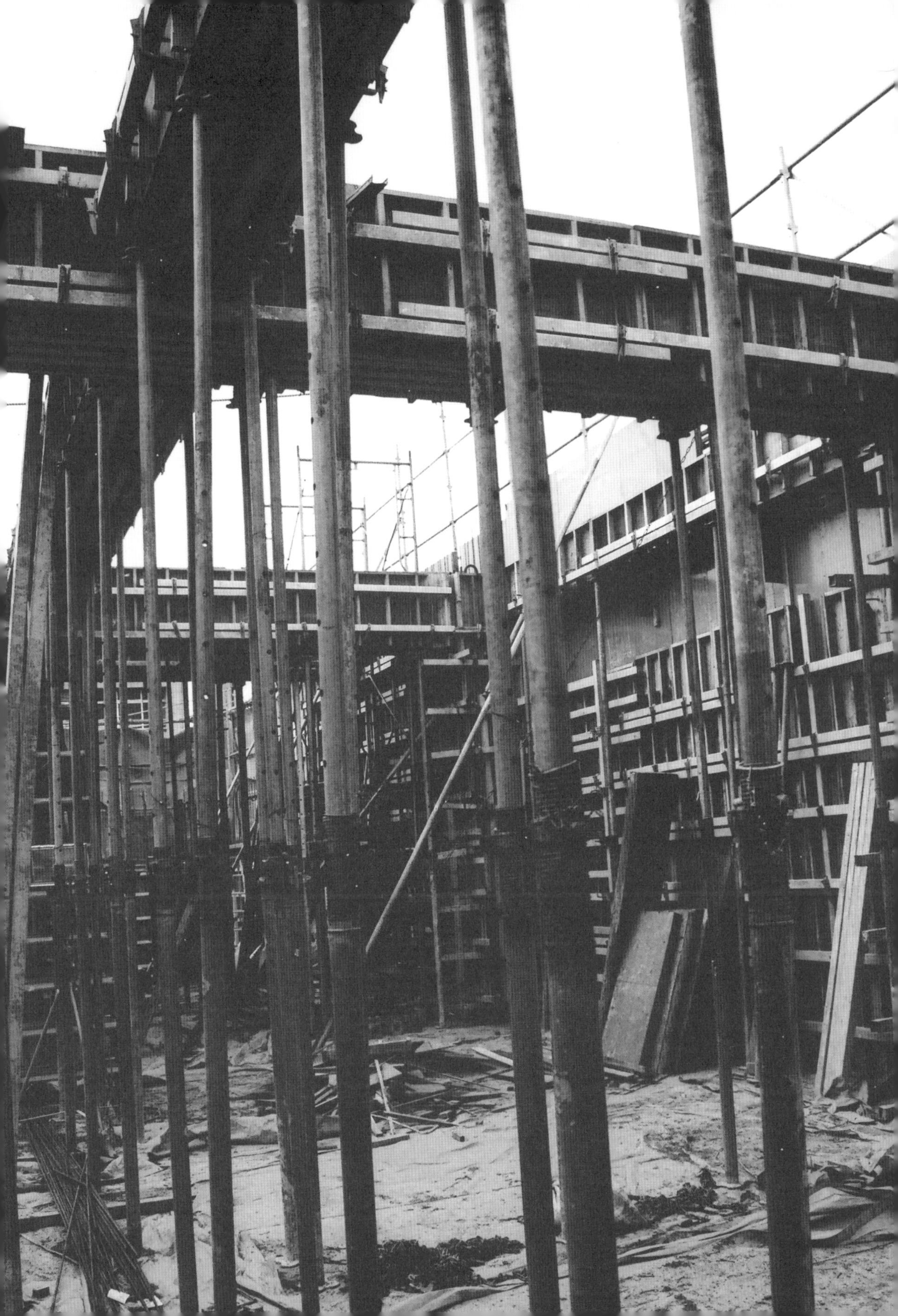

着工から上棟（2）

まずは、できてしまっているせっかく作った基礎を杭だけ残して全て解体。
そして、これからしようとしていることを、作業に関わる人全員が理解できるように、東京から著者を呼んでビデオを見ながらの講習会。長年コンクリートに関わってきた人たち。ベテランたち。その人たちに一から考え方を変えてもらわないといけない。それからは現場に行く理由が変わった。以前は面白がって見学していただけ。それが、正しく作業ができているかのチェックをする日々になった。いくら講習会を受けてもらっても作業員ひとりひとり体の隅々には染み込んでいない。僕自身にとっては自分のこと。素人であっても誰よりも事細かく染み込んでいる。見方が違う。何度も細かい駄目出しを繰り返す。ひとつのミスも見逃せない。

コンクリートを打設する日は朝の朝礼から一作業員として参加。手には型枠を叩くハンマー。1日中叩き続ける。少しでも隙間なくコンクリートを詰めるため。卓上の塩や胡椒の容器をトントンすると、中身が詰まって上が空く、それと同じ原理。水分や空気を押し出していく。バイブレーターやポンプの振動音が響く中、夢中で叩き続けた。少しでもいいコンクリートになるように思いを込めて！

コンクリートの打設が終わった次の日から、また次の階の鉄筋と型枠の組み上げが始まる。組み上がると打設。
店の1階が終わったと思うと今度は家の1階、そして、店の2階、お次は家の2階…。
そんな日々の中でも日曜日の現場はわりと静かなので、日菜を連れて現場日参を続ける。日菜も僕の真似をしてメジャーを持ってあちこち何かを測っている。どこで見つけたのかホースの切れっ端を持ち歩き、マイクに見立てて歌い出す。荒々しい現場の景色と、その中にいる2歳児のギャップが面白かった。

3ヶ月間にコンクリートデイが2棟合わせて計10日。まさか自分がこんなにコンクリートの作業までするとは思っていなかった。でも、これだけ自分自身関わって作れたのは面白かった。意識したことがなかったたくさんのことを知り、経験できた。

年の瀬が近づいた2008年12月27日、無事コンクリート打設が全て終わり、上棟となった。
陽がほとんど沈んだ遠くの空が微かにピンク色だった。

Laying the Foundation (2)

The first step was to destroy the work that had already been done on the foundation. Only the original concrete posts were left. I wanted all the workers to understand what we were going to be doing from now, so I called the concrete expert from Tokyo. He came and gave them a lecture accompanied by a video about how to make concrete using his method. Many of the workers had worked with concrete for a long time, but I needed to get them to change their way of thinking.

From that time on, my reason for visiting the site changed. Previously I had been observing the work because it was interesting. Now I was there to check that it was being done properly. We had many training sessions, but a lot of workers were resistant to change and made mistakes. Their point of view was completely different from mine. This thing we were making was mine. I was only an amateur, but I understood the method we were using better than anyone else. Time and time again I pointed out mistakes. I could not overlook even one mistake.

On the day we poured the concrete we had a meeting in the morning with all the workers. In my hand was a hammer for beating the concrete. The beating continued all day. If you bang a salt shaker on the table, the contents get packed together — it's the same principal at work with the concrete. With the sound of the pump and the concrete vibrator filling the air I became absorbed in the work. I started to really feel that we were making good concrete.

Once we finished pouring the concrete, we had to set up the rods in the cast for the next floor. Then we poured the concrete and beat some more. After we finished the first floor of the shop, we moved on to the first floor of the house, then to the second floor of the shop.

On Sundays during that time, I often took Hina to the site. She used to imitate me by getting a tape measure and going about here and there measuring different things. I remember her singing into a cut off piece of hose she had found somewhere, as if it were a microphone. The contrast between the rough building site and the two year old playing there was amusing.

It took ten separate days of pouring concrete over three months for all the concrete work for the two buildings to be done. When we started building, I hadn't imagined that I would go so far as to actually work on the concrete myself, but I learned a lot of things I hadn't known. It was certainly an experience.

It was December 27, 2008, when all the concrete work was complete and the framework was in place. I remember that evening. The sun had almost set and the sky in the distance had a faint pink tint to it.

December 27, 2008 Raising the Ridgepole

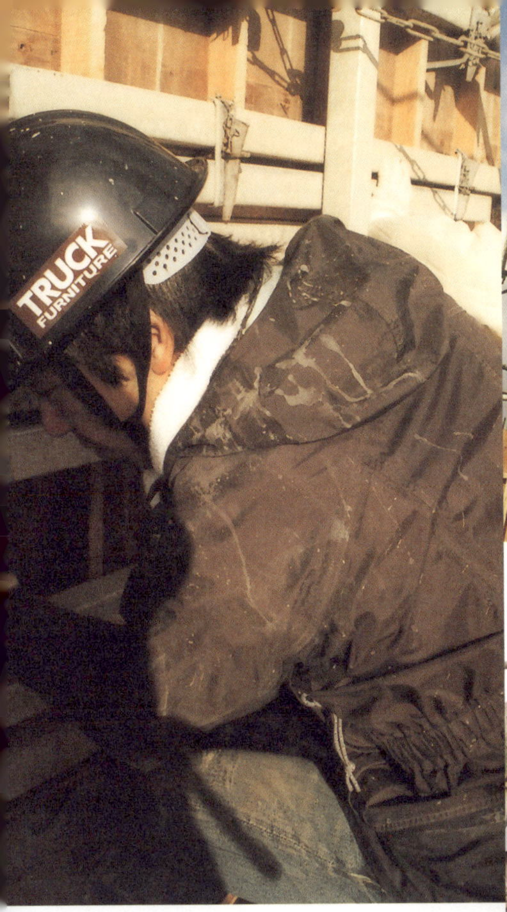
TRUCK
FURNITURE
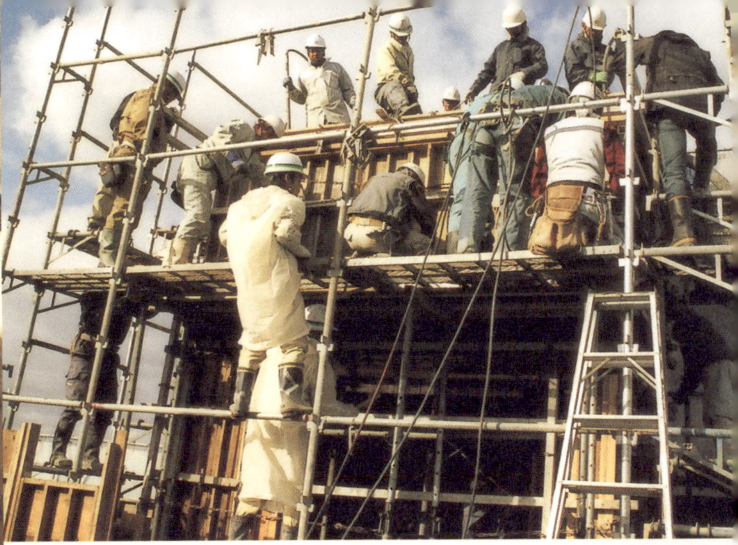
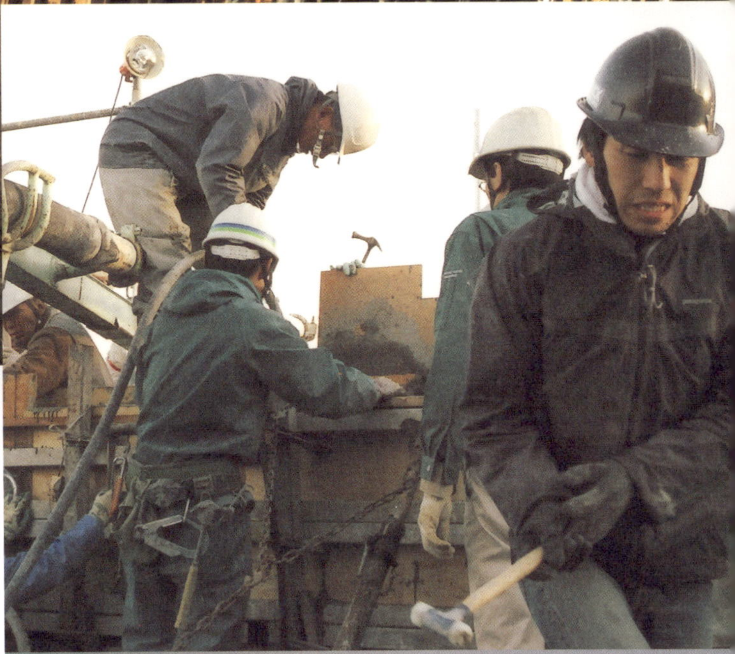
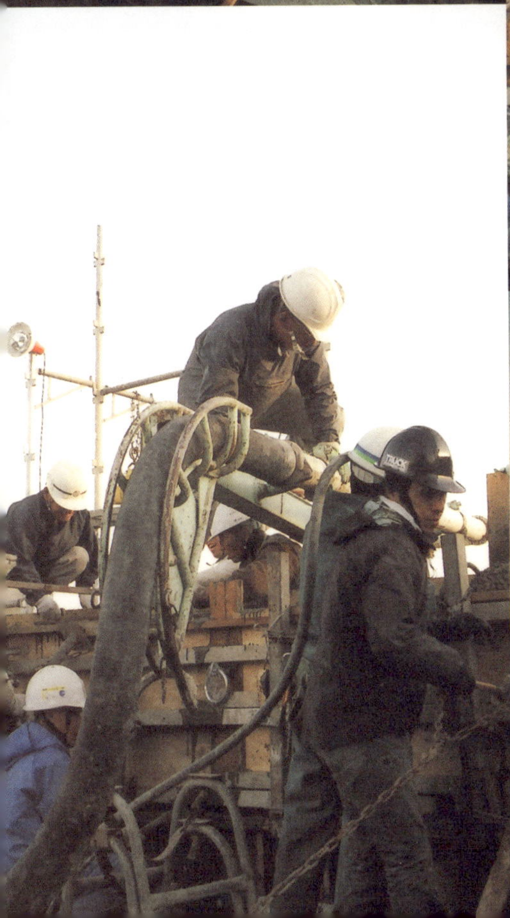
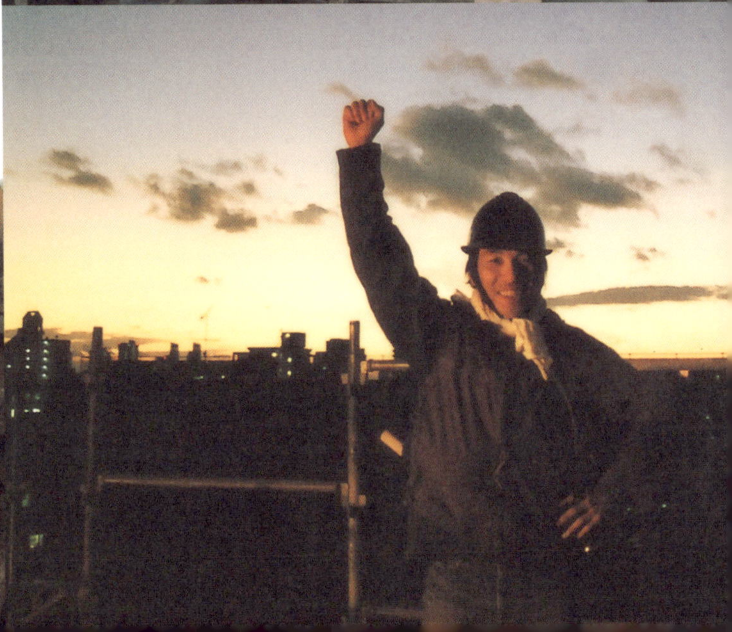

Laying the Foundation (2)

間髪入れず、12月30日、型枠の取れた箇所、1階工場及び仕上げスペースからペンキ塗りを始める。年末にもかかわらずスタッフ総出で塗っていく。窓枠の入っていないうちのほうがマスキングの手間が省けるという作戦。
コンクリートの塊でしかなかった躯体が、自分たちで白く塗っていくと、急に身近な空間に変わっていった。ここが自分たちの、これからの居場所になる！
そう思うと、寒い冬の夜、作業で冷えきった体が少し熱く感じた。

A few days later, on the 30th, we began painting the areas where the wooden molds had already been removed. We started with the first floor of the store, which would become the workshop. Even though it was the end of the year, all of the staff came and helped paint. I wanted to get all the painting done before the window frames were installed to save having to spend time and effort later covering them with masking tape.
As we painted those bare concrete walls, we began to get a real sense that this was really our place, and that it would become a place we could call home. The thought warmed us as we painted on the cold winter nights.

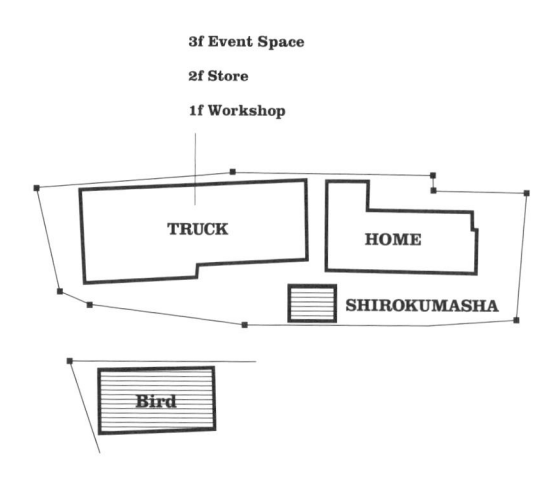

3f Event Space
2f Store
1f Workshop

TRUCK   HOME

SHIROKUMASHA

Bird

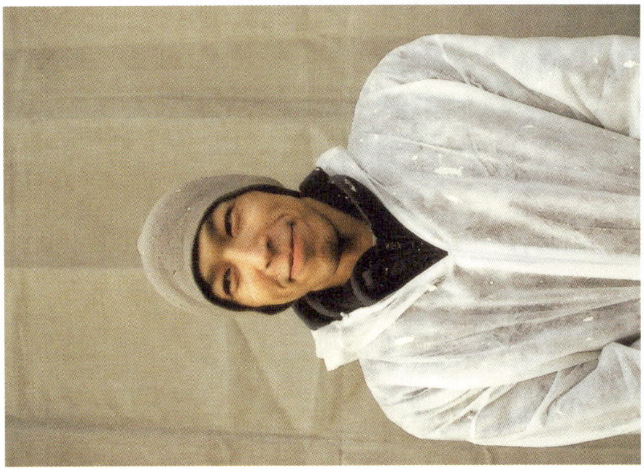
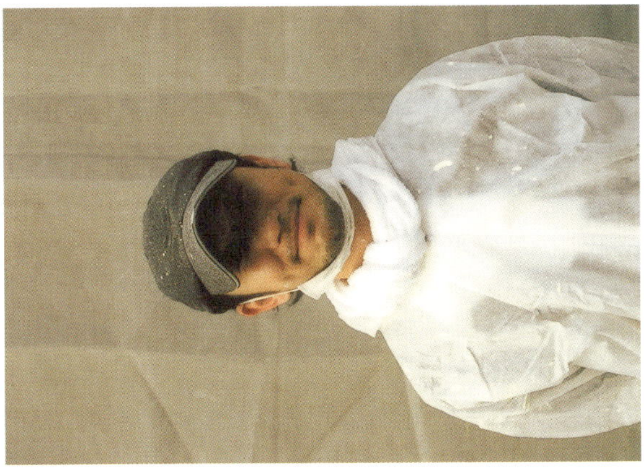
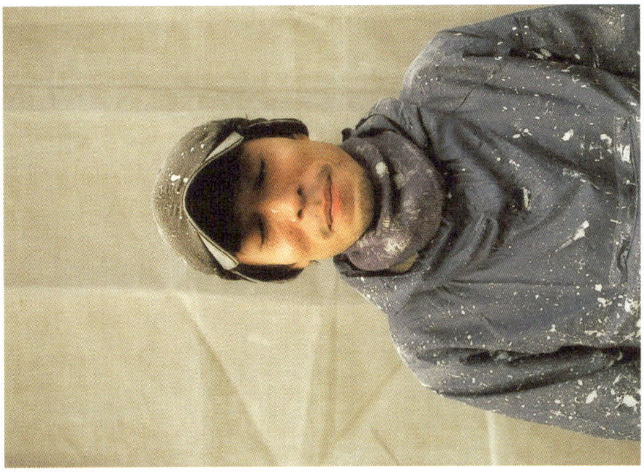
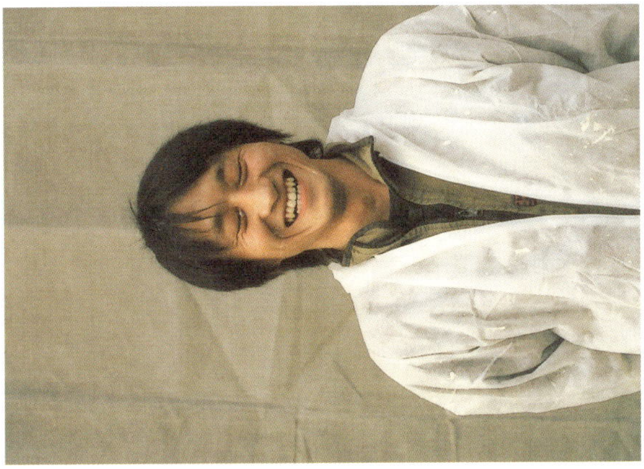
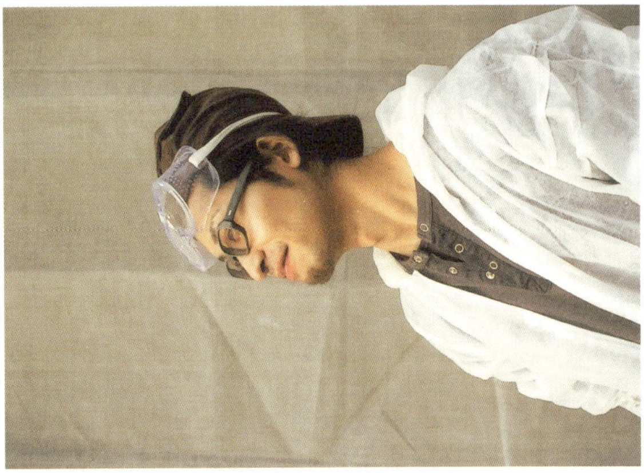
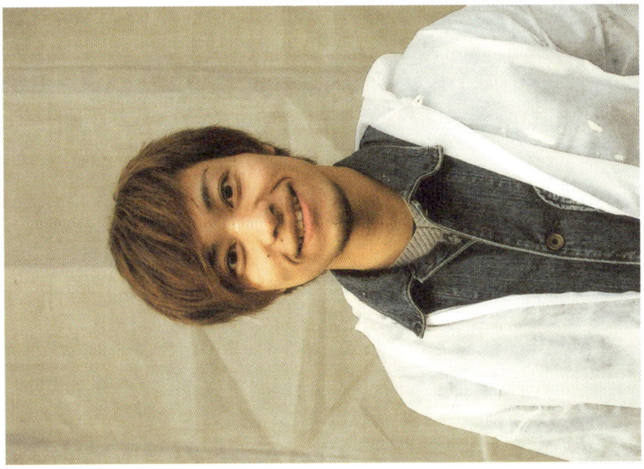
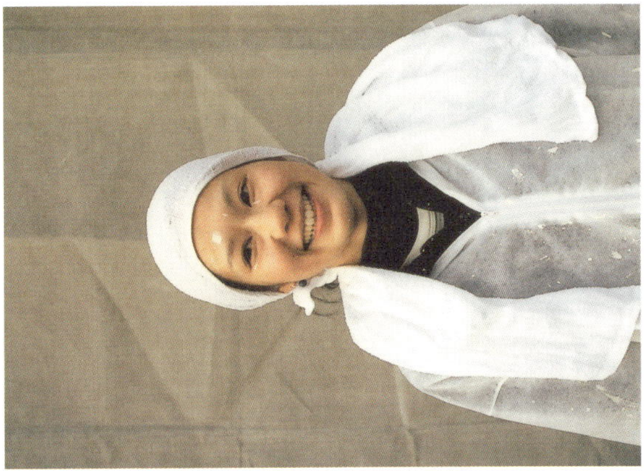
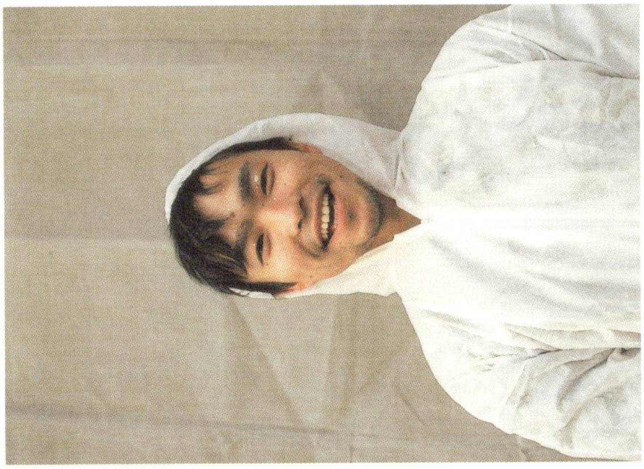

この顔のまま帰り道、ドーナツとコーヒーを買いに立ち寄った。混み合ったレジの行列に並ぶ。
店員さんも他のお客さんも何もなかったかのようなさらりとした態度。
「ポイントカードはお持ちですか？」それが逆に見てはいけない、触れてはいけない扱い的で面白かった。

On the way home with my paint splattered face I dropped by a shop to pick up some doughnuts and coffee.
The place was packed. I was amused by how far the staff and other customers went to act like nothing was strange.
"Do you have a point card, sir?" they asked.

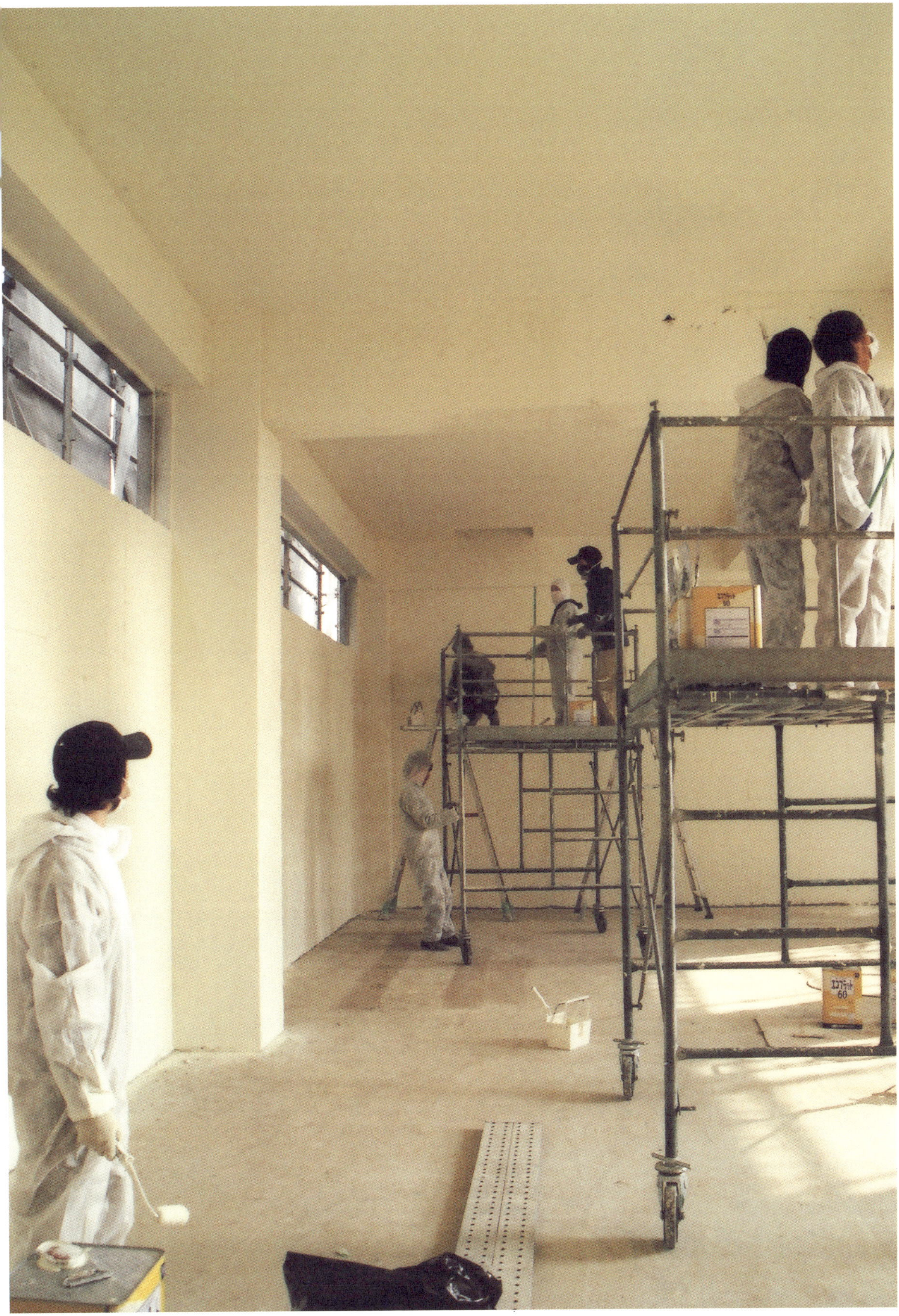
エコフラット
60

STEEL WINDOW FRAME INSULATING GLASS

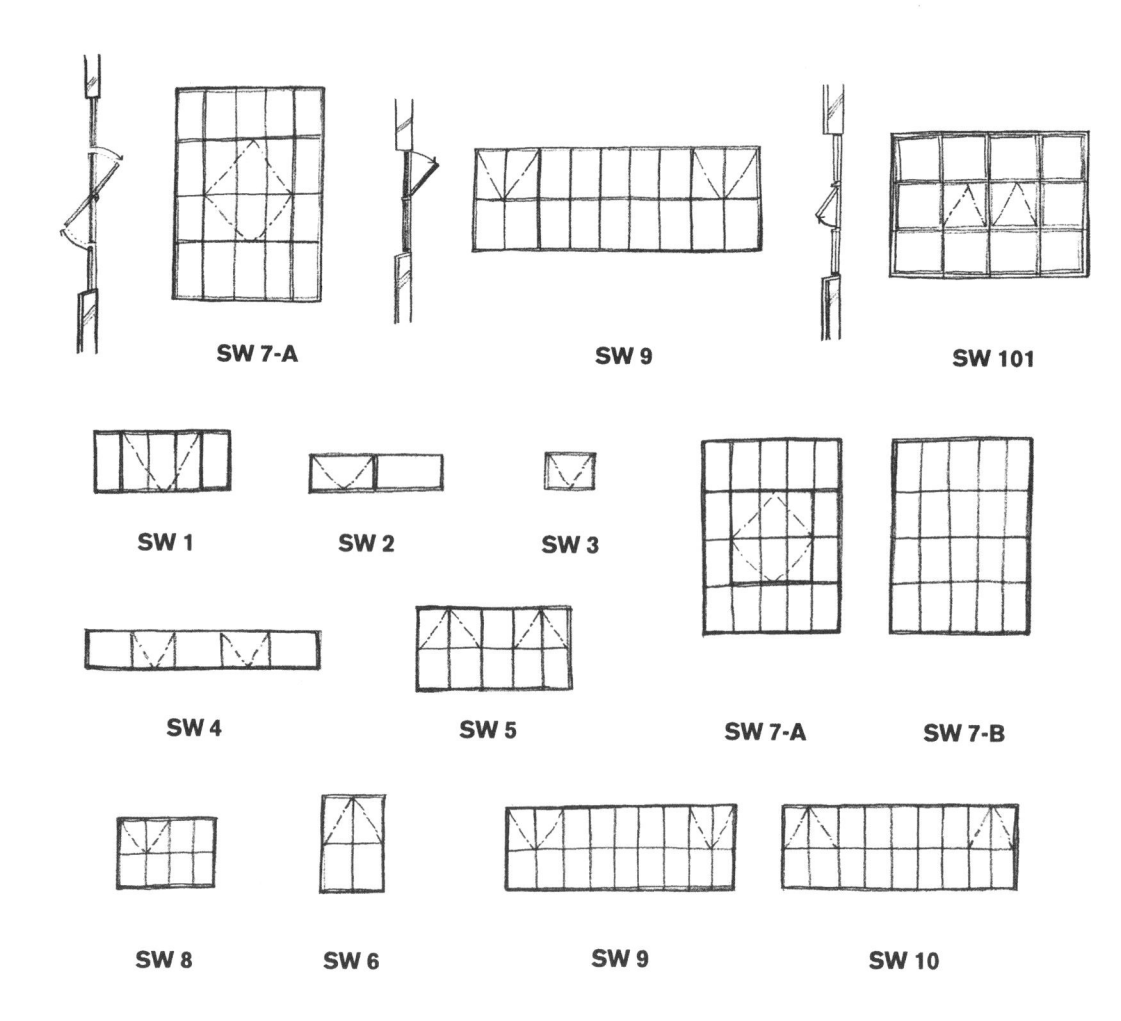

SW 7-A **SW 9** **SW 101**

SW 1 **SW 2** **SW 3** **SW 7-A** **SW 7-B**

SW 4 **SW 5**

SW 8 **SW 6** **SW 9** **SW 10**

Jan. 22, 2009
Window Frames
Arrived

ついに窓枠がやって来た。何度も絵を描き、考えた窓がいよいよ取り付けられる。
I spent many months designing the window frames. They finally arrived.

When the window frames were installed and the scaffolding was taken away,
rays of sunlight cast a grid-like shadow on the floor. It suddenly started to feel like a proper building.
I got the real feeling that we were making progress.

3630円
10%税込

注文カード

帖合・書店印

注文数

冊

発行 集英社

実用単行本

著者 TRUCK

TRUCK NEST

9784083331237

ISBN978-4-08-333123-7
C0076 ¥3300E

定価3630円
本体3300円
税10%

窓枠が入り、建物を覆っていた足場がなくなると、日射しが差し込み格子状の窓の影が床にできた。
コンクリートの箱が急に建物らしくなった。少しずつ前に進んでいることが実感できた。

集英社
東京都千代田区
一ツ橋2-5-10

実用単行本

TRUCK NEST

TRUCK

定価3630円
本体3300円
税10%

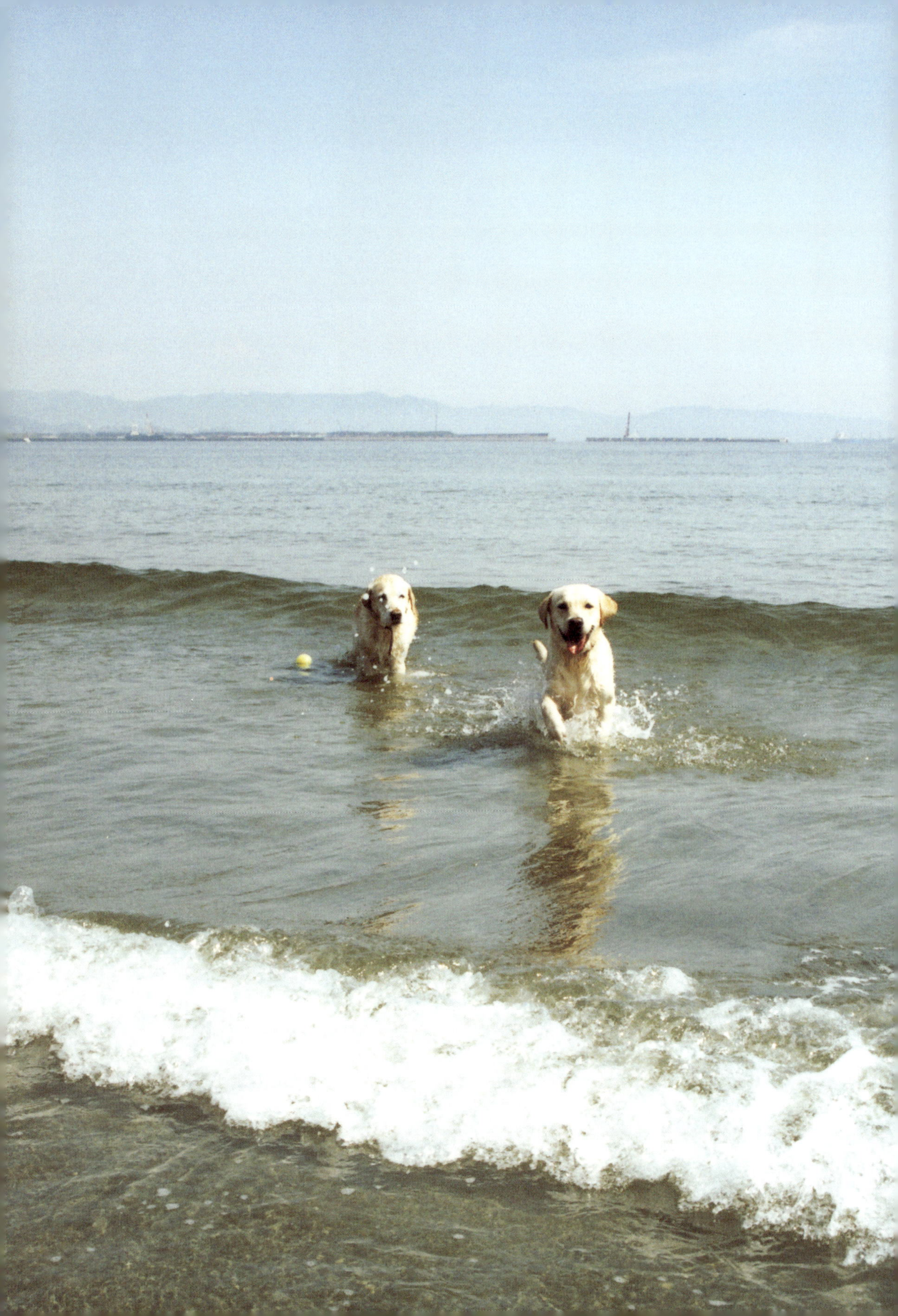

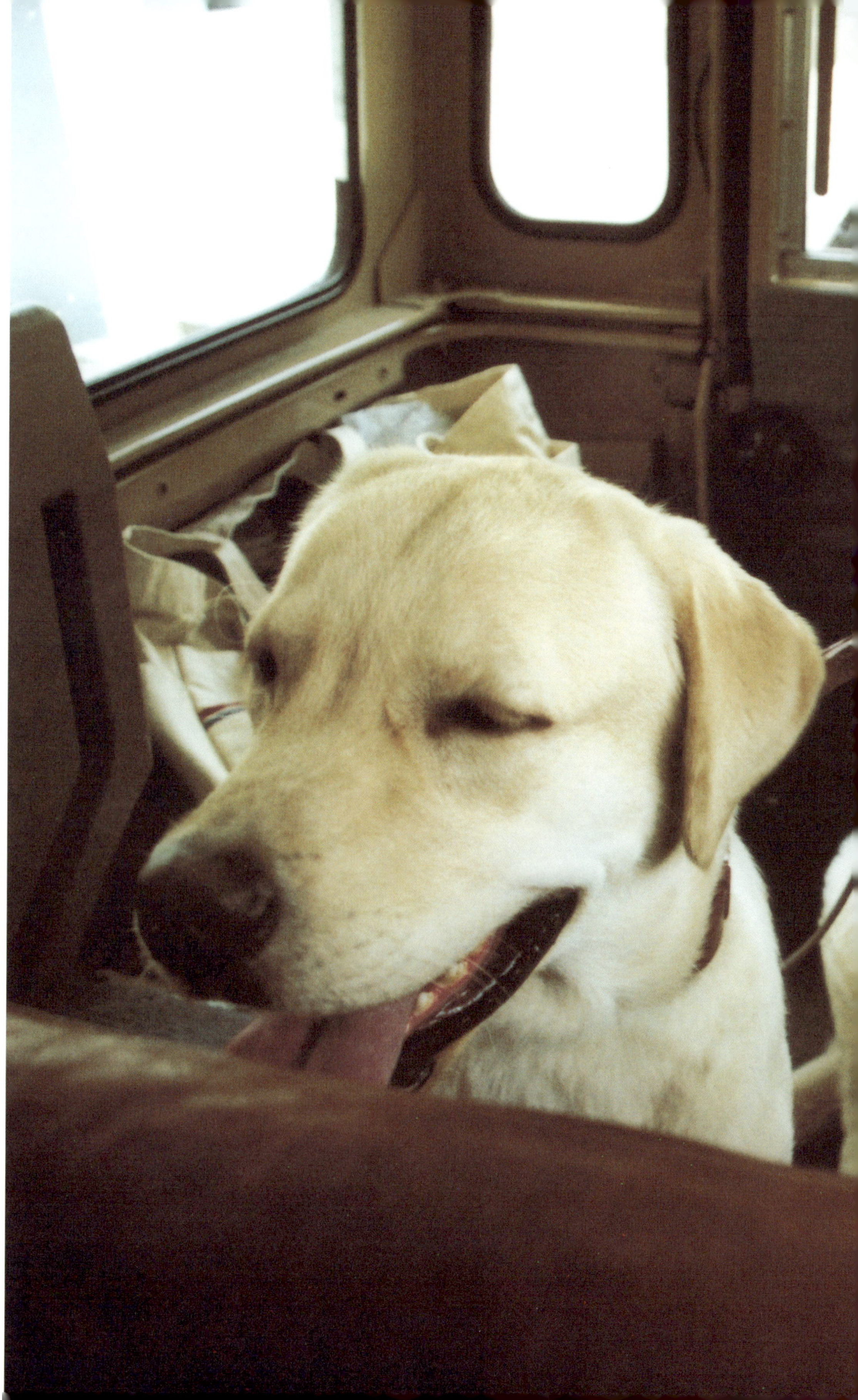

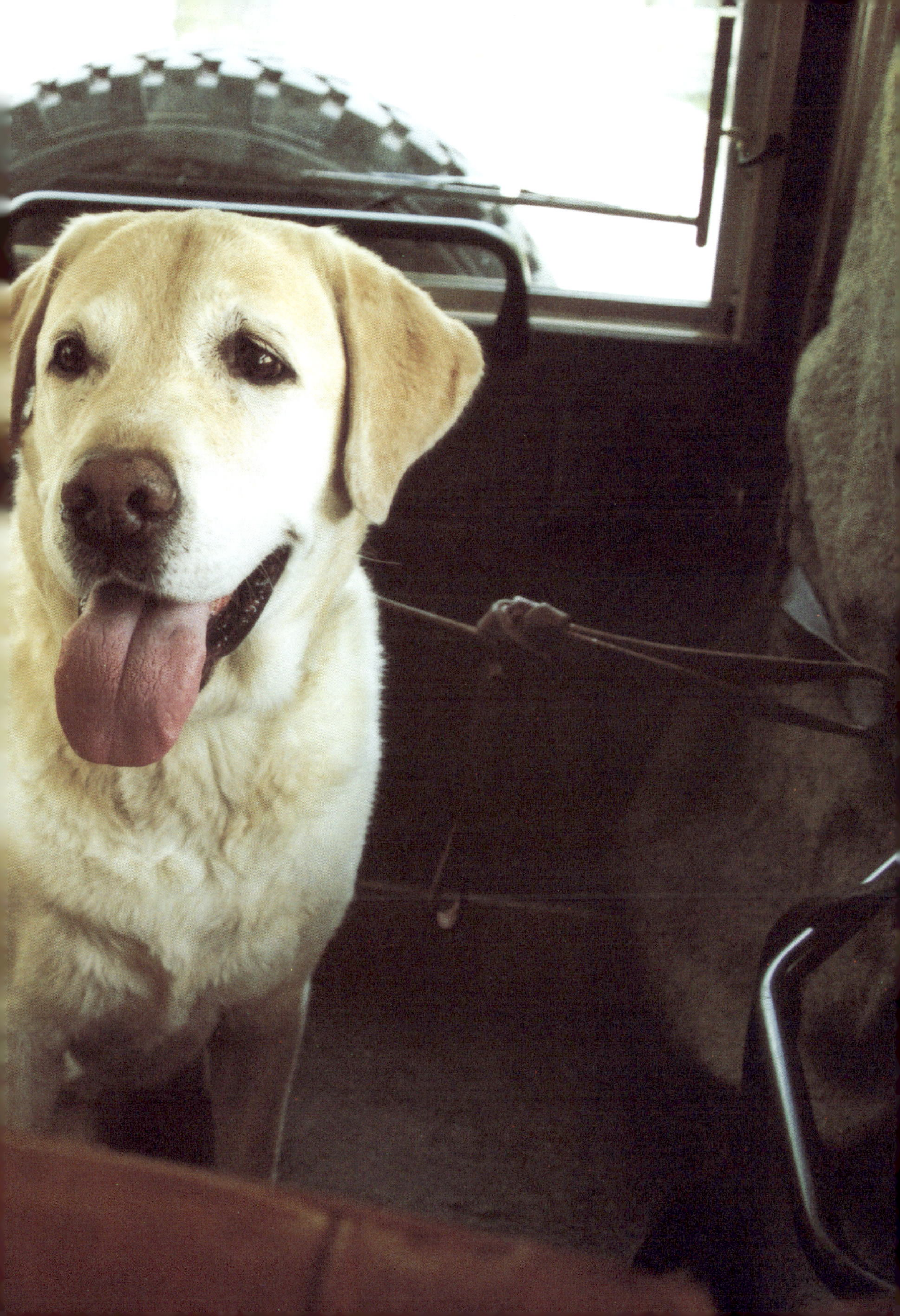

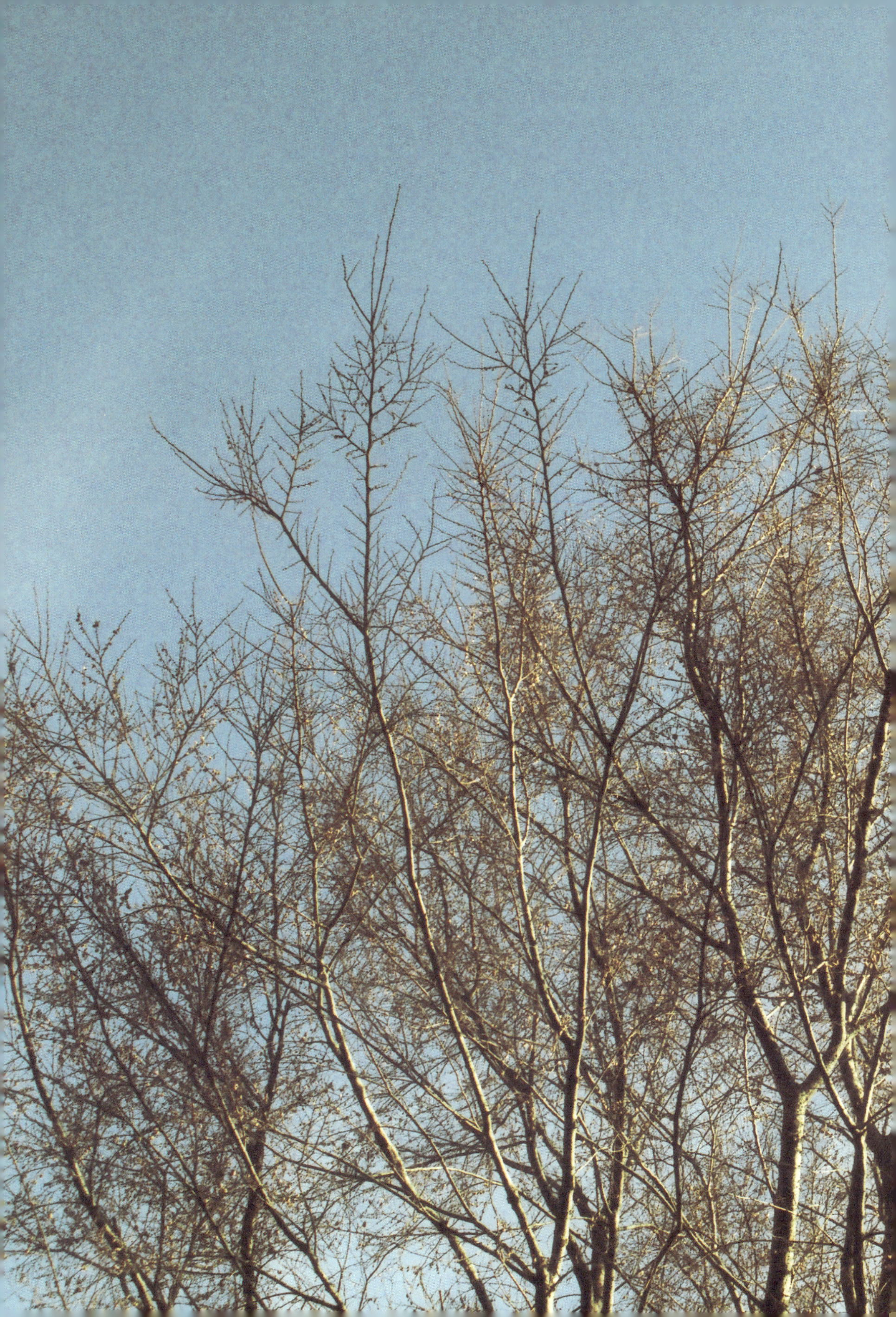

LONGING FOR TREES

樹を考える

なければ植えよう。
そう思ったが、いざ植えるとなると樹のことって全然知らないことに気がついた。明るい落葉樹が好き。それ以外は何もない。鉢植えの植物はいろいろ育ててきたからいくらかは知っていた。でも、大きな樹を自分たちが持つなんて考えたことがなかった。普通はそうだと思う。
そこでどんな樹を植えるのか。どの樹種が好きなのかを考えることから始めた。
最初に頭に浮かんだのはホワイトオーク。
アメリカやヨーロッパで何度も見ていいなあと思っていたし、何よりTRUCKの家具に一番よく使っている。馴染みがある。でも造園屋さんに聞くと、ホワイトオークは大阪には向かない、もっと涼しい所の樹とのこと。大阪の夏は暑い。最近では天気予報を見ていても「沖縄の気温より高いやん」と思うことがよくある。残念。そして、日本にはホワイトオークの大きな樹なんてなかった。

それから2人は、いつどこにいても樹を意識して見た。車で走っていても、信号で停まっていても、犬の散歩に行っても。今までは樹があるってだけの意識だったのが、自分の場所に植えるとどうか、毎日見たいかどうか。そしてその樹の名前は？ 常緑か落葉か。見方が変わった。だいたいの街路樹の名前が言えるようになっていった。
僕が好きと思った樹。5匹の犬の散歩で毎日行っていた難波宮。そこにあったきれいな樹形の大きな樹。葉っぱがいっぱいの季節でも明るい。ひりんこも唐津家のお墓参りの時に池の畔で見た樹。その樹が印象に残っていた。調べてみると、偶然にもそのどちらもがアキニレと分かった。

造園屋さんが商品の樹をたくさん植えている山をあっちこっち見に行った。
商品とは移植可能な状態にして育ててきた樹。細かい根がいっぱいある。
自然に山で育った樹は太い大きなメインの根があってそれを切ったら生きていけない。どうしても移植をしないといけない時は2年とか3年がかりで根回しをしていく。少しずつ根を切って、そこから出た細かい根を増やしていく。
そう、ここから"根回し"って言葉がきている。なるほど。面白い。また新しい知らない世界が広がっている。造園屋さんが使う専門用語も面白がってどんどん真似して使っていく。葉張り、目通り、など。そんな用語を使いながら、2人とも目の前にある樹のサイズを言い当てられるようになっていった。造園屋さんよりも先に言っては楽しんでいた。

気に入った樹は1本1本写真に撮ってサイズを測り、データを表にする。
春、夏、秋、冬と全ての季節、観察しに行った。葉っぱがいっぱいの季節に見るのはもちろん。でも、冬になって葉っぱが落ちた姿がもっと大事。枝振りが丸見えになった時に自然樹形かどうか。夏にいいと思っていても、冬に見ると駄目ってこともあった。

造園屋さん曰く、「最近こんな大きい樹を植えようとする人なんかほとんどいない。たまに駅前なんかのシンボルツリーくらいかなぁ。それに実際に山まで見に来る施主なんていない。設計者が樹種やサイズをファックスで発注してくるだけ」

Thinking about Trees

僕とひりんこは樹のことを、これから毎日一緒に過ごしていく家族のように考えていたから納得いくまで見たかった。
1本のアキニレを見るだけで熊本にも行った。
写真だけでは決められない。造園屋さんもびっくりのしつこさ。

Tracking the trees through the seasons

167

Thinking about Trees

ひりんこのすごいところ。
一度樹を見に行った山、何千本ってくらい樹がある広い敷地、同じ樹種だけでもいっぱいある。そんな中で、前回見て好きになった樹の、幹の太さや枝振り、そしてその樹がどこにあるのかを全て記憶していた。毎日そこにいる造園屋さんよりも。みんな驚いていた。すごい才能。

建物の計画をしながら、同時に植える樹のことも考えていく。いくら山で樹の姿を目に焼きつけてきても、まして写真で撮っても、現場に立ってみると想像がつかない。敷地の図面の中に4つの建物、そして樹を描いてみる。全然実感が湧かない。葉張りが8mといってもきれいな円周で8mではない。枝の形はそれぞれいろんな姿をしている。隣の樹との距離は？ ここの窓から見たらどう見える？ あっちから見たら？？？ 想像できない。鉢植えの植木だとあっちに置いたりこっちに置いてみたりといろいろ試してみられる。でも10mもあるような樹はそんなわけにはいかない。一度植えたらずっとそのまま。もうちょっと右だったかな？ なんて巻き戻せない。緊張感がすごくあった。
公園とか樹のある所で、「この樹とあの樹の間が8mか」と何度も実際に体感してみて想像を膨らませた。

考えに考えてようやく植える樹のラインナップが決まる。
その中の1本、アキニレの根回しを見に行った。地面に立っている10mもある樹の根元を掘っていき、まあるい根鉢を作る。よく植木市で見かける、植木鉢に入っていない樹の根元。大きな樹をあの姿にしていく。職人さんたちがすこぶるカッコいい。見惚れる。手際よく掘り進め、縄でくるくる巻いてあっという間に3人が手を広げても届かないような大きさの根鉢を仕上げる。僕とひりんこ、やーちゃん、TRUCKスタッフのトックンは周りで「すごー！うわー！キャー！」とまるでアイドルを目の前にしたかのような大騒ぎ。職人さんたちも、そんなに見られたことって今までなかったようで、ちょっと得意気だった。

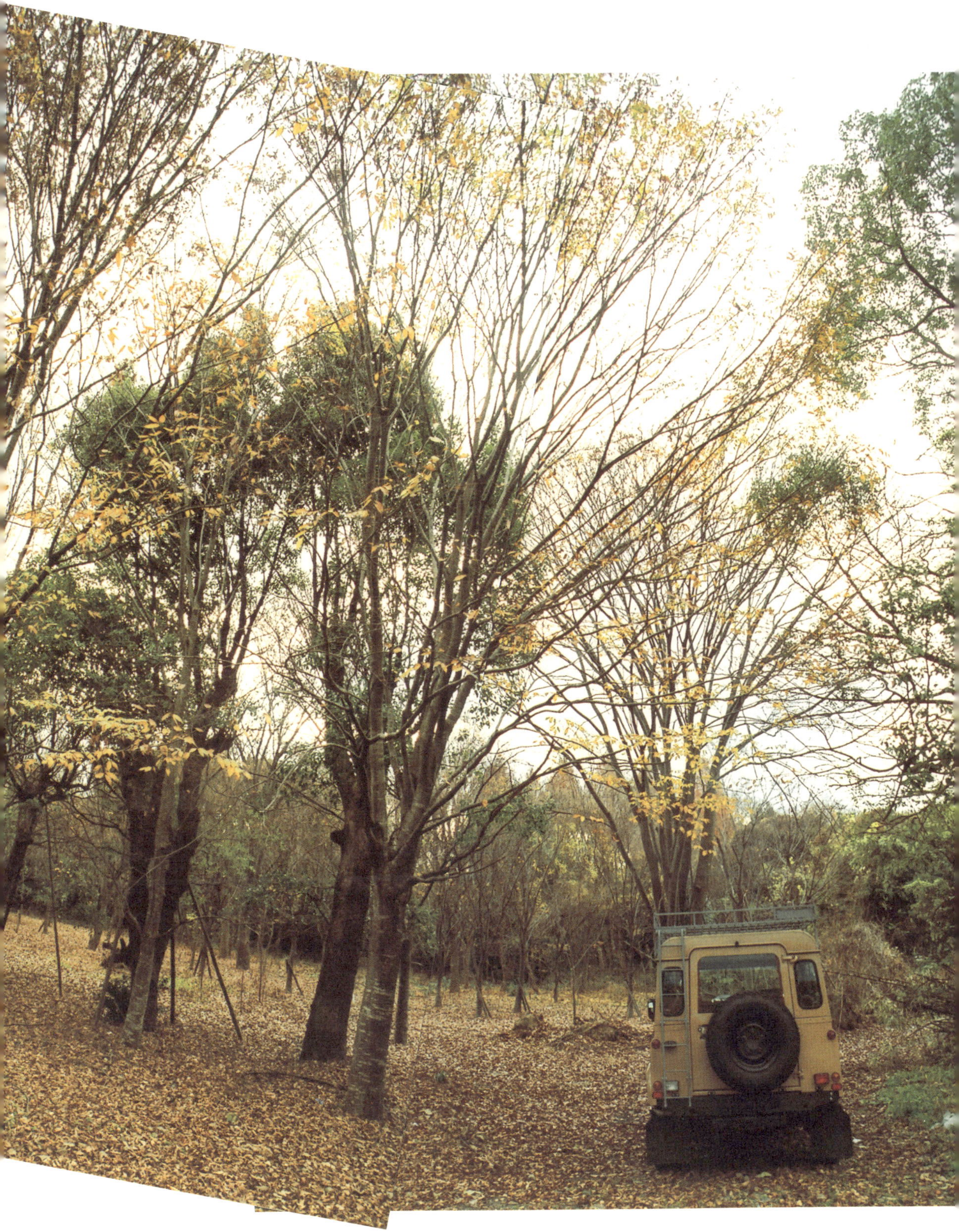

Thinking about Trees

"If there are none, we'll just have to plant them," we had decided, but when we thought about it, we realized that we really knew nothing about trees. I knew that I liked airy deciduous trees, but that was about all. We'd raised a lot of potted plants, so we knew about those, but we really hadn't thought at all about big trees.

We started thinking about what species we liked. At first I had hoped to plant white oaks. I'd often seen them in America and Europe and really liked how they looked. It was the wood that we used more than any other at TRUCK, too. I consulted a landscape gardener, but he told us that Osaka was not suitable for such trees. They prefer cooler climates. Osaka is very hot in summer. Recently on some days, hotter even than Okinawa. Unfortunately, it seemed there were no big white oaks in Japan. Hiromi and I tried to be more aware of the trees around us when we were driving, when we were stopped at traffic lights, and when we were walking the dogs. We learned the trees' names, found out if they were evergreen or deciduous, and considered if we would like to live surrounded them every day. After a while, we could name almost all the trees in the city.
There were a couple of trees we liked. Every day when I walked my dogs, I went to Naniwanomiya Park. There was a tree there that was very big and was airy, even in seasons when it had many leaves. Another was a tree Hiromi had seen next to a pond in her hometown. We looked them up and discovered that they were both Chinese elms.

In our search, we visited many nurseries in the mountains where landscape gardeners had large plantations of trees. The trees were raised so that they would one day be transplantable. They have many tiny roots. If a tree grows wild in the mountains it develops a big main root. If that is cut, the tree will die. If that kind of tree needs to be moved it can take as long as two or three years to prepare it. The roots are gradually cut so they sprout fresh, thinner roots, a process called *nemawashi*. There is a Japanese expression *"nemawashi"* that means to prepare or lay the groundwork for something. Until I started looking for trees, I didn't know the origin of the expression. It was very interesting to find out. We came to enjoy picking up the jargon used by landscape gardeners and tried to use it whenever we could. Some other examples are *"medori"*, which is the diameter of the tree at breast height, and *"habari"*, which describes the circumference of a tree's branches. We would try to use these words to estimate the size of the trees in front of us. It was fun whenever we were able to use them before the landscape gardener did.

When we found trees that we liked, we photographed them, measured them, and recorded the information in a notebook. We visited them again in spring, summer, autumn and winter. We wanted to see how the trees changed with the seasons. Perhaps the most important season to check was winter, when all the leaves had fallen. I wanted to be able to see how they looked when I could see all the branches. Some trees looked good in summer, but less so in winter.

"There aren't many people who buy such big trees these days," the landscape gardener said. "Occasionally they are bought to be planted in front of train stations as symbols, but that's about it. I've never seen anybody come all the way out here to see them. Usually we just get a request fax with the species and the size and send it off." We thought of the trees as being new members of our family, so we were determined to search until we were satisfied. We traveled as far away as Kumamoto (four hours away by bullet train) just to see one Chinese Elm. We knew we couldn't decide just by seeing a photograph. The landscape gardener was surprised at our persistence.

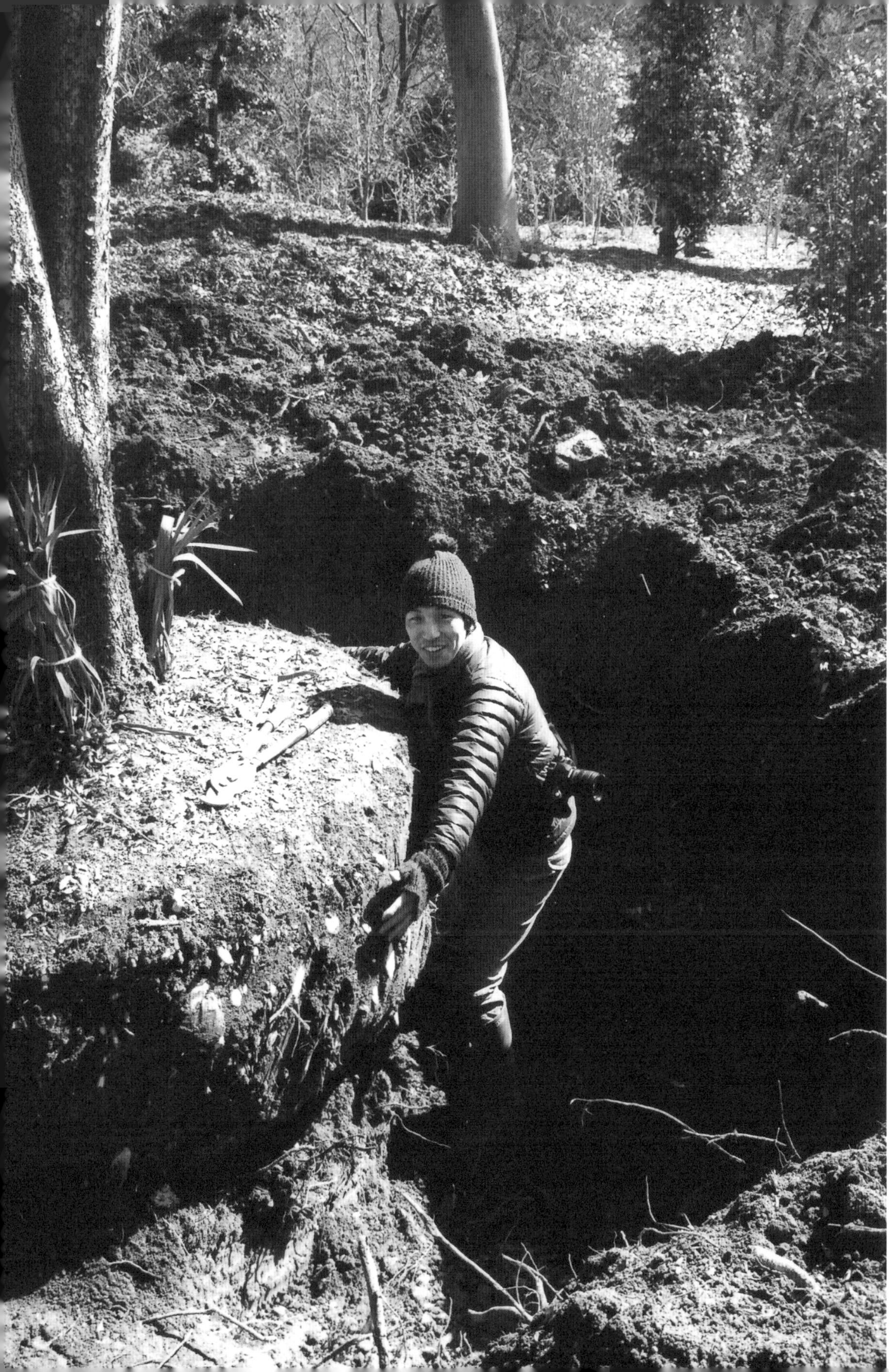

These trips to the mountains revealed a hidden talent of Hiromi's. Many nurseries had thousands of trees spread across a wide area, many of which were of the same species. Hiromi was able to remember not just the measurements of the trees we liked, but was also able to locate them faster even than the landscape gardeners who worked there every day. They never failed to be surprised.

The planning for the trees continued alongside the planning for the buildings. No matter how many times we saw the trees in the mountains or looked at photos, it was difficult to imagine what they would actually look like on our land. We tried adding trees to our drawings, but couldn't get a feel for how they would really look. A tree might have a branch circumference of 8m, but it was never a clean circle, every tree had its own distinctive shape. We wondered how far the tree should be from its neighbors, what it would look like from this or that window, or a particular spot in the garden. It was difficult to imagine. When you're dealing with potted plants it's easy to move them around to get them right.
You don't have that flexibility with a tree that's ten meters tall. Once you decide, that's it. If things look wrong, you can't go back and do it again. When we went to parks and other places with trees, we would look at two trees and wonder, "Are there 8 meters between them?" trying to simulate our plans as far as possible.

Eventually we decided on the lineup of trees. We went to see the root preparation of one of the Chinese Elms. The tree was ten meters tall and it's roots were being dug up and wrapped into a root clump. We couldn't help but admire the skill of the workers. Before we knew it they had deftly dug up the roots and gathered them into a clump. Hiromi, Yasuko, Takashi (a longtime member of the TRUCK staff) and I stood around admiring them like they were pop stars. They had never had such an appreciative audience and seemed grateful for the praise.

fig. **1) Drip Line**
Look down from the top of the tree with the trunk as the center. The drip line is the diameter of a square encompassing the leaves and branches. If there are both long and short, then the average of the longest and shortest is used.

fig. **2) DBH / Diameter at Breast Height**
A measurement is taken by throwing a tape measure around a tree at a height of 120cm from the soil. We liked the way landscape gardeners shortened *senchi* (Japanese for centimeters) to just *sen*. 100cm would be *hyaku-sen*. (*Hyaku* means hundred).

fig. **3) Root Clump**
When you're moving a tree, you have to gradually prune the roots of the tree over a period of one or two years. This encourages small fresh roots to emerge. These help the tree adapt more easily to its new environment. When moving the tree, the roots are gathered together into root clump (containing roots and soil) that is usually about four to five times as big as the trunk of the tree.

DIGGING AROUND A TREE'S ROOTS

(1) DRIP LINE

1. 葉張り
樹を上から見て、樹の幹を中心とし、四方向に伸びた葉と枝の直径幅をいう。長短がある場合は最長と最短の平均値とする。

Root wrapping

DBH
(2) diameter at breast height
120cm

(3) ROOT CLUMP

2. 目通り
地面から120cmの高さをメジャーをぐるっと回して測定した数値。造園屋さんはセンチの"チ"をとって"セン"という。これがカッコいいのですぐに真似して使うようにした。100cmだとヒャクセン。いきなりそれっぽくなる。

3. 根回し、根鉢
樹を移植する時は、逆算して1〜2年前の成長が止まっている冬の時期に根元の周りを掘って根を切っておく。そうすることで新しく細かい根が出る。若い細かな根がたくさんあると移植後、活着しやすくなる。
根回しをして根っことその周りについた土を幹周りの4〜5倍のサイズに仕上げる。それを根鉢という。

そこでまた知ったこと。根回しをする時は枝もある程度切らないといけない。根を切る。すると吸い上げる水の量が減る。葉っぱはどんどん水分を蒸散していく。根と葉の量のバランスを合わせないといけない。なるほど。納得。
なるべく自然樹形を維持するように剪定してもらう。
その時に切った枝がもったいなくて車の屋根にくくりつけて持って帰った。店に持って帰ってびっくり。
めちゃめちゃ大きい。山で見ていると分からなかったけど、街で見るとすごく大きい。
AREA2の前に植えていた2階の高さまであったトネリコ、それよりも大きい。剪定で払われた枝のほうが大きい。
ってことは本体ってどれだけ大きい!? 大丈夫か？ドキドキした。
「いかにも植栽しましたっていう苗木ではなく、初めから気合いの入った大きな樹を植えたい」と言う僕たちに造園屋さんが何度も言っていた「山に生えているとこ見てたら分からんけど、持って帰って植えたら思った以上にでかいで」
その言葉がこだましました。

Feb. 21, 2008
Chinese Elm
Root Clump

Something I learned that day was that when you cut a tree's roots, you have to cut an equal amount from the tree's branches. Cutting a tree's roots reduces the amount of water it can absorb from the soil. If you don't also reduce the number of leaves (which lose water through transpiration) there is a risk of the tree dehydrating. You have to balance how much you take from each. I had them prune so that tree maintained as natural a shape as possible.

It seemed a shame to just throw it away, so I strapped one of the branches they had cut to the top of my car and took it with us. We were surprised when we got it home. It was massive. It was difficult to understand how big it was in the mountains, surrounded by other big trees, but in the city it really stood out. There was a Japanese Ash outside AREA2 that was two stories tall. This was bigger. "How big," I wondered, "would the actual tree look?" Indeed, when we first decided we wanted a real tree rather than something just bought from a nursery, the landscape gardener warned us many times how difficult it was to judge how big it would look until we actually saw it at our house.

団地の樹、救出作戦

難波宮の東と南側にたくさんあった古い団地が取り壊されるという噂を聞いた。そこはとても好きな場所だった。すごく広い敷地に団地の標本と言えるくらい歴史を感じるいろんなタイプの団地があった。何より、カッコいい樹がいっぱい。50年以上前からの年季の入った様々な樹。樹の少ない大阪で、家から近くにそんな場所があることが救いだった。その団地が解体となると樹は？と心配しているうちに、第1期の工事が始まった。嫌な予感が的中。あっという間にその第1期工事区画の樹は全て切られた。何もなくなった。残念すぎるが、どうすることもできなかった。

以前この団地界隈を散歩していて、そこに住んでいるおばちゃんと話したことがあった。
「この樹はこんなちっちゃかったんやけど、ここまで大きくなって。毎年いっぱい夏みかんができるねん」
夏みかんをいくつかもらった。

僕たちが土地を手に入れてしばらくした頃、第2期工事が始まった。
団地があっという間に背の高い塀で囲まれていく。そんな時、いつも通り過ぎていた場所にびっくりするくらい大きなオリーブの樹があることに気づいた。高さ10m、目通り100セン以上、葉張り6m。こんなオリーブ見たことない。ヤバい！これも切られてしまう。
そうだ！ちょうど今、自分たちが作っている新しい場所。樹を植えようとしている場所。
そこに移植すれば救える！そう考えた。
今までたくさんの犬や猫を救ってきた。ゴミとして捨てられていた鉢植えの植物たちもいっぱい拾っては育ててきた。みんな生き物。モノではない。なんとかしたい。いろんな人に相談した。でも、どうも簡単にはいかないみたい。そこは大阪市の敷地。だからそこにあるものは大阪市の財産。たとえ実生（種から自然に生える）で勝手に育ってしまったものでも、市の財産は市民のもの。よって、「はい。好きに持って帰って下さい」とはいかないらしい。入札にするとかして市民に問わないと。えぇ!?　入札？もし万が一、掘り起こしていいとなったとしても、その作業中に何か事故があったら、問題が起こったら誰の責任になるのか、などとお役所は考えて、結局いいとは言わない。あるいは、「樹を助けたいんですね。分かりました。じゃあ、どこかに移植しておきます」と言いつつ処分するかも？とまで聞いた。
すごく手ごわそう。

でも諦めない。
そこで知り合いから元府議会議員という人を紹介してもらう。すぐにその人に会いに行き、かくかくしかじかと思いを説明した。そして団地を管理する機関の人を紹介してもらった。その人と、新しい場所の樹を全てお願いすることになっていた富士造園の桑原さんとで団地の中を見て回った。オリーブも見てもらった。担当者は植物が好きな人で桑原さんとも話が合った。良かった。そして僕たちに言われて改めて見て回って、これだけの樹が伐採されるということに驚いていた。道が少し開けた。桑原さんは「移植はなかなか難しい。それも、こんな好き勝手に育った野生の樹なんて特に。お金をかけて業者使って移植しても8割方枯れるかも。新しいとこに植えるんやったら買ったほうが安いしリスクも低いで」と何度も言われた。

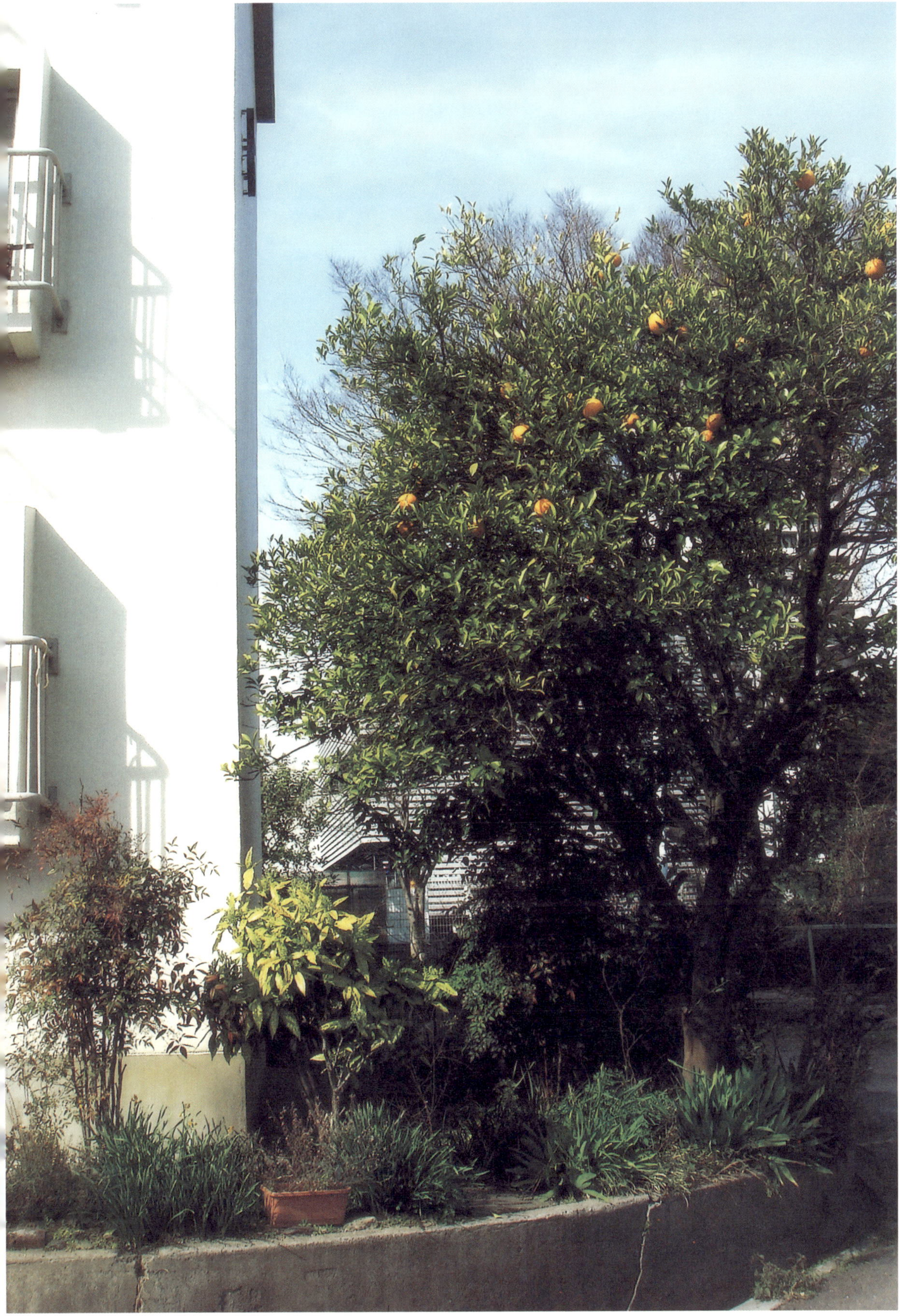

Tree Rescue

でも、このまま見過ごせない。少しでも何とかしたい。移植したら枯れてしまうかもしれなくても、どうせ伐採される。一か八かやってみよう。お金の問題ではない。
何度も桑原さんと団地中を見て回り、移植できそうなのを選んでいった。樹種によっては可能性があるものもあると教えてもらった。歩きながら話していると、桑原さん自身、仕事柄、お施主さんに言われて植木の植え替えを依頼された時など、引っこ抜かれた植物をかわいそうに思い、家に持って帰っていると言う。家の周りはそんな救ってきた植物でいっぱいらしい。さらに、家の屋上ではメダカを1万匹！育てている。面白い。

やっと、お役所や団地の自治体の許可が無事とれて3日間限定で植物救出大作戦を決行することになった。

さあ、これからという救出の日の朝に、日菜を預けている保育園から電話が。
「日菜ちゃん、どうも水疱瘡みたいです。すぐにお迎えお願いします」…負けへんで。

桑原さんと数人の職人さんと一緒に3日間、計31本の樹を掘り起こした。さらに置き去りにされた大小様々の鉢植えも。桑原さんも僕たちと同じように、「この植木はいいなあ」「これもいける！」と同じ温度で楽しそうだった。
桑原さんなしではこの作戦は実現できなかった。ありがとう。桑原さん。
この31本は一旦、富士造園さんの畑に仮植えされて約10ヶ月間育ててもらった。大方の樹は枯れずに生きた。そして、旭区の現場に植えるタイミングが来るのを待った。（この救出作戦のきっかけになった大きなオリーブは将来、公園になる予定の位置にあることが判明。大事に残すと約束してもらう）

May 7-9, 2008
RESCUE OPERATION
31 TREES

Tree Rescue

I heard a rumor that an old housing complex next to Naniwanomiya Park was going to be knocked down. It was a place that I really liked. There were a number of types of building spread around a large area. You could really feel that they had some history to them. There were many wonderful trees, too. In Osaka, which has so few trees, to have such a place nearby was a great help.

Just as I was beginning to worry about what would happen to the trees, the first stage of the construction began. A portion of the buildings and the surrounding gardens were partitioned off. When the fences came down, my gloomy prediction proved to have been correct. All of the trees in the area had been cut down. They were all gone, and there was nothing I could do about it. I remembered one day when I had been walking in the area, an old woman had given me some mandarin oranges from one of the trees, saying, "This tree used to be very small and now it's so big! Every year it grows lots of summer mandarin oranges."

Preparation for the second stage began. Next to the path along which I often used to walk, was the biggest olive tree I'd ever seen. It was 10 meters tall, about a meter round the trunk, and had branches spreading out for 6 meters. "Will this be chopped down, too?" I wondered.

I realized that we were just about to start making a new place, a place where we would be planting trees. Perhaps we could rescue some of these trees as we had rescued so many cats and dogs. We had picked up and raised many pot-plants that we'd found put out with the trash. They are all living things. They are not objects.

I talked with many people and it seemed like it would not be a very easy thing to do. The land belonged to Osaka city. The trees growing there (even those that had grown from fallen seeds) also belonged to the city. Consequently, they couldn't just let us take whatever trees we wanted. They'd have to put it up for tender and we'd have to bid. And what if there were an accident while we were moving them? Whose responsibility would that be? It was a difficult problem to solve.

A friend introduced me to a former member of the prefectural government. I quickly went to meet him and explained the situation and our plans as persuasively as I could.
Through him we were introduced to a member of the organization that ran the housing complex. He agreed to walk around the grounds with Mr. Kuwabara, the landscape gardener from whom we were buying all of our trees for the site. He turned out to be something of a plant lover and got along well with Mr. Kuwabara. He said he had been unaware that so many trees would be destroyed. The way forward cleared a little.

Mr. Kuwabara told us that transplanting trees was very difficult, even more so for those that are wild. Even if it were done by a professional, about 80% of the trees could be expected to die. It would be much cheaper and much less risky for us just to buy new trees. We felt, though, that if there was even a little we could do for these trees, we should do it. Some of them might die, we thought, but they would be chopped down anyway if we did nothing.

Many times we walked the grounds with Mr. Kuwabara. He selected the trees that looked like they might be able to be transplanted. As we walked we got to know him and found out what an interesting person he is. As a landscape gardener he is often asked by customers to replace old plants. He can't bring himself to throw the old ones away, so he takes them home and keeps them there. His house is small and lacks a garden, so it is surrounded by these rescued plants. And on his roof he had 10,000 Japanese killifish.

We finally got approval to remove some of the plants from the housing complex. They gave us three days.

On the first day, just as we were getting ready to start, we got a call from Hina's kindergarten. They told us that it seemed like she had measles, and asked us to come and pick her up. We raced home, picked her up, and arranged for Hiromi's mother to look after her while we were digging up the trees.

With the help of Mr. Kuwabara and other workers we dug up thirty-one trees (and collected a large number of pot-plants) over those three days. It was hard work, but fun. Together with Mr. Kuwabara we enjoyed pointing out to each other the plants that we especially liked. Without his help there is no way we could have done it. Thank you Mr. Kuwabara.

The thirty-one trees were temporarily planted at Mr. Kuwabara's nursery, where they waited for ten months until the new place was ready to take them. Almost all of them survived. The big olive tree that had been the catalyst for the rescue operation was slated to be included in an extension to the park.

ペンを持ってなかったので、救出した樹を指でナンバリングして写真に記録していった。
この31番で無事3日間の救出作戦が終わった。

We had no pencils, so we used fingers to number each tree in photographs.
Number 31 marked the end of our successful three-day rescue mission.

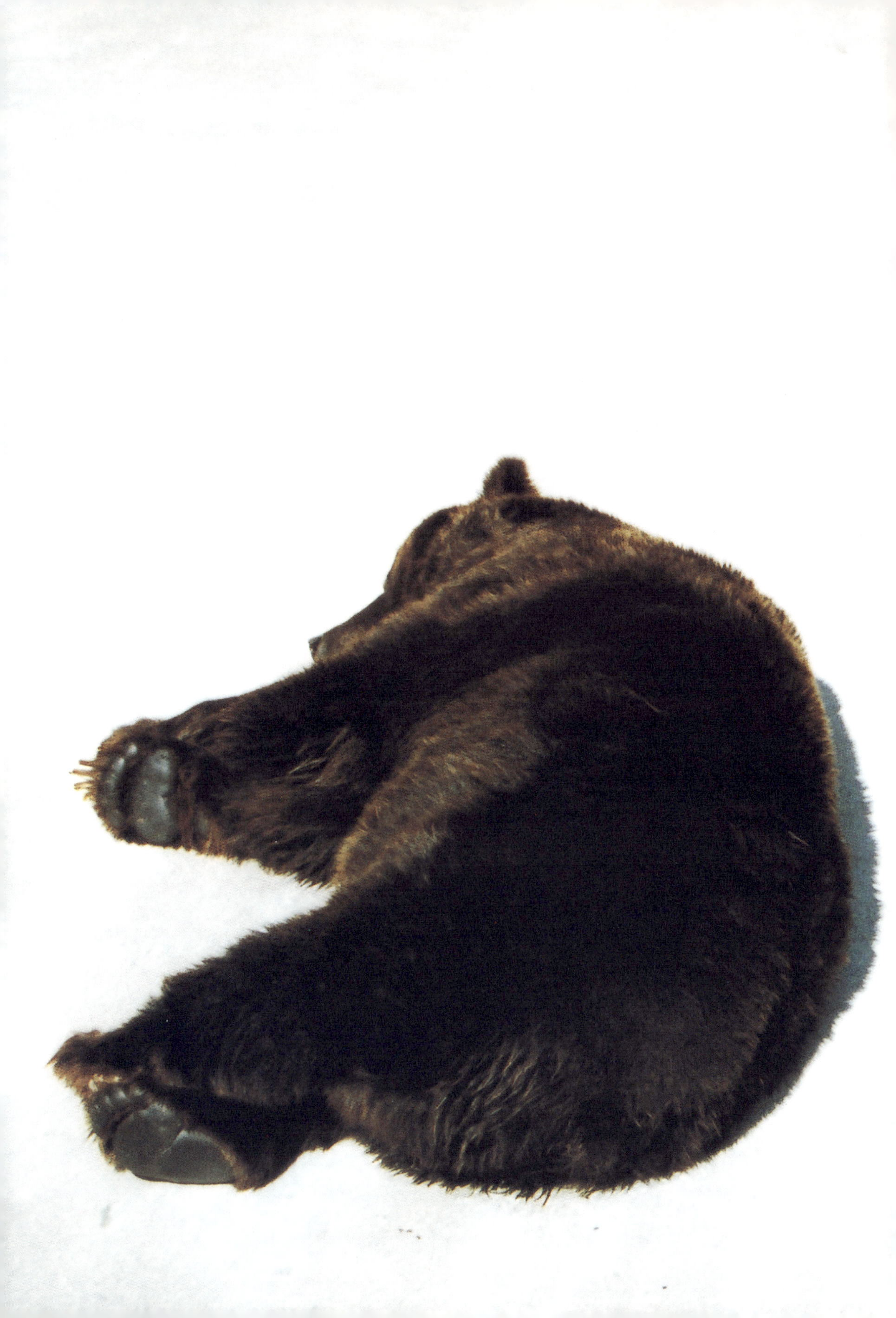

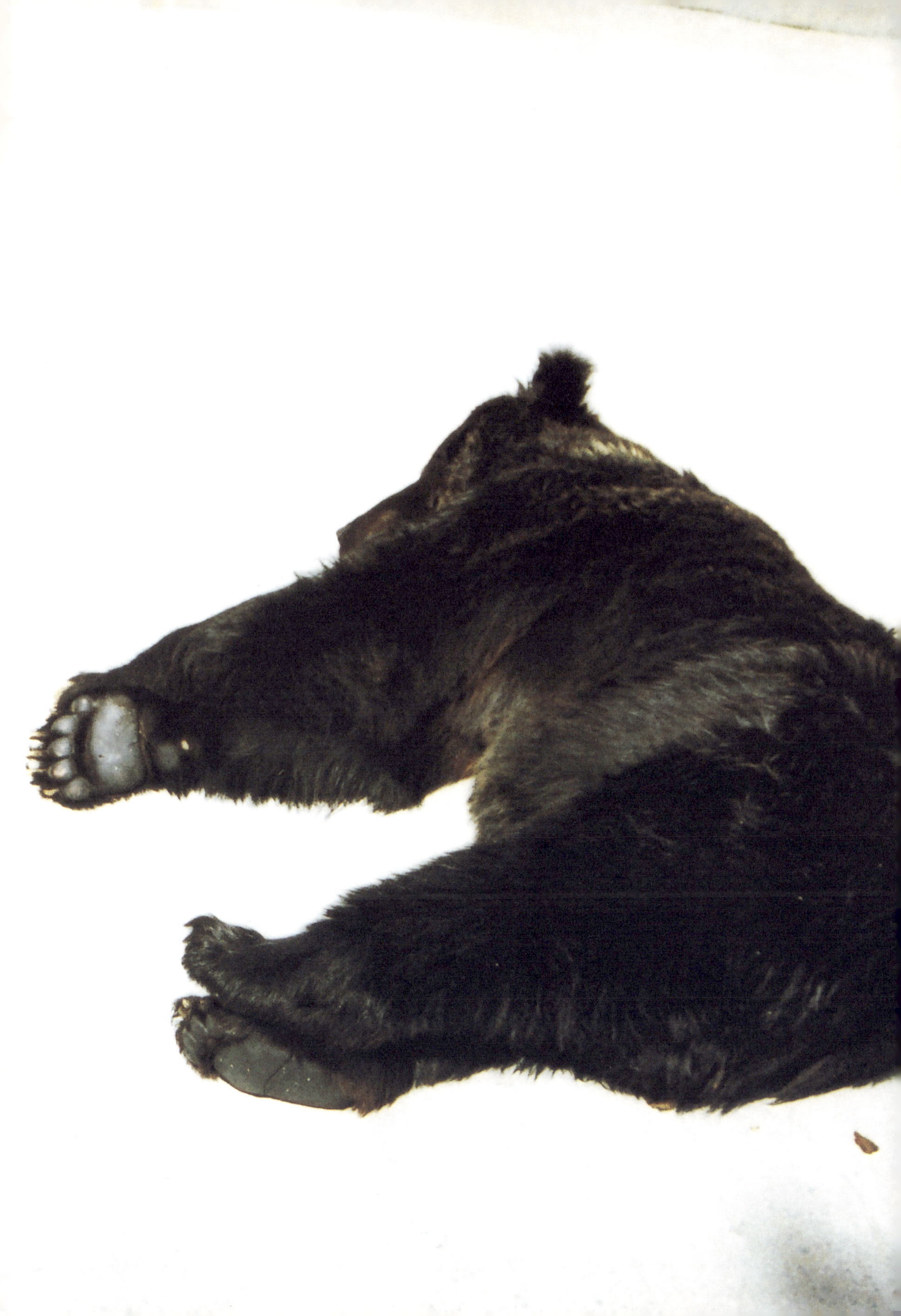

樹を見に行った熊本でクマ牧場を発見。クマだらけ。
日菜よりも親2人が大盛り上がり。瞳孔開きっぱなし。体重10kgの子グマを抱っこして写真に収まる。
その後、ひりんこはクマ牧場で流れていたテーマソングを口ずさむ日々がしばらく続いた。

We visited Kumamoto to look at a tree and found an unusual park; a bear park. We were surprised at just how many bears there were.
I think Hiromi and I were more excited than Hina. We walked around with our eyes wide open the whole time.
We took a picture of us holding a small 10kg bear. There was a catchy theme song playing over the park's PA system.
Over the next few days, Hiromi occasionally found herself singing snippets of it.

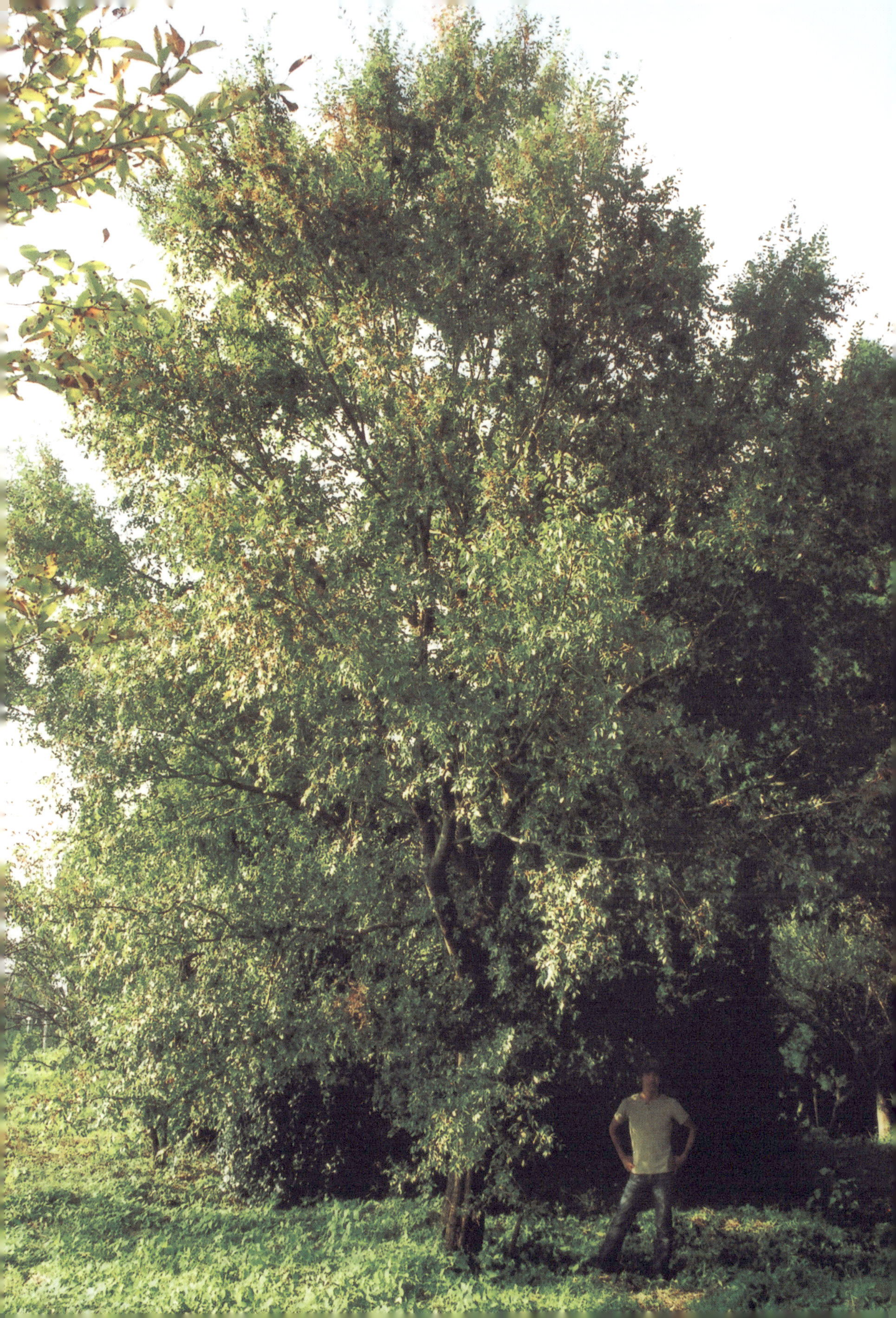

Planting Trees

There's an appropriate time to plant a tree. They can't just be planted in any season. The deciduous trees we were to plant needed to go into the ground just before the temperature started to rise, sometime before the middle of March. However, as March approached, the buildings were still not done and the area around them was full of scaffolding. If we missed this opportunity, we would have to wait another year. We'd have to move in and open the store with no trees. It was unthinkable. Our only option was to take down the scaffolding, plant the trees, and once again put it up. A costly thing to do, but much better than opening without trees.

樹を植える

樹を植えるには時期がある。どんな季節に植えてもいいということではない。
僕たちの植えようとしていた落葉樹は気温が上がり出す前。根が動き出す前の3月中頃までに植えないといけない。困った。工事が間に合いそうにない。建物の周りを足場が取り囲んでいる。これでは植えることができない。でも、この3月を逃すと、次のチャンスは1年後。それでは店のオープン時に樹がない。それはありえない。どうする？
考えた作戦、外壁の仕上げがまだだったが、一旦、足場をバラすことにした。無事、樹を植えてからまた足場を組み直す。植栽のために、こんな大きな建物の足場を2回も組むなんてたいそうなこと。もちろん費用もかかる。でも、何が大事か。

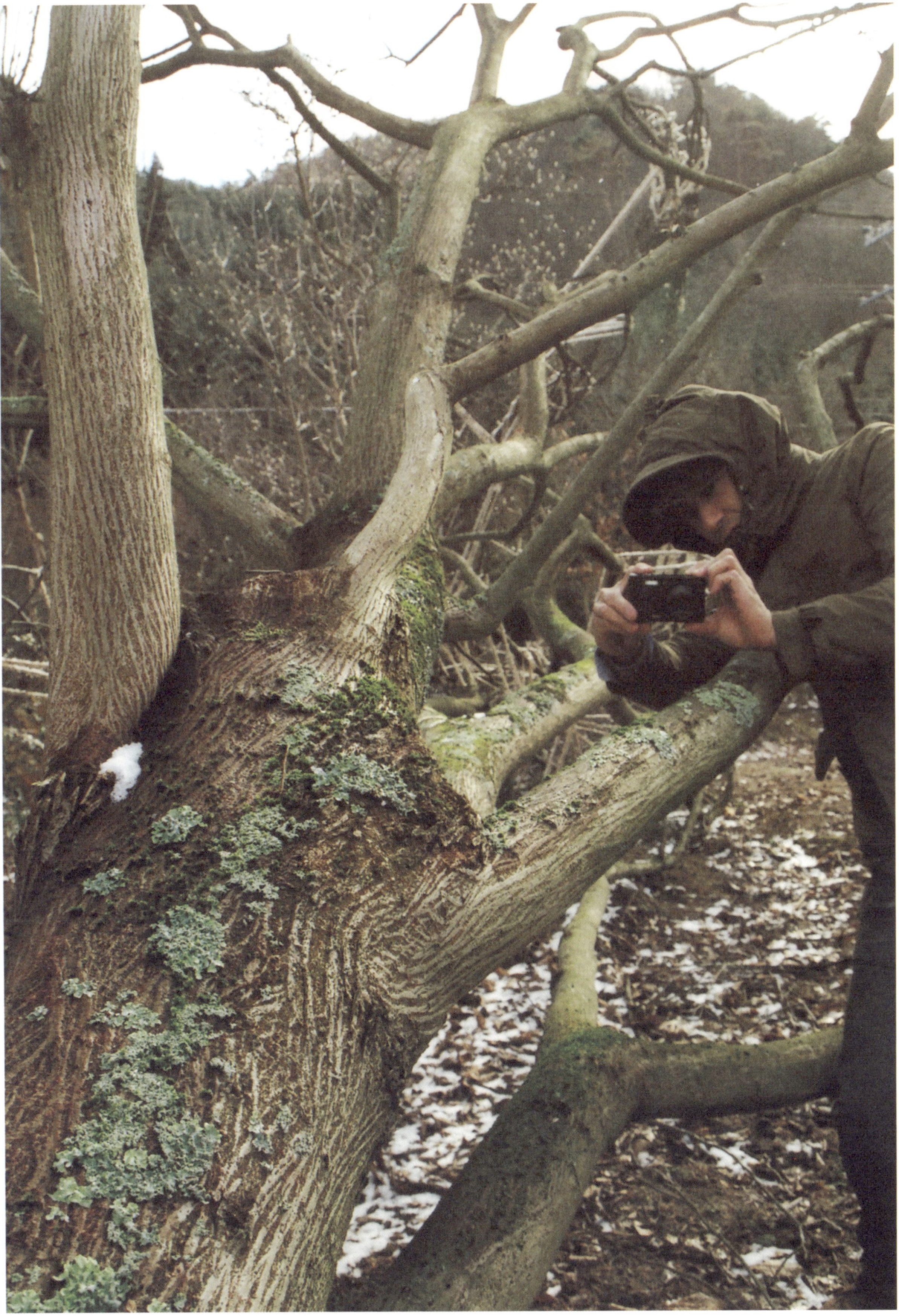

根回しされた樹を見に行った。3月も近いというのに山には雪が降っていた。
アンドリュー・ワイエスの絵の中にいるかのような色合いだった。
We went to see a tree get its root clump tied. Although it was almost March, it was still snowing in the mountains.
The land around us was the color of an Andrew Wyeth painting.

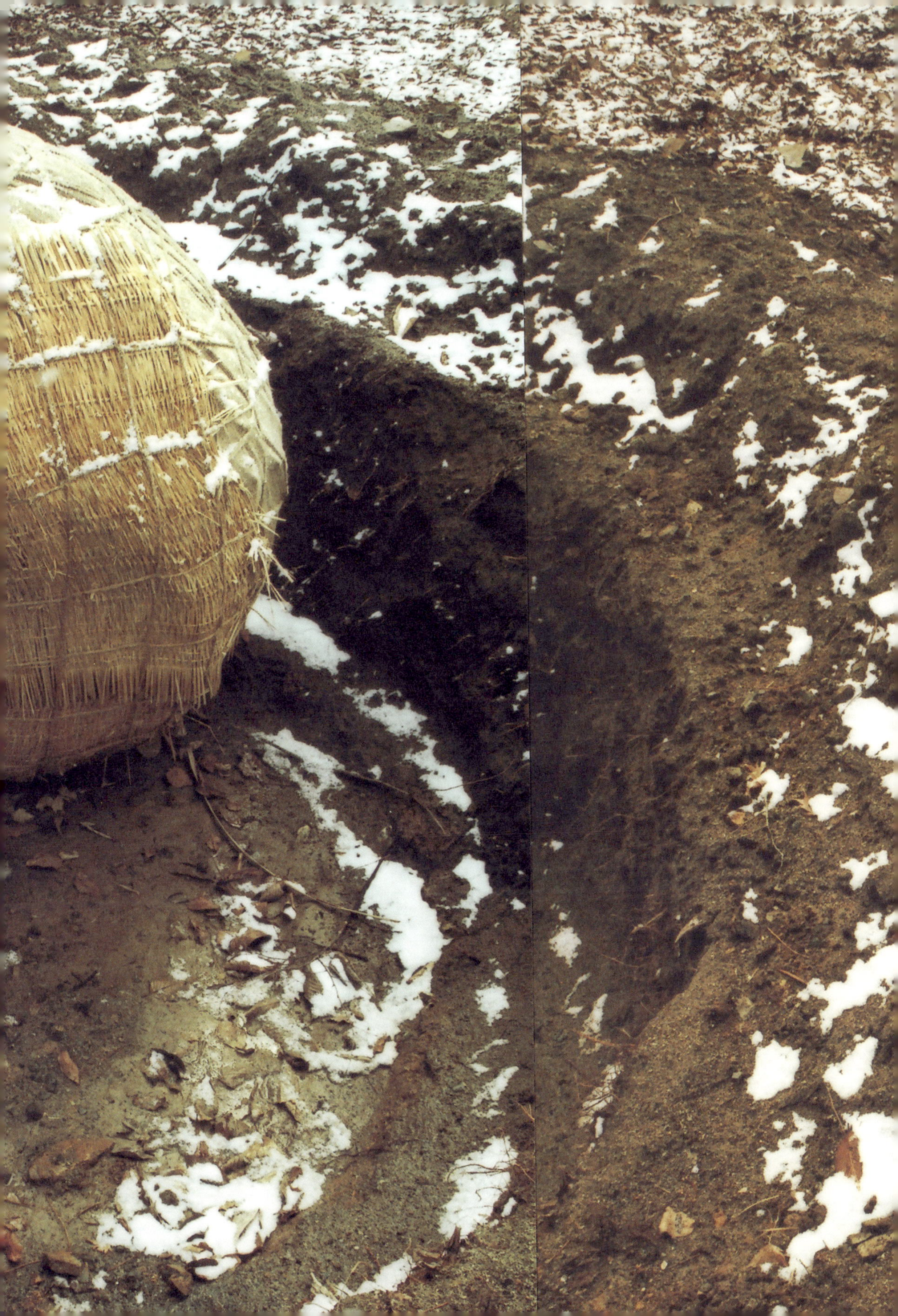

いよいよ樹を植えていく。その前日、それぞれの位置に穴が掘られた。
隕石でも落ちたのかと思うような大きな穴は2歳児の恰好の遊び場。

We were ready to plant the trees. The day before, large holes were dug all over the site.
They looked like meteorite craters, and made perfect places for two-year-old Hina to play.

重さ5tもある樹がクレーンで吊り上げられる。すごく非現実的な光景。
でもこれが数時間後には元々そこにあったような現実へと変わる。
This five-ton tree was lifted into place for planting by a crane. It was a surreal sight.
A few hours later, however, it looked like it had always been there.

Planting started on the 28th of February.

団地から救出したザクロの老木はTRUCKの入り口に移植した。この樹の根元に椿が生えていたので、それごと持って来て植えた。早春、ピンク色の花が咲いた。自分ではあえて選ぶことはないピンクの花。ちょっと似合わない気もするが、これは特例。目が合うと助かって良かったなと、ちょっと嬉しい。

At the entrance of TRUCK there is an old pomegranate tree. It is one of the trees we rescued from the housing complex. Near the end of summer it becomes loaded with fruit. This tree had a camellia growing at its base that was brought along too. We were surprised when it bloomed with pink flowers. It's not a color we would have chosen, but seeing them makes us happy.

JAPANESE ZELKOVA
14M

CHINESE ELM
10M

APHANANTHE
10M

I was very happy when we finally started planting the trees.
A massive crane hoisted them into the holes we'd dug.
The biggest tree was a 14m tall Zelkova that weighed 5 tons.
The 2m root clump meant it measured 16m in total. It felt like we were transporting a bullet train car.
Seeing it near our house I began to wonder if had overdone it.

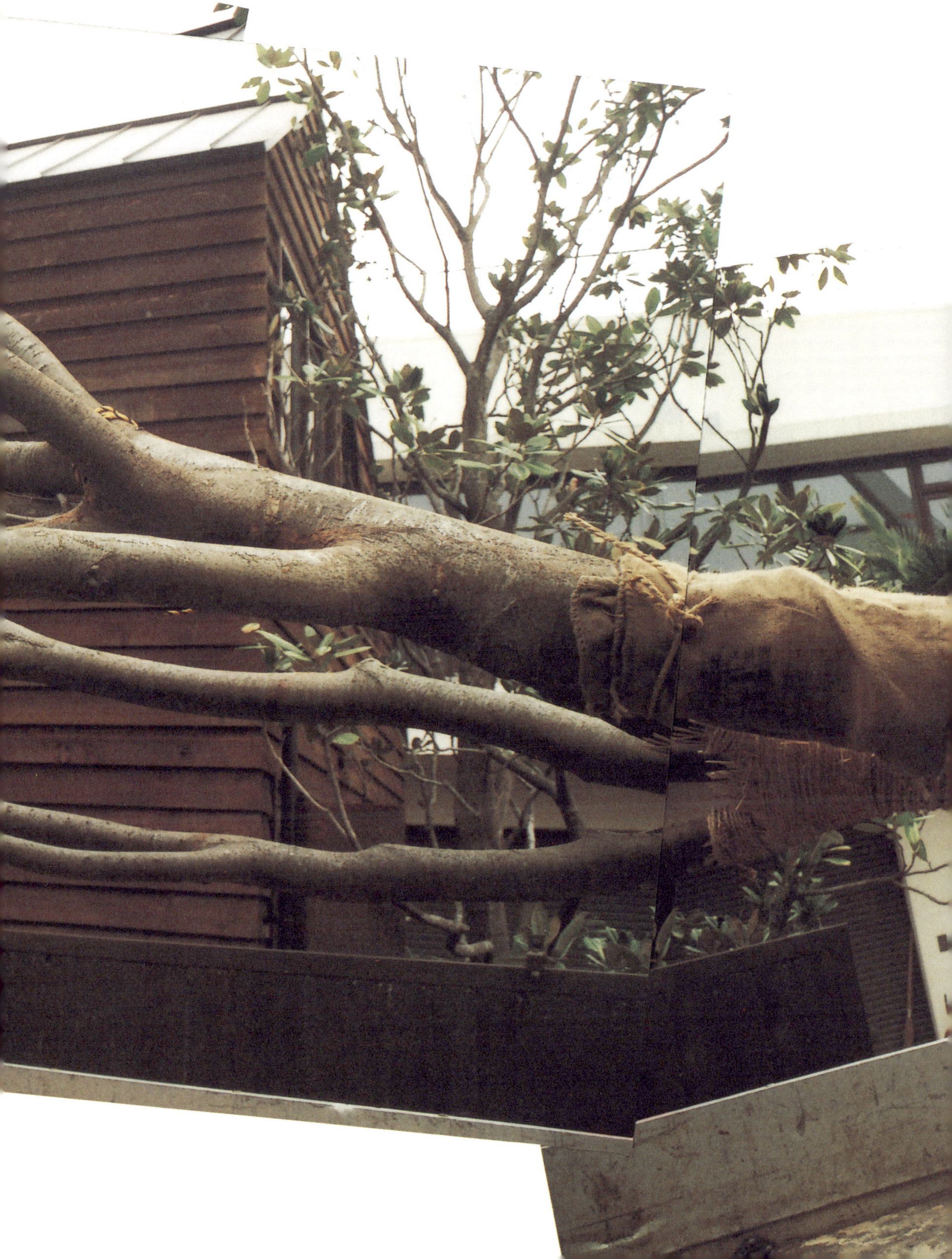

JAPANESE ZELKOVA
ROOT CLUMP
Approx. 2M in diameter

いよいよ始まった。嬉しい。樹を植える日が来た。予め掘っておいた大きな穴に、大型クレーンで吊り上げた樹を立てていく。一番大きなケヤキだと高さ14m、そこに根鉢が2m近く。トラックに横たわっていると16mもの長さ。新幹線の車両でも運んでいるような雰囲気。重さは5t!!ちょっとドキドキした。
「おっきすぎたかな？やりすぎたかな？」少し不安になる。

1日に2、3本ずつ。約10日以上つきっきり。それぞれの樹の微妙な位置、角度、向きを調整しながら植えていく。
一度植えたらずっと毎日見ることになる樹。妥協はできない。たくさんの職人さんに細かく気持ちを伝えていく。
ちょっとだけ右に傾けてと言っても、大型クレーンで吊られた10m以上の大きな樹。ちょっとと言ってもグワッと動く。
加減が難しい。
樹には表と裏があるらしく、造園屋さんとしては通りから見える側を表にするのが習わし。でも僕たちはこの部屋からこの窓から、この樹をどう見たいか、が大事。だから、自分たちの思いを信じて植えていった。
団地からの救出チームもラインナップに加わった。
これらも、すっとまっすぐなのでなく、自然に育ってきたワイルドな感じがカッコいい。

いい。やっぱりいい。時間をかけて探した自然樹形の大きな樹。植えてしまうとすんなりと収まった。
樹を植えたことで建物が馴染む。理想としていた元々そこにあった建物のように見えた。

12mのケヤキでこの大きさ。(パノラマでしか撮れない)
Even this 12m Japanese Zelkova was imposingly large. (It could only be photographed in panorama.)

#	Name	Details
1	Chinese Elm	H9 C0.75 W6 m — Deciduous
 2	Griffith's Ash	H3 C0.35 W2 m — Evergreen
 3	Japanese Hackberry	H6 C0.5 W4 m — Deciduous
 4	Aphananthe	H10 C0.96 W7 m — Deciduous
 6	Chinese Elm	H8 C0.58 W5 m — Deciduous
 7	Chinese Elm	H11 C0.65 0.63 0.59 W8 m — Deciduous
8	White Oak	H5 C0.5 W3 m — Deciduous
 9	Japanese Hackberry	H9 C0.75 W6 m — Deciduous
 10	Japanese Zelkova	H14 C0.87 W8 m — Deciduous
 11	Chinese Elm	H10 C0.90 W6 m — Deciduous
 12	Southern Magnolia	H6 C0.55 W4 m — Evergreen
 13	Glossy Privet	H6 C0.6 W3 m — Evergreen
 14	Konara Oak	H8 C0.55 W5 m — Deciduous
 15	Pomegranate	H4 C0.4 0.5 W3 m — Deciduous
 16	Japanese Zelkova	H14 C0.9 W6×4 m — Deciduous
 17	Japanese Maple	H5 C0.5 W4 m — Deciduous
 18	Glossy Privet	H6 C0.5 W3 m — Evergreen
 19	Japanese Privet	H3.5 C0.3 W2 m — Evergreen
 22	Chusan Palm	H3 m — Evergreen
 23	Chusan Palm	H4 m — Evergreen
 26	Yucca	H0.5 m — Evergreen
 27	Japanese Sago Palm	H1.6 W1.6 m — Evergreen
 29	Oleander	H2.5 3 m — Evergreen
 30	Olive	H4 C0.4 0.3 0.2 W2.5 m — Evergreen
 34	Chusan Palm	H5 m — Evergreen

TREE LAYOUT 2009

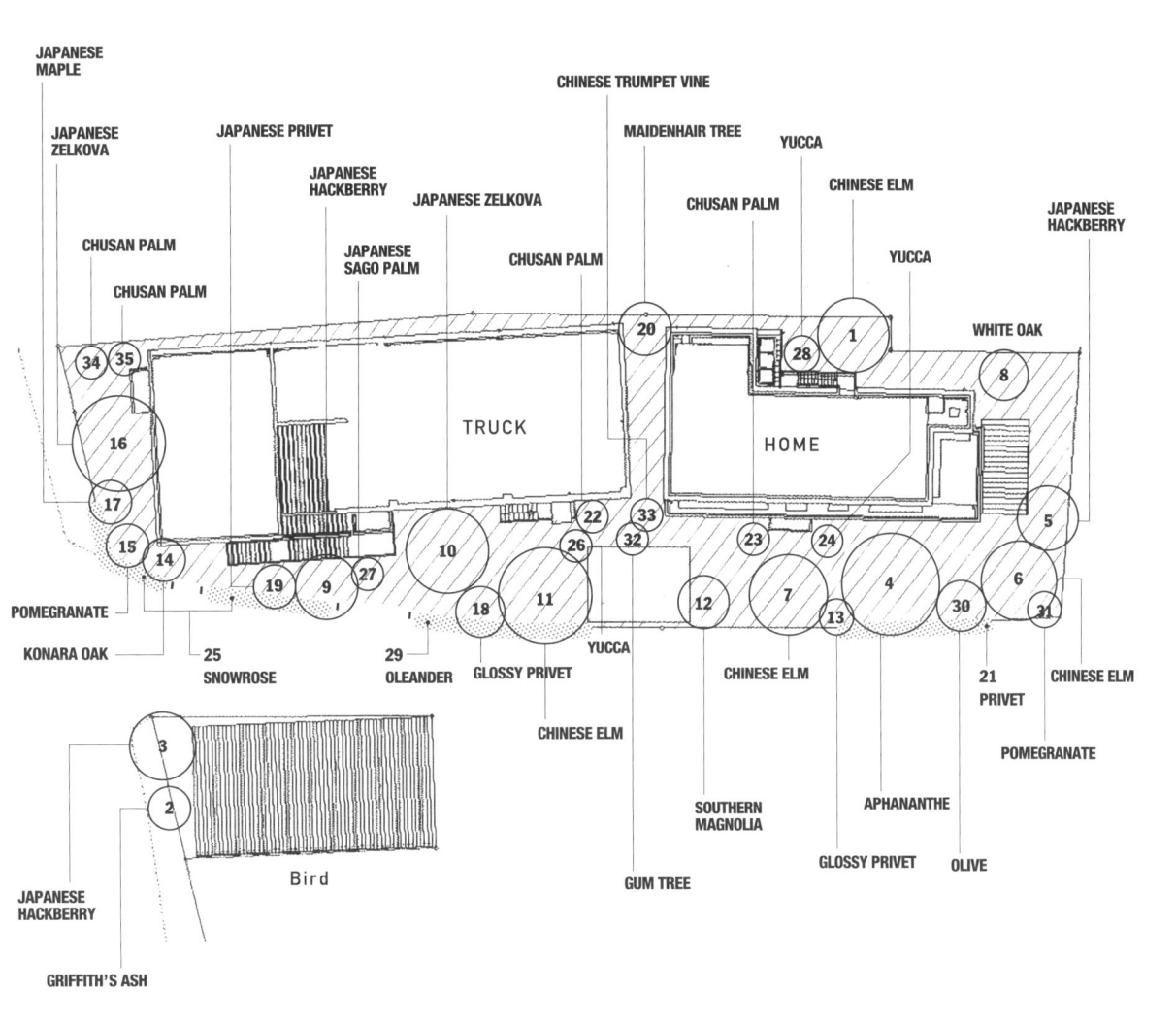

JAPANESE MAPLE
JAPANESE ZELKOVA
CHUSAN PALM
CHUSAN PALM
JAPANESE PRIVET
JAPANESE HACKBERRY
JAPANESE SAGO PALM
JAPANESE ZELKOVA
CHUSAN PALM
CHINESE TRUMPET VINE
MAIDENHAIR TREE
CHUSAN PALM
YUCCA
YUCCA
CHINESE ELM
JAPANESE HACKBERRY
WHITE OAK

TRUCK
HOME

POMEGRANATE
KONARA OAK
SNOWROSE
OLEANDER
GLOSSY PRIVET
YUCCA
CHINESE ELM
SOUTHERN MAGNOLIA
GUM TREE
CHINESE ELM
APHANANTHE
GLOSSY PRIVET
OLIVE
PRIVET
POMEGRANATE
CHINESE ELM

JAPANESE HACKBERRY
GRIFFITH'S ASH
Bird

1. アキニレ	11. 熊本アキニレ	21. プリペット	31. ザクロ
2. トネリコ	12. タイザンボク	22. シュロ	32. ユーカリ
3. エノキ	13. トウネズミモチ	23. シュロ	33. ノウゼンカズラ
4. ムクノキ	14. コナラ	24. ユッカ	34. シュロ
5. エノキ	15. ザクロ	25. ハクチョウゲ	35. シュロ
6. アキニレ	16. ケヤキ	26. ユッカ	
7. アキニレ株立ち	17. モミジ	27. ソテツ	
8. ホワイトオーク	18. トウネズミモチ	28. ユッカ	
9. エノキ	19. ネズミモチ	29. キョウチクトウ	
10. ケヤキ	20. イチョウ	30. オリーブ	

2009年に考えたこのプラン。現在植わっている樹種と違っているところが数ヶ所ある。植える時に変更したのと、植えた後しっかり根付かなくて、残念ながら他の樹に差し替えなければ駄目になったもの。いくら商品として動かせるように育てられた樹であっても、これだけ大きい樹を移植するのは難しいことがよく分かった。若い樹は馴染むのが早いが年を取った樹はなかなか馴染みにくい。人間でも同じかも。

Our 2009 plan. There are some differences with the current garden. Some were due to changes we made while planning. There were also some trees that didn't adjust to the new surroundings and had to be removed. Even when dealing with trees that have been raised specifically for sale, there is a risk that they won't make it. As with people, it seems that young trees adjust more easily to a change in environment. It can be very difficult for older trees.

やりたかったことのひとつ。
毎朝、2階にある洗面所で歯を磨きながら、窓からアキニレを見ること。
このトイレの窓からもすぐそばにアキニレが見える。そこに止まっている鳥たちもよく見える。
見られていることを知らない油断した姿を見るのが楽しい。

One of the things I wanted was to be able to see the Chinese elm while brushing my teeth.
I enjoy watching the birds perching there unaware.

a. CHINESE ELM
The tree I see every morning while I brush my teeth. The bathroom window is just the right height. It would have been difficult to plant after construction had finished, so we planted it in March 2008, while the land was still bare.

b. WHITE OAK
This is the tree whose wood we most often use to make TRUCK furniture. I had wanted to be surrounded by white oaks, but they don't grow well in the hot Osaka weather. There are no big white oaks in Japan. On the north side, I planted just the one. We pray that it gets used to Osaka's hot summers. It's a young tree and is growing quickly.

c. THREE-BRANCH CHINESE ELM
We put the Chinese elm we liked best where it could best be seen from the living room. When we were planting, we discovered that one of the branches was diseased. We went ahead and planted it anyway, but it didn't survive. We replaced it with a Japanese ash. Planting big trees is not simple.

d. THE CHINESE ELM FROM KUMAMOTO
We couldn't find a big Chinese elm near Osaka. We heard there was one in Kumamoto and went to see it. We planned to live with our trees forever, so we didn't want to decide just based on a photograph. After we saw it we found a bear park nearby.

e. THE OLEANDER WITH WHITE FLOWERS
I've liked this plant since I first saw it in Vienna. It's an evergreen and in summer blooms with white flowers. These are rare in Japan, where most oleanders have pink flowers.

f. JAPANESE HACKBERRY
Its leaves and branches cover the stairs that lead up to the store. When people visit TRUCK or Bird I don't want them to rush inside immediately. I want them stand on soil and pass beneath branches. I think it's important. Many birds gather to eat the red fruit.

g. KONARA OAK
TRUCK is in a school zone. Many children pass by every day. We thought the children passing by on their way to school might enjoy picking up chestnuts, so we chose this place for this tree. There is a chestnut reference book on the bookshelf in Bird, too.

h. POMEGRANATE
It's an old tree, but quickly took root. Every year, the branches are loaded with fruit. There's something very cool about this tree's wild-looking branches.

i. JAPANESE SAGO PALM
We rescued this tree from the garbage when we were still in Tamatsukuri. We planted it in the ground when we moved to Asahi Ward. It's doing very well.

j. 14m JAPANSESE ZELKOVA
Standing on the roof you can touch its leaves and branches. You can also look down happily at the birds below. When it arrived on the truck on planting day, I was taken aback by its size.

We planted mainly deciduous trees. I like them because you can get a clear sense of the four seasons passing. In summer they bring shade, blocking out the sun, and in winter, they drop their leaves and let the sunlight through.

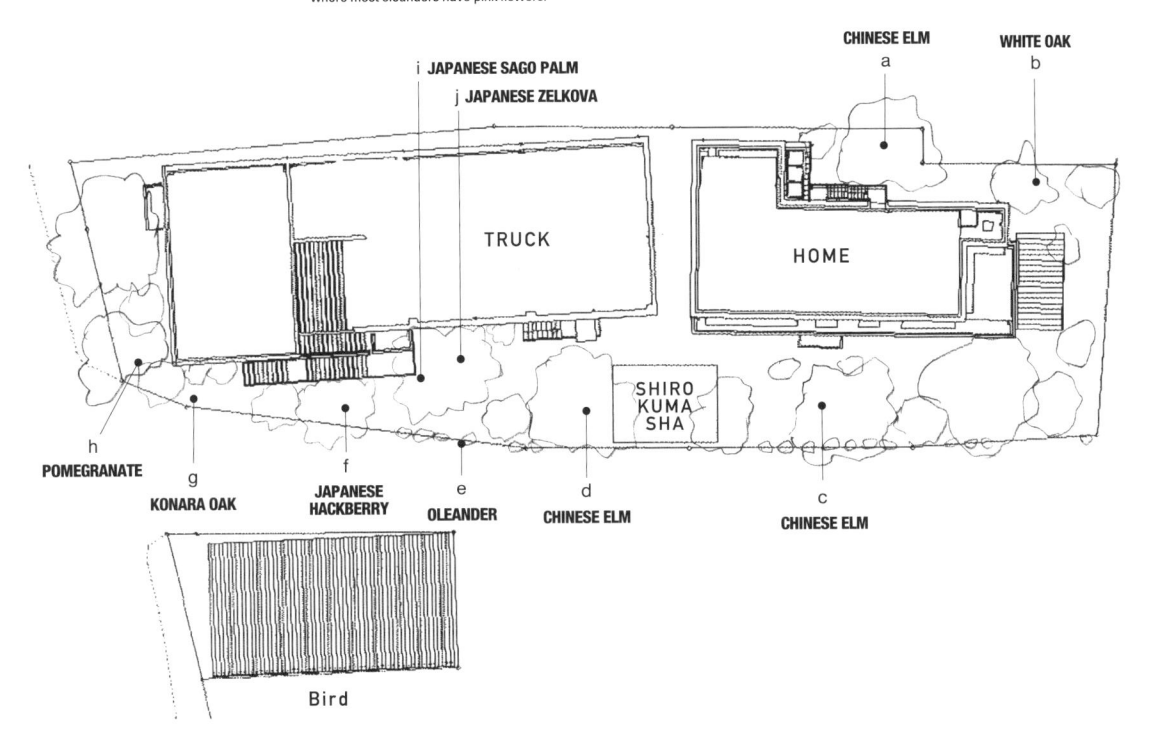

---

a. アキニレ
歯磨きをしながら、1日の始めに眺めたい樹。窓もちょうどいい高さに作った。この位置は、建物が建った後では植えることが難しいので、2008年3月、更地に先行して植えた。

b. ホワイトオーク
TRUCKで家具を作るのに一番よく使う木。ホワイトオークの大きな樹に囲まれて暮らしたかった。ところが気温の高い大阪には合わないし、日本には大きなオークはなかった。だから北側の位置に若い樹を1本植えることにした。暑い大阪に馴染んでくれることを祈りつつ。若い樹はその土地に順応しやすい。それが良かったのか、すくすくと育っている。

c. 3本立ちのアキニレ
リビングからよく見える場所にも一番好きなアキニレを選んだ。3本立ちの大きな樹でも、植える時に虫が入っていることが発覚。そのまま植えたがやはり活着せず、今はトネリコが植わっている。大きな樹を植えることは、簡単ではない。

d. 熊本から来たアキニレ
大阪近辺では見つけることができなかった大きなアキニレ。熊本にあると聞き、見に行った。ずっと一緒に暮らしていく樹を写真だけでは決められない。対面が済んだ後、近くに「クマ牧場」を発見!

e. 白い花のキョウチクトウ
ウィーンで初めて見てからずっと気になっていた、珍しい白花のキョウチクトウ。(日本でよく見かけるのはピンクの花)

f. エノキ
お店に上がる階段に、葉っぱが覆いかぶさるように植えている。TRUCKもBirdも、訪れる人には、道路からすぐに入るのではなく、地面の土を踏んで樹の枝の下をくぐって来てもらいたい。それがとても大事なことだった。たくさんの赤い実を食べに鳥が集まる。

g. コナラ
TRUCKは通学路にある。店の前を通る子供たち、店に来る子供たち(もちろん大人も)がどんぐりを拾えたら楽しいと思って、入り口の階段横に植えた。Birdの本棚にはどんぐり図鑑も置いた。

h. 団地から救出したザクロ
老木なのにすぐによく根付いて、毎年、枝もたわわにザクロが実る。気合いの入った枝振りがカッコいい。

i. 拾ったソテツ
中央区に店があった頃、ゴミとして捨てられていたのを拾ってきて育てた。旭区に一緒に引っ越して来て、地べたに植えたらずいぶん立派に成長した。

j. 14mのケヤキ
屋上に立つと上のほうの枝葉に触れる。鳥の様子を俯瞰で眺めることができて嬉しい。植栽の日、トラックに横倒しで運ばれて来た姿は圧巻だった。

主に落葉樹を植えた。元々、四季の移り変わりを感じる落葉樹が好きなことが理由だが、夏には木陰を作って熱を遮ってくれ、冬には葉が落ちて、日射しがよく入る。

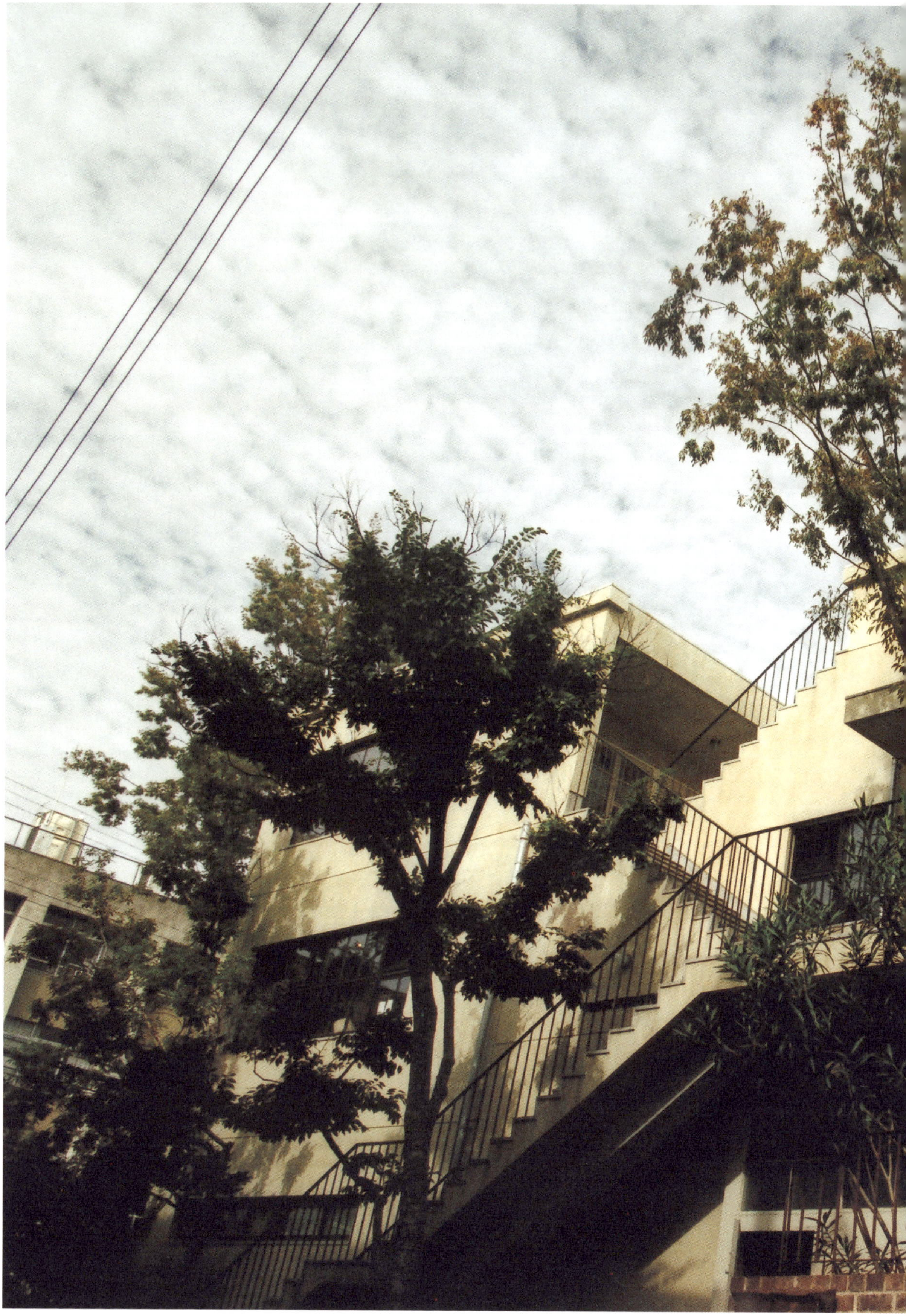

Each day we planted two or three trees. In total it took over 10 days. As we planted the trees, we looked at them and decided if we were happy with their placement. If I wanted one adjusted, I told the workers and they got the crane going. It was difficult to make fine adjustments. For landscape gardeners, trees have a front and a back. Customarily the front is what they consider the most attractive side to view and they placed the trees accordingly. That didn't matter so much to us. We wanted to make sure they looked good from different places around our house, from this room or that window. We trusted our own idea of how they should be planted. I was especially pleased by how the trees we had rescued looked. Their trunks were not straight and they had a wildness about them.

The time and effort we spent finding the right trees was worth it. Once they were in, they looked like they'd been there forever. The trees matched the building well, helping it also look like it had been there for a long time.

Completing the House and Store

On December 27, 2008, the framework had been completed and the concrete structure was done. After removing the wooden mold from the concrete, we began painting. It took hundreds of liters of paint to do both the house and the store. As we painted the concrete, the place became brighter, a monochrome world turning to color. The low-water concrete we'd used made the walls and ceiling look like shiny black mirrors. I almost thought it was a waste to paint over them. There were a few flaws in the concrete but, considering the effort everyone had put in, I could overlook them.

We decided that making our house livable would be our first priority. We had decided with the construction company that they would put up the frame and install the basic fittings and that we would take care of the rest ourselves, thinking about each part as we went along, without a blueprint.
There was a mountain of work to be done. We had to choose lots of materials: tiles, paving stones, flooring, and the like. We had to install flooring in a number of rooms, lay stones for the porch, and plaster the walls. Things that needed painting kept popping up here and there. I also wanted to build a brick wall to surround our land and top it with an iron railing. We needed to make doors, finish the two toilets, and get the seven water outlets ready for use by installing sinks and faucets. The number of things to be done seemed endless, and they kept springing up everywhere. The work we had done to prepare TRUCK and AREA2 in Tamatsukuri was nothing compared with the task we now faced.

At the same time, construction began on Shirokumasha and the storeroom. There was also the store, the workshop, the staff room, and Bird to prepare. They all had to be started and kept going till they were done.

After a few days of laying floorboards in the bedroom, I began to question the value of doing it myself. There were many other things that I needed to do to. Was I wasting my time doing this manual work? Then I remembered what a friend, an experienced craftsman whose opinion I respected, had said when he visited the site. That doing it yourself creates a stronger bond between you and the place. "All of this work is connected to tomorrow." I told myself and continued laying the boards. I saw the staff doing the painting themselves the same way. Being there before the start and working on it would create a stronger emotional bond between them and the store than if they just walked into a completed building.

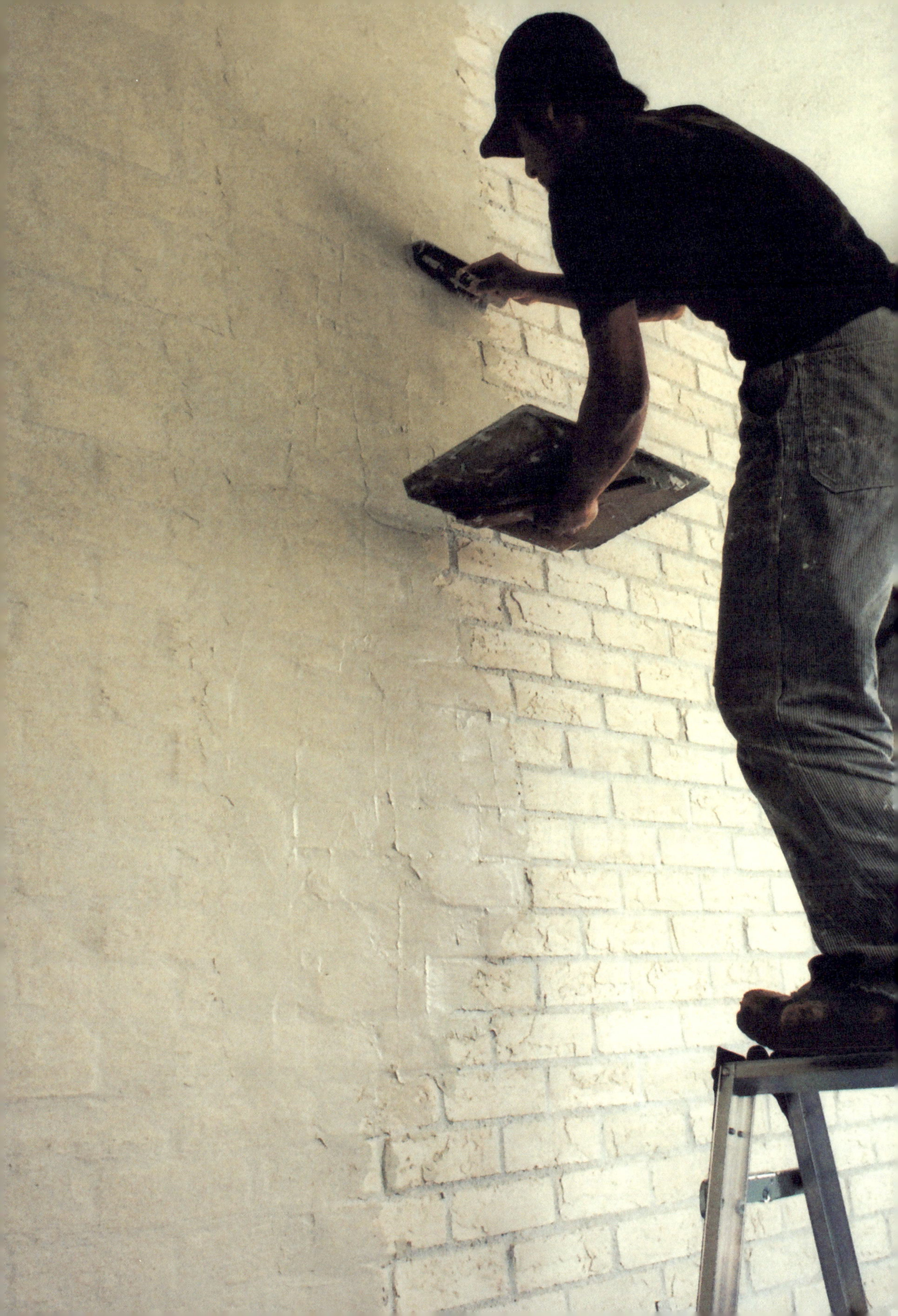

家と店を仕上げる

2008年12月27日に上棟し、コンクリートの躯体が形になった。型枠が外れた所から順次、ペンキ塗りをしていく。家と店の2つの建物全て。一斗缶のペンキを20缶単位で何度も買う。グレーのコンクリートが白く塗られて明るくなっていく。視界がモノクロからカラーに変わっていく。
水分が少ないコンクリートに挑んだ結果、型枠が外れた壁や天井がまるで鏡のように黒光りしている。ペンキを塗ってしまうのがちょっともったいないと思うくらい。数ヶ所ジャンカ（コンクリートが上手く入っていない所）があったが、あれだけ頑張ったんだからと納得して見られる。

まずは家を優先して進めて、とりあえず住めるようにしよう。
設計段階で工務店に発注して決まっているのは、躯体と基本の設備のみ。あとは全て2人でその場その場で考えながら進めていく。図面はない。

タイル、敷石、床材、細かいパーツ、たくさんの中から素材を探し出す。
いろんな部屋の床を張ったり、壁を作ったり、ポーチに石を敷いたり、壁に漆喰を塗ったり。どんどん出てくるペンキを塗る箇所。外回りのレンガの塀、その上に拾ってきて置いてあった鉄の柵を初めての溶接で取り付けたり、板を張り巡らせたり。ドアを作り、2つのトイレを仕上げ、7ヶ所の水道回りをそれぞれ使えるようにシンクやカランを選び設置…。
家だけでもきりがない、やるべきことが湧くように出てくる。
TRUCKやAREA2の店を作ってきたのとは比べ物にならない。

同時進行で、シロクマ舎の建築、倉庫の建築もある。店や工場、スタッフルーム、そして、今までなかった場所、カフェのBird。たくさんのことを進めなければいけない。どれもこれも考えながら、作りながら。

数日かかって寝室の床を張っていた時、ふと、「これって自分でやる意味ある？」と頭によぎった。
この単純作業。他にもいろいろやることが山ほどあるというのに。
そんな時、僕がもの作りにおいてすごく信頼している人が現場に来て、作業している僕に言った言葉
「そうやって思いを入れていくのって大事やんね」
その言葉を思い出し、こんな作業全てが明日につながる。と自分に言い聞かせ床板を張り進めた。
スタッフのペンキ塗りも一緒。出来上がった建物に、さあどうぞってそのまま入るより、スタート前から自分たちで関わった店はきっと思い入れのある職場になるはず。

BRICKWORK BONDS

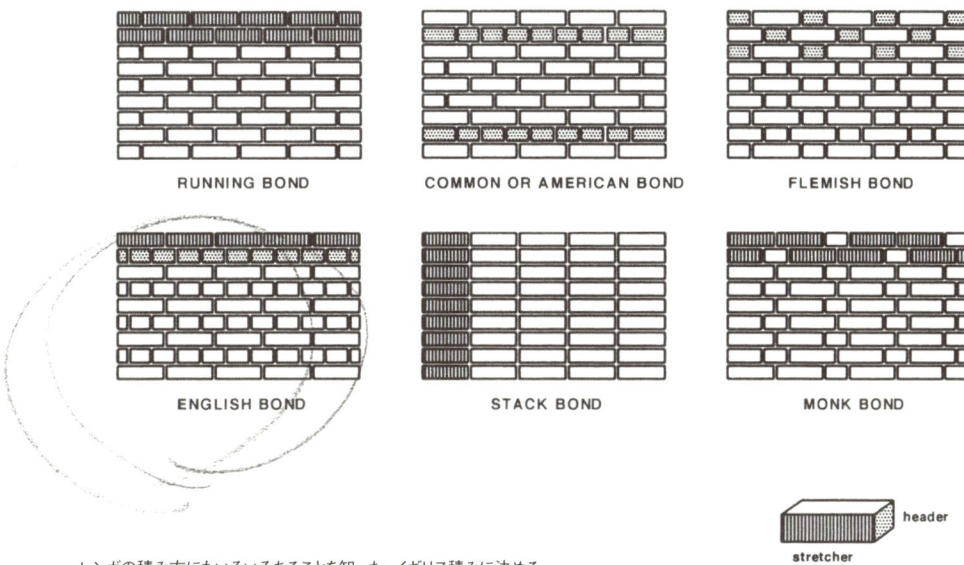

RUNNING BOND COMMON OR AMERICAN BOND FLEMISH BOND

ENGLISH BOND STACK BOND MONK BOND

header
stretcher

レンガの積み方にもいろいろあることを知った。イギリス積みに決める。
I discovered that there are many ways of stacking bricks.
We decided on the English bond.

ENGLISH BOND

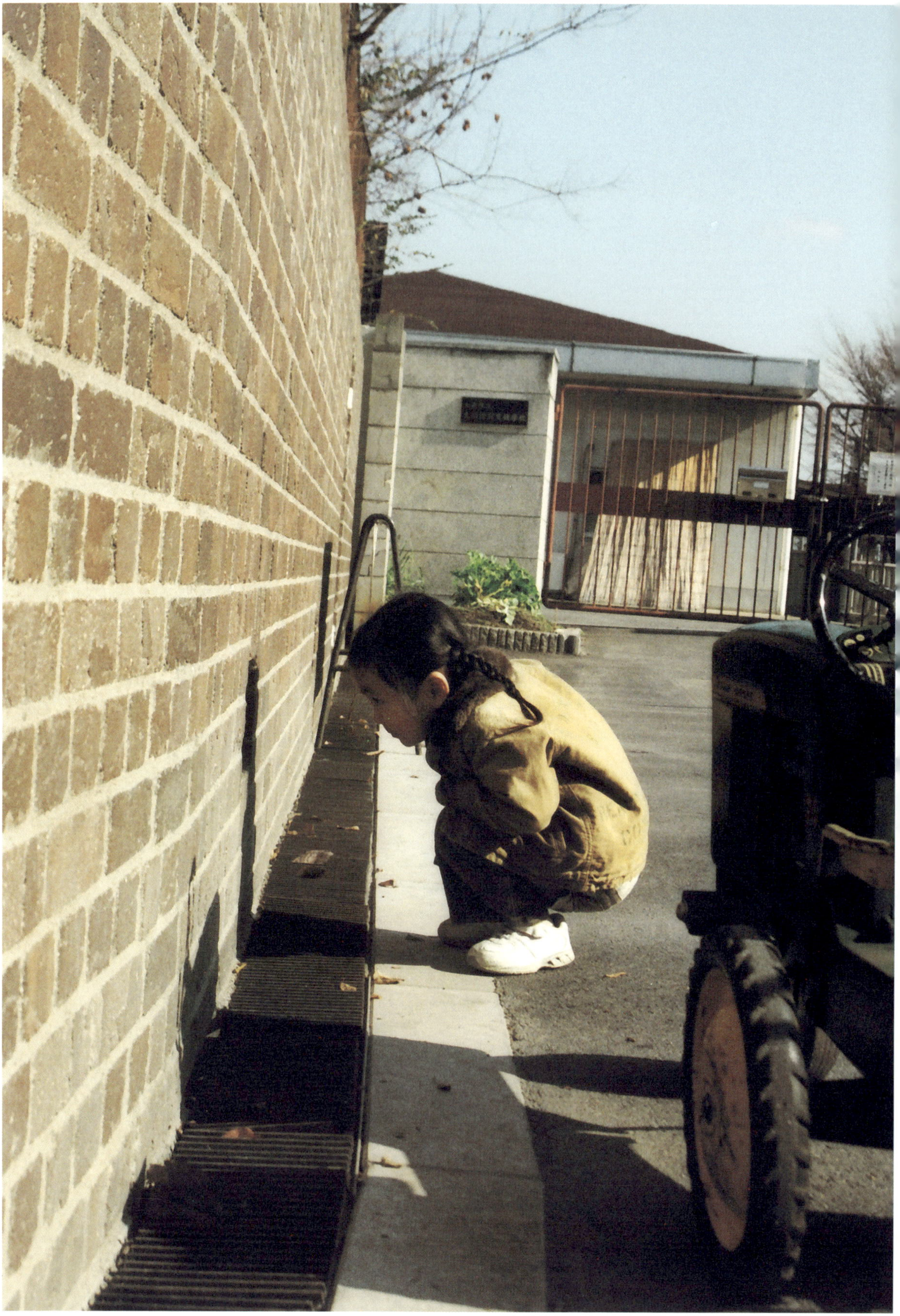

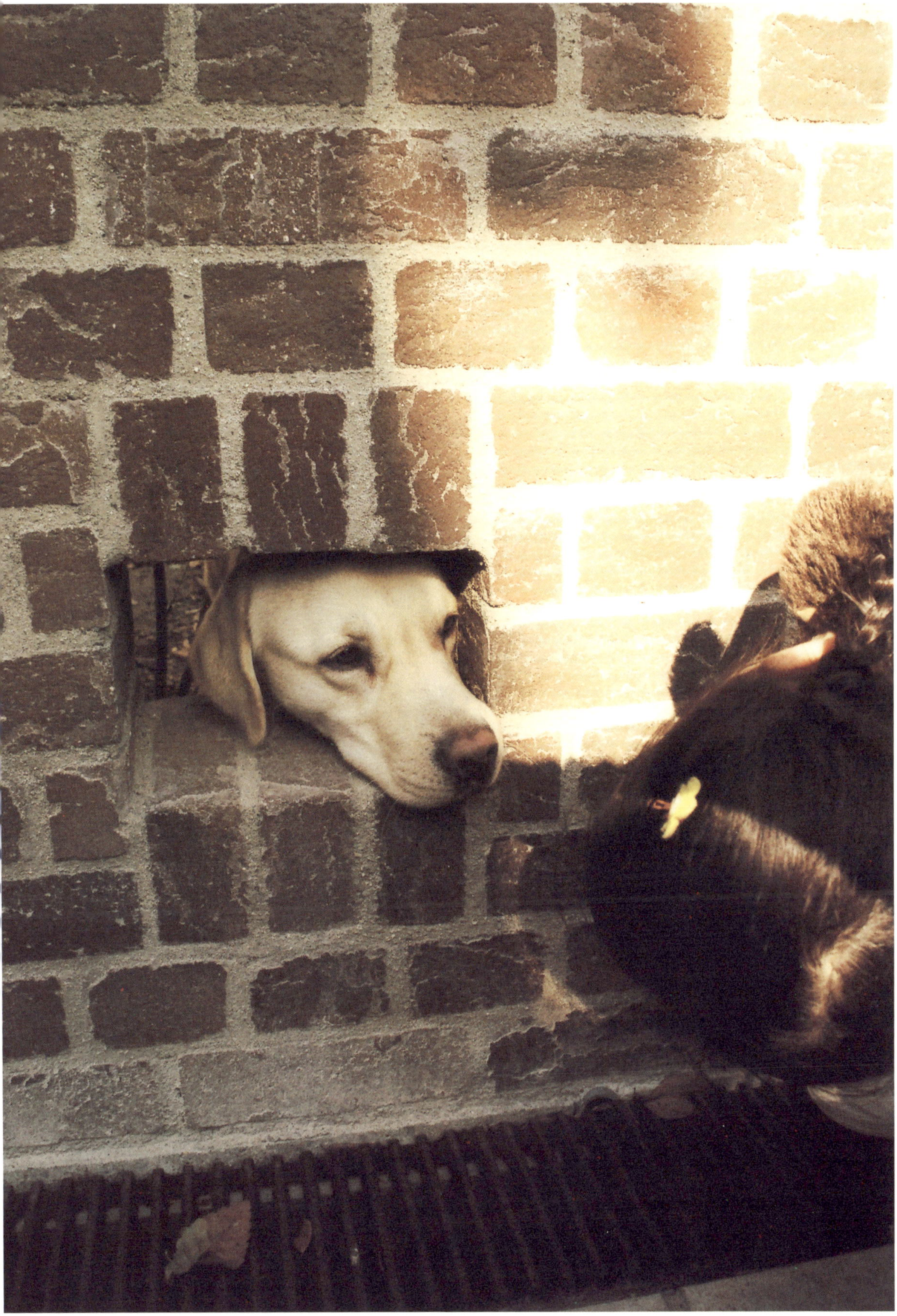

May 11, 2009
Exterior
Welding

工事が始まるずっと前から、何かに使えると思い拾って置いていた団地の窓の柵。出番が来た。レンガの塀の上に初めての溶接で取り付けていく。師匠タカシタ君と。

Some time back I had salvaged some window railings from an old apartment building. Now the time had come to use them. In my first attempt at welding, under the watchful eye of master welder Takashita, I attached them to the top of the brick wall surrounding our home.

May 25, 2009
Designing
Bird's Plates

現場作業が続く中、Birdで使うお皿なども型からオリジナルで
作る。店全体のイメージを想像しながら。

**As construction continued, we chose the tableware for
Bird. We designed it all ourselves, keeping in mind the
ambience we wanted.**

May 13, 2009
Exterior
Door

May 15, 2009
Exterior Door

Completing the House and Store

Jun. 8, 2009
Planting Grass

芝の種を2種類蒔いてみる。10日くらいすると芽が出た。蟻が運んだのか蒔いたつもりのない所にライン状に並んで芽が出ている所があった。

I planted two types of grass seed. In about ten days it had sprouted. Here and there I found lines of sprouts in places I hadn't been near. The work, I think, of hungry ants having made off with the seed.

May 20, 2009
Drawing in the Garden

親2人が作業を続ける中、2歳児は日射しの気持ちいい場所でお絵描き。これで数十分は時間が稼げる。手が離れる。
While the two of us worked on the site, two-year old Hina often spent her time coloring in the sunshine. It bought us some time and kept her out of harm's way.

May 7, 2009
Bedroom
Plastering
by Team Kusumi

寝室の天井に漆喰を塗り進める久住チーム。すこぶる手際がいい。
Mr. Kusumi's team at work, plastering the bedroom ceiling. I was awed by the speed and skill with which they worked.

Completing the House and Store

その頃たまたまTVの「情熱大陸」で見た左官の久住さんが、すごく印象に残った。なんとか会いたいと思っていると、ちょうど大阪で個展を開くと聞き、会いに行った。その日のうちに玉造まで来てもらいTRUCKも見てもらった。早速、本人を連れて帰って来たのを見て、ひりんこはびっくりしていた。

せっかく出会えたのだから、どこかの壁を久住さんに塗ってもらいたいと考え、家の寝室と将来の子供部屋の壁と天井を、ざらっとした漆喰に仕上げてもらうことにした。

たくさんの塗りサンプルを見せてもらい、いろいろ相談して素材と塗り方を決めた。初日、下塗りが完了。2日目、子供部屋の天井が仕上がった後、見せてもらった。いい。いいけど、昨日見た下塗りの荒い壁のほうがかっこ良かった。正直にそう言うと、「ええよ。やり直すし。そっちでいこう」と、こともなく、せっかく塗った天井を剥がし出す。その潔さに感動した。結果、すごく好きな仕上がりになった。

店の建物の外壁の仕上げも悩んだ。素材感、色、コスト。悩んだ結果、久住さんに洗い出しを依頼することにした。玉造のTRUCKの前回りにも取り入れていた洗い出し。子供の頃の記憶。学校の校舎の壁、どこかの銀行の建物の壁。表面を水洗いすることでザラザラした小さいベージュの石の表情が出る、あんな壁にしたい。

久住さんチームは約1ヶ月間、経費を抑えることができるからと言って、まだ空っぽだった工場部分に泊まり込みで作業をしてくれた。ベニア板の床に、職人さん7、8人が布団を敷き、トイレのドアや手を洗う洗面場すらなかった環境で。ありがとう。

洗い出しの洗い方には2通りある。ポンプで水をかけて洗う方法と、昔ながらのブラシで洗う方法。もちろんブラシのほうが手間がかかるし金額も上がる。でも仕上がりサンプルを見比べると、やっぱりブラシのほうが好き。じっくり見ると素材の見え方が違う。うーん。と考え、メインの壁はブラシにして、少し妥協して（今まで妥協なんてひとつもしてこなかったのに、さすがに懐が寂しくなり）西側の家との間で誰からも見えない壁一面だけは、ポンプ式でいくことにした。

洗い出しが進んでいったある日、久住さんが「やっぱり、この壁だけ違うのは違和感あるから、ブラシでやるわ。値段はそのままでいいし」と言った。素人目には、それも離れて見たらそんなに差が分からない。でも職人としていいものが作りたいとの気持ち。カッコいい。しびれる。

ようやく1ヶ月かかった外壁の左官が終わった。と思ったけど、久住さんチームの動きが何かおかしい。何かなと思うと、「西側の壁、夕方の〇時辺りの光で見たら歪んで見える。だからやり直したい」と言われた。
素人が見る分には全く気にならない。でも、プライドのある職人にとっては納得がいかないこと。びっくりした。
「分かりました。納得いくまでやって下さい」と言った。すぐに壁をハツり始めた。数日後、やり直しも終わり無事店の外壁が完成した。
いきなり、すでにそこで歴史を重ねてきたような、雰囲気のある建物になった。

May 19, 2009
Laying
the Paving Stones

敷石を並べてポーチを作る。一輪車を押す。どっちも初めてで楽しい。
Using a wheelbarrow for the first time. So much fun!

Completing the House and Store

I had seen Mr. Kusumi, a plasterer, on the Japanese TV program "Jonetsu Tairiku". The show left a deep impression on me and I hoped someday to meet him. Luckily, he soon came to Osaka to do an exhibition and I went to meet him. That same day he was kind enough to come and visit TRUCK in Tamatsukuri. Hiromi was rather surprised to see that I had brought him.

Having met him, I hoped he would be able to do some work on our new house. He agreed to plaster the walls and ceiling in Hina's room and our bedroom. After being showed many samples, we decided on a material and a plastering method. On the first day, he did the undercoat. The following day he finished the ceiling in the Hina's room. I liked it, but preferred how it had looked the previous day. I was reluctant to tell him, but when I did, I was surprised at how coolly he took it. He simply said, "Okay, I'll do it over." Without even a hint of annoyance he stripped the ceiling he'd just done and set about starting over. I was moved by his depth and, when he was done, thrilled with the results.

I was also concerned about what to do with the exterior wall for the store. There were many things to consider, the feeling of the material, the color, and the cost. In the end, I requested that Mr. Kusumi cover it in *araidashi*, a wall covering made with clay mixed with colored stones, that used to be popular in Japan, but has given way to cheaper, quicker methods. The top layer of clay is washed away to reveal the stones beneath. Whenever I see it I am reminded of my youth. I remember seeing it on the walls of my school and buildings such as banks.

There are two ways to prepare *araidashi*. One way is to wash the top layer away using pumped water. The other, older, way is to use a brush. The brush method requires more time and labor (and is more expensive), but after looking at the samples, I decided that I preferred it. If you look at it carefully, the materials look better. I decided to use the brush technique for the main walls that customers would see. I made a slight compromise, as funds were running low and the list of things we needed kept growing. For the western wall, one that few people would ever see, I decided to use the pump method.

However, after work on the walls was underway, Kusumi said there was something unbalanced about having one wall different. He said he'd do the other wall using the brush technique too and not charge any more. From a distance, and to the untrained eye, it was almost impossible to tell the difference, but a true craftsman wants to make things as good as they can.

After a month, the work on the outer wall seemed to be drawing to a close. However, Mr. Kusumi was uncomfortable about something. He said that the western wall, that faces the main road, at a certain time of late afternoon, looked crooked. He said they wanted to do it again. My amateur eyes couldn't see anything wrong with it, but I know that craftsmen take pride in their work and asked them to work on it until they were satisfied. They stripped it and started again. Some days later, work on the exterior walls was complete. Suddenly, the building looked like it had some history to it and started to take on some real character.

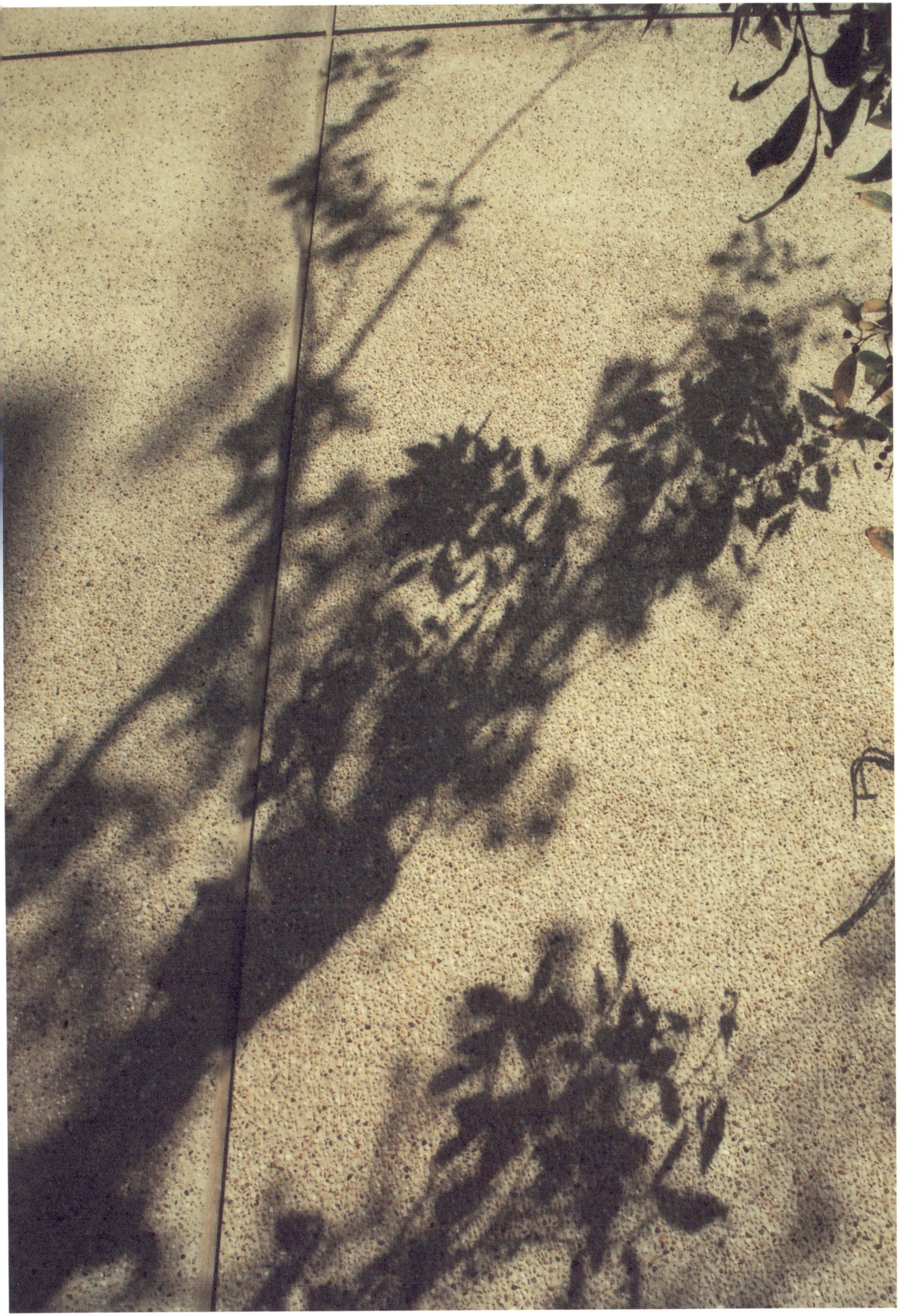

Completing the House and Store

ここ旭区の現場で工事を始めてから関わってきた工務店は、基礎をやり直したことに続き、躯体が上がった後も約半年間、大小様々な、納得いかない仕事の連続連発だった。毎回、現場監督ではない僕たちが見つけては指摘、やり直し。ふと、「自分たちのほうがおかしいん？ 欠点見つけすぎ？」と、思ってしまうことがあったほど。
TRUCKで家具を作ってきて、いつも少しでもいいものにしたい、と考え実行してきたつもり。そんな自分たちとのギャップに苦しんでいた。そんな中に見た久住さんたちの、プライドを感じる仕事ぶり、心意気に感動した。清々しかった。この現場でやっと本物の職人を見た思いがした。

After the concrete framework had been completed, there were still a lot of tasks for the construction company. It took six months for them to finish everything to my satisfaction. It was a constant struggle. Time and time again I found mistakes and careless work. I wasn't the foreman, but it seemed like I was the only person paying attention. After a while I began to wonder if it wasn't me that was strange. Was I finding too many flaws? At TRUCK, when we made furniture we want it to be as good as possible. It was painful dealing with people whose approach was so different. Seeing the pride Mr. Kusumi and his team took in their work was very refreshing. It made me feel that there were others with similarly high standards.

イベントスペースの中にあるキッチンの壁に板を張っていく、ひりんことやーちゃん。初めてのインパクトドライバーにドキドキしながら。
Hiromi and Yasuko installing panelling. It was the first time they had used a power screwdriver, so they were a little nervous.

Jun. 25, 2009
Installing Panelling

Jun. 16, 2009
Building
the Kitchen

これができたら引っ越しだと思っていたのに後回しになっていたキッチンのカウンター。
ひりんこの思いをいかに形にするかで悩んだが、いよいよ決行。2日間で形になった。急に家らしくなった。

We had planned to move in as soon as we had the kitchen done,
but I spent a lot of time wondering about how to make a kitchen counter that Hiromi would want.
When I finally decided and got going, it took just two days. The place soon seemed more like a home.

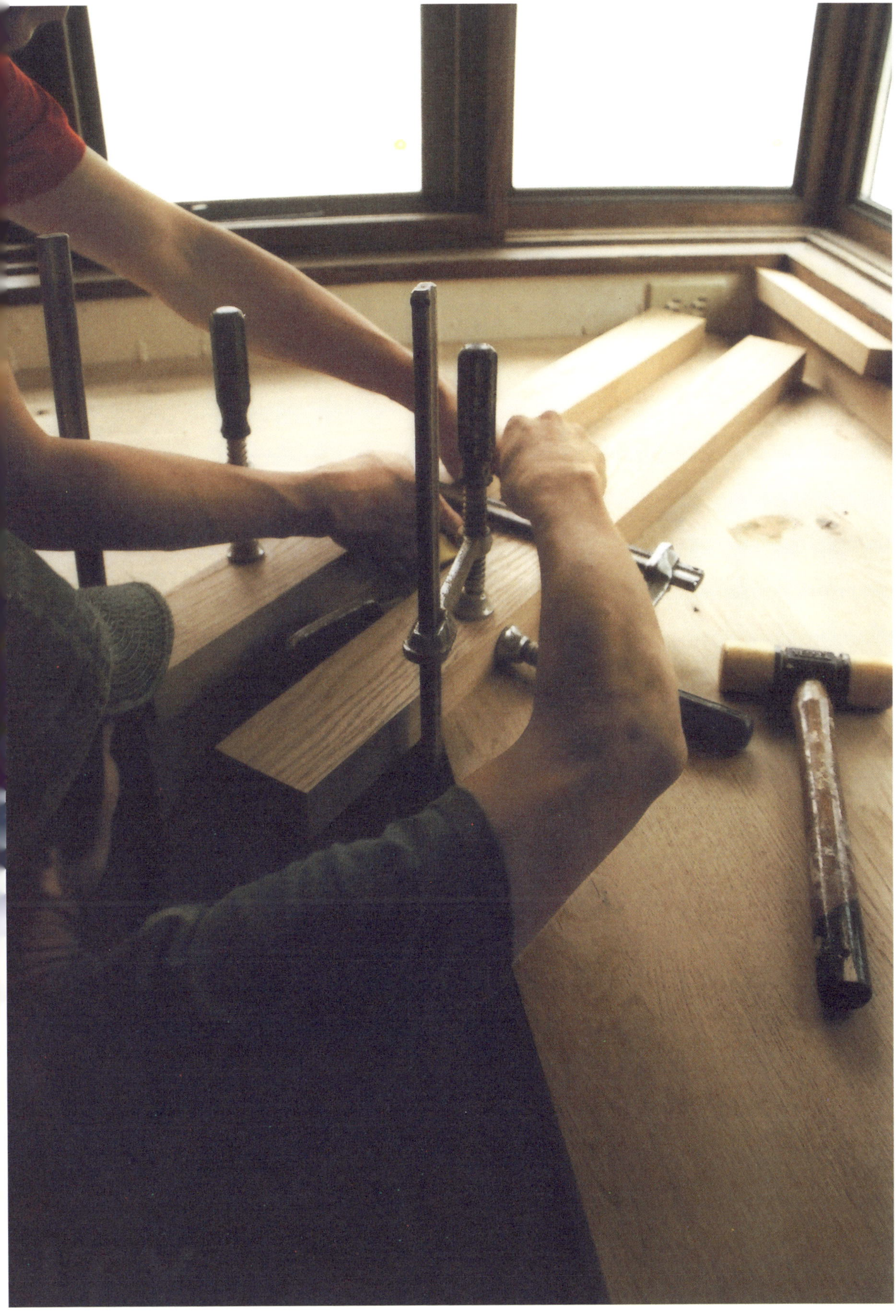

Progress of Construction 2009

February

March

April

June

October

November

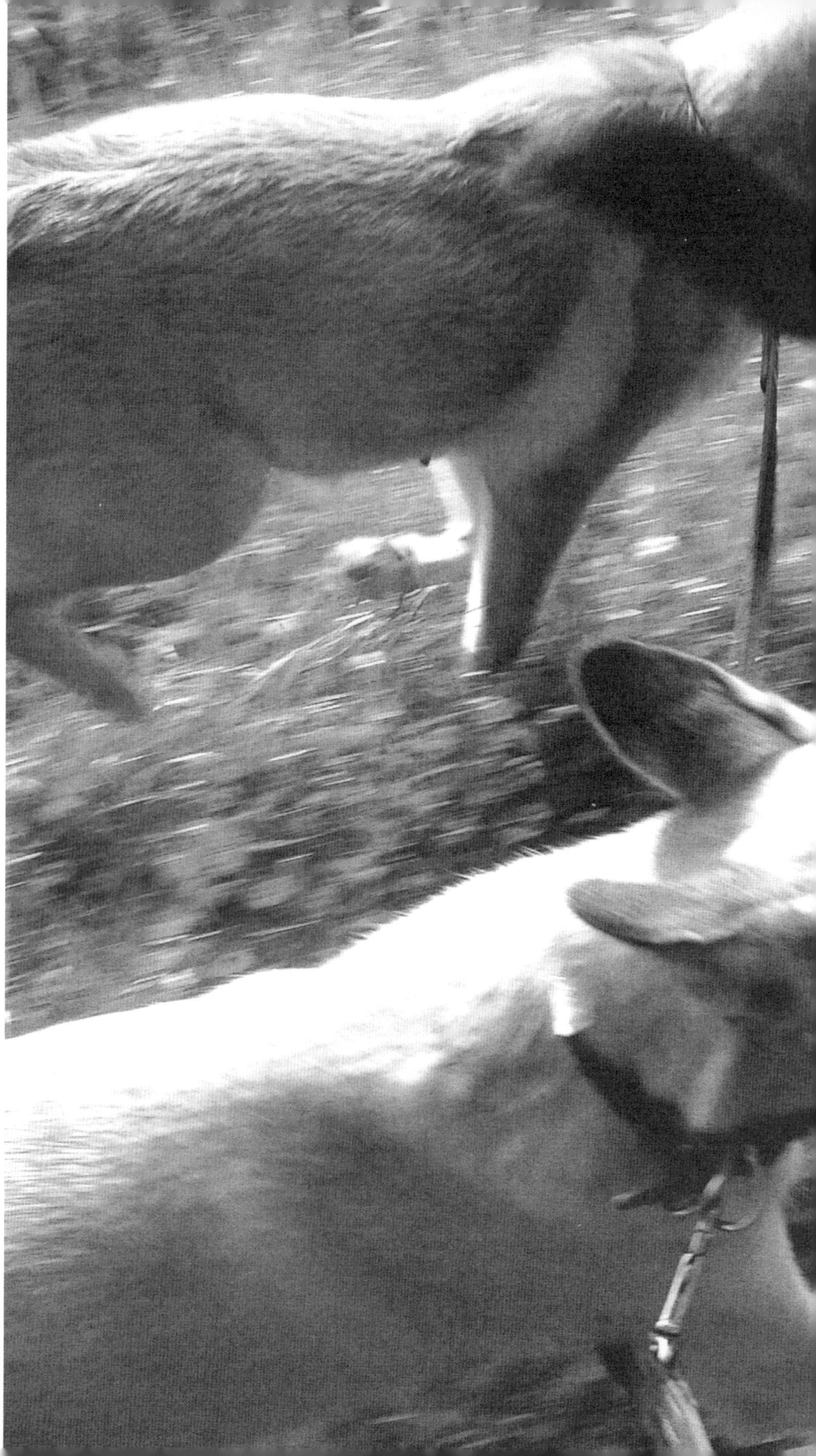

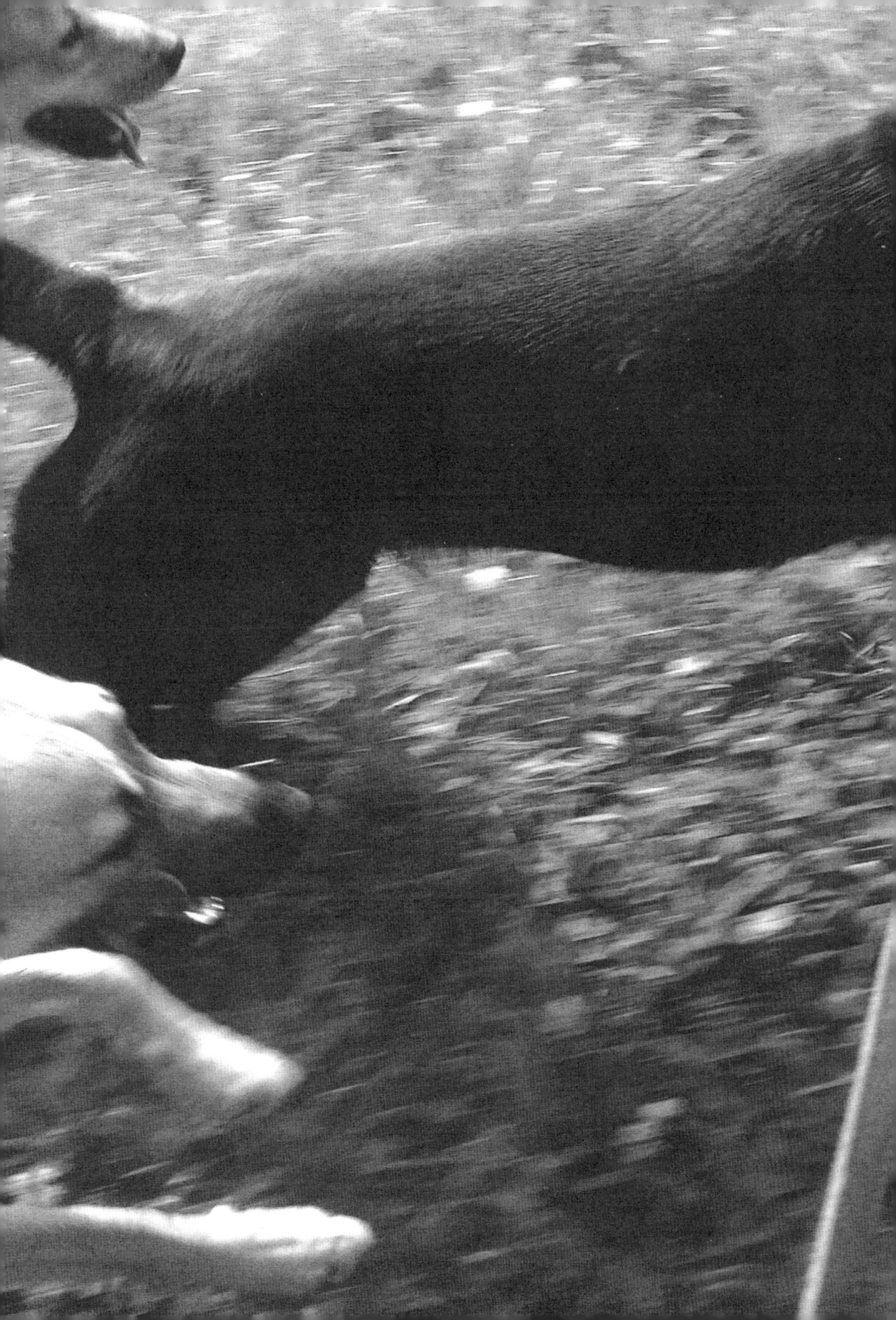

Moving

毎朝、店を通り抜け難波宮まで走っていった5匹のワンたちの散歩も今日が最後。
In Tamatsukuri, I used to take our five dogs through the store and out to Naniwanomiya Park for a walk every morning. This was the last day.

TRUCKの入り口のドア。取り外してBirdで使う。好きなものはずっと好き。新しい場所での出番が待っている。
The front door from the old store went on to serve as the door for Bird. I never lose affection for the things I like.

Jul. 6, 2009
Last Walk with the Dogs

家の引っ越し

毎日、玉造と旭区の往復。やることは、まだまだいくらでもある。
きりがないので、家のキッチンができたら引っ越ししようと決めていた。住みながら工事を進めるほうが効率がいい。
そのキッチンが形になった2009年7月。
13年間住んだ玉造から家だけ一足早く引っ越しした。5匹のワンと8匹のニャンと共に。

家の引っ越しは、ひりんこが書くほうがいい。

引っ越し。モノの多いうちの場合、それはそれは大変なもの。「トランクひとつで」なんて言ってみたい。
なんせ自宅のベランダの植物だけでも2tトラック1台分以上ある。
それに、ワンニャン13匹。
おまけに拾ってきた石ころやら、錆びた針金やら、油断したらゴミと間違えられそうなものまで持って行くんだから。
とりんこが「今日、引っ越しの見積り呼ぶで」と言った時、嫌な予感がした。
セカラしいとりんこのことである。きっとじゅうぶんな荷造り期間はとってもらえないと。
「引っ越し1週間後に決まったで」
やっぱり。
それまでは毎日2人で現場に通ってペンキ塗りやらなんやらしていたが、
翌日から私1人でこの引っ越しの荷物、(段ボール200箱はくだらない) 梱包しまくった。

箱に詰めるしりから、横で先月3歳になったばかりの日菜が放り出していく。仕分けして入れたはずなのに、わけの分からんもんが混じって入っている…。ガムテープで段ボールのふたを閉めようとしてよく見ると、ニャーが気持ちよさそうに中で寝てたり、クマとサビが荷造り用のヒモをチョイチョイしてみたり。
忙しすぎて猫の手も借りたいと言うが、8匹もいる猫たちは、どちらかというと足手まといなのである。
怒濤の1週間だった。

「朝8時に積み込んで、昼過ぎには旭区に荷物を下ろします」引っ越し業者の予想は甘すぎた。
朝8時に積み込み作業開始、玉造を出発したのが夕方5時。旭区で荷物を下ろし終わったのが夜10時過ぎ。
応援に駆けつけた引っ越し業者の人員もどんどん増えて、最終時は10人以上いた。
無事荷下ろしが終わったあとは、これをまた全て開梱、片付け。
引っ越しから1週間後の朝、急に原因不明の高熱が出て、そのまま8日間も入院するハメに。今まで病院なんてほとんど行くこともなかったのに。
私の寝かしつけでしか眠れない日菜のことを思うと、「入院なんかしたくない！」と病院でゴネたがダメだった。
ところが、その間一度も「ママ」と言わないで、ぐずることもなかったととりんこに聞いてびっくりした。
日菜なりに、すごく頑張ってくれたんだと思う。ありがとう。ひなっこ。

Moving House

以上、ひりんこでした。

引っ越しを待つベランダにあった植物たち。それだけでトラック1台が満杯。みんな揃って新しい場所へ。
The plants waiting for their trip. They took up a whole truck to themselves. They all went together to the new place.

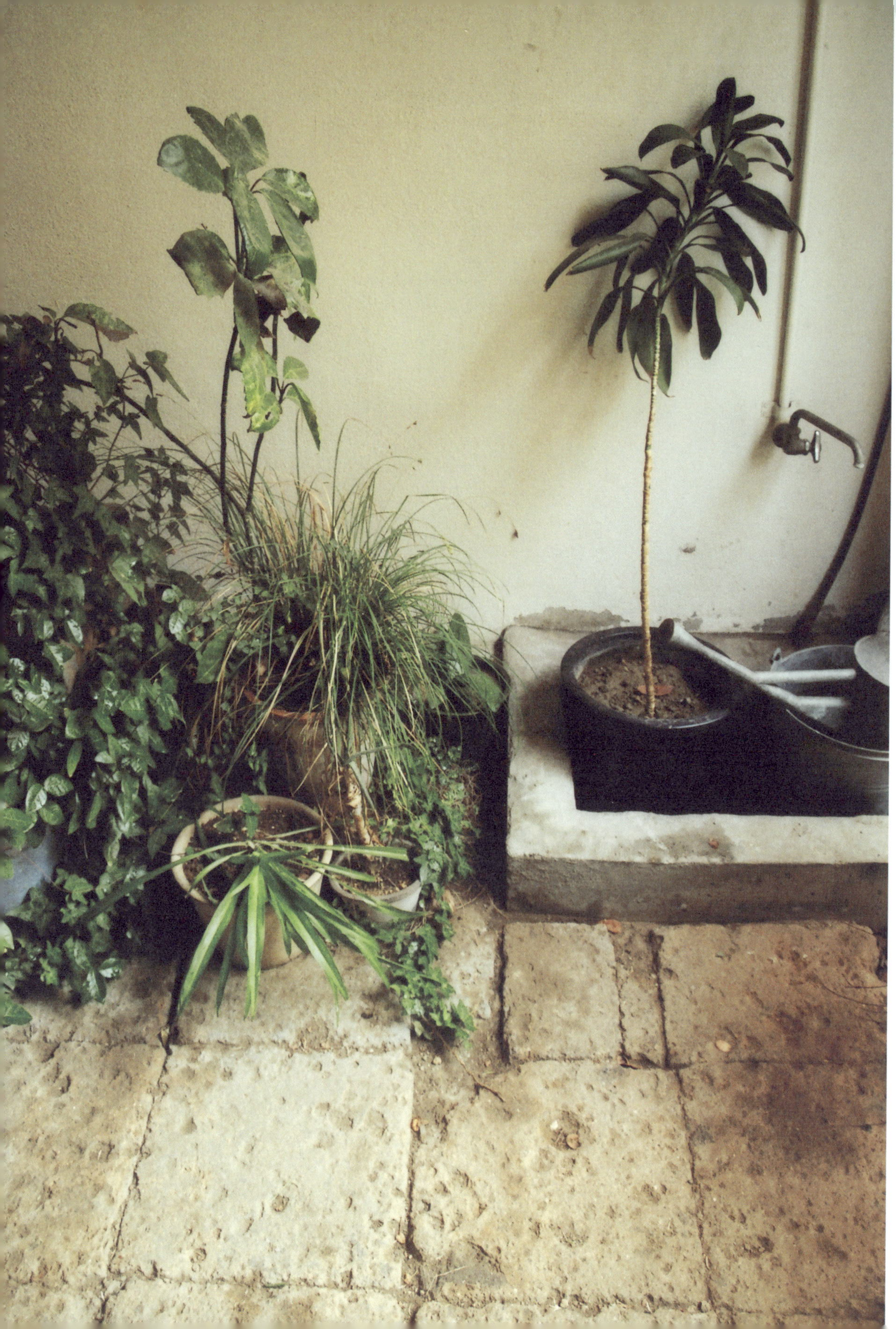

Moving House

Every day we were going back and forth between Tamatsukuri and Asahi Ward. There were still many things to do, but we decided that once we had the kitchen done we would move in. In July 2009 the kitchen was finished and we moved with our 5 dogs and 8 cats from our home in Tamatsukuri where we had lived for the last 13 years.

It's better if Hiromi takes up the story here:

When you have a lot of things, moving is a difficult thing to do.
I wanted to say, "Let's take just one trunk."
But we have enough plants on our verandah that a 2 ton truck isn't big enough to carry them.
And then there are the 13 dogs and cats.
What is more, there are stones I've picked up, and bits of rusted wire. Things that might carelessly be mistaken for garbage.

When Tokuhiko said, "Today I'm calling for a quote from a moving company," I had a foreboding. He likes to move quickly and sets tight schedules. I was sure he wouldn't give us enough time for packing.

"I told them we'd move next week." he said.
Typical.

Until then, we had gone to the site to work on the house together, but from that day on I stayed home and packed. There was so much stuff. Even 200 boxes weren't enough.

As I packed the boxes, Hina, who had just turned 3 years old, had to fend for herself. I had wanted to organize as I packed, but there were many things I wasn't sure how to sort. They ended up getting mixed in with other things. I often went to tape up a box only to discover Nya napping peacefully inside. Around me, Kuma and Savi played with packing string. Perhaps the cats were trying to help, but they were more of a nuisance than anything else. It was a turbulent week.

"We'll load the van from eight o'clock and we should be ready to start unloading in Asahi Ward just after lunchtime." the moving company workers told me, overly optimistically.

Sure enough, we started at 8 am and didn't leave Tamatsukuri until 5 pm. We weren't done unloading the trucks until 10 pm. Once they realized how big the job was, the company sent out more and more staff to help, ending up with a team of more than ten people.

The boxes were all unloaded, but the task of unpacking everything and putting it away loomed in front of me.

One week later, I came down with a high fever. Until then I had hardly ever been to hospital and loathed the thought of being admitted. The doctor was adamant, though, and I ended up staying for eight nights. I was worried about Hina, who normally couldn't sleep if I wasn't near. However, according to Tokuhiko, She went the whole time without grumbling or calling for her "mama" even once. I was surprised. It must have been hard for her. Thank you, Hina.

— Hiromi.

The floorboards in our home in Tamatsukuri before being pulled up.
Countless photographs were taken on these floorboards and against these walls.
This is where our three catalogs were born.

床をめくる前。TRUCKの2階にあった自宅の部屋。
たくさんの写真を撮ったこの壁、この床。3冊のカタログがここから生まれた。

The scent released when we pulled up the floorboards took me back 13 years to the time we started TRUCK.

床板は剥がして持って行く。床下からは13年前の思い出が匂いと共に蘇る。

The floorboards being installed at the new place,
where they will absorb more memories.

When we moved from Tamatsukuri, we brought along our long-used floorboards. This caused a bit of a problem. Until all the boxes were removed from our place in Tamatsukuri, we couldn't pull up the floorboards. And until we put in the floorboards in the new place, we would have nowhere to put the many panda-marked boxes supplied by the moving company. It was like a game. The room slated to receive those floorboards was the cat's room. If I didn't get the floorboards laid quickly we'd have no place for the cats. It was puzzling. The eight cats moved to the new house one day before us. We kept them locked up in Hina's room. Nico and Kuma had recently been on very bad terms, so we put Kuma on her own in the toilet.

As soon as the movers had moved out the boxes, some TRUCK staff helped me pull up the floorboards. I felt a deep attachment to these boards. 13 years ago Hiromi and I had laid them together. On them we had taken the many pictures we'd used to make our three catalogs. On these floorboards we had welcomed Buddy when he was just a 41-day old puppy. You could see his teeth marks here and there in the wood. We couldn't just throw them away. As soon as we pulled them up, the air filled with an old smell, it was the same smell that had penetrated the place when we were pulling it apart all those years ago. 13 years had passed, but it felt like yesterday.

Without the furniture or floorboards it looked extremely empty. Debris was strewn about here and there. The ceiling looked lower and the whole place looked smaller than it had ever looked before.
This place had been everything to us. It was the place with 13 years of precious memories. I carefully bundled up those memories and brought them with me to our new place.

Moving House

玉造の部屋。
年月を共にした味のある床板は移植する。
荷物を全部出してからでないと床板がめくれない。
一方、新しい家では床が仕上がっていないと、大量にあるパンダマークの段ボール箱の行き場がない。常に勝負だ。
その床板を張る新しい部屋は、ニャンたちが暮らす予定の部屋。急いで仕上げないとニャンたちの行き場もない。
ややこしいので、ニャンたち8匹は引っ越し前日に新居へ。将来、子供部屋にする部屋に監禁。ニコとクマは最近犬猿の仲なので一緒にできないから、クマだけはトイレに隔離する。

引っ越し業者によって荷物が運び出されるやいなや、TRUCKスタッフにも手伝ってもらって床板をめくる。
この思い入れのある床、13年前にひりんこと2人で張った床。この床の上でたくさんの写真を撮影してカタログを3冊作った。初々しい床に生後41日のバディを迎え入れた。子犬バディのつけた歯形も残っている。この床板は捨てることはできない。
めくり出すと、当時の匂いが出て来た。初めてこの部屋に来た時の、解体していた時の匂い。13年も経っているのに、あまりにもリアルで、昨日のことのような錯覚を覚える。床下に張り巡らせている根太のレベルを調整するために隙間に詰めたクサビ状の薄いメープル。これは当時よく作っていたテーブルの脚、下に行くほど細くなっている脚を作る時に出た端材。
並びのめし屋で、素うどんをすすっていた毎日。全ての感覚が蘇る。

家財道具が出尽くして、床板もめくられた空っぽの空間。何かの残骸がいくつか転がっている。
思っていたよりも意外と狭い。天井も低い。この場所が全てだった。
家具とカタログ全てを作り出していった場所。改めて見ると少しちっぽけにさえ見える。よくここで頑張ったんやなぁと、13年分の思い出がいたる所にある。でも、すごく遠い記憶にも感じる。そんなもの全てをギュッと集めて大事に持って外に出た。

剥がして持って来た板を新しい家に張っていく。ここでまた記憶を重ねていく。

New Address

一緒に引っ越してきたワンたち。真新しいこのサンルーム。嬉しさからか不安からか、みんな揃って笑顔でしっぽふりふり。

The dogs in their brand-new home. Whether it's from happiness or from anxiety is a mystery, but they are all smiling and wagging their tails.

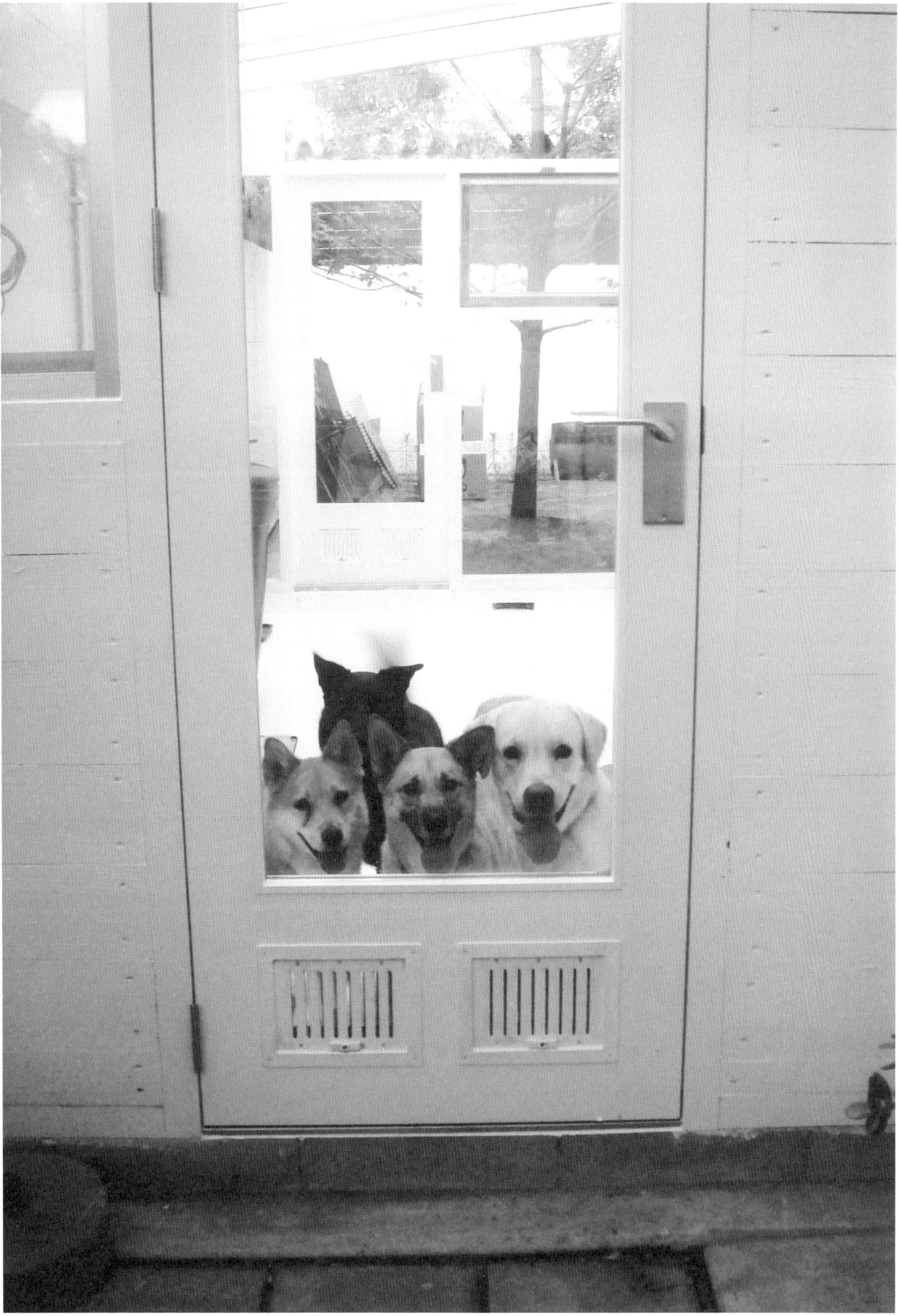

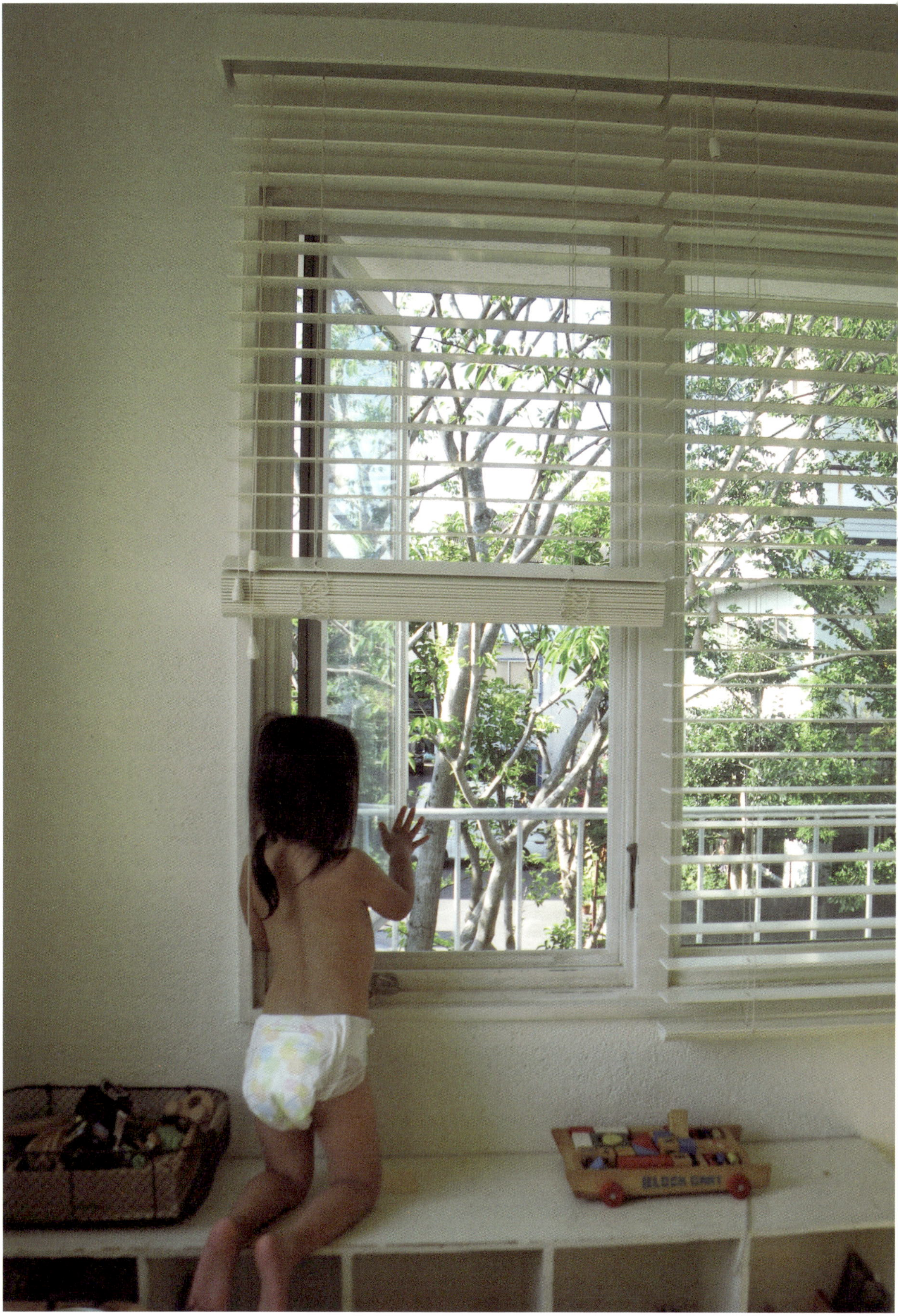
BLOCK CART

New Address

そんな怒濤の引っ越しデイの翌朝、目が覚めると、ヌーサのいつもの部屋、朝日が樹々を縫って入ってくるあの部屋にいるのかと、勘違いするくらい気持ちいい朝だった。
自分たちで植えた樹々。明るい朝を迎えたいと南東の角に作った寝室。まだブラインドもついてなかった窓からの朝日が眩しかった。1階に降りてきても、どこかヌーサ感が続く。こんな朝がこれから毎日あると思うと、いいのが作れたなぁと喜びがじわっとくる。

でも、落ち着いている時間はない。
家の引っ越し後、家の未完成な所はいったん後回しにして、今度は住みながらTRUCKとBirdとシロクマ舎を仕上げていく。まだまだ作業は続く。いつ頃出来上がるのか、全く先が読めない。妥協知らずの2人は納得いかないと、容赦なくやり直す。時間はかかるが、家具作りも工事も前向きな後戻りは慣れたもの。
玉造で営業を続けているTRUCKとAREA2には、初め「2009年春頃、新しい場所にTRUCKがオープンします」と張り紙をしていた。それが、「夏頃」に書き変えられ、そして「秋頃」に書き変えられた。その秋もとっくに深まり過ぎようとしてきた。

先にオープンの日を決めてしまって、突貫工事になるのは嫌だ。これで良し、というものができるまで工事は続く。

引っ越し後、旭区では保育園がどこも定員オーバーで、日菜はしっかり待機児童になってしまった。
毎日朝から晩まで作業が続く現場にずっと、3歳になったばかりのちびっこがいる。傍らで遊んだり、時にはいっちょまえに頭にタオルをキュッと巻きペンキや漆喰を塗ったり。
3歳児連れでの作業は思うようにはかどらず、かなりややこしくて大変だったけど、親のこれだけのもの作りな日々を見て育ったのは日菜にとって良かったなぁと、今となっては思えるし、いろんなことが日菜の体に染み込んだはず。

The day after our hectic move, I woke up in our new house for the first time. When I opened my eyes, I had the feeling that I was in Noosa. The light and the trees had me confused for a moment. They were the trees we had planted, though. The bright sun had come to greet us in the new bedroom in the southeast corner of the house. The windows had no blinds yet, so the sun was dazzling.

When I came downstairs, I still felt like I was in Noosa. That I'd be able to enjoy this every morning gave me the feeling that we had made something good.

There was no time to relax. Now that we had moved, we had to postpone the things needed to do to finish our home and focus on finishing Bird, Shirokumasha, and TRUCK. There was still a lot to be done, and it was unclear when we would be finished. Neither of us were willing to compromise. We would do things over until we were satisfied. It would take a lot of time, but in both making furniture and making our house we were used to going back to go forward.

New Address

All this time TRUCK was still doing business in Tamatsukuri. I put up an announcement saying that TRUCK would be moving to a new place in spring of 2009. After a while, I changed it to summer. Then it changed to autumn. Now we were getting deeper into autumn.

I didn't want to decide on a day in advance. That would force us to do a rush job. I wanted to make sure we did it properly. We would keep working until we were done. When we were done we would open.

When we moved, the day care center to which we planned to send Hina was over capacity, so she was put on a waiting list. From morning to night, while we worked on the site, there was a barely three-year old child there working (and playing) beside us. Sometimes she played under supervision. Other times she wrapped a towel tightly around her head and helped with the painting and plastering. Having her there certainly made the work more complicated, but in the long run I think it was good for her, to see us making so many things and to absorb so many experiences.

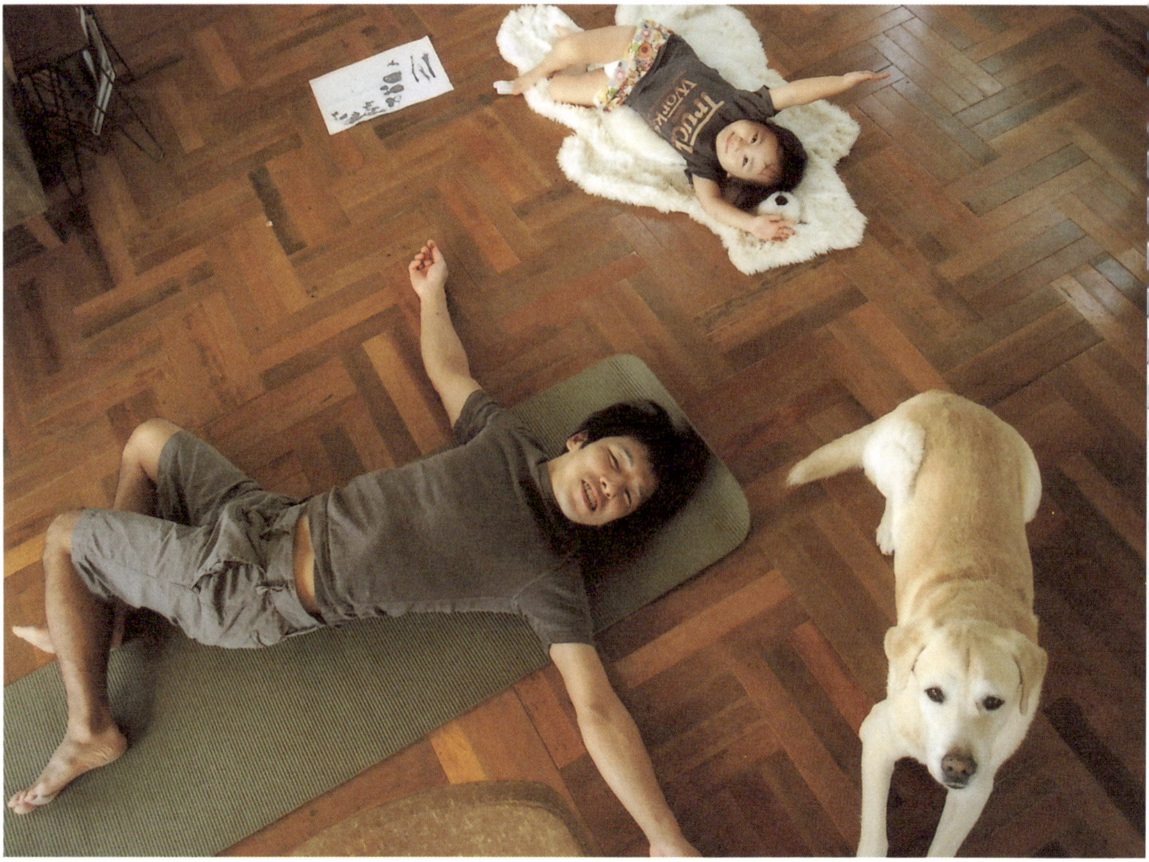

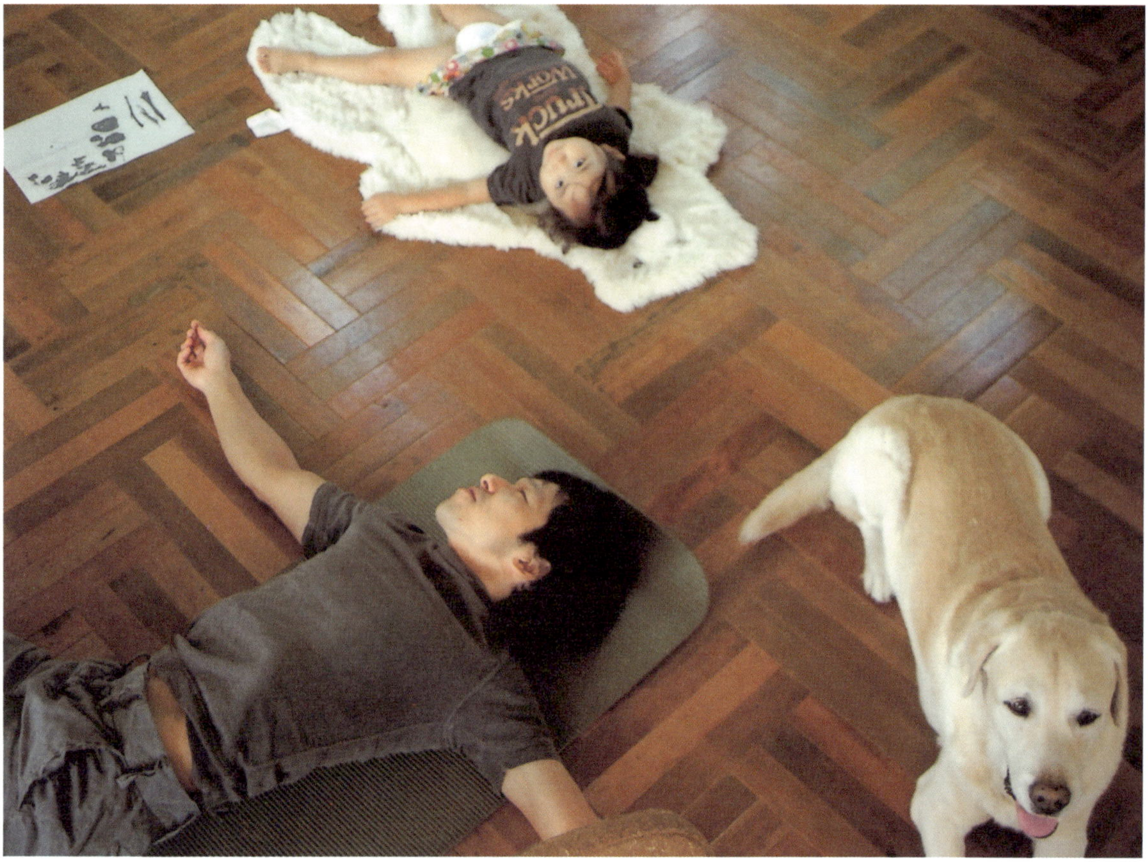

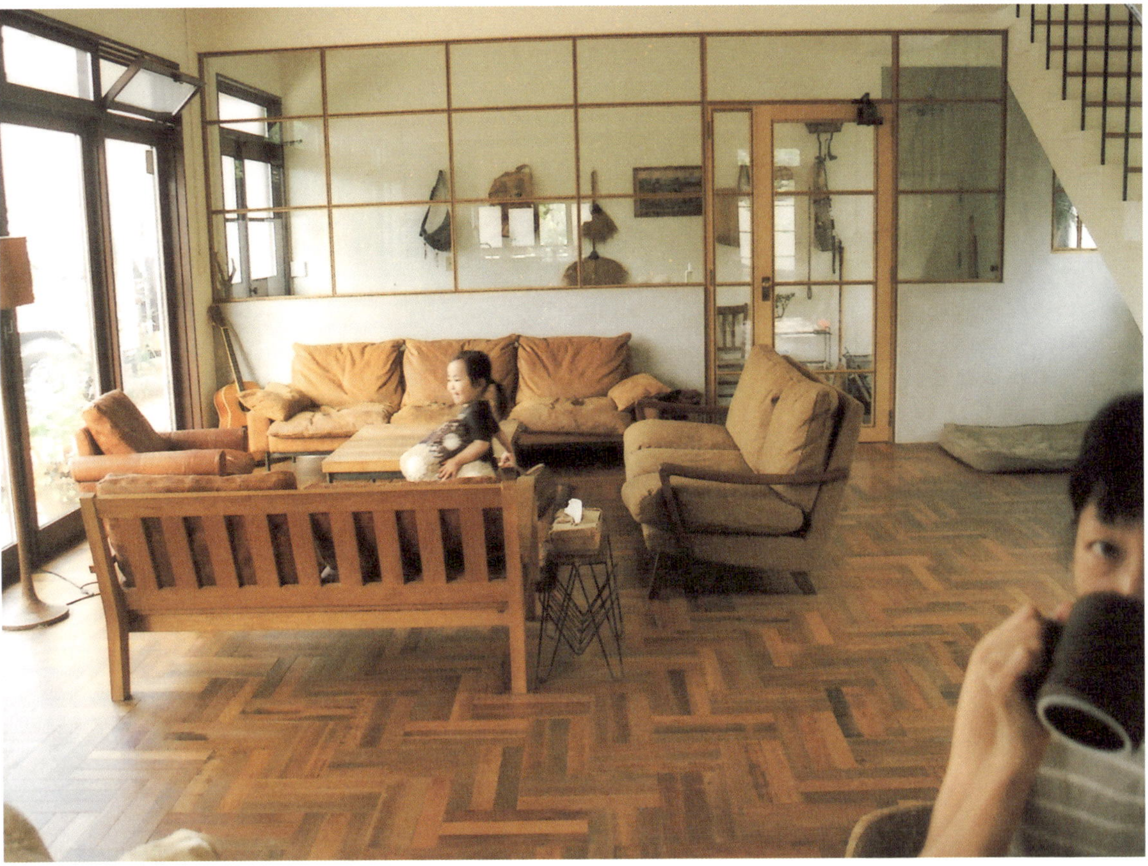

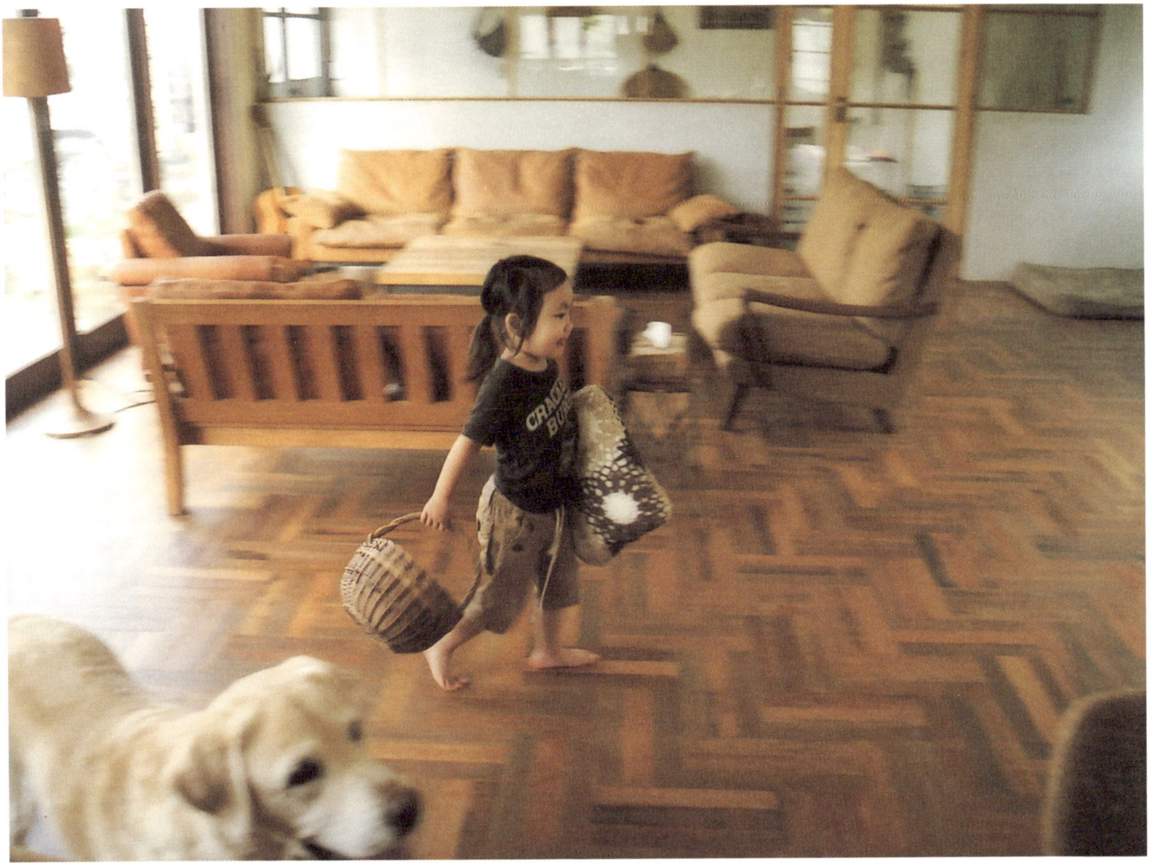

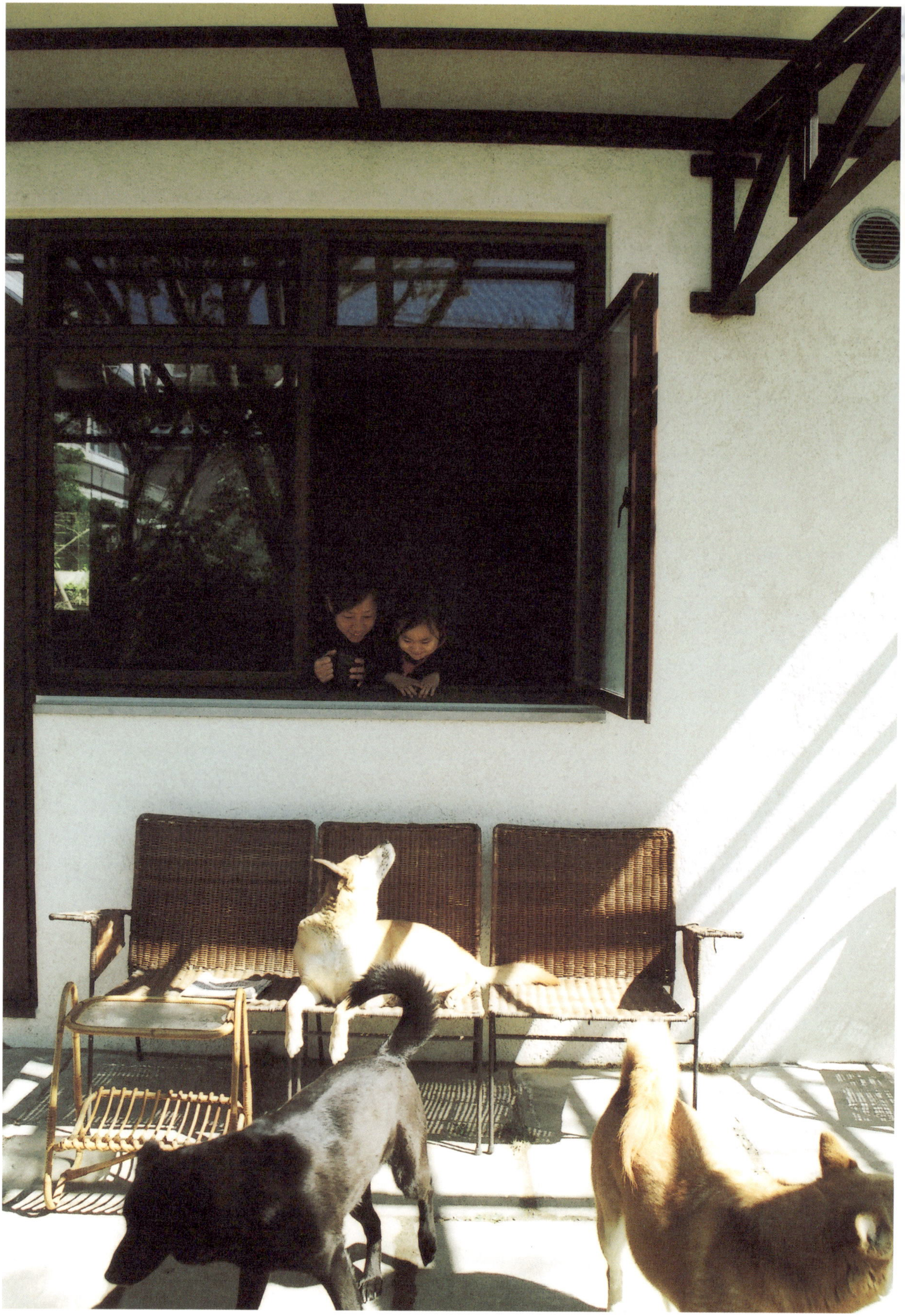

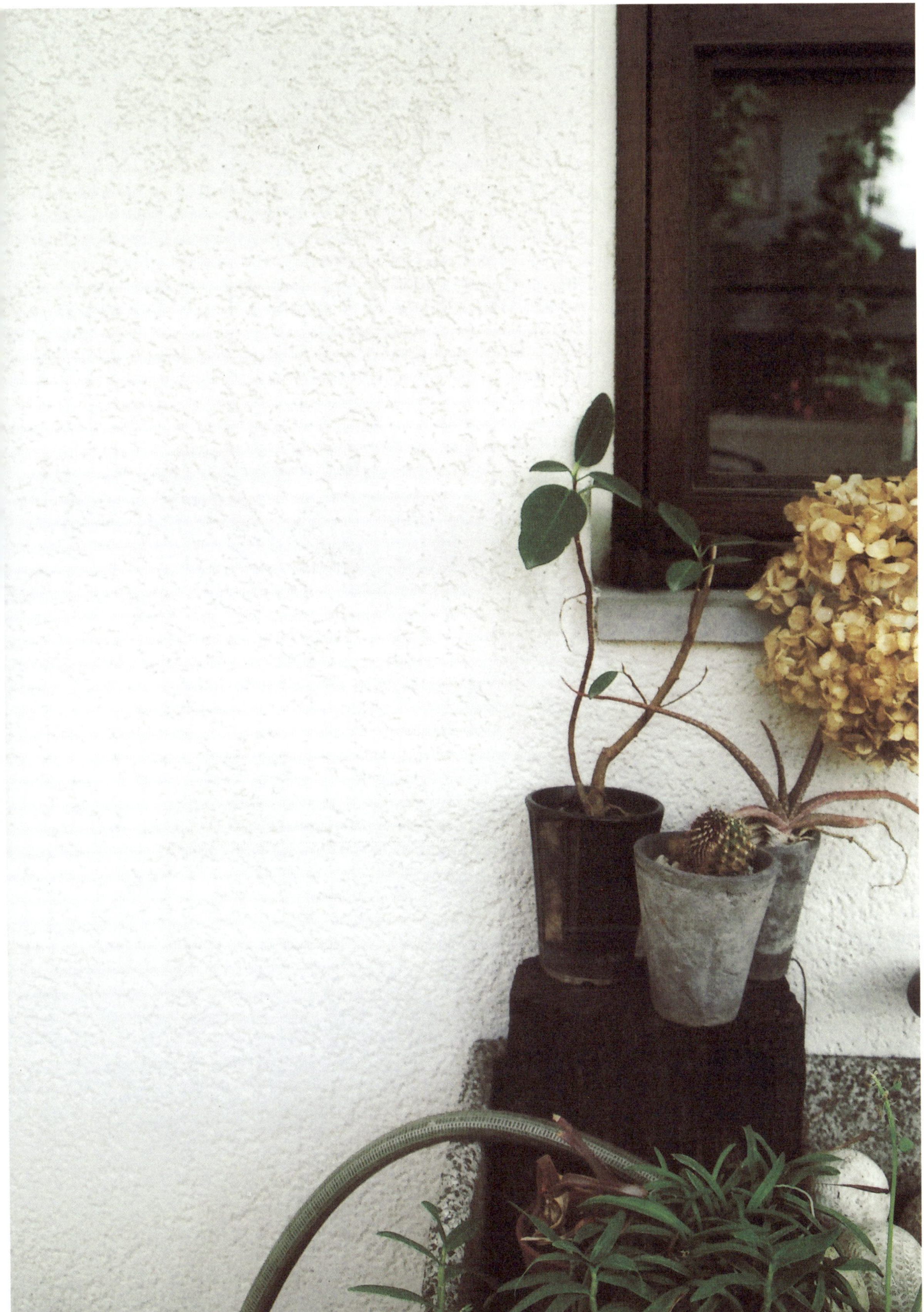

Halfway up the Mountain

and then,
"Shirokumasha" "Bird"

まだまだ頂上は遠い。さらにシロクマ舎とBirdも。

なんでもやりたい3歳の日菜。空の容器と刷毛では納得しない。実際に塗料が入ったものを要求、そして一緒に塗っていく。
Hina was keen to help out. She wasn't satisfied making believe with an empty paint container. She insisted on doing it for real.

Sep. 5, 2009
Shirokumasha
Painting the Wall

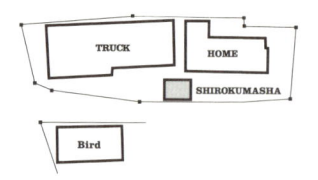

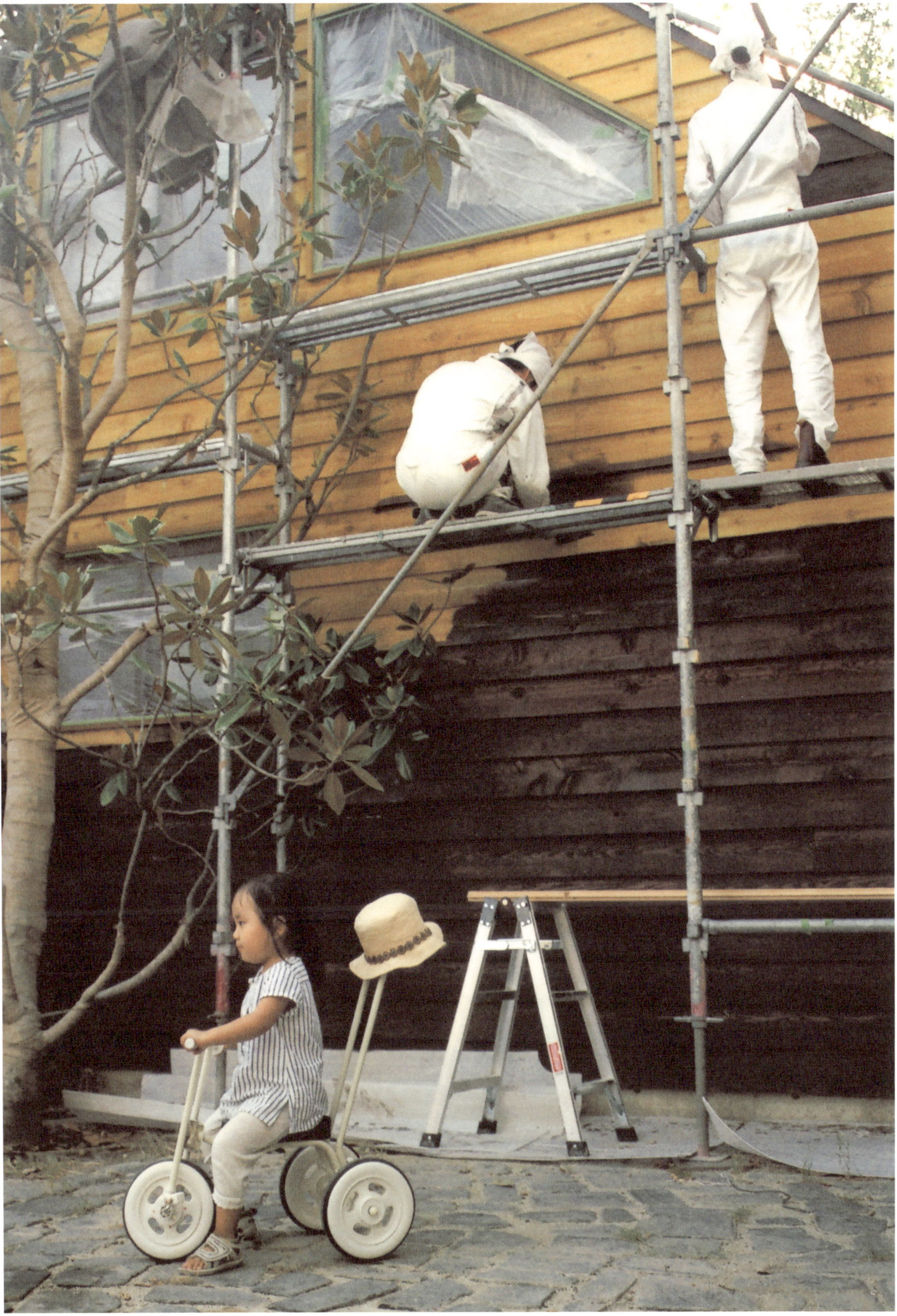

日菜、卒乳

今まで寝る前だけはまだ儀式のようにおっぱいを吸っていた日菜。
9月27日、突然、卒乳した。
毎日現場でヘトヘトになって、(いっちょまえに日菜も) ベッドに入って、3人とも即、爆睡。儀式もなく。
こんなバタンキューな日が続いたある夜、ちょっと何日かぶりにおっぱいをあげようとしたら、吸い方を忘れていたそうだ。
ひりんこは、断乳は全く考えておらず、もっともっとおっぱいをあげたかったらしく、すごく残念がっていた。
お姉ちゃんになったなと、ちょっと寂しい気もした。

An Unexpected End

On September 27, Hina suddenly stopped drinking breast milk. Until then she had breast fed every night before bed. We were working so hard during the day (and that includes Hina) that when we were ready for bed we fell asleep almost immediately.
Until then, she had always been fed before going to sleep. After a few days of falling asleep immediately, it seems like she had forgotten how to suck. Hiromi was saddened by this change. She had not intended to stop breastfeeding her so soon.

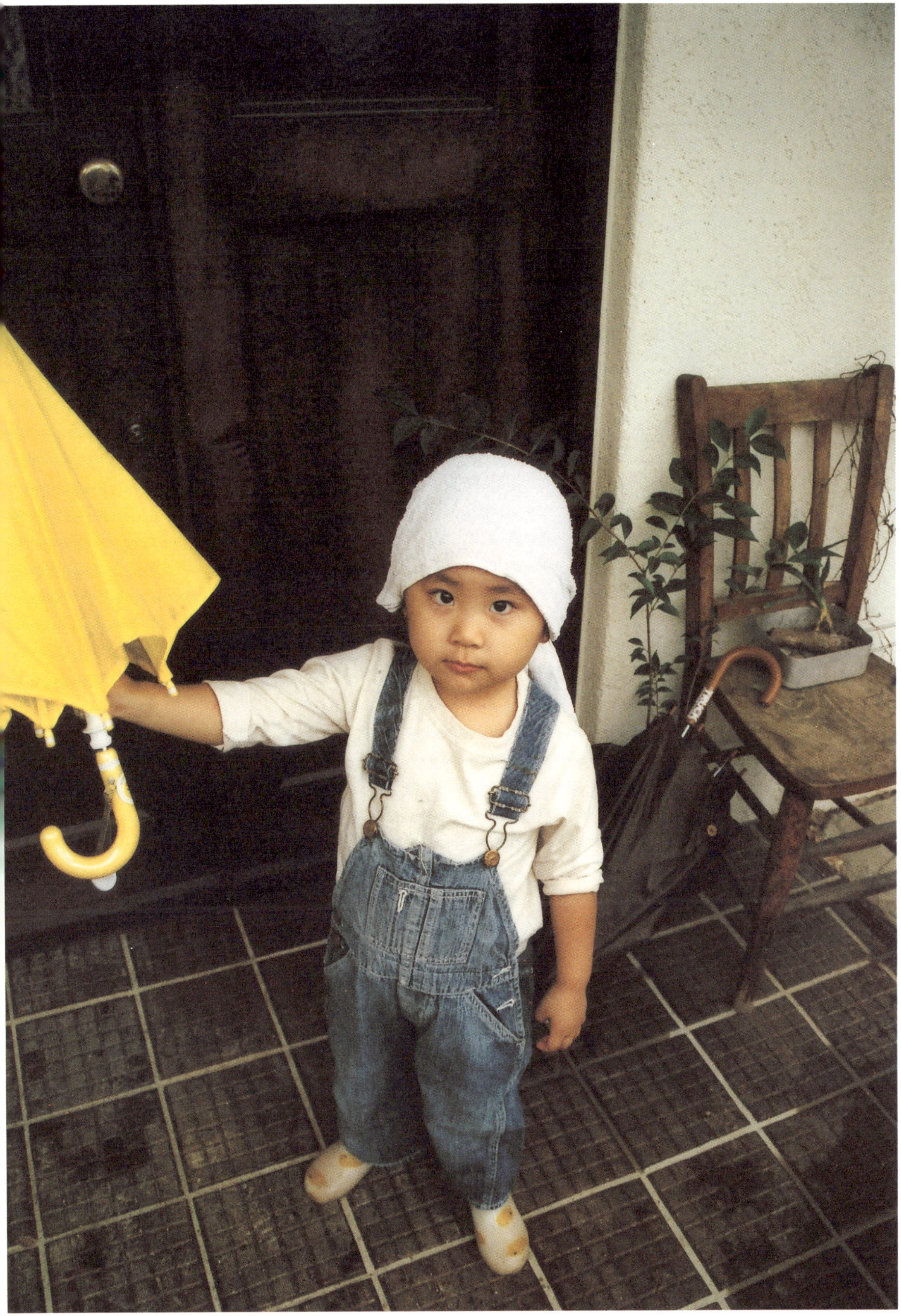

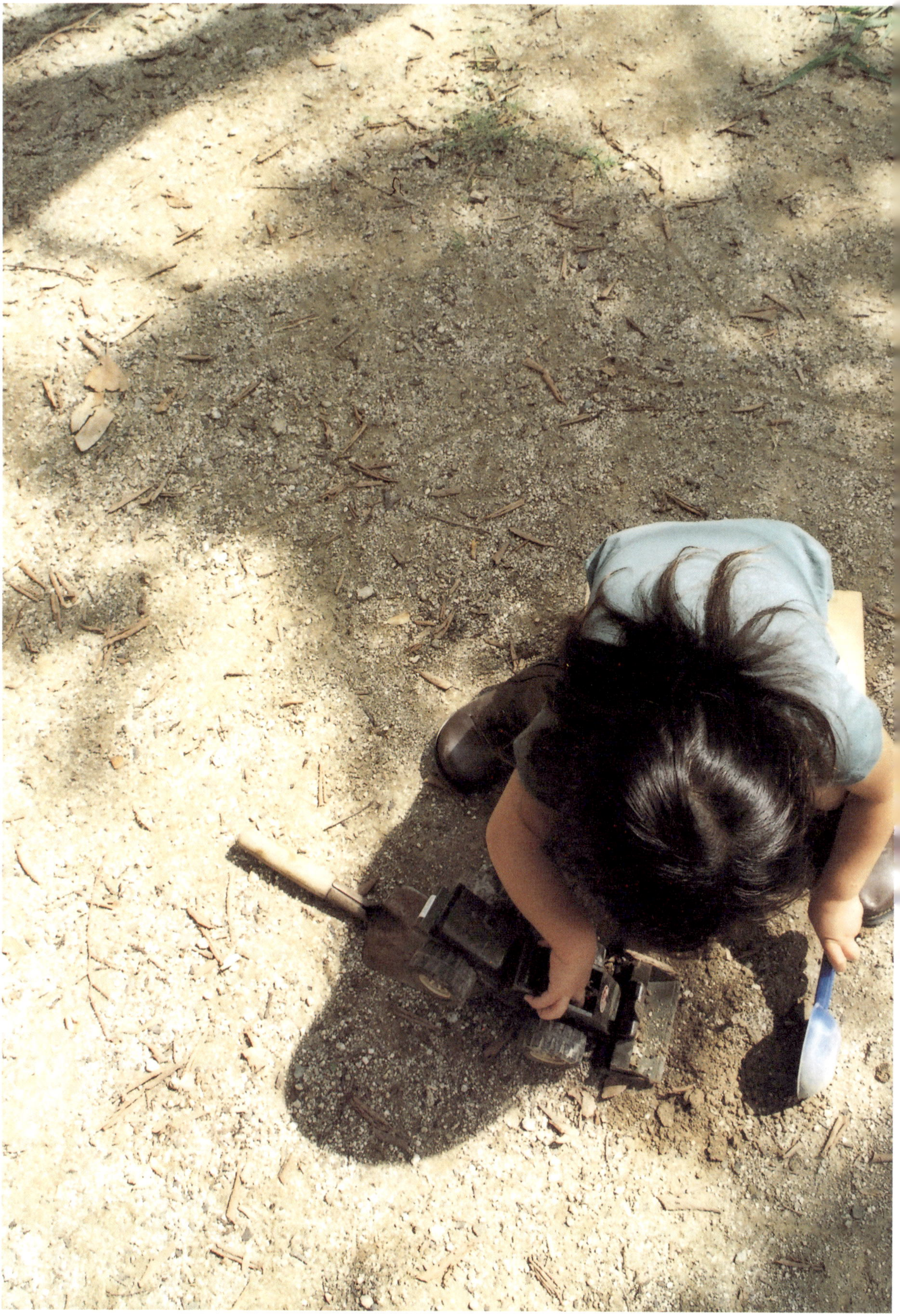

庭でどんぐりが拾えれば嬉しいと植えたコナラ。植えてから初めてのどんぐり。
We planted a konara oak hoping to be able to gather acorns in our garden. These are the first acorns it produced.

木目の並び、その見え方にこだわるひろみが悩みながら並べた引き戸に張る板。
その上をカタカタと三輪車が通り抜けて行く。

**Hiromi laid these planks out to determine the best way to arrange them.
Hina decided it looked like a nice bumpy track for her tricycle.**

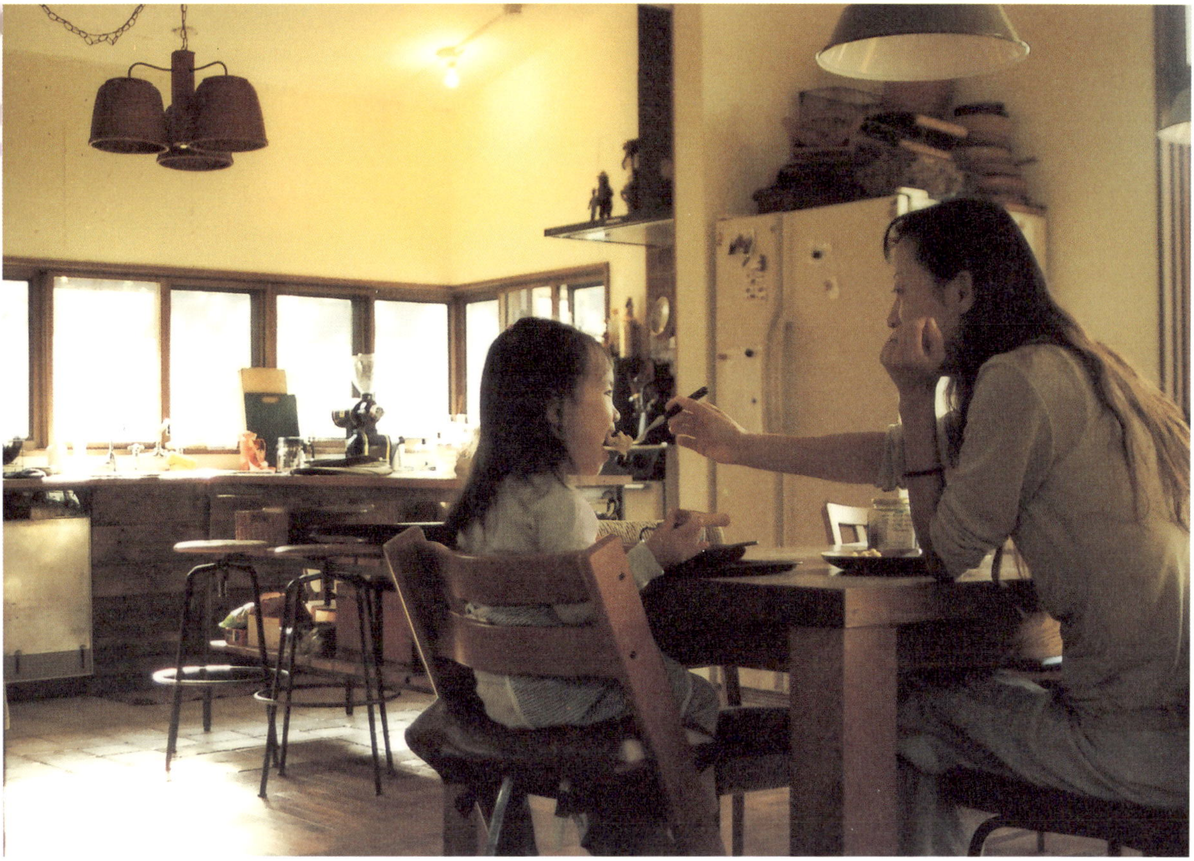

Oct. 22, 2009
Making
the Car Gate

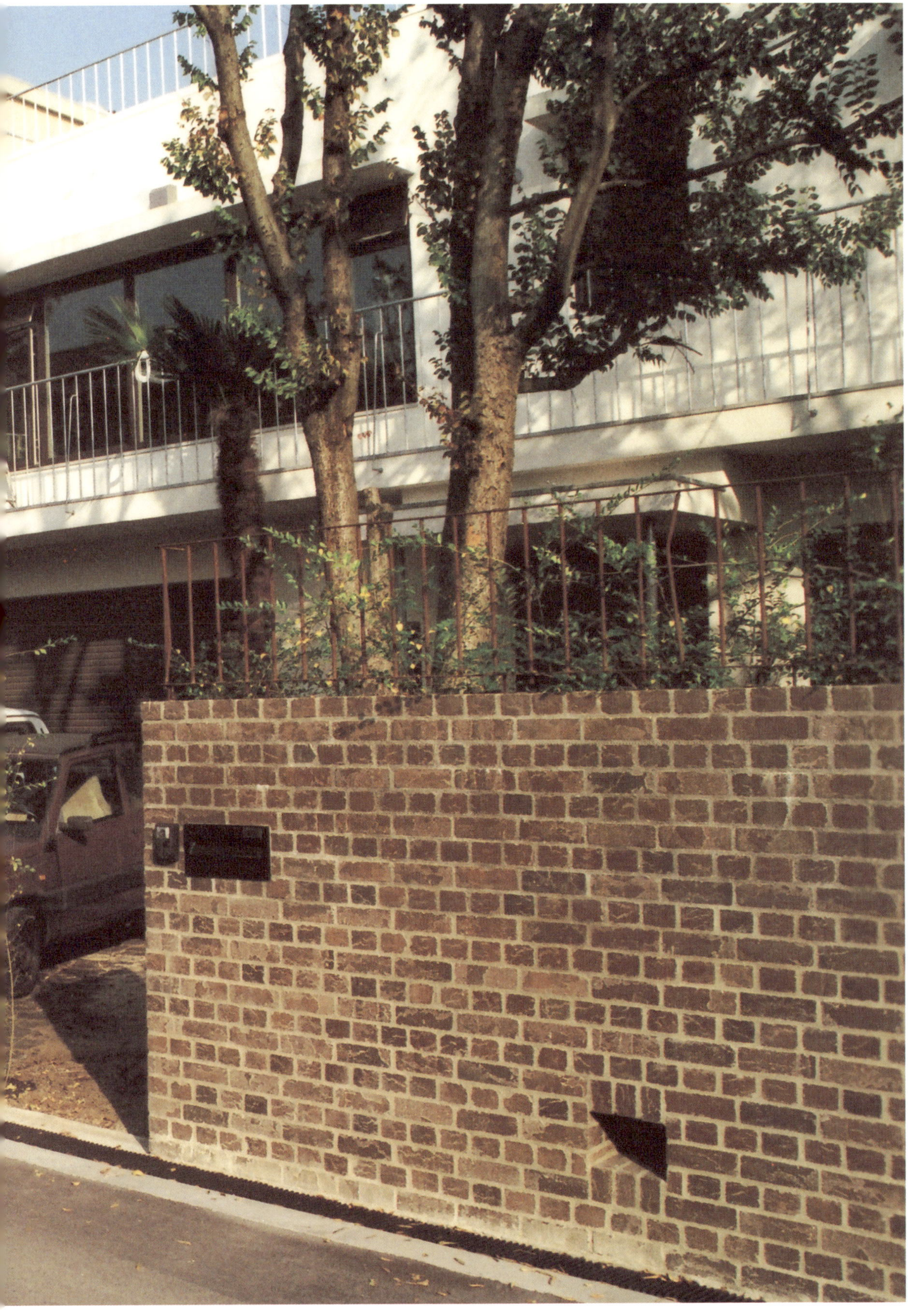

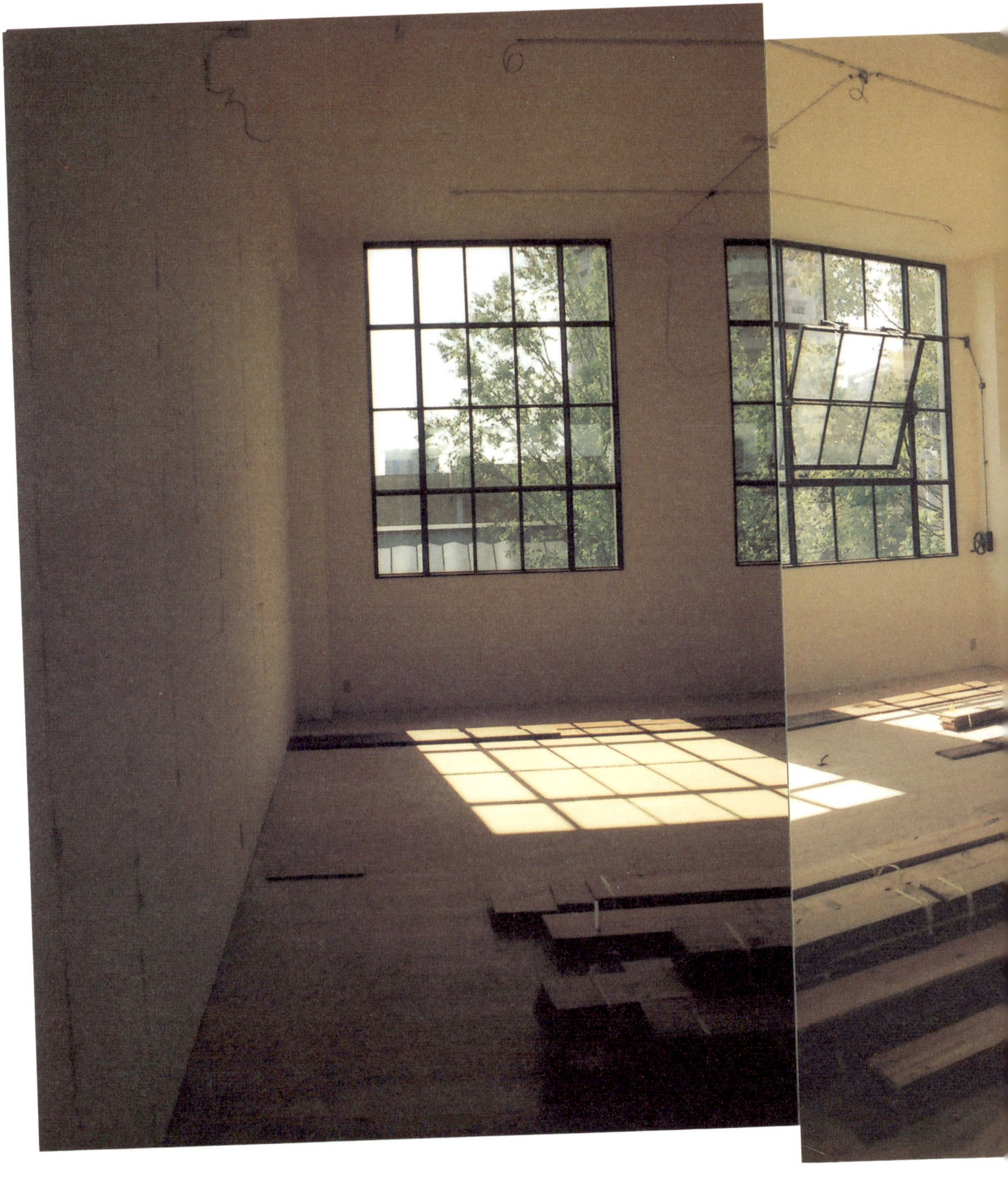

最終まで白いコンクリートにするつもりだった店の床。急遽、木のフローリングに作戦変更。材料が揃うのに1ヶ月待つ。
We'd intended to leave the floor in the store just as white concrete, but decided at the last moment that it would look better with wood flooring. We had to wait a month for the wood to arrive.

オープン間近、時間のない中、ひりんこが相変わらず全て
手描きで看板を書いていく。13年前とやってることは変わらない。
These signs were made just before we opened.
As with all our signs for the last 14 years, they were hand-painted by Hiromi.

Dec. 9, 2009
Hanging
the Frames

1999年、AREA2をオープンした時に押し葉で作ったフレームを、
壁に掛けていく。新しい壁が見慣れたものになっていく。
These frames had been hanging in AREA2 since it opened in 1999.
They made the new walls somewhat more familiar.

Opening TRUCK and Bird

On November 29, 2009, TRUCK and AREA2 in Tamatsukuri closed. It was a place we had built over a period of 12 years. There was sadness as it closed, but we stepped forward with a smile on our faces.

There were many things to which we were attached that we put to use in the new store: the lights, the register counter, and the elevator door. We would use the door of TRUCK as the door of Bird and the door of our old home as one of the inner doors inside the new store. We never thought that because we were moving to a new store we needed a new concept. Our tastes remained the same. We had never had anything like a "concept" for the store. When we had opened AREA2, many writers had asked us what the concept was for the new store. We were surprised. It wasn't "Asian" and it wasn't "Scandinavian". It was just TRUCK.

Our previous store had gradually become too cramped. Our new store looks very similar, though. If there are any big differences, I don't know what they are. Our taste remains consistent. It doesn't matter if it is the shop or the house. People writing about us for magazines have often said, "Oh, your house is just like your store." We prefer to think that it's our store that is just like our house.

Finally, it came time to move the store. Hiromi and I had our hands full getting things ready at the new place. Fortunately, we could rely on our staff to get things done. Tatsuki and Akko worked around the clock to get everything packed up at AREA2. Takashi did the same at TRUCK. There was an incredible amount of stuff to get ready. They didn't have enough time, but did a great job. Thank you.

A short while before we moved the store we moved the workshop, storeroom, and Shirokumasha. Each of them involved packing and moving an immense number of things. Almost all of the arrangements and work for this was handled by the staff. How lucky we are to have such dependable people working for us. Finally, the new store was ready to receive furniture. All of the TRUCK staff worked side by side with the movers. There were no slackers. They moved a massive amount of furniture. "We want them for our company!" the movers said when they saw our guys at work. I knew I could leave it in their hands. I can't say how grateful I am to them.

In the end it took two and half years to make the store in Asahi Ward, from the time we decided to buy the land to the opening. During that time, I had thought of nothing but building and construction. When I saw the furniture on display the new store, though, I was happily reminded, "Oh yeah, I'm a furniture maker."

Just because we had all the furniture and other goods laid out didn't mean it was ready for customers. They make the effort to come all the way here and there is no excuse for a slapdash experience. We wanted to make sure every detail was precisely right.

I couldn't tell when we would truly be ready to open until we were, so we couldn't print out the kind of announcements or invitation cards that a store would normally send out. When I was ready, I just put something on our website saying that we'd be opening in three days. When we'd chosen the location we hadn't really thought about attracting customers but, now that we were ready to welcome them, we were a little concerned. Would anyone come?

It was a crisp, clear morning on December 14, 2009, when TRUCK and Bird finally opened their doors. Everything looked bright and shiny.

Dec. 13, 2009
Hand-drawing
the Signs

TRUCK、Bird オープン

2009年11月29日、玉造のTRUCKとAREA2を閉める。
13年間、自分たちの思いを目一杯注いできた場所。寂しさが溢れる。でも、また1歩前に進もうと笑った。

TRUCKの入り口のドアはBirdのドアに、TRUCKの店の中にあった僕たちの家の入り口のドアは新しい店の中で使う。AREA2で使っていた照明、レジカウンター、エレベーターの扉など、移設して使うものがたくさん。どれも愛着がある。新しい店だからといって、気分一新、今度はこんなコンセプトで!! みたいなことは一切ない。気持ちはずっと同じ。好きなものは変わらない。そもそもコンセプトなんて初めからない。
玉造のTRUCKの裏にAREA2が増えた時。取材に来たライターに「もう1軒の店はどんなテイストですか?」と聞かれて、かなり驚いた。別に、2店舗目はアジアンテイストですとか、北欧テイストです。ってわけないやん!! と。
1軒目が手狭になったので裏にもう1軒増えただけです。
何が変わることがあるのか、分からない。今回も一緒。何も変わらない。ついでに言えば、2人とも好きなものが一貫しているので当然、店も自宅も変わらない。これもまた取材の時に「お家もお店と一緒ですね! ステキ!」なんて言われるが、「どっちかというと店が家と一緒なんです」

いよいよ店も引っ越し。
でも、僕とひりんこは、新しい店の、まだまだ残っているたくさんの作らないといけないものに追われていた。スタッフの馬場君とあっこが徹夜でAREA2の雑貨や備品をまとめあげてくれた。TRUCKの店はトックンが。すごい量だったと思う。しかも前日まで営業していたのに! 時間もない中で、よくやった。サンキュー!
忘れないために書いておこう。店の引っ越しより一足先に、工場と倉庫とシロクマ舎も引っ越しした。どれもがおそろしい物量。それらのほとんどをスタッフが仕切って収めた。頼もしかった。
ついに新しい店に初めて家具が入っていく。TRUCKのスタッフはみんなよく動く。のろのろ歩いている奴なんて1人もいない。引っ越し業者と共に家具をどんどん運ぶ。負けてない。「うちの会社に欲しいなぁ」とスカウトされそうになったくらい。店の引っ越しも安心してみんなに任せることができた。自慢のスタッフが揃っている。

結局、旭区の店作りには土地を決めてからオープンまで2年半かかった。
この間、建築のことばかり考えてきた。時間をかけて、一から作ったその空間に家具が並んだ時、
ふと、「そうや、自分は家具屋やった」と妙に懐かしく、そして嬉しく感じた。

引っ越しはしたものの家具や雑貨が並んだだけでは人に見せることはできない。100%言い訳のないものにしないとオープンはできない。せっかく、わざわざ来てもらうのに、中途半端な状態では申し訳ない。細かい所まで精度を上げていく。こんな調子。引っ越しは済んだものの、まだまだいつできるかなんて分からない。自分たちが納得できた時がオープンの時。だから、開店日を知らせるDMなどの印刷物は作れなかった。3日前にHPで告知しただけ。集客を考えた場所選びなんて気にしない2人も、さすがに本当にお客さんが来るのか正直不安だった。

2009年12月14日、一転晴れてキリッと澄み切った空気の朝、TRUCKとBirdがオープンした。
全てが眩しく見えた。

photo_Kozo Ono

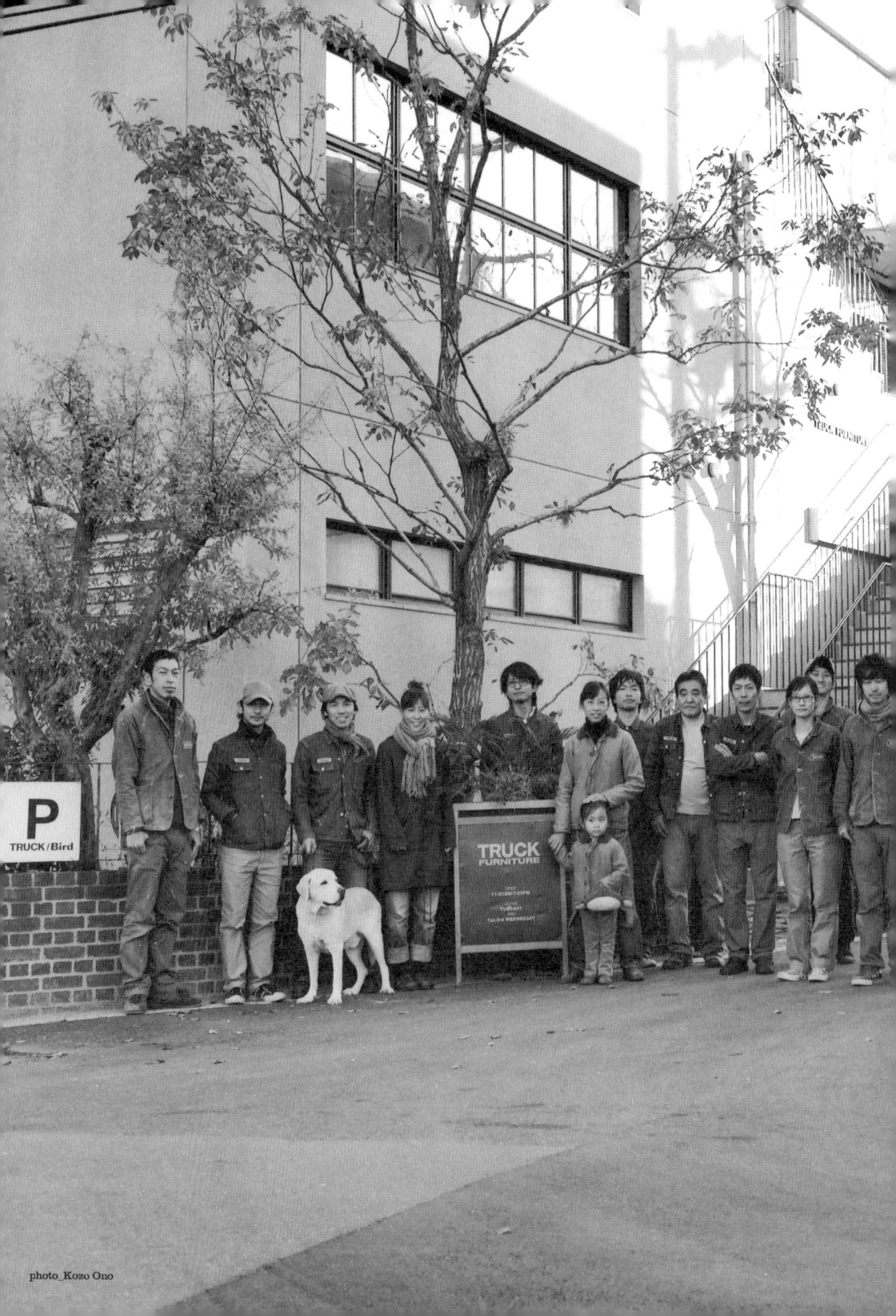

December 14, 2009　Opening Day

TRUCK
FURNITURE

OPEN
11:00AM-7:00PM

CLOSED
TUESDAY
AND
1st, 3rd WEDNESDAY

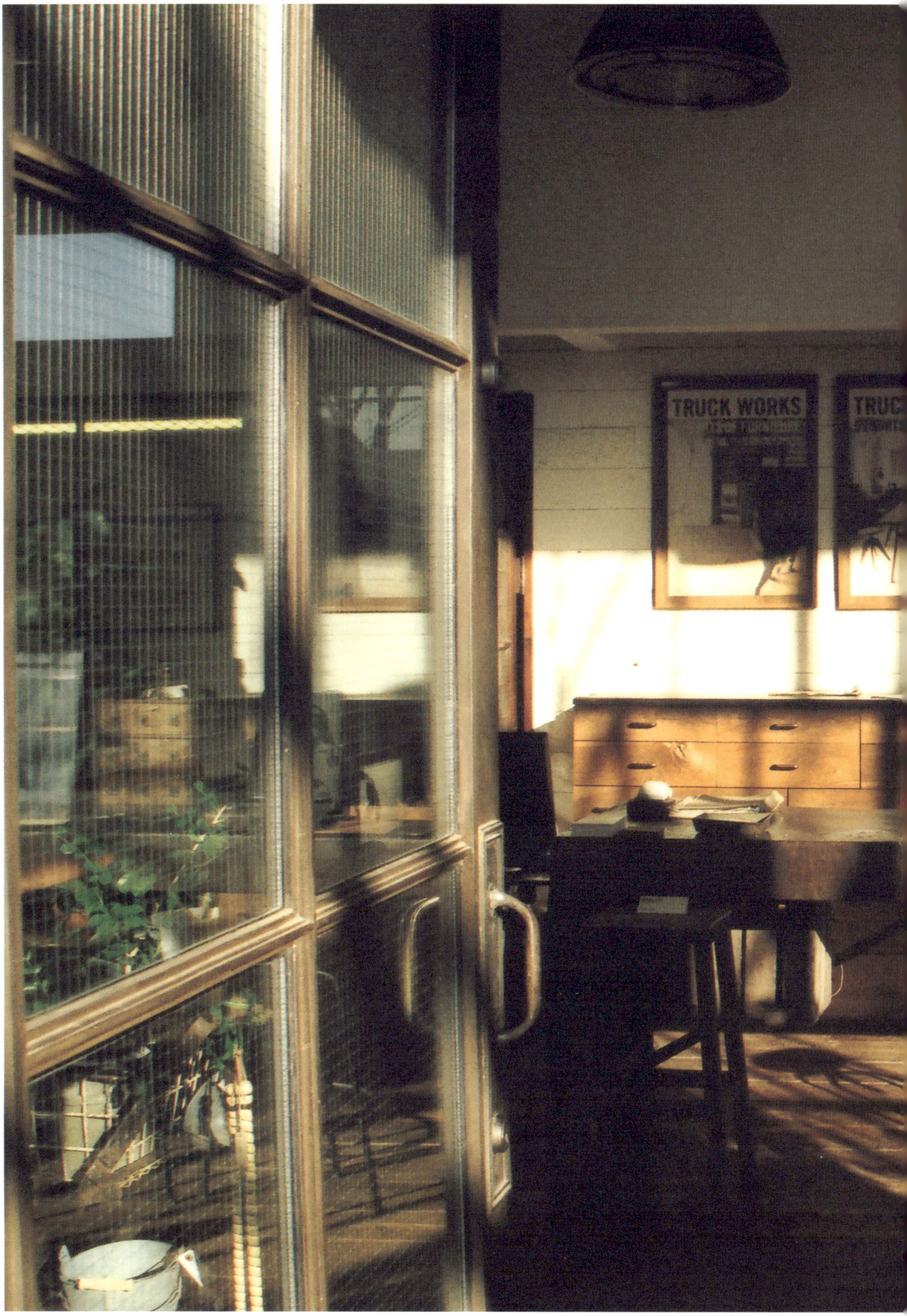
TRUCK WORKS

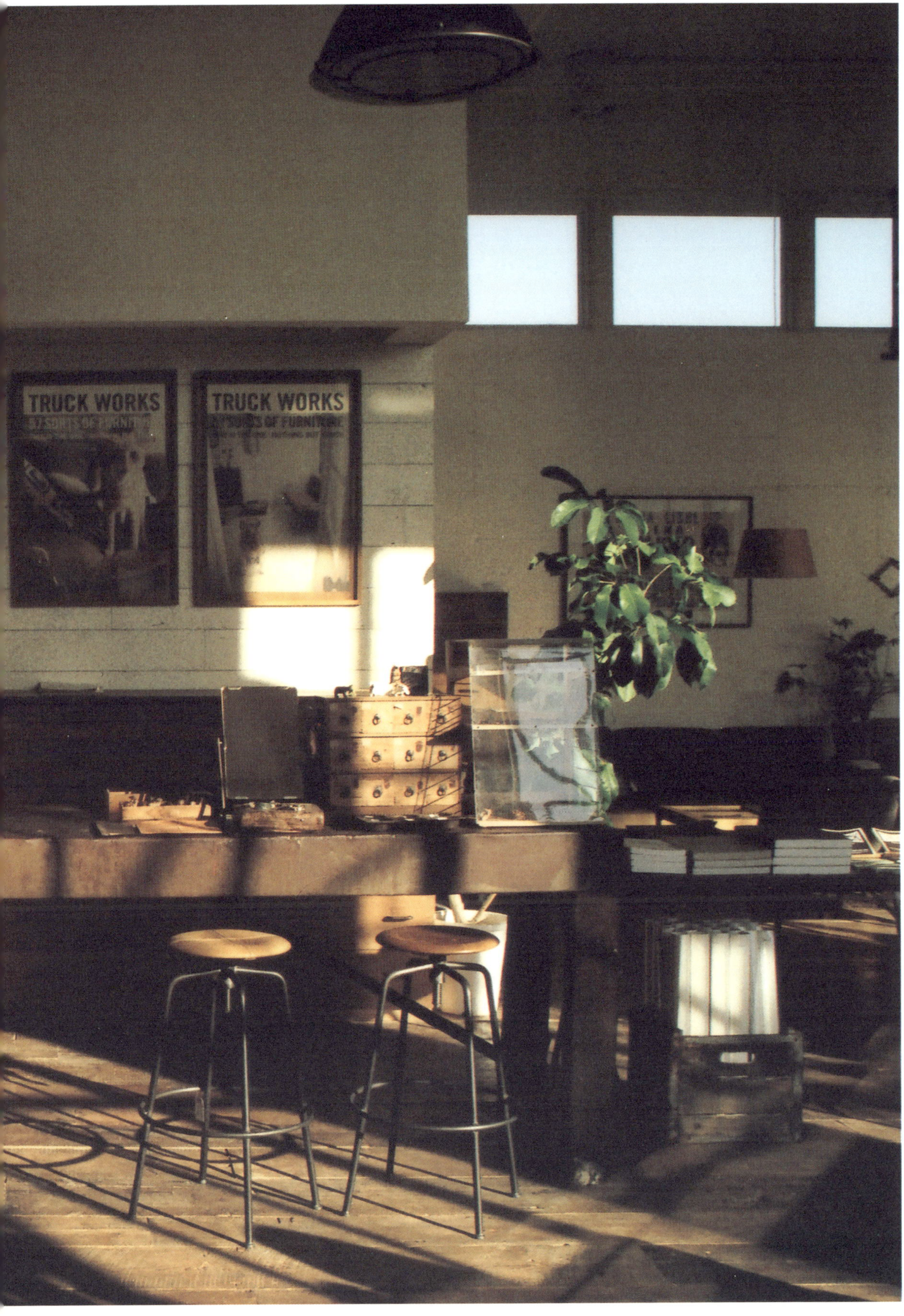
TRUCK WORKS
TRUCK WORKS

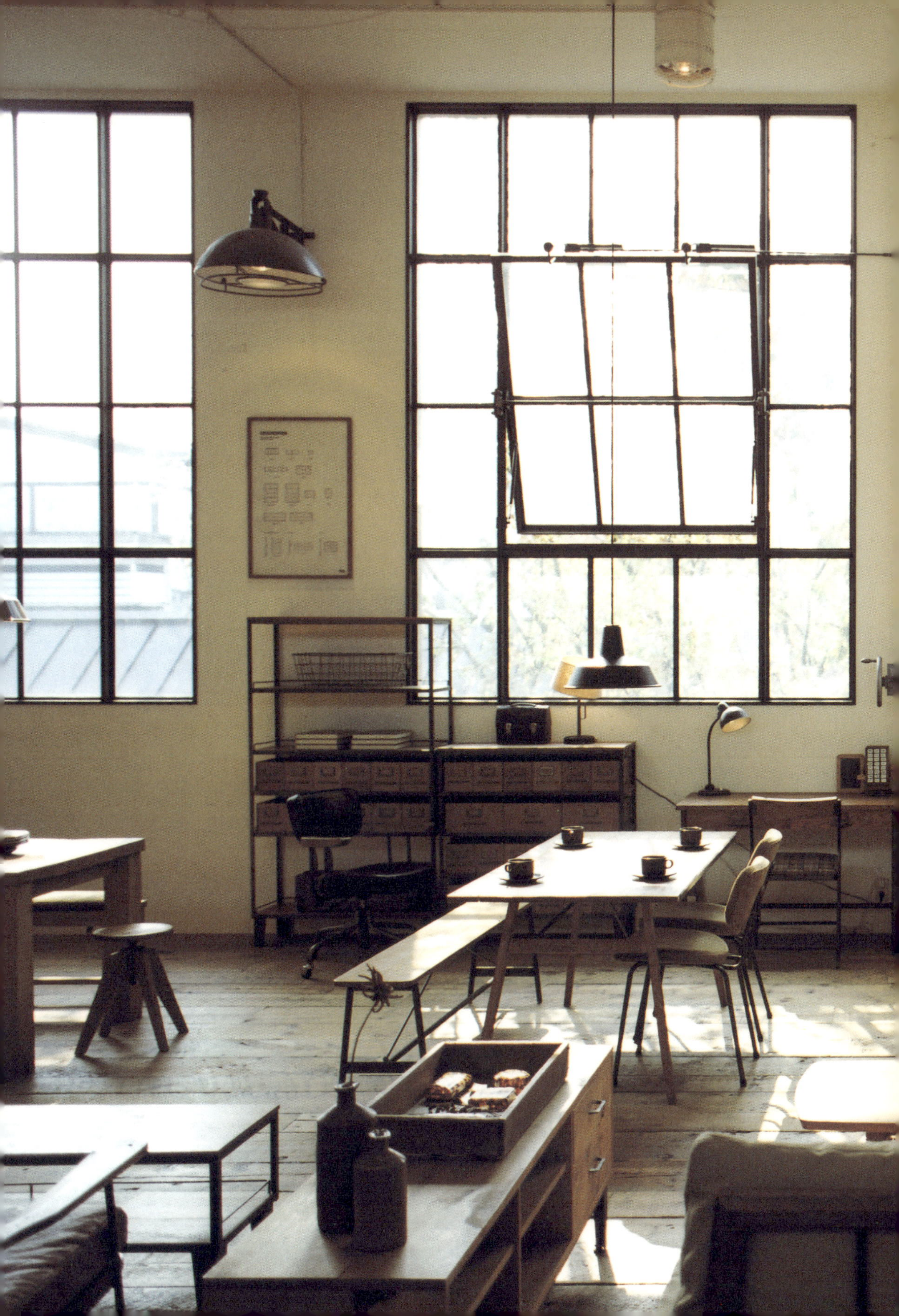

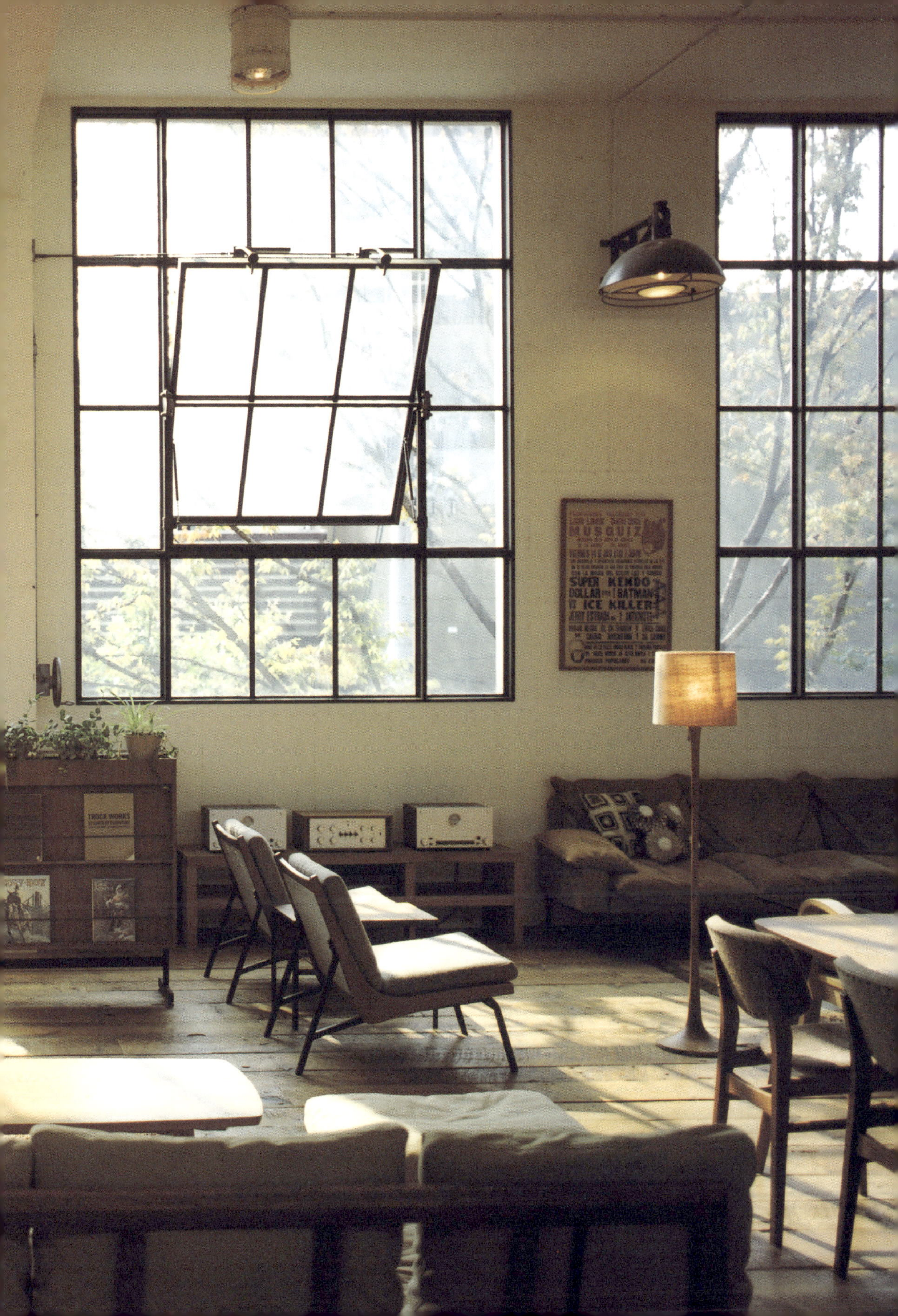

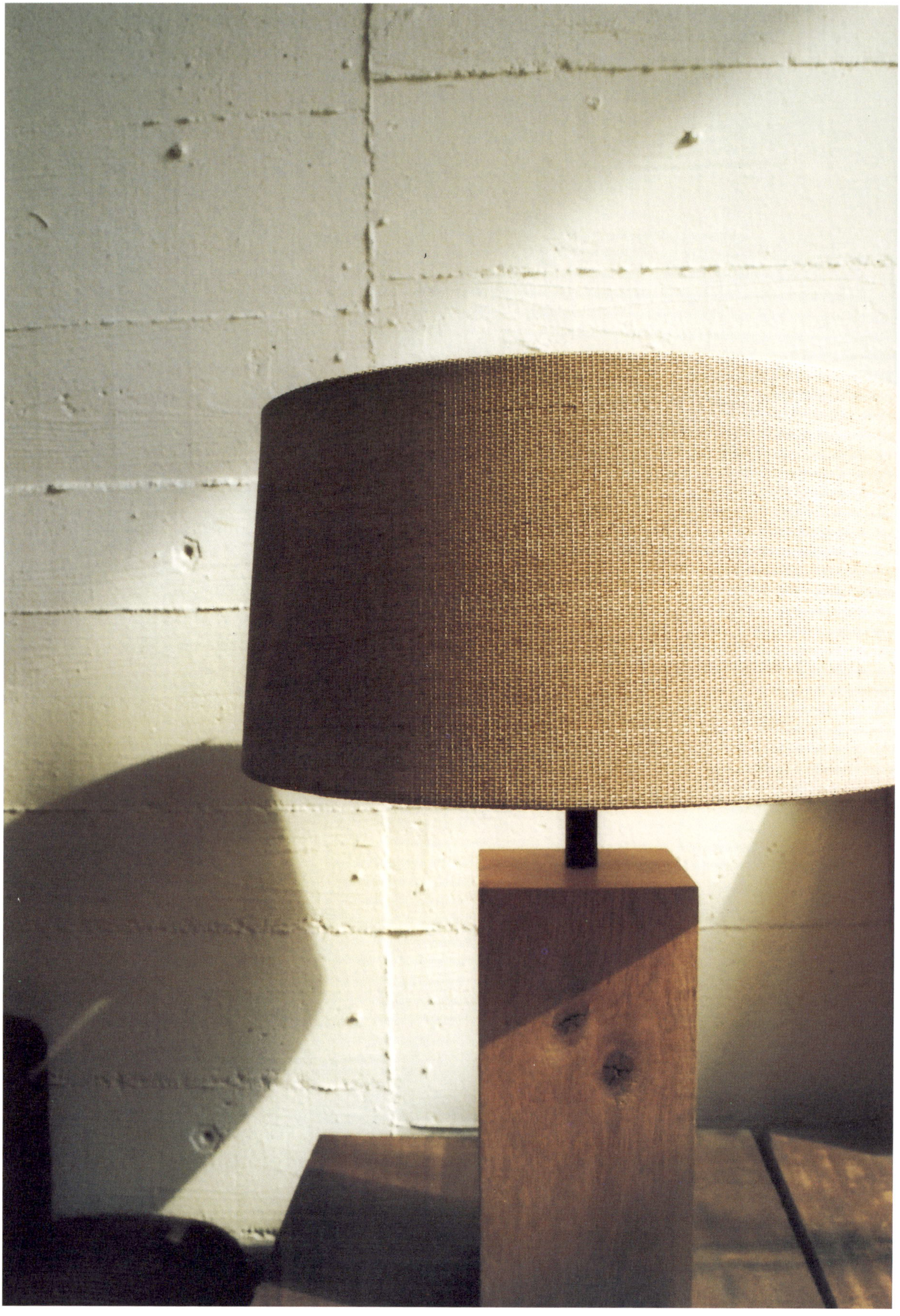

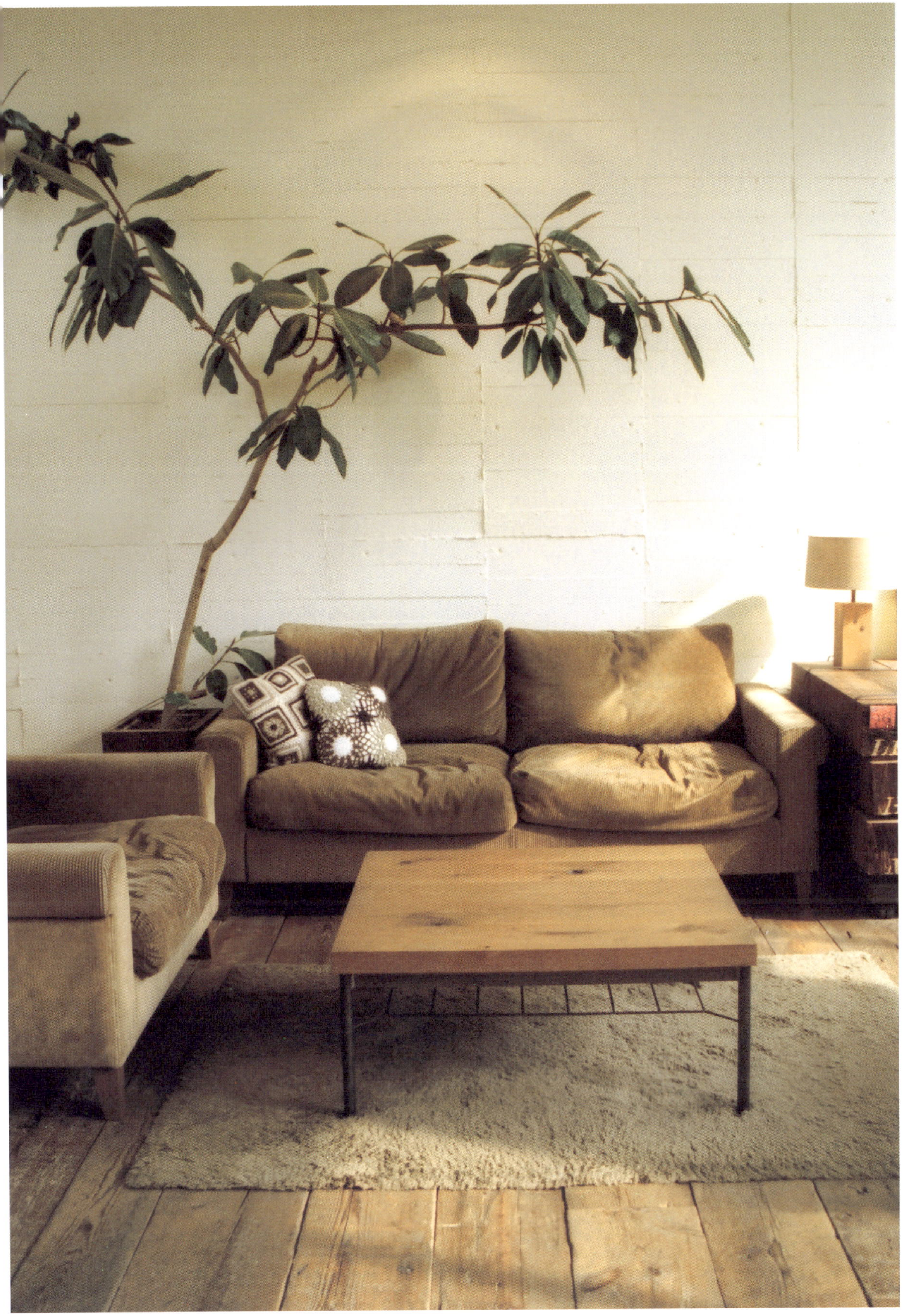

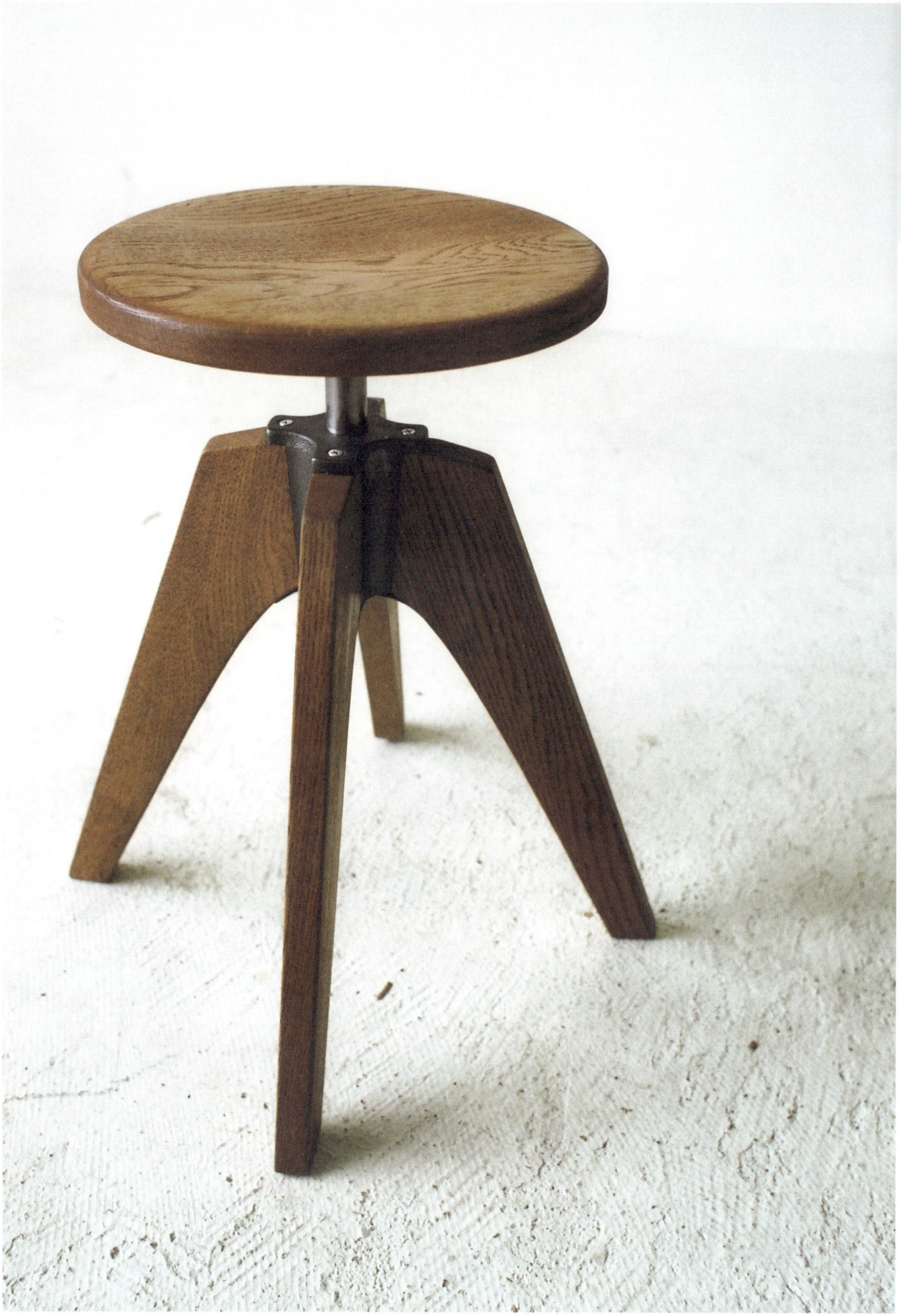

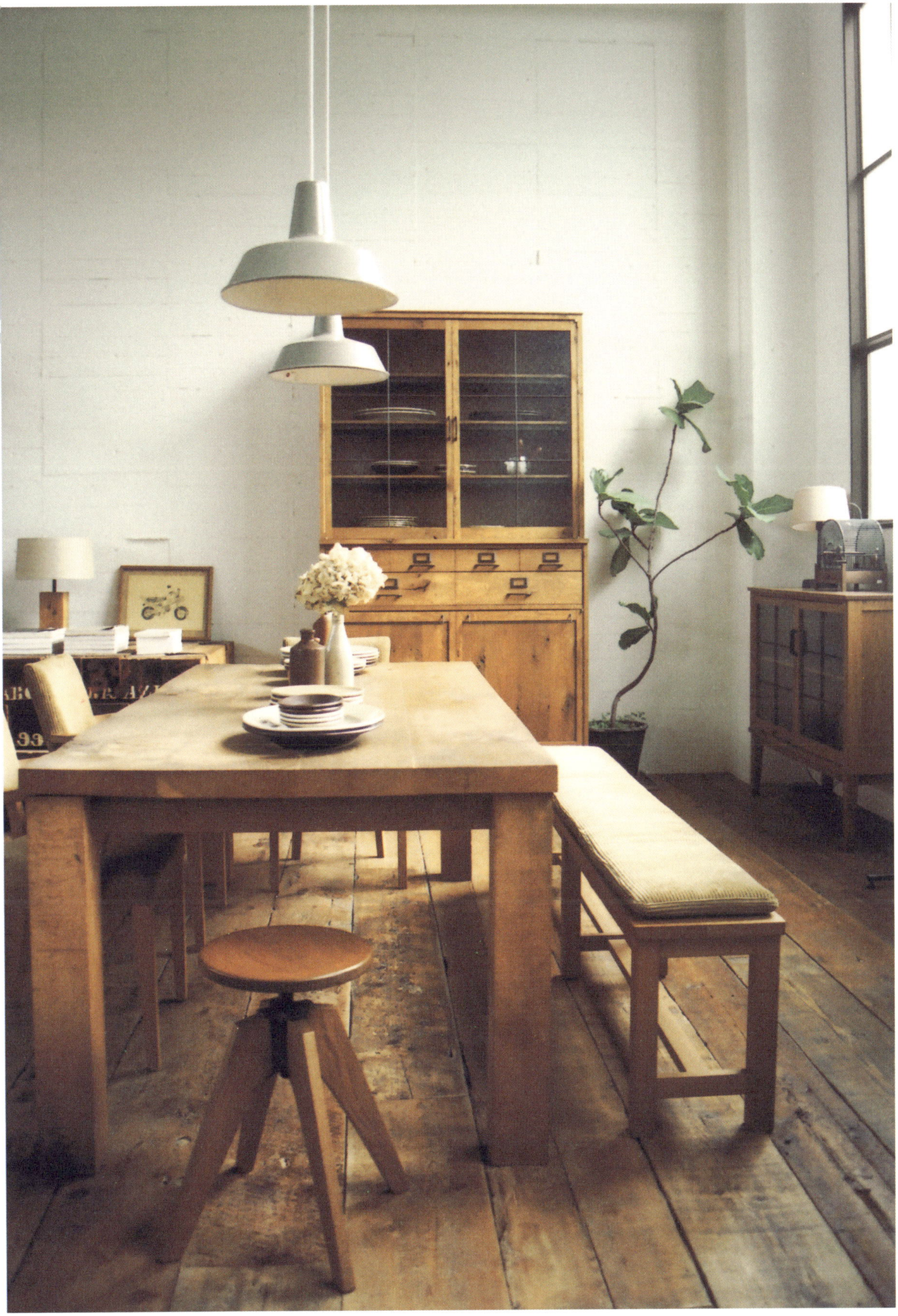

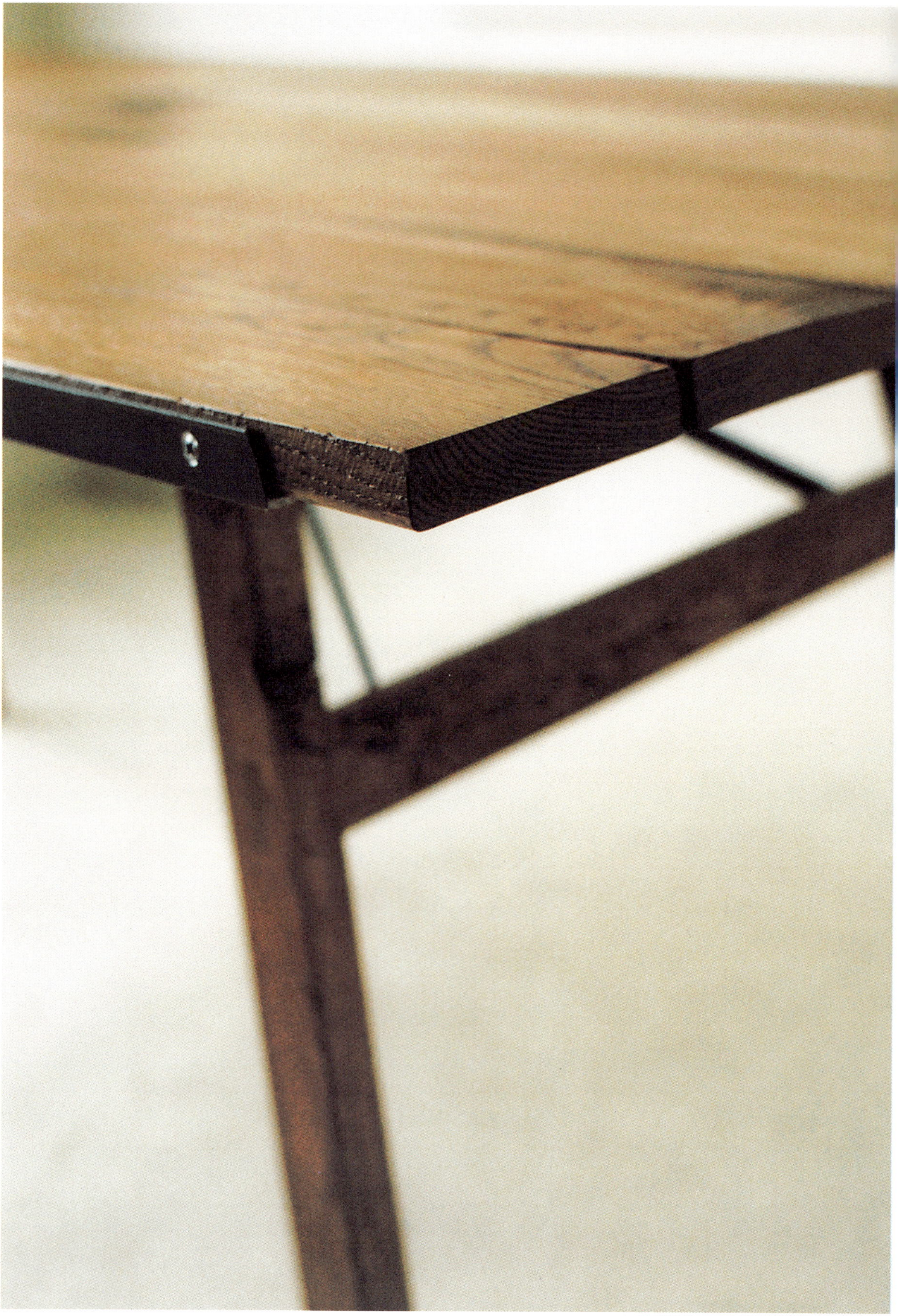

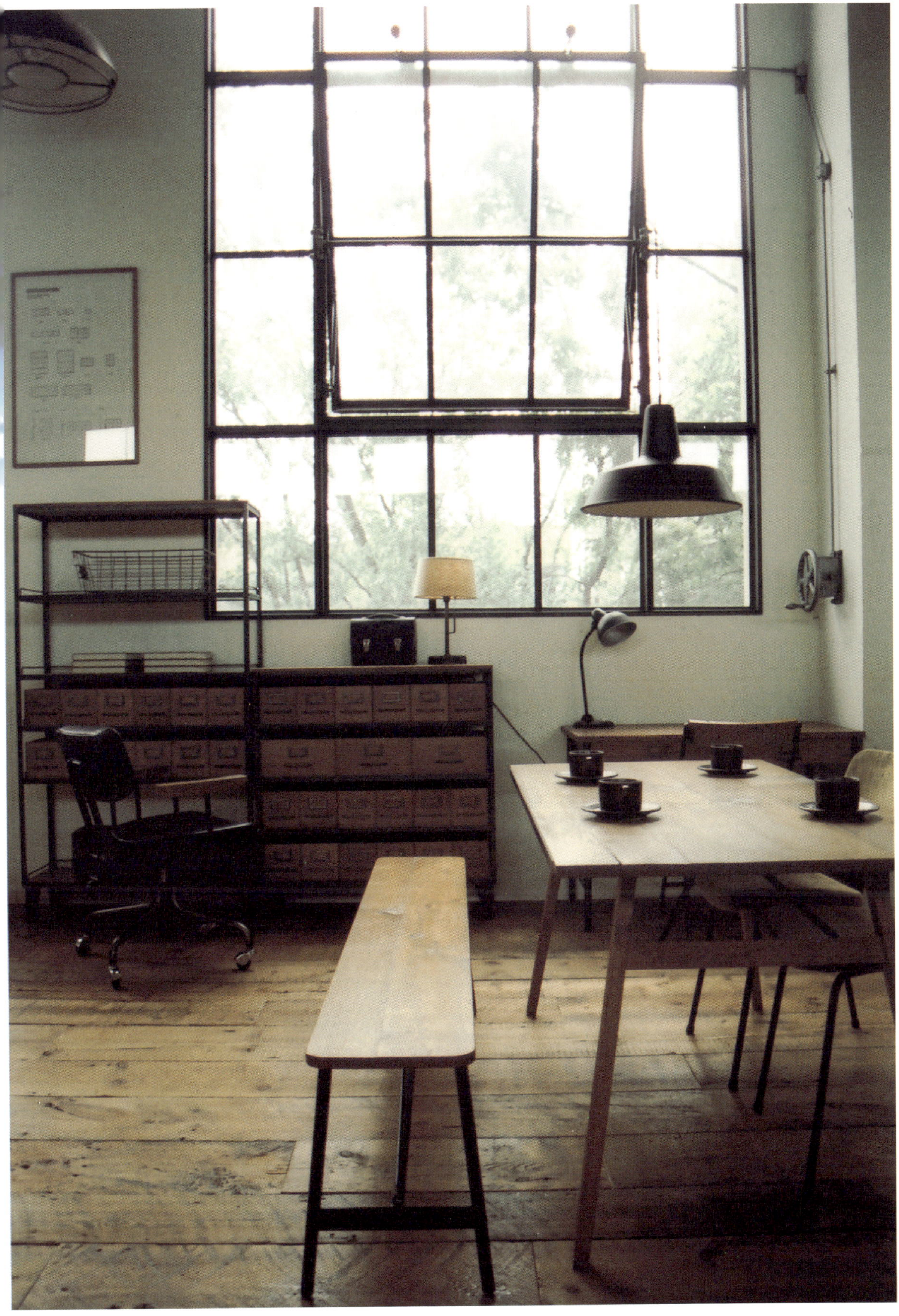

TRUCK FURNITURE
→ THIS IS BUDDY. TRUCK IS COMPLETELY UNDER HIS CONTROL.

TRUCK PRODUCTS
TRUCK PRODUCTS
TRUCK PRODUCTS
TRUCK PRODUCTS
TRUCK PRODUCTS

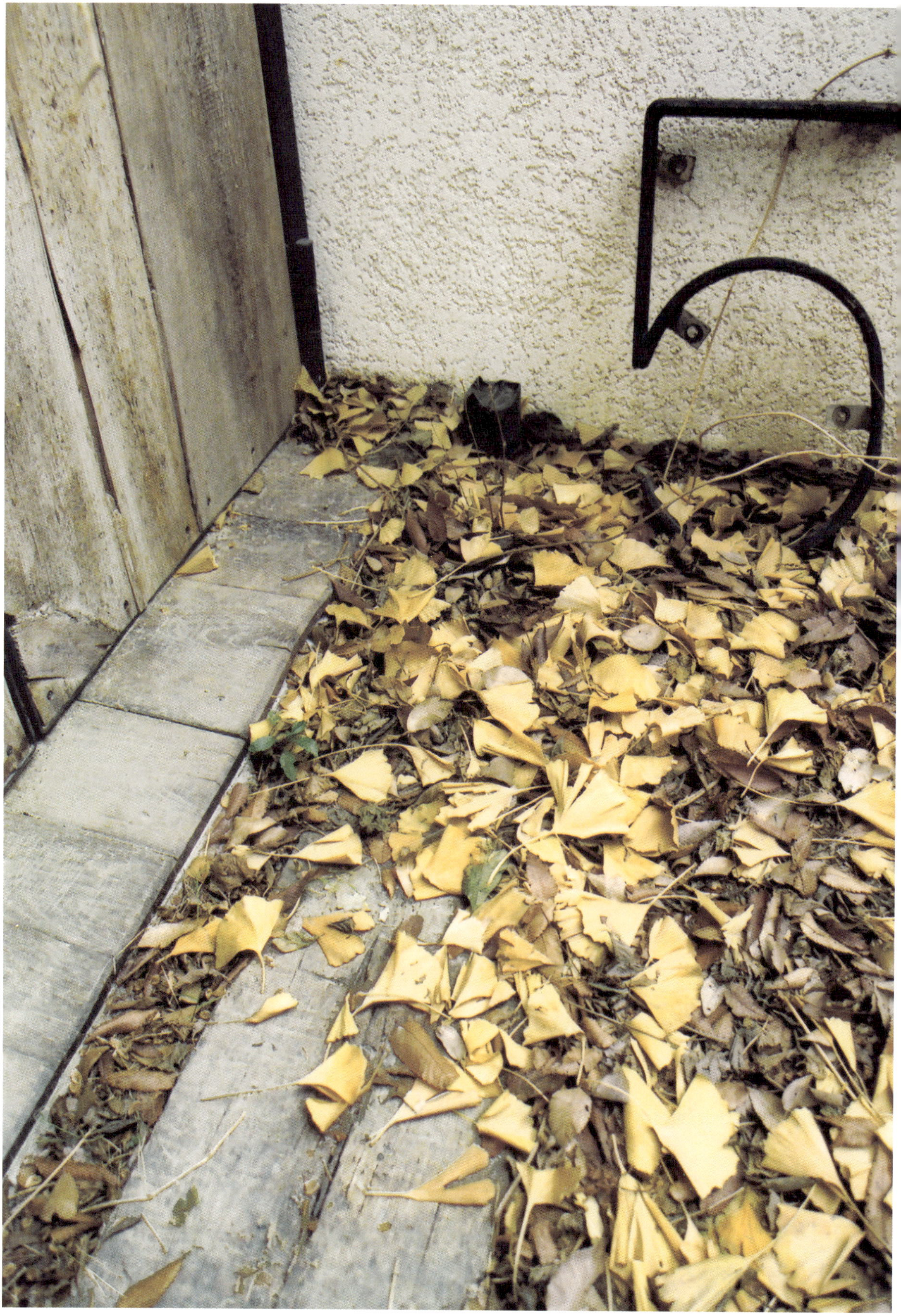

Bird COFFEE
Paper

www.bird-coffee.com

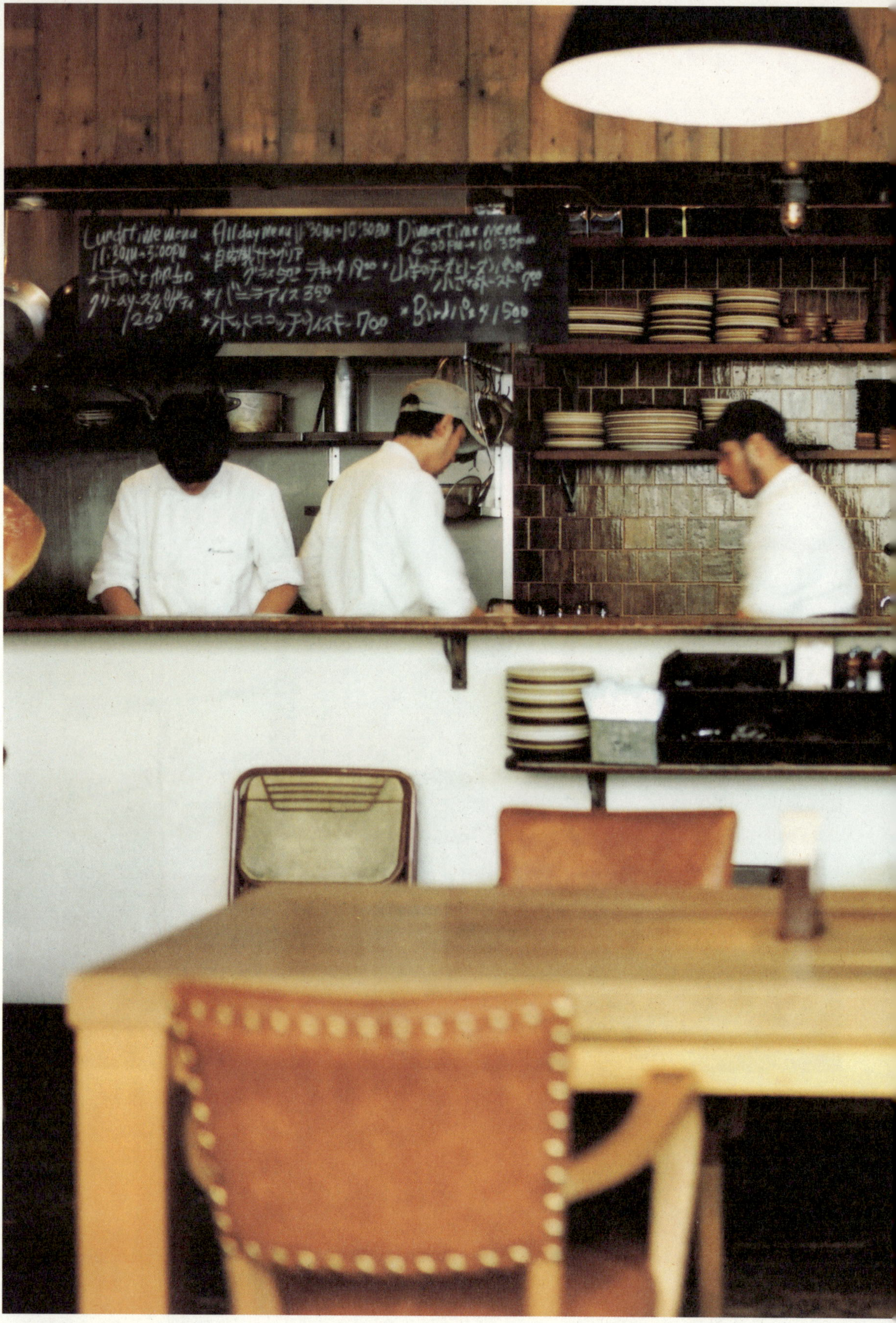
Lunchtime menu
All day menu
Dinnertime menu

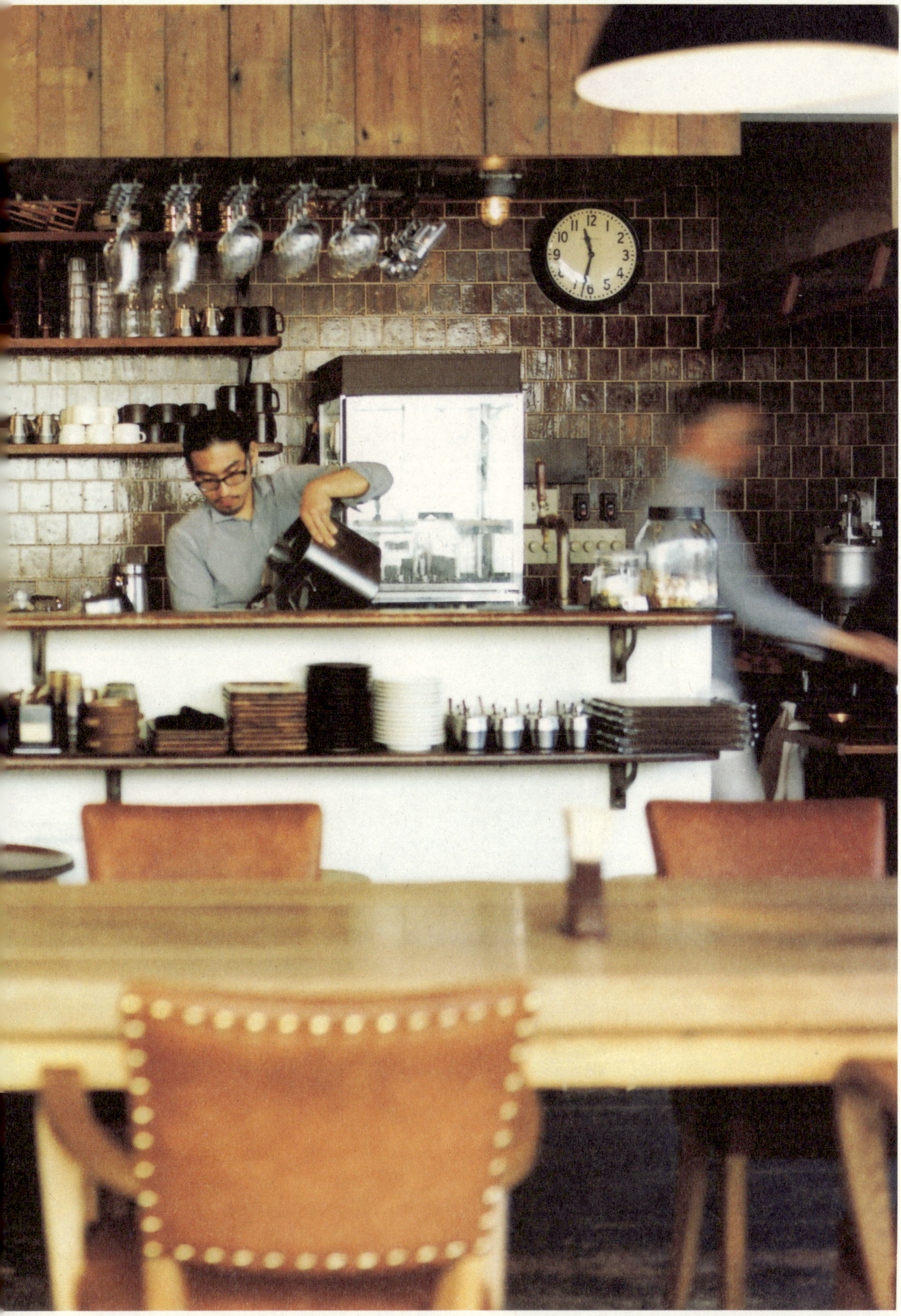

Bird Paper

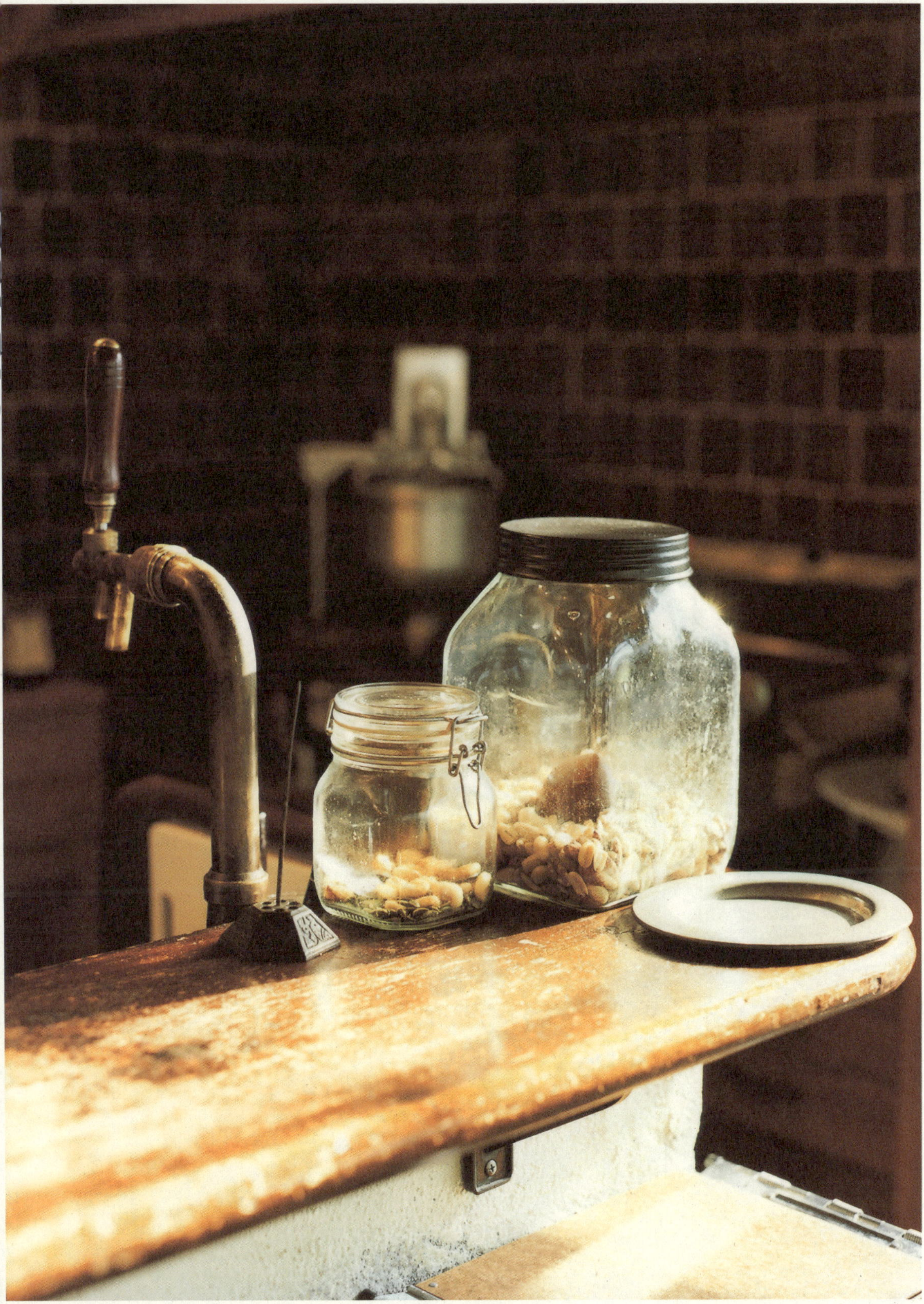

Bird COFFEE

OPEN
11:30AM-10:30PM
CLOSED
TUESDAY
1st,3rd WEDNESDAY

Birdのこと

カフェがやりたかったのではない。衣食住を提案したいとかでも全くない。提案なんてしたことない。本当は、畑違いの飲食店の経営なんてしたくなかった。ただ、わざわざ来てくれるお客さんに、ちょっと座ってもらえる場所が欲しかった。

玉造に店があった頃。TRUCKの斜め前にあったバス停。そのベンチに座ってTRUCKのカタログを見ながら相談しているお客さんの姿をよく見た。はるばる遠くから（近くからでも）来て家具を買うなんて大きな買い物、お客さんにとっては一世一代的な決断事。僕たちも、気持ちをリセットしてよーく考えてもらったほうがいいと思っていた。ちょっと座って休憩できる場所があったらいいのになぁと、ずっと思っていた。
TRUCKを始めた頃、世間はまさにカフェブーム。でも天の邪鬼な僕たちは、そんな簡単に異業種に手は出さない。遊びに来た友達にコーヒーをいれるのとはわけが違う。やるからには中途半端なものは嫌だった。
新しく店を考えている時も、ずっとそのことを考えていた。バス停のベンチがいつも頭にあった。最初は、セルフサービスのコーヒーを置き、休憩できるスペースを店の中に作ろうと考えた。いく通りも絵を描いてみた。でも、機械で作って保温されて煮詰まったコーヒーなんて嬉しくない。じゃあ自動販売機？なんてことも考えた。

そして、もうひとつずっと頭にあったもの。ドーナツ。
2003年に初めてヌーサに行った時、大きなスーパーの前にあったチェーン店のドーナツ屋。そこで見たドーナツマシン。ケンタロウとひりんこと3人。大の大人がガラスにへばりついて釘づけになった。1mほどの油のプールにポトンとタネが落とされ、ぷかぷか流れて行き、半分地点でパタンと見事に裏返る。そこで全員絶叫。その後、残りの距離を流れて行き最後に坂を上ってポトンとお皿に落ちる。その動きに3人の心は鷲掴まれた。「欲しい！」えっ？ドーナツマシンが？なぜか3人同時にそう思った。でもそんなもの一般家庭にあってもしょうがない。「やっぱり、ケンタロウ事務所でいるんちゃう？」「そらやっぱりTRUCKやろ」なんて6年間も言い合っていた。ヌーサに行く度に見に行っていた。

家具屋の中に突然、ドーナツマシンと自動販売機のコーヒー？なんかイマイチ。で、誰がドーナツマシンの相手するん？？
どうせやったらご飯も食べたい。ちょっとビールも。それやったらワインも。自分たちやスタッフにとっても、嬉しくおいしい場所になったほうがいいんちゃう？
こうなったら、中途半端に店の一角にスペースを作るんじゃなくて、向かいに建てる予定の倉庫の1階をカフェにしよう。と、どんどん話は盛り上がり、なんだかちゃんとした店を作ることになってきた。そんなこんなで紆余曲折あり、ケンタロウに相談した。いつもいろんな所で一緒にご飯を食べてきた。お互いの好みもよく分かっている。そしてケンタロウが料理監督になった。やっと、思い続けてきた場所が形になる。

初めてのBirdミーティング。ケンタロウもやって来た。メニューのことを話し合う。僕のイメージしているものがどうも洋にばかり走りがちだった。「○○定食ってのは違うなぁ」と僕は言った。ケンタロウはご飯粒も食べたいとの思い。ちょうどお昼時、ケンタロウが黄瀬家の冷蔵庫にあった材料を使ってみんなの昼ご飯を作ってくれた。白いご飯と、いろんな味付けのいろんな野菜や肉を一皿の上に盛った一品。おいしかった。ケンタロウは「ご飯を使ってもこんな風に見せれるで」とやってみせたのだ。これがBirdライスの原型となる。

料理人として決まったアッキーとタム。2人でケンタロウ事務所に1週間の泊まり込み合宿に行った。昼間はケンタロウの普段の仕事を傍らで見る。アシストできることはする。技術とかではなく、ケンタロウの思いや心意気を学ぶために。ちょっとでも、感覚的なところを吸収してほしいとの思いから。
夜中からはBirdのメニューの試作が始まる。まずは、ハンバーグ。今まで一緒に行ったいろんな旅先、時には大阪の僕の家でいく度となく食べてきたケンタロウのハンバーグ。カツ代さん直伝のそのハンバーグ。受け継いだ息子ケンタロウは僕とひりんこがいると、どんどん調子に乗って悪ふざけともいわんばかりに、そのサイズを大きくしていった。いつも大盛り上がり（ハンバーグのサイズも僕たちも）だった。もちろんすこぶるおいしい。
そのBird版を作ろうとなっていた。とにかくハンバーグを仕上げたら道が開けるとの思いで、ケンタロウ、アッキー、タムの3人は来る日も来る日もハンバーグ。1日何食もハンバーグ。明けても暮れてもハンバーグ。作っては食べ作っては食べ、時には他のお店のハンバーグも食べに行き。そしてついに完成した。
ケンタロウから電話があった。
「できた！ついにやったで。僕らのハンバーグ。愛情たっぷりのハンバーグ！」

Turkish Bread for Bird
blended wheat flour

Width 5", Height 2.5", Depth 4"··················Weight 5.1OZ

ケンタロウは、自分の料理を店に出すという話は今まで断ってきていたらしい。だからこのBirdに関わったこと、そこにはたくさんの愛情と思い入れがあった。アッキーとタムを、自分の息子か兄弟か、はたまた分身くらいの思いで向き合ってくれた。横で見ていてちょっと悔しいって思うくらい、料理人だけが分かるチーム感ができていった。

毎年みんなで行く、オーストラリアのヌーサ。地元のスーパーでステーキ肉を買って焼いて食べていた。その赤身のおいしさにいつも絶叫していた。その頃から僕たちは断然赤身派になっていた。そうだ、「あんなステーキが食べたい」となった時、ケンタロウは自分のノートをさっと取り出した。そこにはそのステーキの入っていたパッケージのラベル。ケンタロウはそれをちゃんと剥がして持っていたのだ。すごい。最高!けんちゃん。
そしてそのラベルをヒントに調べていくと、それは日本ではない部位。だけど、オーストラリア産の同じステーキ肉が仕入れられることが分かった。そうしてスコッチステーキがメニューに加わった。

ヌーサ続きで、サンドイッチ。よくランチに行っていた店がある。すごいボリュームでいろんな種類のサンドイッチが食べられる。とびきり最高!ってほどではないけどヌーサでは必ずその店に立ち寄った。そこで食べたパンのうちのひとつにターキッシュブレッドというのがあった。日本では馴染みがないが、ヌーサの街ではパン屋でもスーパーでも見かけるパン。それを思い出した。
ターキッシュといっても七面鳥とは関係なく、多分トルコ風のパンってことだと思う。厚みは7cmくらいあるけど、がぶっと噛むと、皮がサクッと軽く、中も軽い。噛み出して噛み終わるまでの間に立ち止まることがないような。そう、あのパン。あれが食べたい。

パンと言えばブランジュリタケウチのタケウチさん。(大阪にある大人気のパン屋さん)すぐに相談しに行った。
僕がサンドイッチの話を力説する。「ターキッシュ」と言った瞬間、タケウチさんの目の色が変わった。いつもパンのことを考えているタケウチさん。聞き慣れないパンの名前に、見ていて分かるほど、スイッチが入った。目の中に炎が上がっていた。ように見えた。
思い立ったら即行動したい僕と同じタイプのタケウチさん。今すぐにでも1泊でヌーサに食べに行こうかということになりかけた。でもとりあえず「1週間待って下さい。1回考えて作ってみます」となった。僕が見せたのは、テーブルの前に座っている日菜の写真。その傍らにかろうじて写り込んでいるパン。手がかりはそれだけ。

1週間後、電話があった。「できました」すぐに駆けつけると、2種類のサンドイッチがスタンバっていた。それらを見せながら「こっちがターキッシュという名前を元にひも解いて作ったもの。でも写真のものとは明らかに違います。で、もうひとつのほう、それは写真から見た目で考えて作ったものです」
食べてみた。前者、それはそれでおいしい。でも感触は思っているのとは違う。写真からのほう、それをがぶっと口に入れたとたん「そうそうこんな感じ!」となった。ヌーサで食べた時の感触味覚嗅覚聴覚それら全部が舞い戻る。恐るべしタケウチさん。
(「パンの表面の色から材料を、横に写り込んでいるフォークなどの大きさからパンの厚みを、想像で作った」タケウチさん談)
その日からさらに何度も実験と試食(東京にいるケンタロウにもその都度送って)を重ね、現地のとは見た目も違うBirdのターキッシュサンドが完成した。
ありがとう。タケウチさん。カッコいい!勉強になります。

メニュー作りと並行して、店の工事とBirdで使うお皿やコーヒーカップの制作も進める。Birdなんて想像もしていなかった時から、自分が欲しくて進めていたマグカップ。1年以上も試行錯誤が続いていた。なかなか思った色と質感が出なかった。
ようやくできたマグカップ。その延長でBirdのお皿とコーヒーカップを作った。業務用のような厚み感。でも色は白ではなく茶系のグラデーション。これらもまた何度も試作を繰り返す。
そしてできたお皿はしっかり重い。Birdのスタッフの腕は逞しくなっていく。

店の工事も半年以上続いた。図面は1枚もない。ひとつずつ考え、作りながらまた考える。その繰り返し。断片的なイメージをつなぎ合わせながら、何度もやり直し、だんだんと形にしていった。大きな窓から、大きな樹が見える。店に入るのに、樹の下を通る。TRUCKのテーブルと椅子をここで実際に使ってもらえる。
ちょっとした本棚も作ろう。
さらに欲しい要素として、薪ストーブは欠かせない。TRUCKの工場で毎日出る木っ端。しっかり乾燥したオーク。今までゴミとして捨てるしかなかった。それが燃料として生かせる。わざわざ薪を買ってくるのではなく、捨てられていたものが暖かさに変わる。それだけで嬉しい。

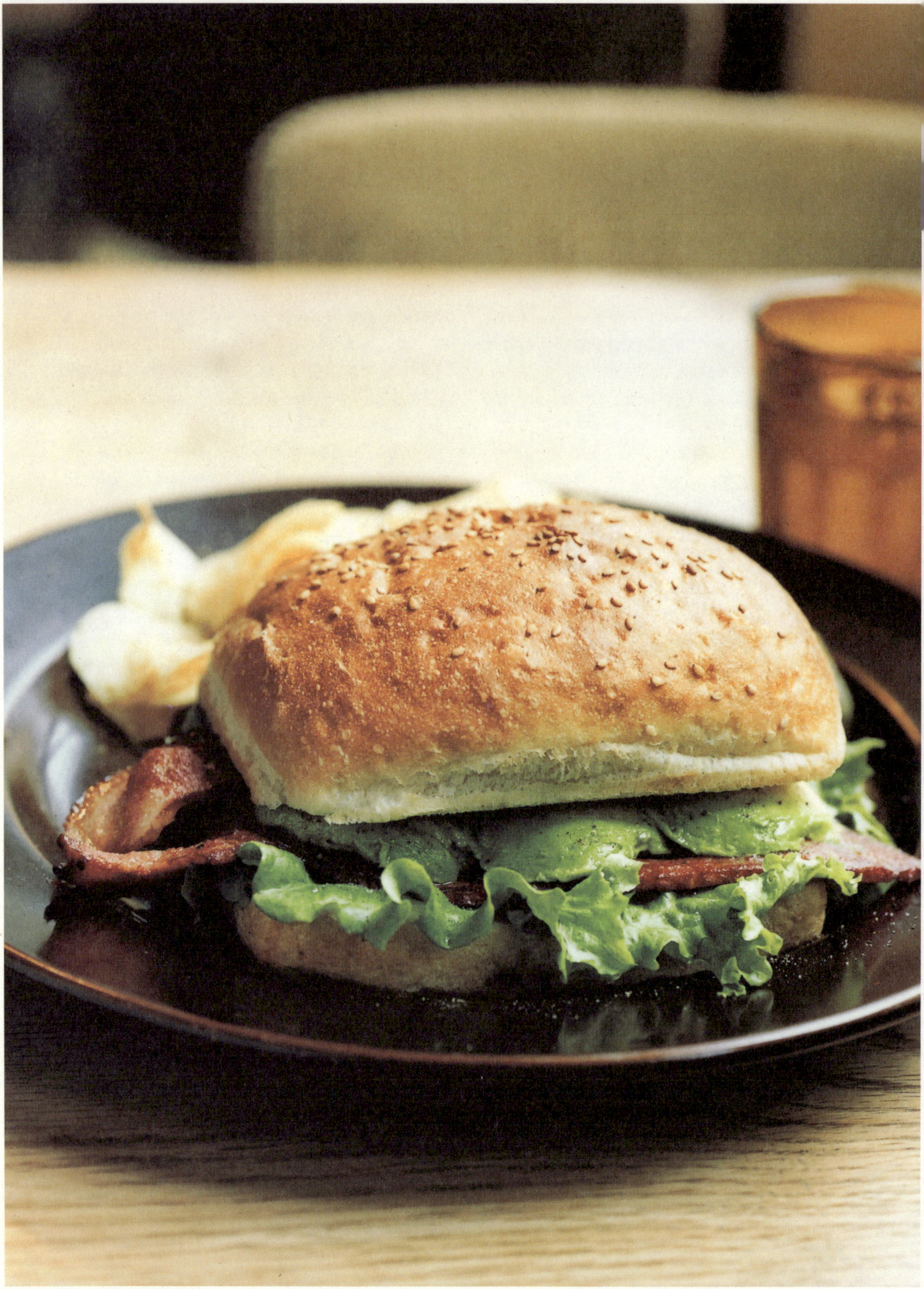

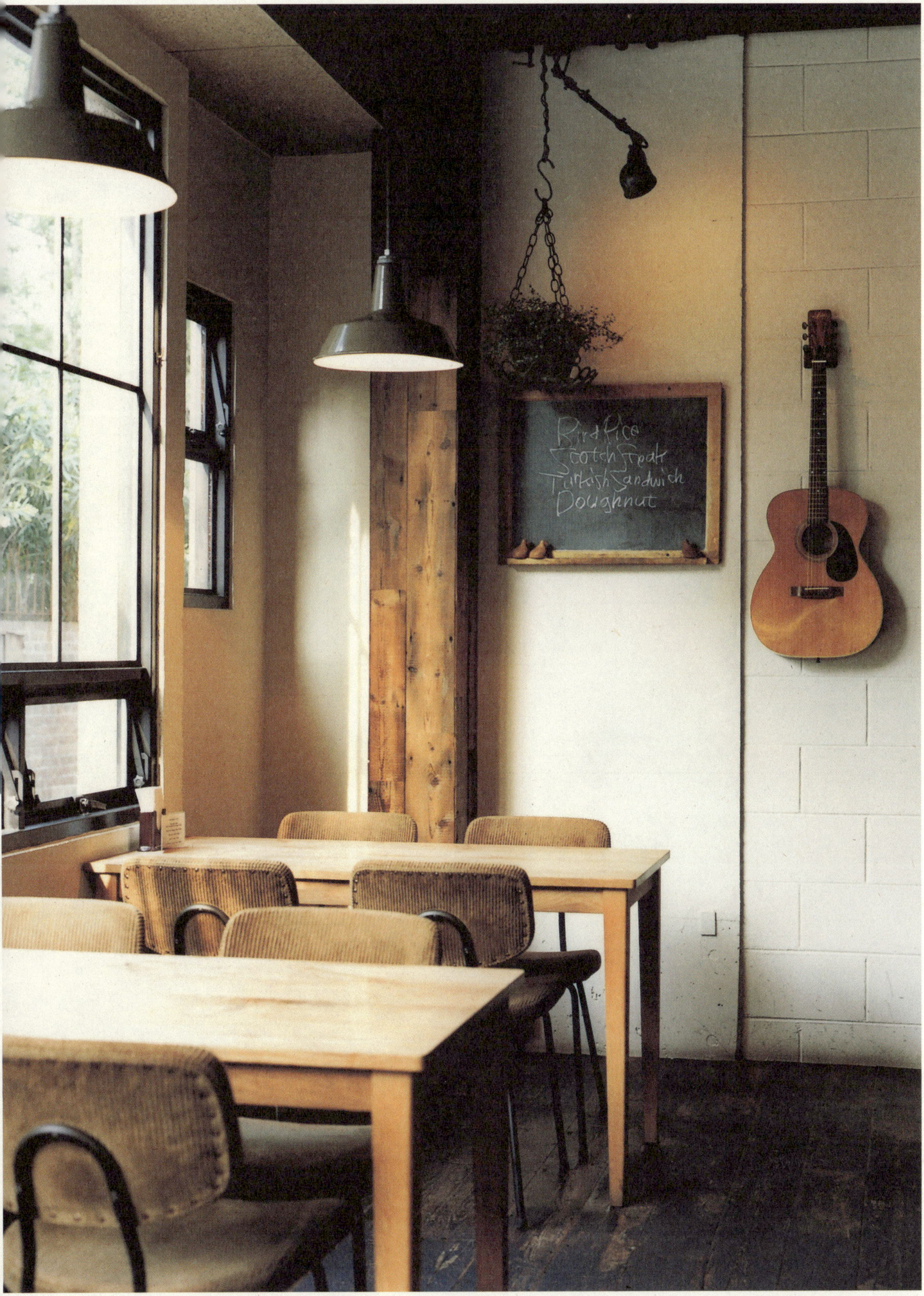
Bird Rice
Turkish Sandwich
Doughnut

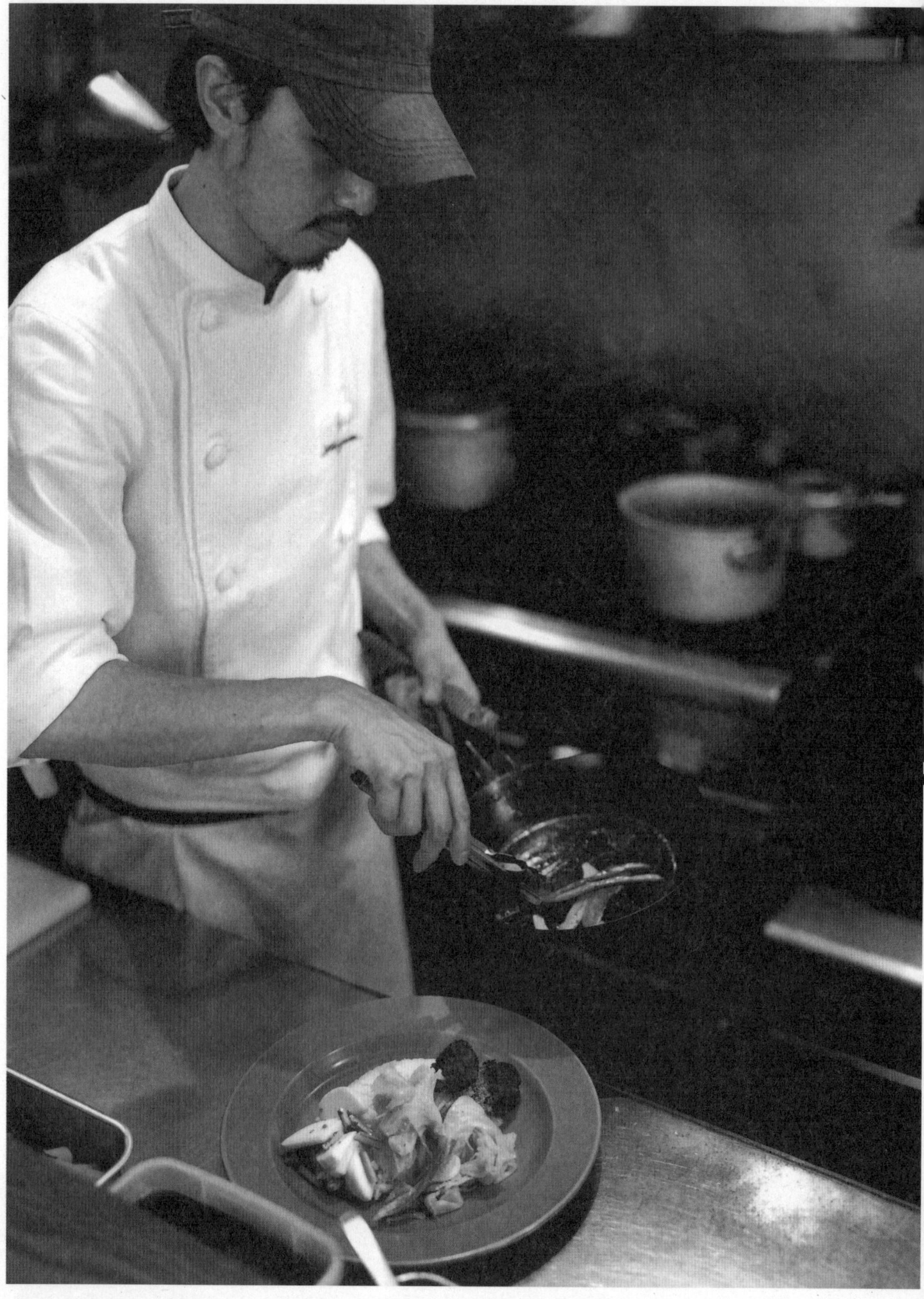

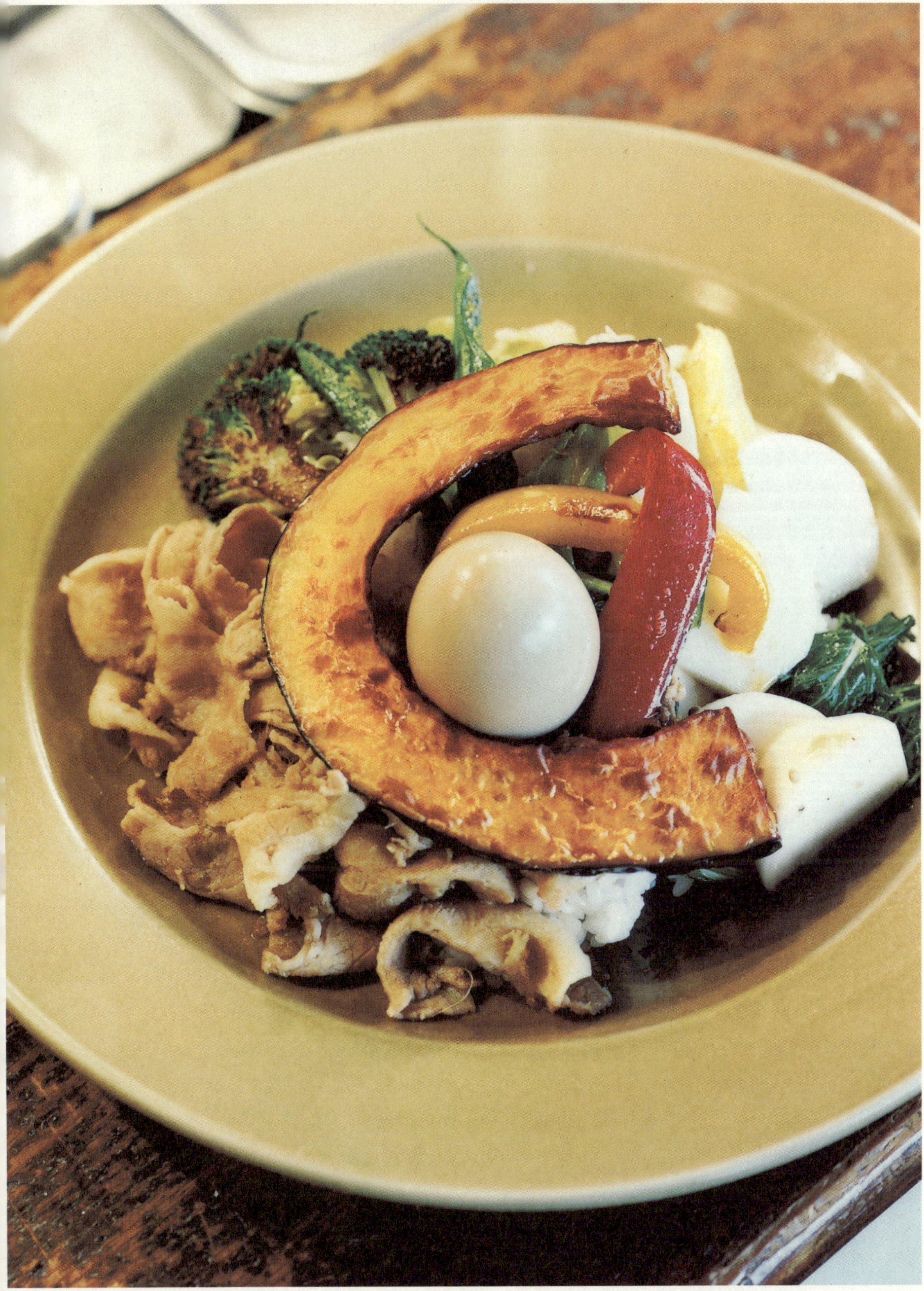

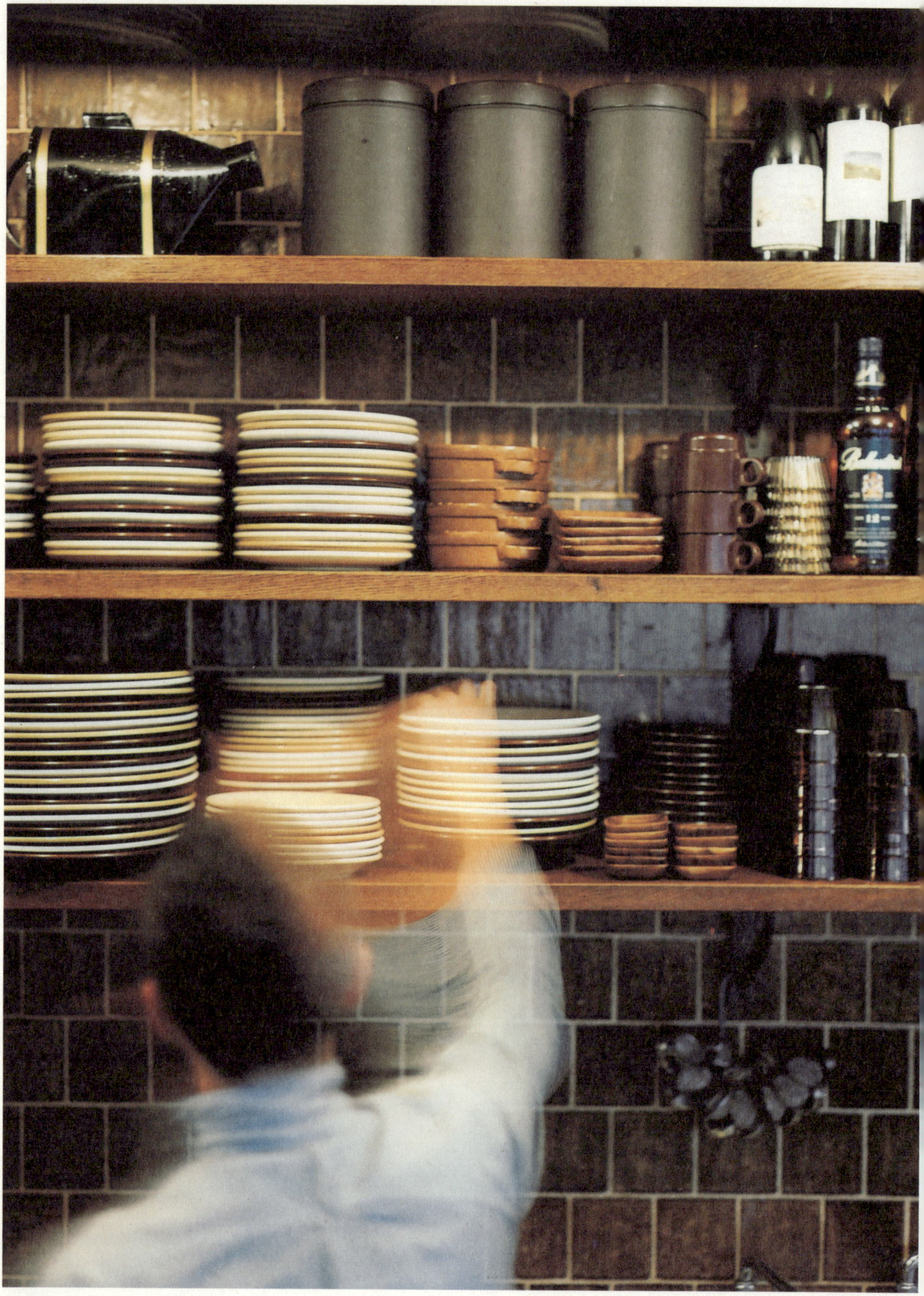

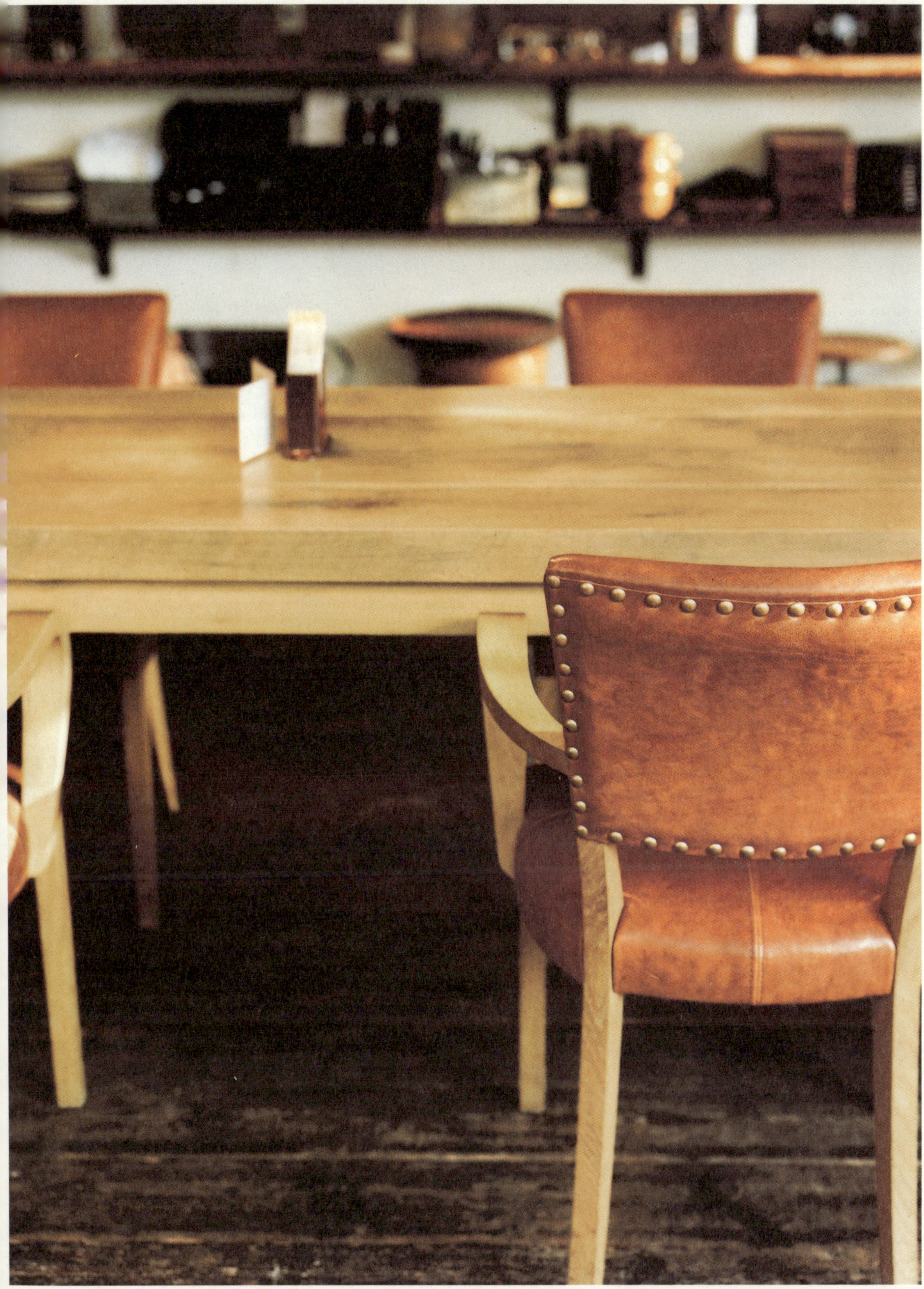

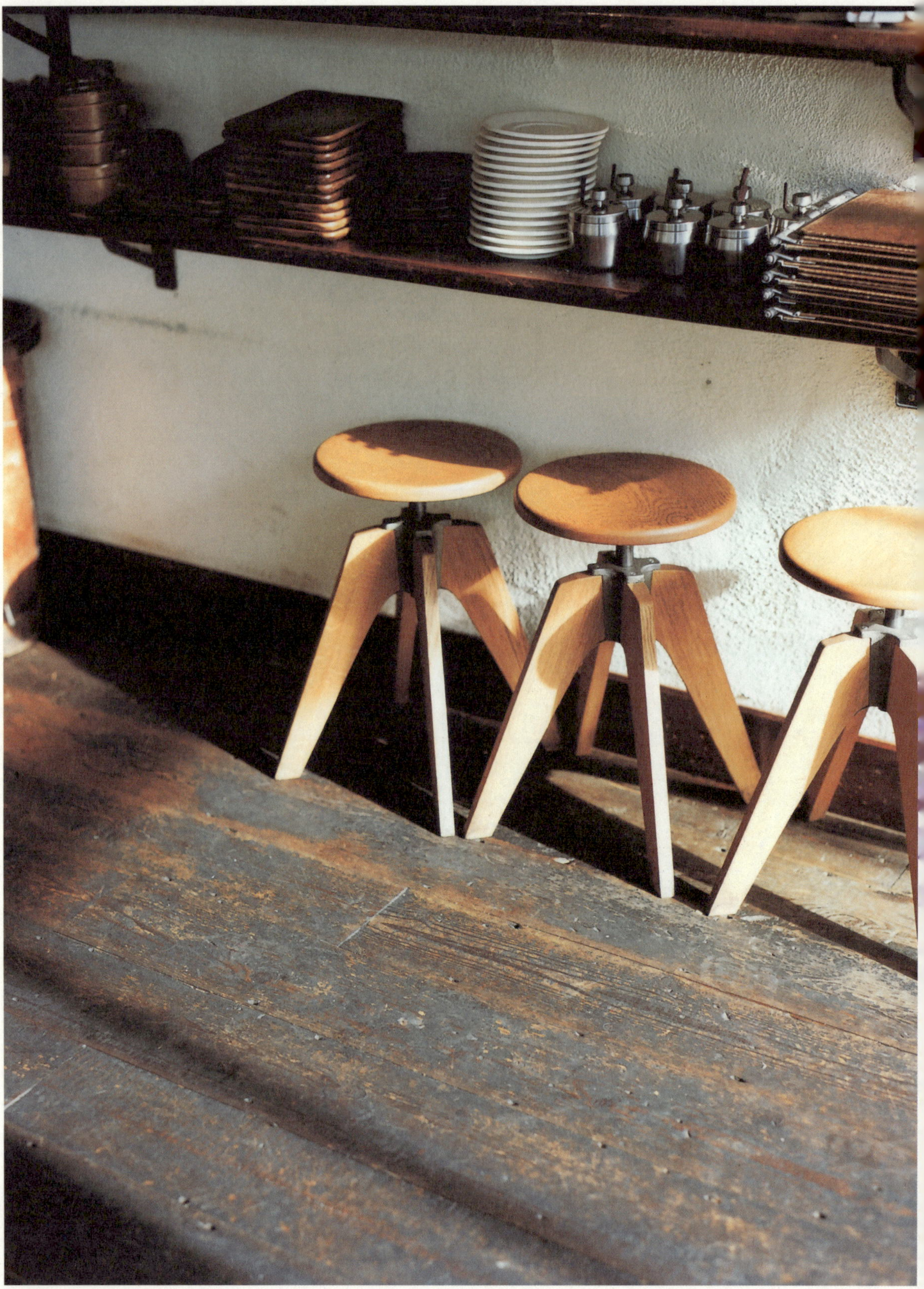

I didn't start Bird because I wanted to start a café. I'd never dreamed or hoped to be in the restaurant business. It was simply that I wanted a space for people who came to our shop to be able to sit down for a while.
In front of our shop in Tamatsukuri there was a bus stop. I often saw couples or families sitting on the bench there poring over our catalog. Many of them had come from very far away and deciding to buy a piece of furniture is a once in a lifetime decision. Basically, I wanted to create a space where they could sit down and think in a relaxed manner. At the time we opened TRUCK there was something of a café boom in Japan, with new shops popping up all over the place, but we weren't interested ourselves. We didn't want to do anything half-baked and running a café is very different from making a cup of coffee for your friends.

While I was planning the new store, the image of customers sitting at that bus stop remained in the back of my mind. At first I considered setting up a little relaxation zone in the store with a self-serve coffee machine. I drew up a few concepts, but I never really liked the idea of serving our customers stale, warmed over coffee made by a machine. "Perhaps we could install a vending machine," I thought.

There was another thing on my mind: doughnuts. On my first trip to Noosa I'd seen a doughnut machine in action outside a supermarket. I'd stood, with Kentaro and Hiromi, our noses pressed to the glass, watching it in operation. Seeing the dough drop into the hot oil, flow along, do a flip halfway, ascend the little escalator and finally drop into the draining basket. After seeing this, we longed to own one. It was, of course, an absurd idea. No house needs a doughnut machine. "Don't you need one for Kentaro Studio?" I often half-seriously suggested. "No, you need it for TRUCK." he replied, joking. This back and forth went on for six years.

I briefly considered setting up the doughnut machine and a vending machine, but I soon realized that I'd need someone to operate the machine. I decided that if I was going to do it, I wanted to do it properly. I abandoned the idea of setting aside a corner of the shop and set about planning a proper café. In addition to coffee and doughnuts, we would have good food, good beer and good wine. Although I knew nothing about the restaurant business, I was fortunate to have the assistance of my friend Kentaro, who was eager to help. He had been approached many times to set up or collaborate on a restaurant, but had so far been reluctant. To have his help was an enormous advantage.

At the first Bird meeting, Kentaro and I discussed the menu. I was pretty sure that I wanted it to be mainly western food. I had no desire to serve anything like a traditional Japanese set lunch with rice and miso soup. Kentaro thought people might also like to have rice, but I was reluctant to consider it. As we talked, it was nearing lunchtime. Kentaro went to our kitchen and started preparing lunch using whatever ingredients he could find in our fridge and cupboards. What he came up with was some variously seasoned vegetables and meat served on the same plate with white rice. "See," he said "rice can look like this, too." And so Bird Rice was born.

I sent Aki and Tamu, the two guys I'd chosen as chefs to go to Tokyo and work with Kentaro for a week.

During the day they helped him with his regular work. It wasn't so much that I wanted them to pick up any special techniques. I wanted them to see how he approached cooking and food, and hopefully to absorb some of his food sense.

One of the dishes we most liked Kentaro to cook for us was *Hamburg steak*, a popular Japanese dish, similar to Salisbury steak made with ground meat, egg, chopped onions and breadcrumbs. He used a recipe passed down to him from his mother (Katsuyo Kobayashi, a famous celebrity chef) that made it possible to make them really big. Basically it involved adding bit of water to the pan. As the *Hamburg steak* cooked, it absorbed the steam, ensuring that no matter how big it was, the inside was properly cooked. We sometimes fooled around making them bigger and bigger. Kentaro decided that, in making the Bird menu, and preparing Aki and Tamu to cook it, he would start by getting the *Hamburg steak* perfected. He worked with them first to develop a good, consistent recipe, then had them practice over and over again. The week they spent with Kentaro was like visiting a country with only one dish: *Hamburg steak*. They cooked and ate them for breakfast. They cooked and ate them for dinner. Sometimes they went to other restaurants and ate their versions. They made them many times until they were finally ready.
Then I got a call from Kentaro " The *Hamburg steak* is ready!" he said "It's full of love!"

Until that time, Kentaro had resisted the pressure to open a restaurant serving food he had created. He was happy creating recipes for his books. When he got involved in creating Bird, he poured all his passion and energy into it. He was clearly proud of the way Aki and Tamu had developed and worked together. When I saw the three of them working in the kitchen it was clear that they shared a special bond. He treated them like an older brother more than a trainer or boss. It was hard not to feel a little like an outsider.

Another thing I was sure I wanted on the menu was steak. In the supermarket in Noosa we often bought delicious lean cuts of beef that Kentaro would grill on the barbecue. Whenever we ate it, we realized how much we preferred lean beef to the fattier kinds that are more popular in Japan.

I mentioned to Kentaro that we should have that on the menu too, but I couldn't remember the exact name. To my surprise, he took his notebook from his bag, opened it up, and there was the label from the meat package. He had carefully peeled it off and put it away for future reference. Good stuff, Ken.

We looked around for a similar kind of steak in Japan, but couldn't find one. We finally found a meat supplier who could import them from Australia and Scotch Steak joined the Bird menu.

Another thing I remembered from Noosa was an excellent sandwich shop we always used to go to. They had a large variety of sandwiches with many different fillings and kinds of bread. We made sure to go there at least once every time we visited.
There was one kind of bread that we particularly liked: Turkish Bread. In Australia it was nothing special. You can find it in any bakery or supermarket, but nothing like it is available in Japan. It had a crispy but light crust so you could bite through it easily. "That bread," I thought," I want to eat that."

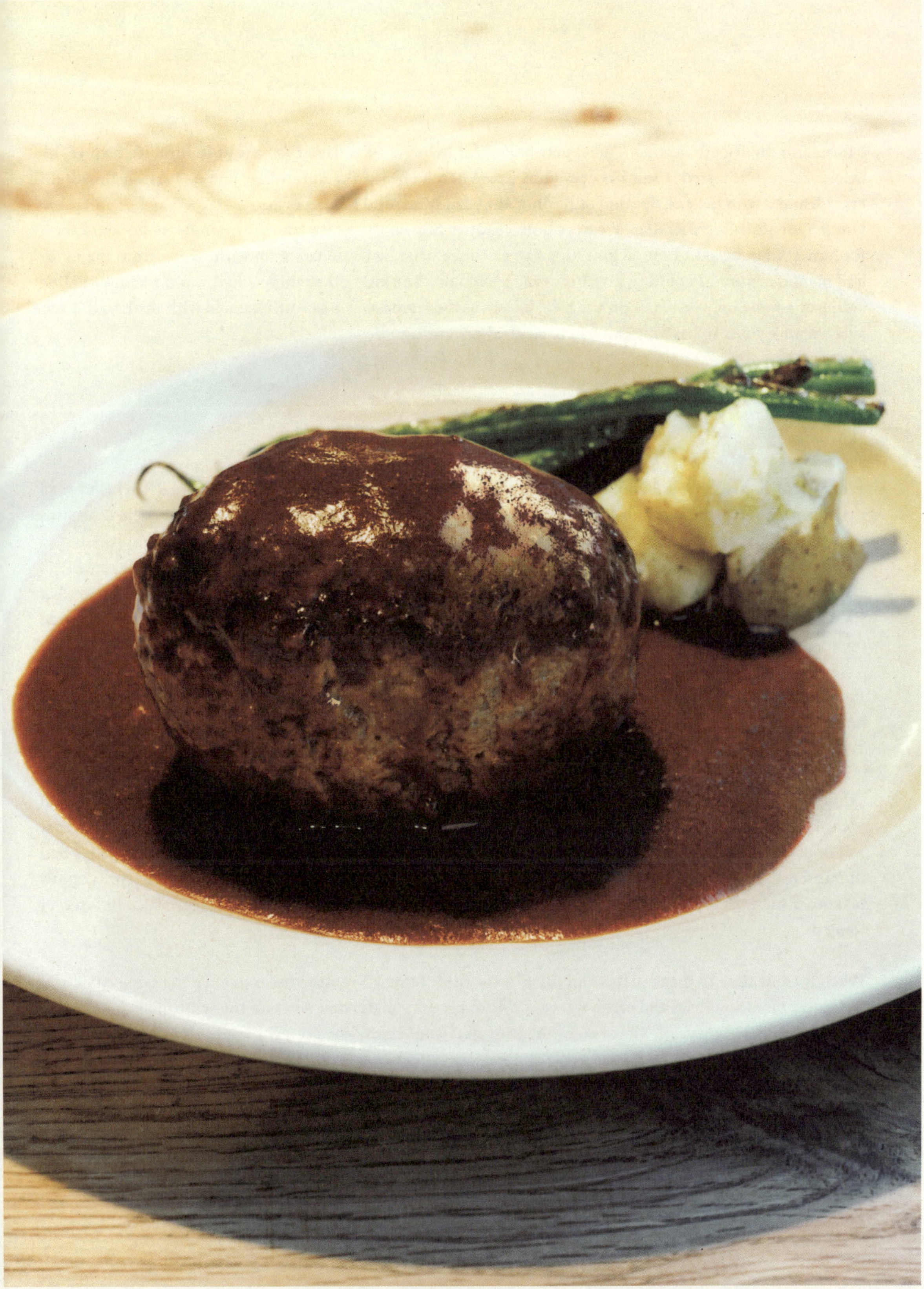

I turned to my friend Takeuchi, an expert baker, for help. As I described the bread to him, it's texture, it's color, and how it tasted, I saw his eyes light up. When he heard the unfamiliar name, Turkish Bread, his eyes gleamed with the anticipation of finding out what it was and how to make it.

Our personalities were similar. We were both ready to hop on the next plane down under so he could try it for himself, but he asked me to give him a week to see what he could come up with. Aside from the name and my description, I couldn't give him much to go on. The only other thing I had was a picture of Hina sitting at a table in Noosa. Off on the side, barely in the frame, was a sandwich made with the bread. I was sure we were going to have make a trip to Australia.

A week later I got a call from Takeuchi.

"I'm done."

When I got to his kitchen I found two sandwiches waiting for me. The first one was real Turkish bread made from a recipe he'd found. It obviously looked different to the one I'd told him about. The other was the result of his experiments in trying to match what he saw in the photo.

I tried the first one. It was delicious, but not what I was looking for. I tried the second one. "Takeuchi!" I thought "You're amazing!" It tasted just like the bread I'd eaten in Australia. To this day I'm still amazed at what he'd been able to make with so little information. He told me that he'd guessed at the ingredients based on the color of the bread in the photo. The size he'd estimated by looking at the fork that was next to it.

It was great, but Takeuchi was sure he could make it even better. After a lot more trial and error (and some help from Kentaro), we came up with the bread we would use in the Bird Turkish Sandwich. Thank you, Takeuchi.

While we were putting the menu together we were building the restaurant and preparing all the cups and utensils. A few years before, I'd wanted to make some cups for our family to use. I wanted something that was of professional grade, that could be used without worrying about it getting cracked or chipped. I had in mind a simple shape with a particular brown gradation. It took over a year of working with various tableware manufacturers before I could find someone who was able to consistently reproduce the color I wanted.

When it came time to make plates and the like for Bird, I knew I wanted them to have the same color and feel. After months of trial and error, we were able to produce plates and bowls of the same quality. They had the same solid, weighty feel. The arms of the Bird staff would certainly get a workout.

The interior construction of Bird took more than six months. Rather than drawing up blueprints, we worked inside the shop simulating a layout that would be practical and look the way we wanted. If there was something that we thought was unsatisfactory, we moved everything out and started again. After doing this many times, the interior gradually took shape.

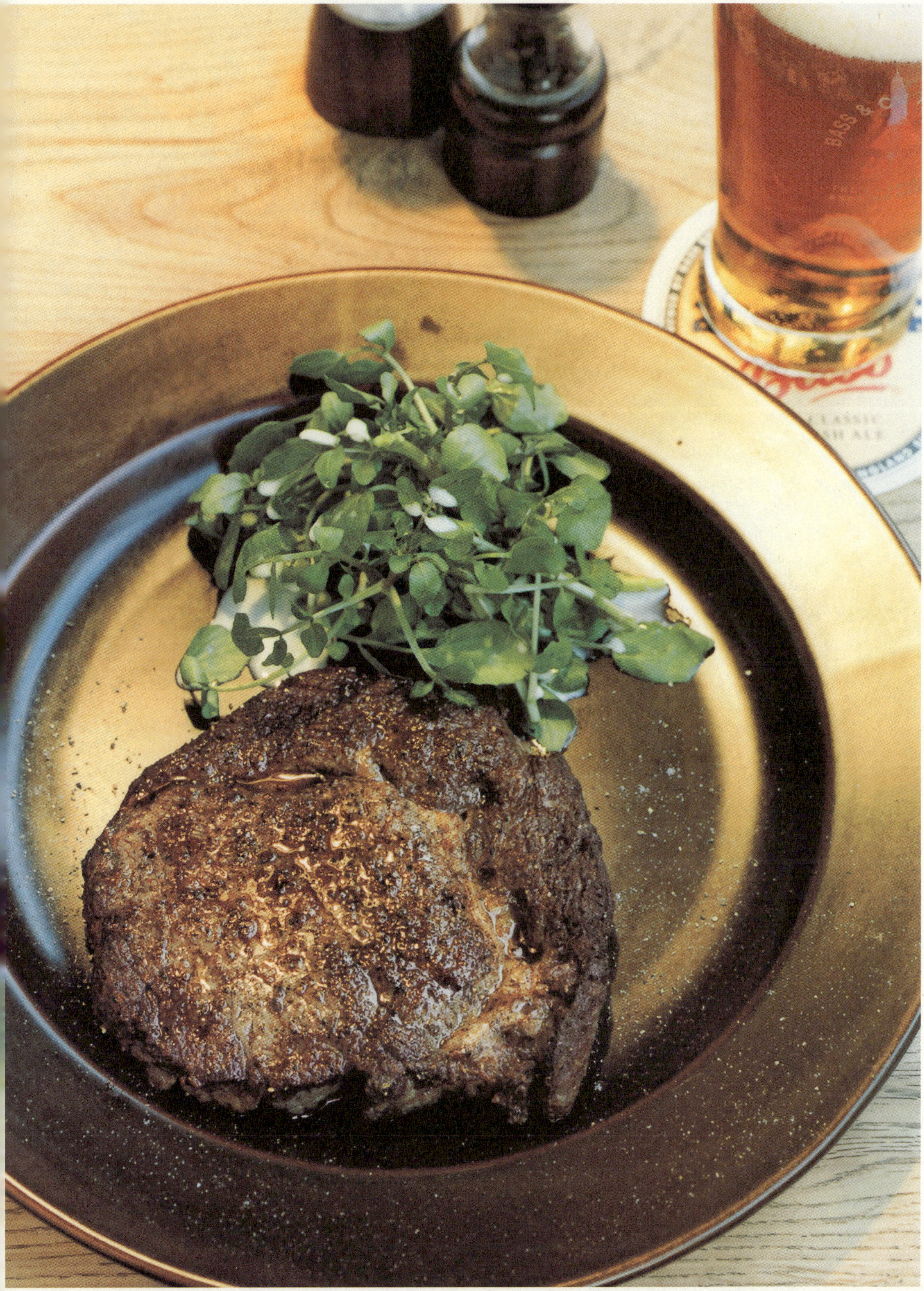

厨房機器の見積りが出た。そして念願のドーナツマシンの値段も。びっくりしたことに、全ての厨房機器よりも、小さいドーナツマシン1台のほうが高い！厨房機器は予想していたよりも安かった。それでなくてもザルのようにお金がなくなっていく厳しい中で、そこにそれだけかけていいのか？何万個売ったら元がとれるのか？ちょっと現実的ではないんじゃないか？と雲行きがあやしくなりかけた。そんな時にひりんこが言った。
「厨房機器が思ったより安かったからこそ、ドーナツマシンが導入できるんやん。これは喜ぶべきことやろ!!」
いつも、「ひりんこが正しい」とケンタロウも言っている。そう、潔い。カッコいい。

思い描いていたBirdの雰囲気。カフェといってもかわいい店ではなく、おっさんくさい大人な店にしたかった。そして、そんな店にちょっとまぬけなドーナツがあるのがいいと思っていた。2003年の初ヌーサ以来、もうかれこれ6年越しに3人があこがれ続けたドーナツマシンを、やっと導入できる口実ができたというのに。そう、元がとれるとかどうとかではない。計算ではなく姿勢だ。Birdの姿勢を無言で語る大事な要素だ。いかに自分たちが面白がれるか、が大事。やっぱりケンタロウも言うように、ひりんこが正しい。
「やろう！ドーナツ！」

ドーナツの生地もタケウチさんに相談。どんなドーナツが食べたいのかを伝えた。粉も揚げる油も全てタケウチさんの考えに基づき試作を繰り返す。
タケウチ師匠が作ってみせるといつも100点のができる。ふわっと軽くて、見事なドーナツ。でも、他の誰かが作るとどうも上手くいかない。仮に、今日上手くできたとしても、翌日また上手くいかなかったりする。
師匠の使う素材は、その日の温度や湿度によって微妙に調整しないといけない。混ぜ方などによっても出来上がりが大きく変わる。非常にデリケートで難しい。誰が作っても簡単に均一なものが出来上がる粉もあるらしいが、そこにはいろんな添加物やらなんやらが入っていると。安心でおいしいものがやっぱりいいので、みんな師匠について練習に励む。見た目はさり気なく懐かしい雰囲気のBirdのドーナツ、でも実は奥が深い。

料理はもちろん、コーヒー、紅茶、ビールにワイン。全てにおいて、自分たちが食べたいもの、飲みたいものを基本に決めていった。多分偏ったところもあるかもしれない。でも、TRUCKで作る家具や雑貨も同じで、自分が欲しい、使いたいと思うものだけでやってきた。自分が本当に好きと思うからこそ、人に自信を持って「いいでしょ」って言える。裏も表も何もない。素直な気持ち。Birdを作ってみて、業種が違っても基本は同じことやなぁと思った。

メニューのラインナップが決まり、毎日練習が続く。約1ヶ月間、昼に夜に毎食Birdで食べる。一皿一皿、それぞれはかなり完成度が高まった。でも、本番は同時に次々と注文が入ったのをそつなくこなさないといけない。混み合った状況の中、一品一品が勝負。オープンしたてだからとドタバタは許されない。だから何度も満席状況を作って練習した。TRUCKのスタッフをはじめ、友達、親戚、近隣、最後には知り合いでない人たちまで。いろんなパターンで昼に夜に席を埋め、好きなように注文をして食べてもらった。お金は受け取らないけど、レジで計算をし「ありがとうございました！」と見送るところまで、一晩だけで客席が2回転以上ってこともシミュレーションした。少し自信が持てるようになった。

オープン前日、期待やら緊張やらが充満の中、仕込みや準備をしている時に、ケンタロウが現れた。「いよいよやな。頑張りや」って言うだけのために東京から。ケンタロウもキッチンに入り、アッキーとタムと一緒にハンバーグを捏ねていく。
我が子の門出を見守っているようだった。ありがとう。けんちゃん。

ちゃんとした予告やお知らせができないまま、いきなりオープンしたTRUCKとBird。お客さんに来てもらえるのかと心配していた。それが驚いたことに、初日から、びっくりするくらいの人が来た。ひりんこと2人「なんでこんなに来てもらえるんやろ？」と何度も言い合った。Birdもなんと2時間待ち状態。スタッフ4人でのスタートだったので全然手が足りない。様子を見に来てくれたタケウチさんがドーナツを、Tea House MUJICAの堀江さんがなんとホールに出て接客を買って出てくれた。助かりました。ありがとう！

いろんな思いを込めて出来上がったBird。
TRUCKを見たあとBirdで休憩、というお客さんを見ると「あぁやっぱり作って良かった」と毎日思う。バス停に座って相談していたあの人たちにも「やっとできました」と言える。
自分もいつでもコーヒーが飲めて嬉しい。ハンバーグにステーキ、サンドイッチにドーナツ。どれもこれも毎回嬉しい。

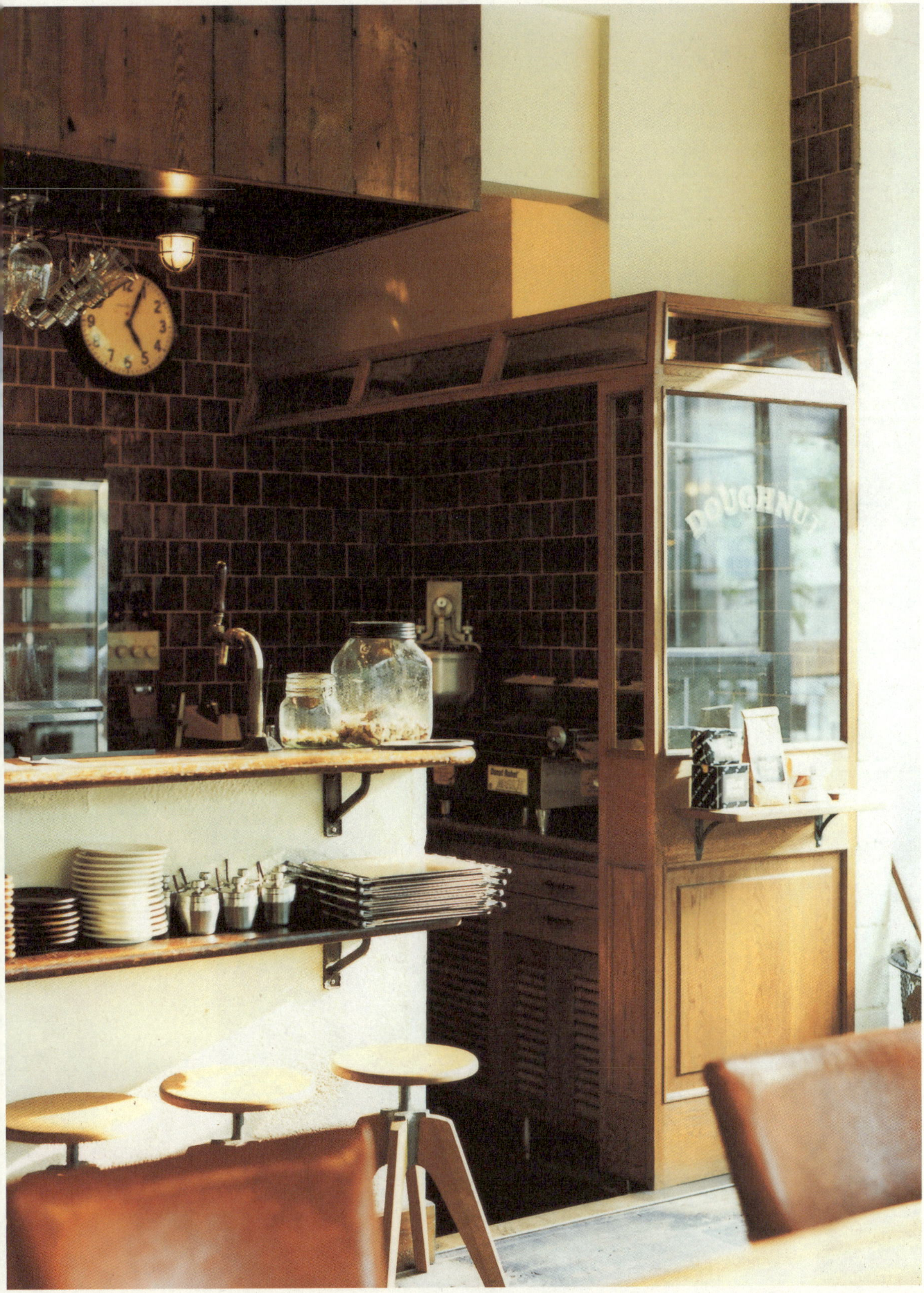
DOUGHNU

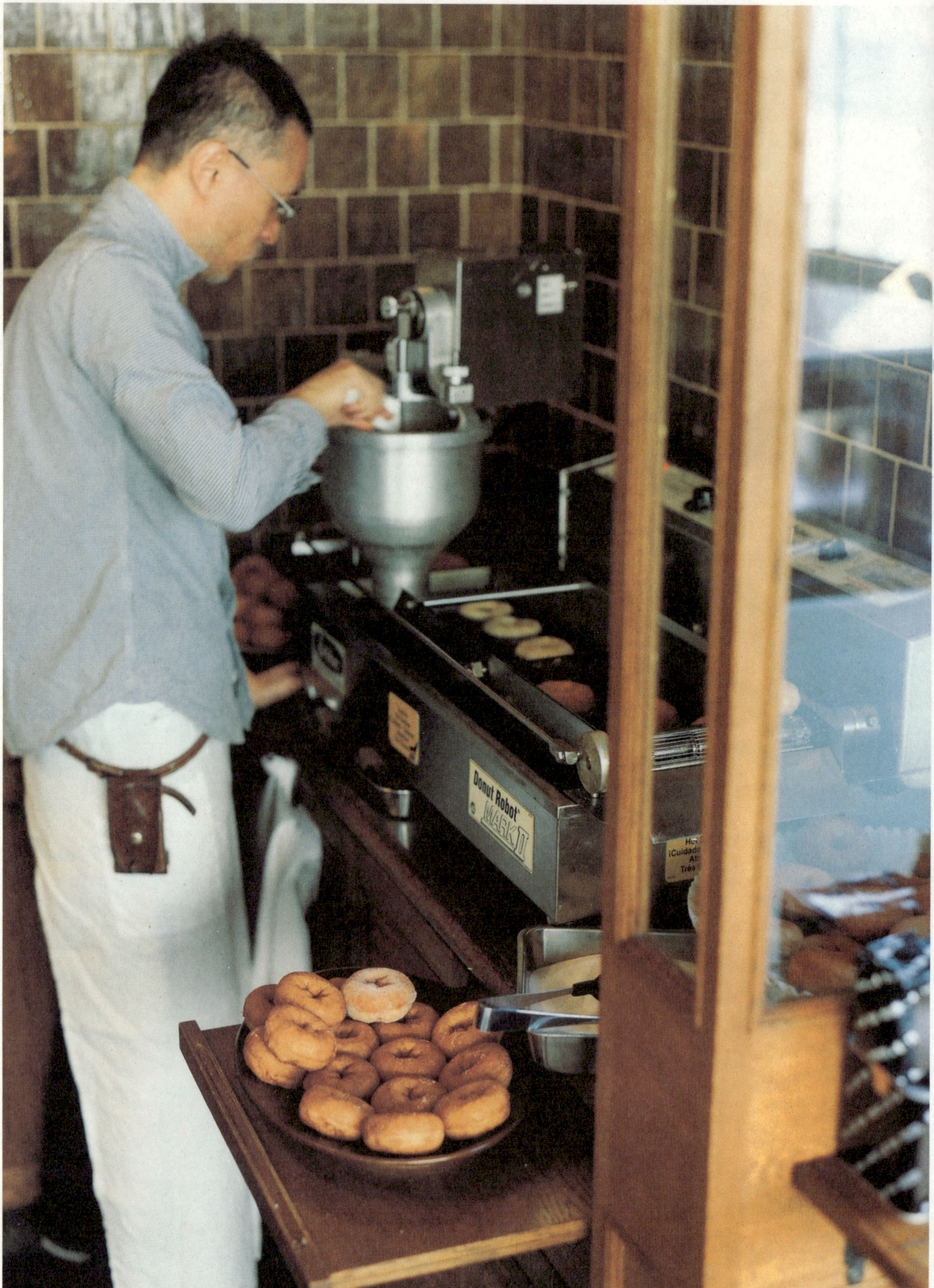
Donut Robot
MARK II

mixing bowl

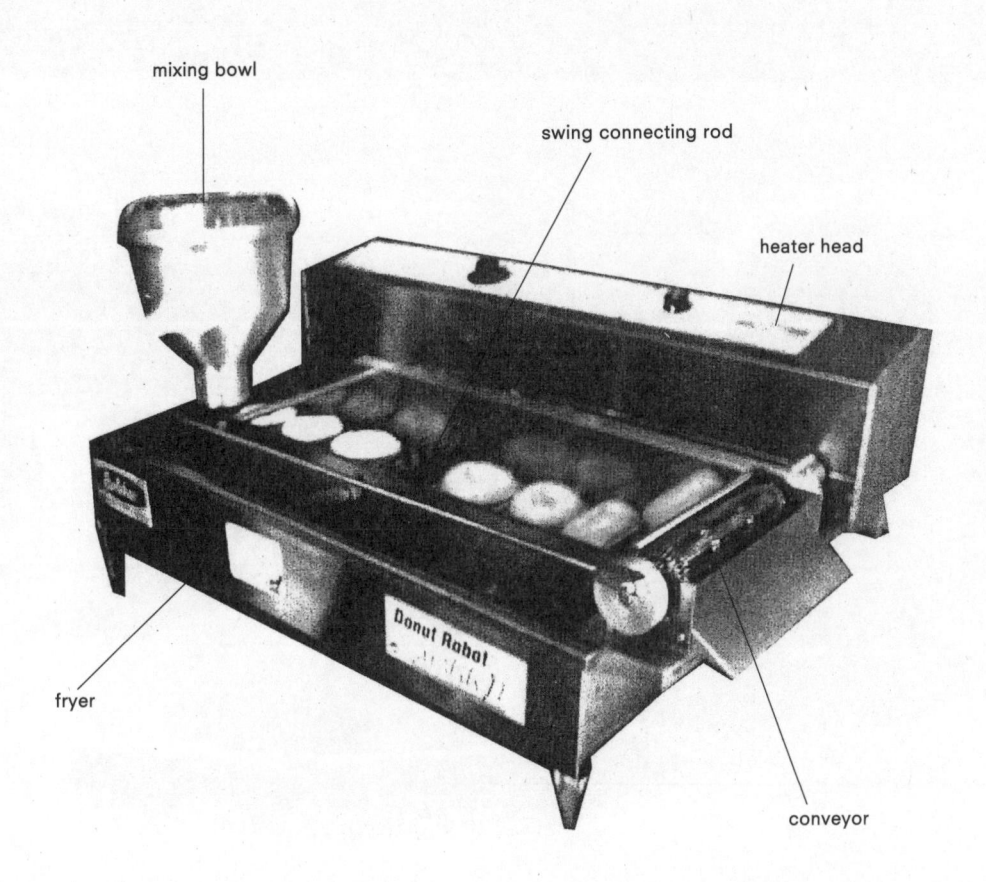

swing connecting rod

heater head

fryer

conveyor

The Doughnut Robot is working every day.

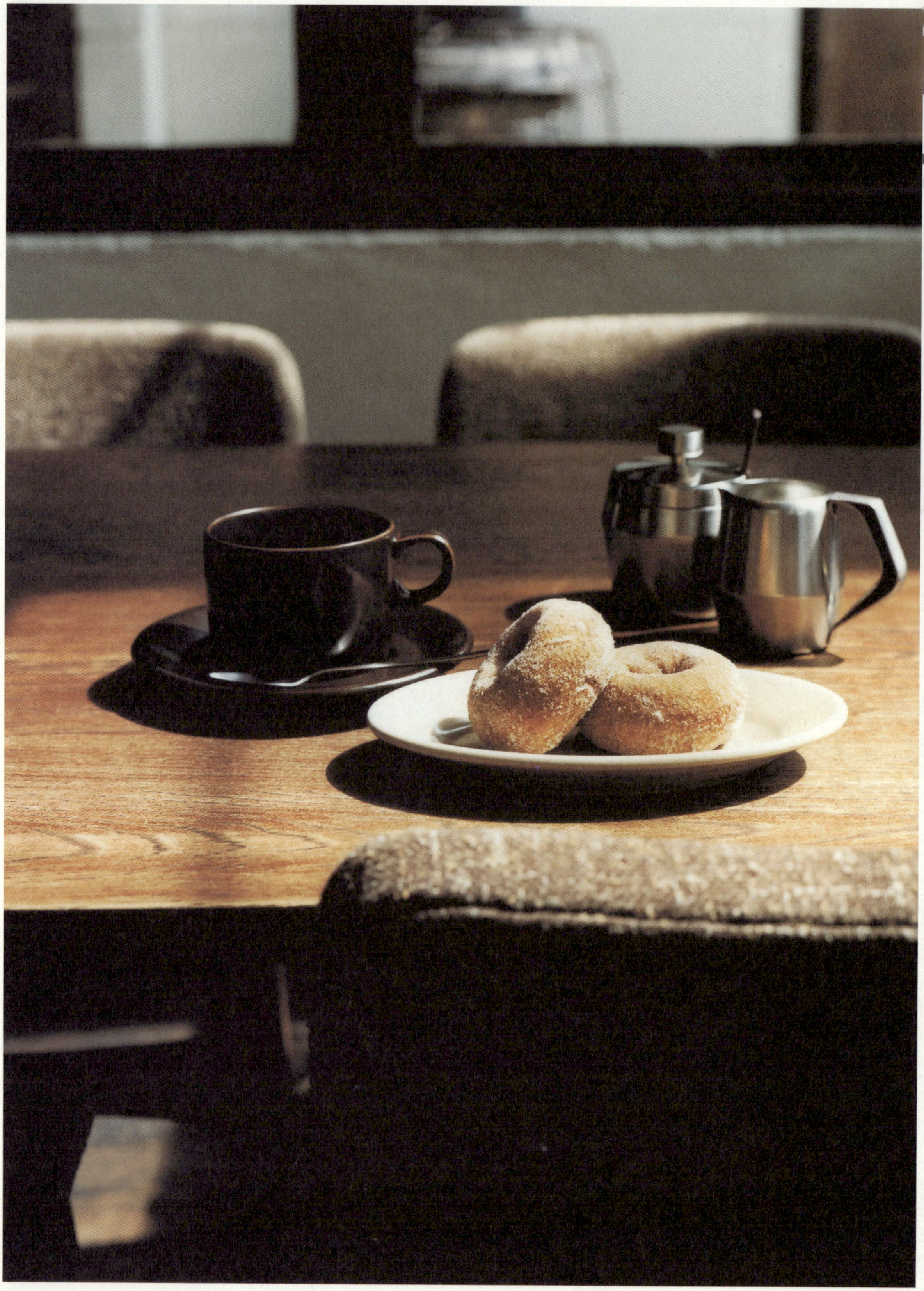

Through the large windows, people would be able to see our big trees. Even inside it would be like they were beneath branches. Customers would be able to use TRUCK chairs and tables for themselves.

One thing I was sure I wanted was a wood burning stove. It would add to the ambience and character of the restaurant, but also serve a more practical purpose. Our furniture workshop produces tons of scrap wood every day. It's mostly sturdy, dried oak and until now we had no choice but to throw it away. A wood burning stove would give us a way to put that scrap to good use. That alone would make it worth installing. That it adds to warmth and ambience of Bird during Osaka's cold winters is almost like an added bonus.

When it came time to start buying equipment for Bird we had a bit of a shock. The estimate for all the stoves and burners and cooking utensils was lower than we had expected. The price of the doughnut machine was not. In fact, although we had chosen the smallest model, it would cost more than all of the other kitchen equipment combined.

I started to have doubts about how wise it really was to buy this machine. How many doughnuts would we have to sell just to make our money back? I wondered if it made sense to spend so much money on just one thing.

Hiromi said "The other equipment is cheaper than we thought it would be. That's why we *can* buy the doughnut machine."

When we imagined the atmosphere we wanted for Bird, the last thing we wanted was to make something cute or trendy. We wanted it to have a mature, adult feel to it. We thought that making and selling doughnuts in such a serious looking place would be a nice contrast. We finally had an excuse to buy the machine we had wanted for the last six years. In the end I had to agree with Hiromi. We decided to buy it.

To create the dough for our doughnuts I again turned to Takeuchi. I described the kind of doughnuts I wanted to make and he started experimenting with different kinds of flour and oil to create the kind of thing I was looking for.

One problem we had was that Takeuchi was an expert baker. When he makes something, he considers dozens of factors and variables. He might choose different amounts of each ingredient depending on differences in the temperature or humidity. Even how the dough is mixed can have a big effect on the final product. There were some kinds of flour that were full of additives that we could have used to be able to make a dough recipe that anyone could follow. But we chose not to. Once he had come up with what we agreed was the doughnut we were looking for, he set about training the Bird staff in how to change and adapt the recipe depending on the day. Thanks to his hard work and the dedication of the Bird staff, we were able to do it.

All of the things we serve in Bird, the food, the tea and coffee, the wine and beer, are all things that we like

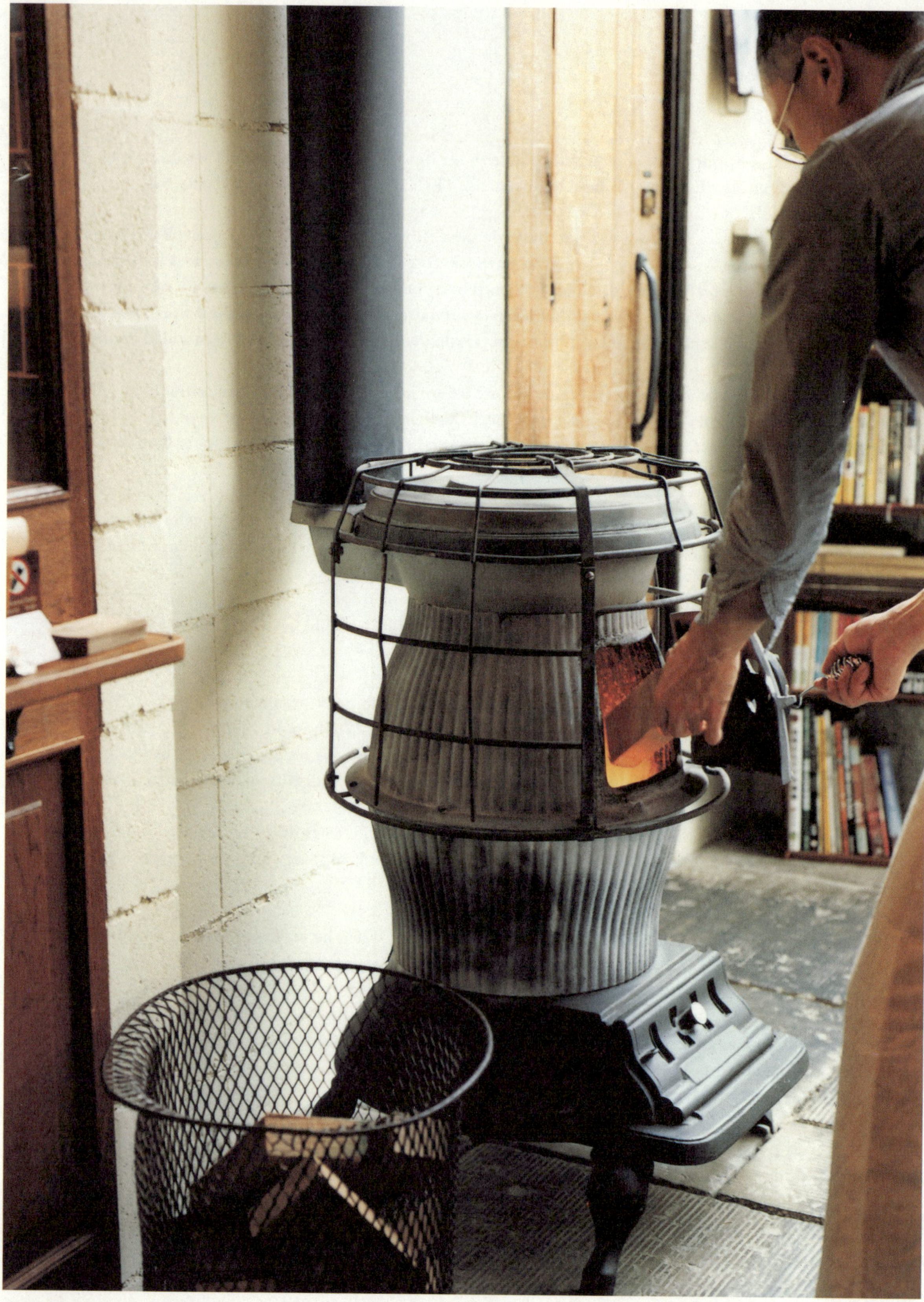

ourselves, things we like to eat and things we like to drink. The menu might not appeal to everyone, but that's okay with us. Since starting TRUCK we had only made furniture that we wanted to use ourselves rather than trying to make furniture to appeal to other people. That way we could say without hesitation about anything in our store, "This is good." Although the restaurant business is different we followed the same principle.

Once we had decided on the menu, the team practiced every day. I ate lunch and dinner at Bird every day for a month. Cooking each dish one at a time they were getting closer to perfection. However, in real situations, they would have to create many different dishes at the same time, with new orders constantly coming in. There would be no room for flaws. I wanted each dish to be a success. I didn't want them to use the excuse that they had just opened if things were less than perfect. To get the staff ready, I prepared simulations over the course of about a week. We got all the seats filled and had people order whatever they liked. Although the food was free, they went through the process of paying to give the staff experience of doing this too. We started with TRUCK staff, friends and family, then gathered groups of strangers. Finally, we tried a night with two successive runs of full seats. This gave the staff confidence that they could deal with a real working situation.

The day before we opened was full of stress and anticipation as we rushed about trying to complete the final preparations, In the middle of this we had an unexpected visitor. Kentaro had come from Tokyo to wish us well. He joined Aki and Tamu in the kitchen and helped them prepare the *Hamburg steaks*.

Finally, Bird opened.

We opened both TRUCK and Bird without having done any advertising or even announcing it properly. We were a little worried about whether any customers would show up at all. We were shocked by how many people came. From the first day, and for months after, there was a two hour wait. There were only 4 staff at first, so they were very busy. Takeuchi visited on the opening day and ended up manning the doughnut machine for a few hours. Horie-san, the owner of MUSICA, a tea house in Osaka, came and took it upon himself to help serve the customers for a while. Takeuchi and Horie-san, thank you for your help.

When I see customers come and look in the TRUCK showroom then go and take a break in Bird I think to myself, "Yes, we did the right thing." I can say to the people I had seen sitting outside sitting and talking on the bus stop bench, "We finally made it."

And of course I'm happy, too. I can drink good coffee whenever I want. And I know that delicious steaks, *Hamburg steaks*, sandwiches, and doughnuts are just a short walk away.

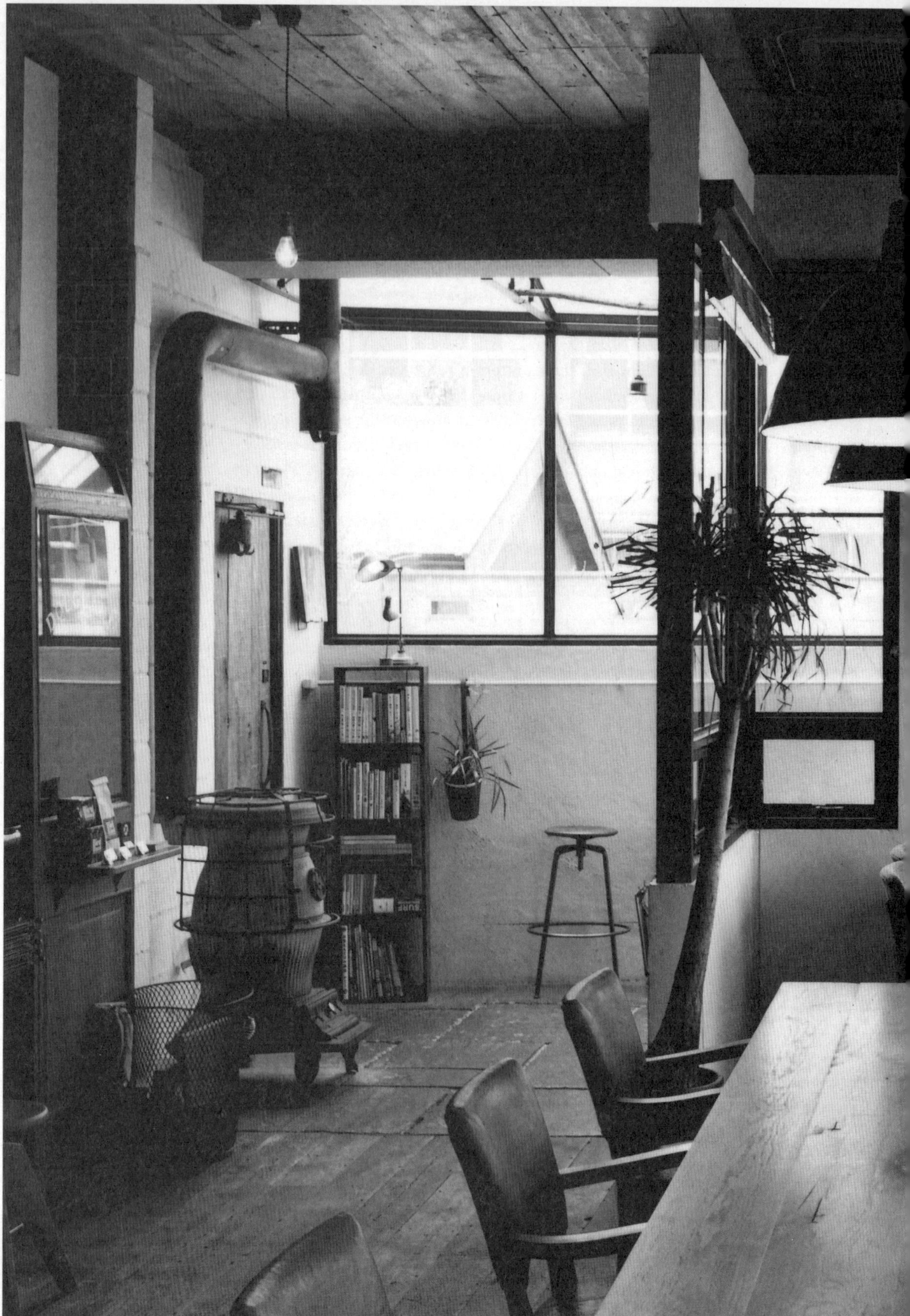

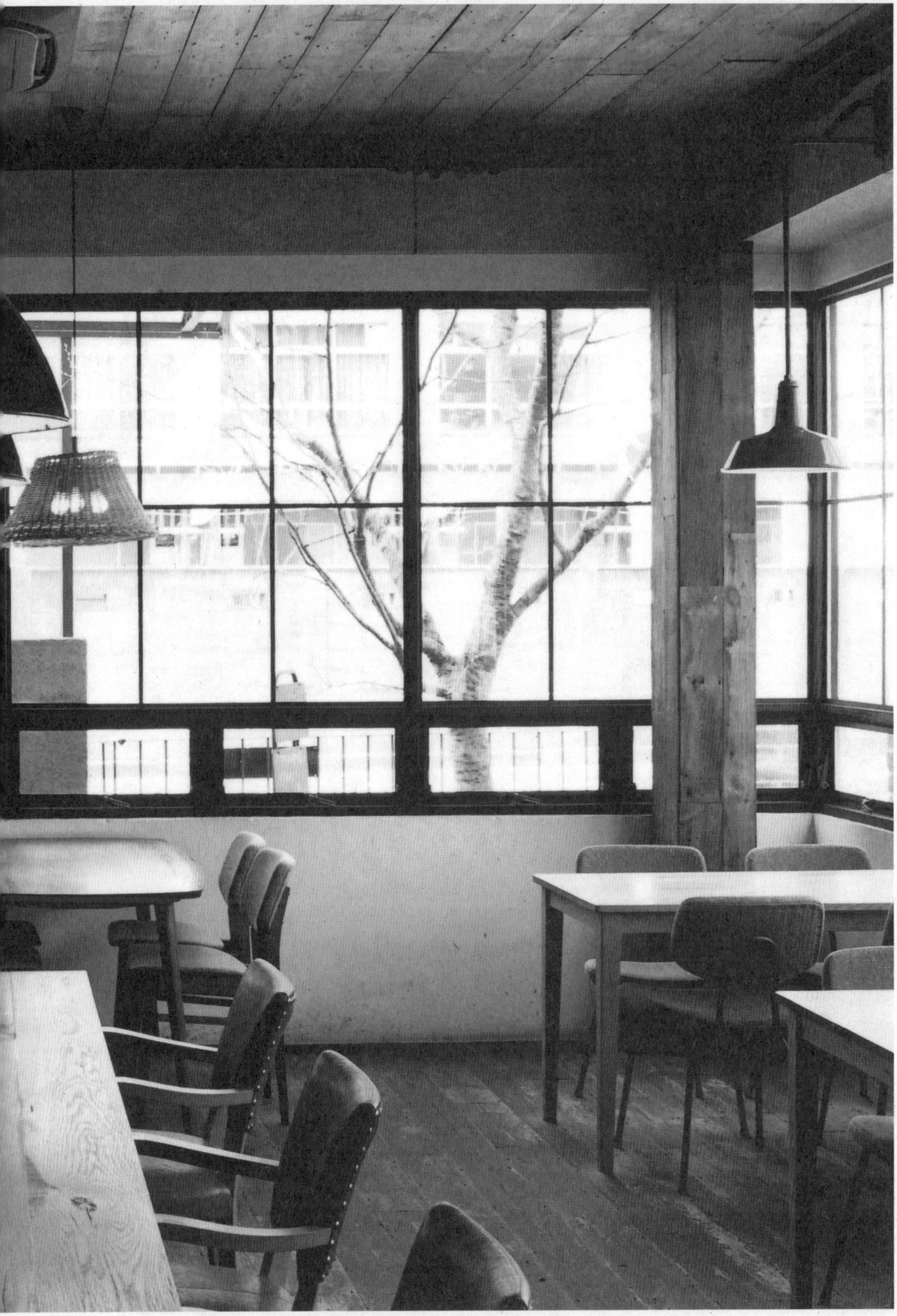

Bird

TRUCK NEST

**BASEMENT, WORKSHOP, GARAGE
ATELIER SHIROKUMASHA, HIRI-COLLE**

新しい場所での毎日が始まった。樹の下を通って敷地内の4つの建物を行ったり来たり。

BASEMENT
**TOKUHIKO'S ROOM, LOCATED IN THE SEMI-BASEMENT.
THIS IS WHERE NEW PRODUCTS ARE DEVELOPED.
FROM THE WINDOW YOU CAN SEE HIS MOTORCYCLES.**

半地下にある黄瀬部屋。ここで新商品を煮詰めていく。窓からはオートバイが見える。

TODAY IS A GOOD DAY

WORKSHOP
**THE WORKSHOP IS LOCATED BENEATH THE STORE.
THIS IS WHERE TRUCK'S FURNITURE IS MADE.**

店の下の階にある工場。ここでTRUCKの家具は作られる。

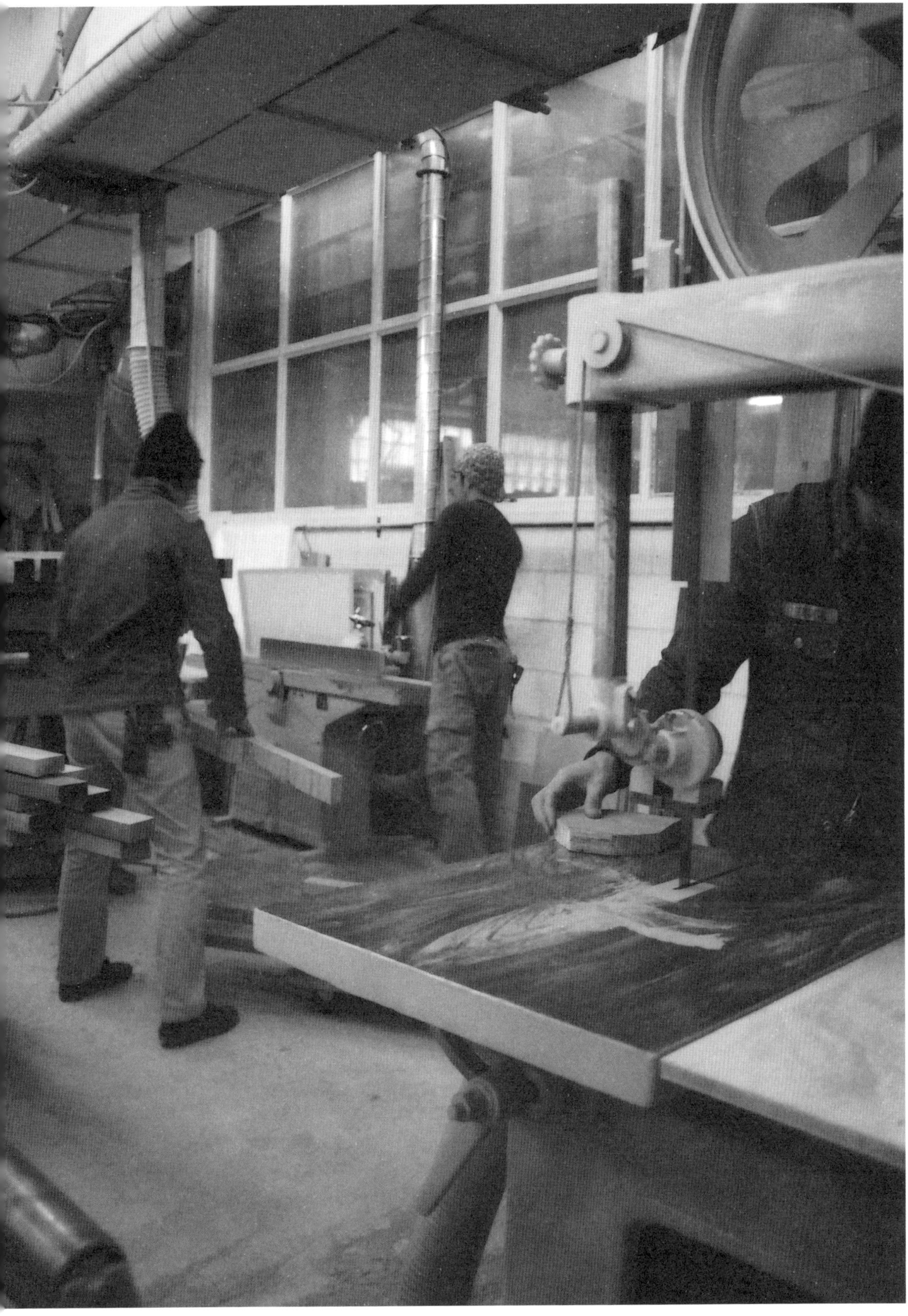

TODAY IS A GOOD DA

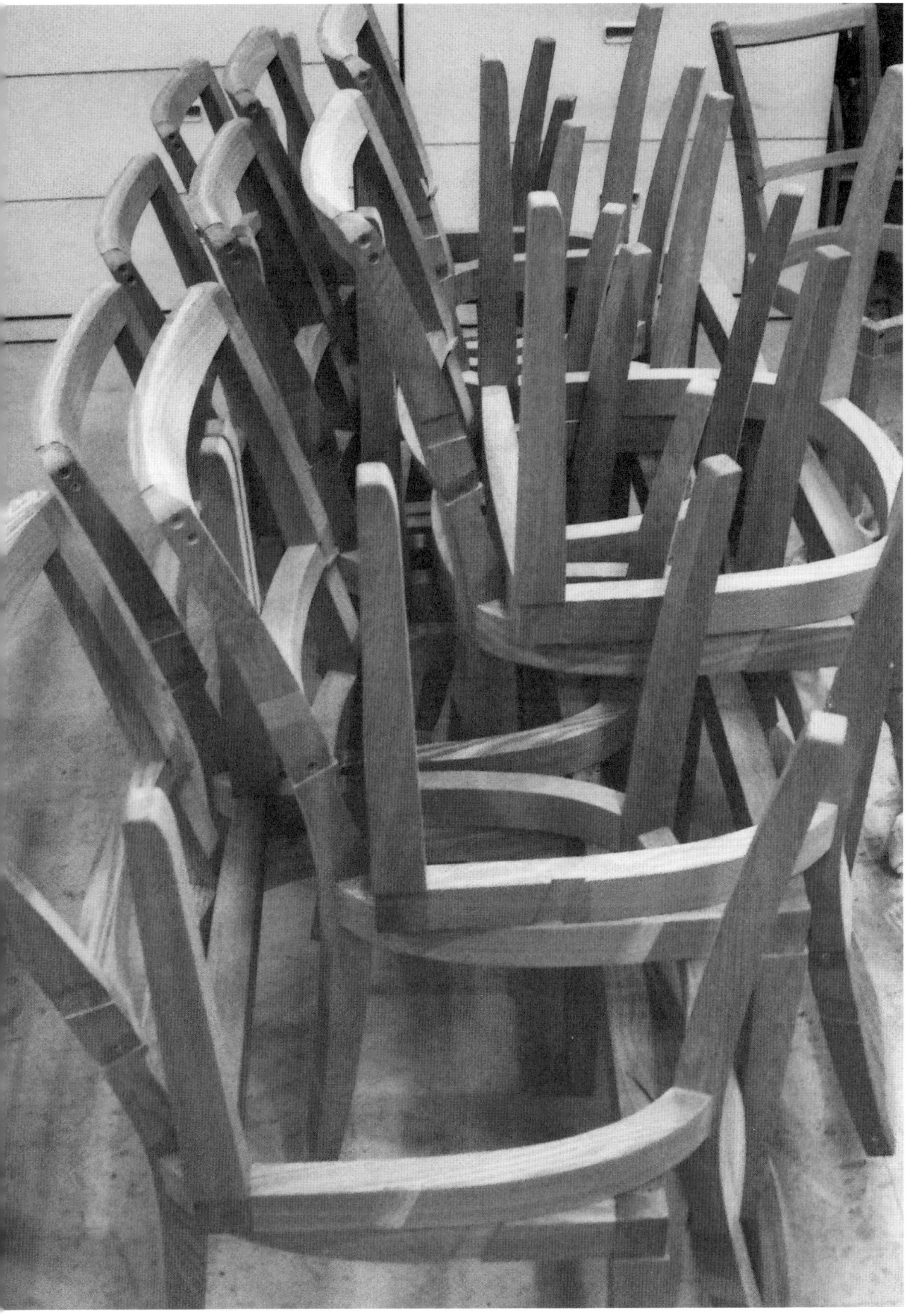

GARAGE WORK

THE GARAGE: HOME TO BICYCLES, MOTORCYCLES, CAMPING GOODS, SURFBOARDS AND MANY OTHER THINGS. IT ALSO HOUSES WELDING EQUIPMENT, A LATHE, AND OTHER EQUIPMENT, MAKING IT SOMETHING OF A PERSONAL WORKSHOP.

家にあるガレージ。自転車やオートバイ、キャンプ道具やサーフボードなどでいっぱい。そして、溶接機や工具、木工旋盤などもあって工作もできる。

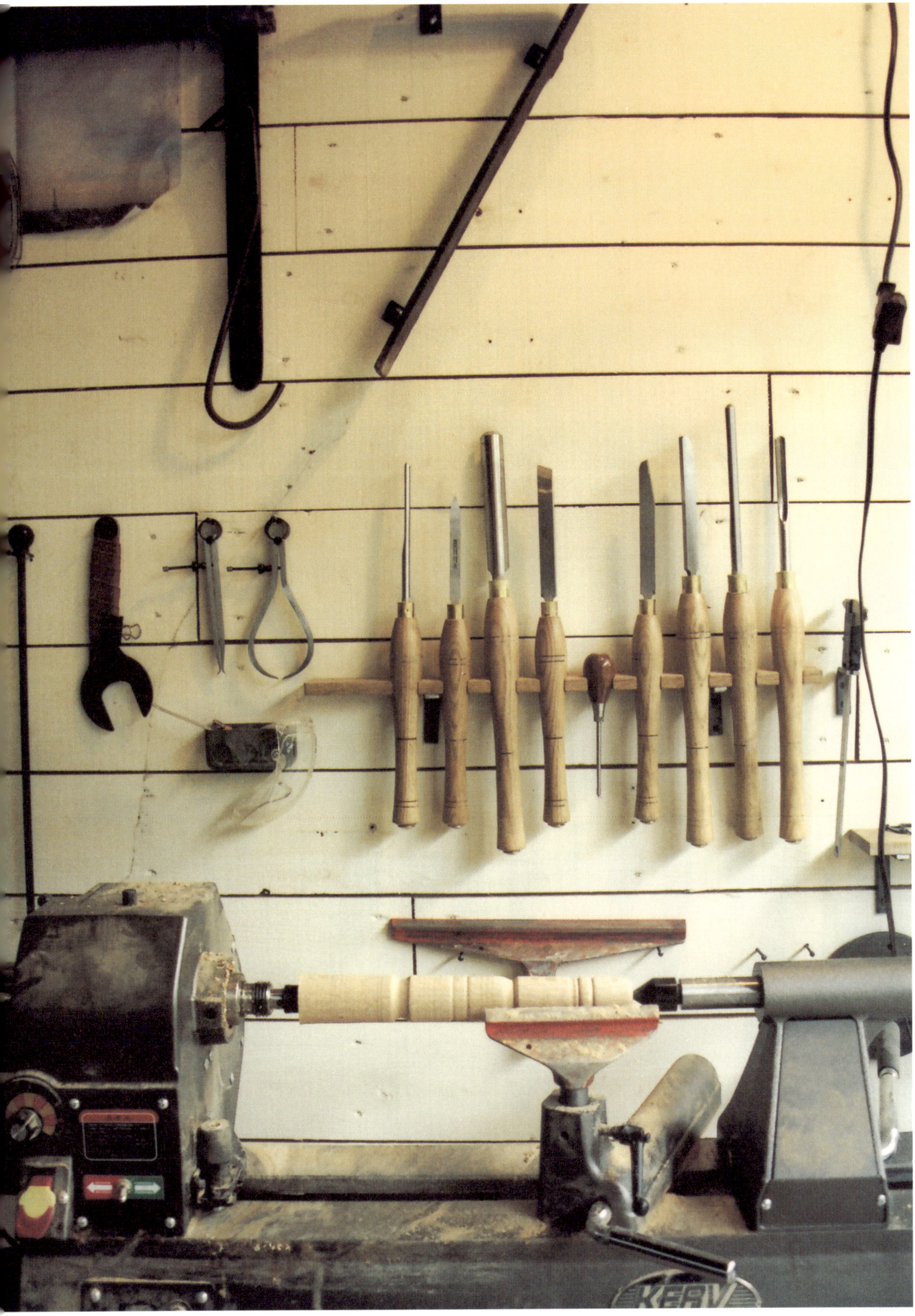
KERV

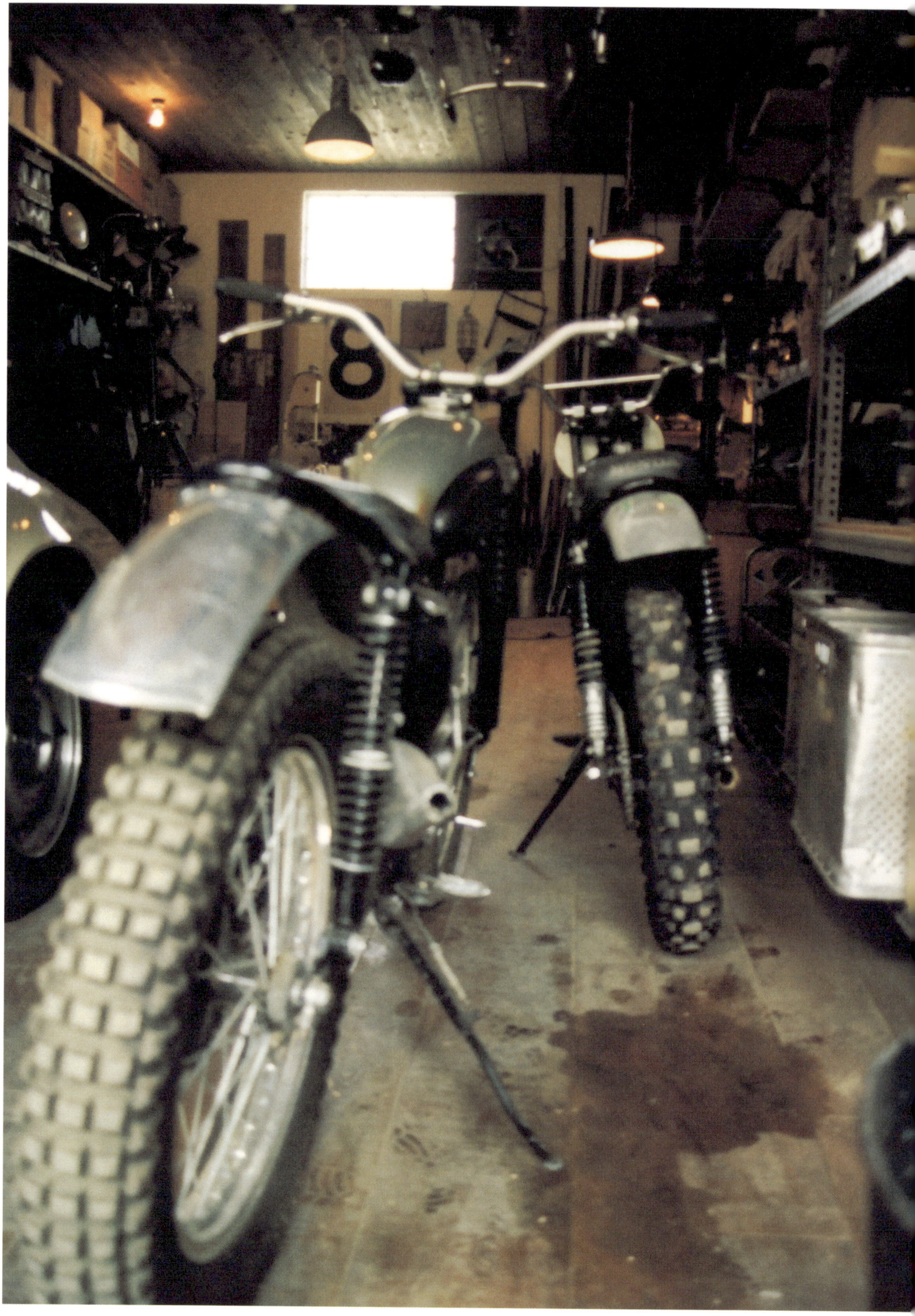

OUR DONKEY PARTY

ATELIER SHIROKUMASHA

**HIROMI'S SISTER, YASUKO, IN SHIROKUMASHA.
SHE SPECIALIZES IN LEATHER PRODUCTS, SEWING EACH ONE BY HAND.**

シロクマ舎でひりんこの妹、やーちゃんがひとつひとつ手縫いで商品を仕上げていく。

オリジナルの革の切れっ端を使ったシロクマ舎の商品。財布や手帳カバーに名刺入れなど、
日々使っていくと、どんどんいい色に変わっていく。味わいも愛着も深まる。

Some of Shirokumasha's products.
Wallets, book covers, card cases, and the like. The longer they are used, as the color changes, the more they become your own.

ATELIER
SHIROKUMASHA
http://www.shirokumasha.com

HIRI-COLLE ELEMENT

MOST PEOPLE WOULD DESCRIBE THESE THINGS AS SCRAP. FOR HIROMI, HOWEVER, THEY ARE VALUED POSSESSIONS. SOMETIME IN THE PAST HER COLLECTION OF SUCH ITEMS BEGAN TO BE REFERRED TO AS HER "HIRI-COLLE" *(SHORT FOR HIROMI COLLECTION).*

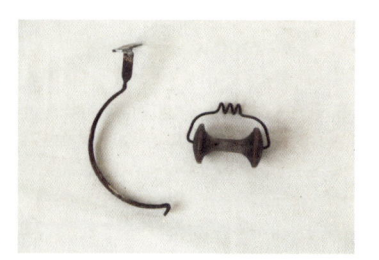

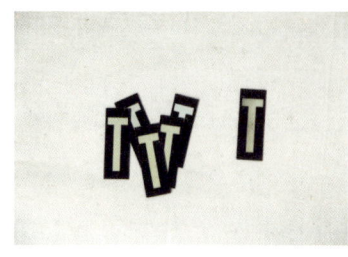

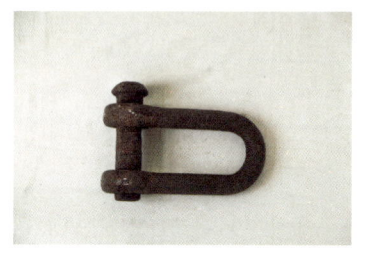

他人にとってはガラクタでも、大好きなもの。それらのコレクションはいつしか"ヒリコレ"と呼ばれるようになった。

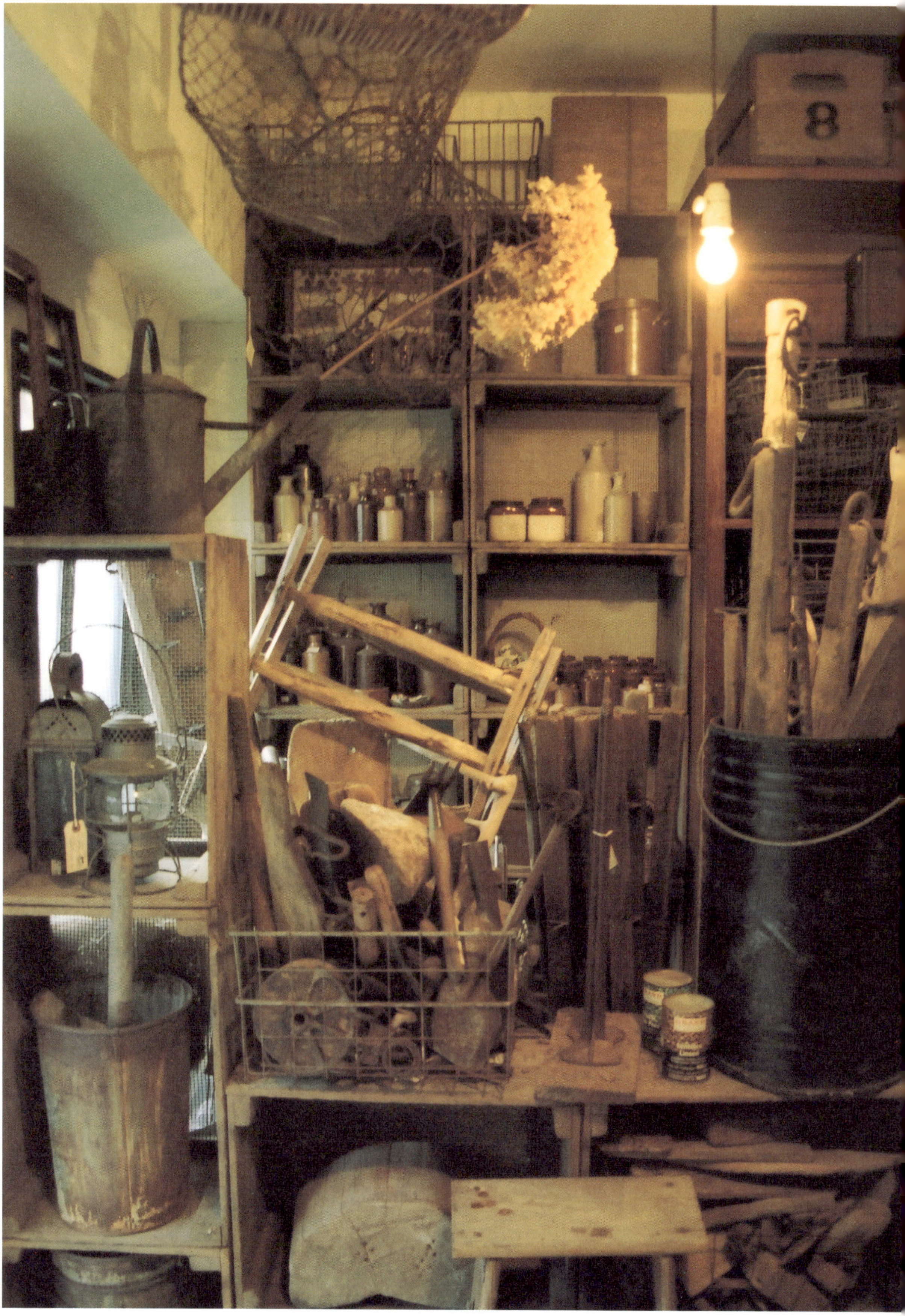
8

特にすぐ使い道がないものでも、好き！って理由だけでストックしているいろんなもの。
それらが申し合わせたかのようにピッタリとはまって、店作りやカタログ作りに生かされる。
このゲートと木の棒、鐘も出番が来た。

Hiromi loves to add things to her stock of objects when she sees something she likes, even if it doesn't have immediate or apparent use. In the course of putting together the store and the catalogs there are many times when something jumps out as being just the right thing. This gate, the wooden pole, and the metal bell here take their turn.

City Trees, Fallen Leaves

In October in London, the trees in the city are very beautiful. There are many yellow leaves. There are trees in parks and along footpaths. Walking on the footpaths near Blackheath station is like walking in a forest. They are entirely covered in leaves. The sound of the leaves crunching beneath my feet is charming. I can barely see my shoes. A small mountain of acorns sits atop a gatepost which a squirrel is using as a dining room. There are squirrels all over the place. If you look up at any tree, you can see its beautiful shape and feel at ease. It's a feeling of richness.

As I walk along, I can't help think of Osaka and something I was told by Mr. Kuwabara. In autumn, when trees lose their leaves, many residents complain that they fall onto their land, that cleaning them up is troublesome, and that they collect in gutters. That's why, even before the leaves have a chance to change color, the trees are pruned. Even though the red and yellow leaves will make it the most beautiful season.

The pruning starts just as summer is ending. Pruning should be done for a tree's benefit, for its health, or to keep it tidy. This pruning, though, is *not* done with the tree's interests in mind at all. The branches are blindly cut with the viciousness of someone seeking revenge for a wrong done to their parents. So many of the branches are chopped away! All that's left is the horrible sight of the trunk stripped just like a pole. It seems to get worse every year. It even happens to trees in parks. Hiromi's parents live on the fourth floor of an apartment building. From their south-facing window, in a nearby park, you can see a big camphor tree. It was one of the main reasons they chose that apartment. It too has been savagely pruned. It looks like an ugly stick. This year the harsh rays of summer sun will edge into their room.

The ugly poles stick up in a line on both sides of the road. You can't even call them trees. Is there another city like this in the world? Deciduous trees shade us from the sun in summer and their leaves fall away in winter to let the light and warmth of the sun shine through. If they are promoting more ecological living why cut the trees like this? To use their budget for the year? I don't understand it.

I didn't think that anyone in London considers the fallen leaves to be garbage. I never saw anyone sweeping them away. I can't say that is necessarily true, though. It's just a feeling based on what I've seen.

Are Japanese people so concerned with neatness? Do they think the fallen leaves look messy? Do they want them to be cleared away? The city government is scared of complaints, so they use tax money to cut the trees. What do these people think when they see the pruned trees? Does it make them happy? Apparently there are some people who look at the banks of a river, all concreted up, and think it looks good.

I prefer the natural looking trees of London. I think they look much better. Am I in the minority here? Perhaps, but in autumn in Japan, people flock, cameras in hand, to country areas to see red maple leaves. They buy maple leaf sweets and eat maple leaf tempura. Why do they think it is so different from the trees in front of their houses and in their neighborhoods? The trees they see every day?

街の樹、落ち葉

10月のロンドン。街なかの大きな樹がすごくきれい。黄色くなった葉っぱでいっぱい。
公園はもちろん、歩道も葉っぱが敷き詰まっていた。ブラックヒース駅近くの住宅地を歩いていると、森の中を歩いているように感じるくらい、落ち葉が歩道を覆っている。サクッサクッと葉っぱを踏む音が楽しい。靴が見えなくなるくらい。家の門柱の上がリスの食堂になっていた。食べかけのどんぐりがのっている。いたる所にリスがいる。
上を見上げると、どの樹も枝振りがきれい。のびのびしている。ほとんどが自然樹形に見える。豊かな気分になる。

歩きながら大阪のことを思い出す。以前、造園屋さんから聞いた話。
秋に街路樹の葉っぱが落ちると近隣の家から苦情がくる。敷地に落ちてくる、掃除が大変、樋に溜まると。
だから葉っぱが落ちる前に枝ごと切ってしまう。これから赤や黄に色が変わって一番きれいな季節だというのに。
この話を聞いてから数年、気になっていつも見ている。夏が過ぎた頃から始まる。剪定が。剪定というと樹のことを考えて、健康を取り戻すためだったり、樹形を整えたりすること。でも、行われているのは決してそんな樹のことを考えたものではない。痛々しい。ブチブチ、めちゃくちゃに切っているようにしか見えない。親の敵討ちかと思うくらい。ほとんどの枝がなくなっている。残ったのは無惨な姿、棒のような幹だけ。それが、年々、度を増しているように思う。
公園の中の樹まで同じようなことがある。ひりんこの両親が住むマンションの4階の部屋。南向きの掃き出し窓からは、公園の大きなクスノキが見えていた。近くに緑の葉だけが見える景観だった。部屋を決めた大きな理由だった。それが、切られてしまった。ブチブチに。ただの醜い棒になった。悲しい。多分、今年の夏は直射日光がジリジリと部屋に入るだろう。道路によっては、両側の歩道に棒がずらっと並ぶ。棒。樹とは言えない。こんな街、他の国であるだろうか？ 落葉樹があると、夏は影を作って直射を遮り、冬には葉を落とし、太陽の明るさ、暖かさが届く。
地球温暖化、エコ、節電とかを唱えるなら、なぜ樹を切ってしまうのか。年度末の予算の消化？ 理解ができない。

ロンドンの街。落ち葉をゴミとは誰も考えていないのかなと思った。落ち葉を掃いている人なんて見なかった。
調査や聞き込みをしたわけではないし、勝手な想像だけどそう感じた。大阪(日本?)の人のほうがキレイ好き？ 落ち葉が入ってきたら汚く思う？ 掃除をしたくなるのか？ で、掃除が大変と苦情を言う。苦情が怖いからお役所は税金を使って樹を切る。切られた樹を見て、その人たちは「ああきれいになった」と喜んでいるのか？ 川がコンクリートで固められた護岸工事を見てきれいになったと言う人がいるように。僕は自然樹形の大きな樹がいっぱいある、秋には落ち葉で覆われた道や公園があるロンドンのほうがずっときれいだと思う。これって少数派なのか？
でも、日本人も紅葉の季節、いろんな紅葉の名所にはカメラを持って押しかける。
紅葉饅頭を買う、紅葉の天婦羅まである。別のものなのだろうか？ 家の前、近所にある、毎日見る樹とは。

もうひとつロンドンで感じたこと。
元からある樹を残すのが前提で物事が考えられているように思った。いたる所で目にした。
歩道沿いにある大きなお屋敷。歩道との境界線にある石かコンクリート製の塀。ちょうど境界線を跨ぐ位置に立っている幹周り2m以上のメープル。その樹の所だけ塀の仕様が違っている。鉄の柵で、樹を上手くよけて作られている。塀を作る時、邪魔だからと切られなかった。公園のぐるり、歩道との境目に高さ50cmくらいの壁がきれいなラインで続いている。そのライン上に樹がある。壁はそこで途切れ、樹の向こうからまた続く。当たり前のように、何もなかったように。
前からずっと、樹を切らないで残す方法で事が進められてきたんだなぁと思う。だから、あんなに都会にいて大きな樹がたくさん身近にある。羨ましい。大昔の開拓時代、森林を伐採して、畑や酪農地、街が作られたのだと思う。それは分かる。家具も木で作っている。生きて立っていた樹で。でも、現代の都市で残っている樹、生えている樹をちょっと邪魔だからと簡単に切らないで、残すことを考えればいいのにと思う。

Hina

Another thing that impressed me about London is the effort they've taken to preserve trees that are already there. I remember seeing a stone fence running along the footpath. Behind the fence was a large building of some kind. Standing in the path of the fence was a maple tree with a circumference of more than 2m. At just that point, the stone fence stopped and changed to a metal one that curved around the tree. On the other side of the tree, the stone fence continued. The tree hadn't been cut down to make way for the fence.

In another place, I saw a fence about half a meter high surrounding a park. Again, the line of the fence was broken by a tree, continuing on the other side. It seemed to be done in a very natural way, as if to stop at the tree was the most obvious thing to do.

It really seems as if the city has been developed so as to avoid having to chop down trees. That's why there were still so many trees in the city. I felt envious of the people who lived here.

As civilization developed, forests were felled to make way for farms and towns. I understand that, after all, I make furniture from wood, but in modern cities, rather than just cutting down trees simply because they are in the way, maybe it would be good to think about keeping them.

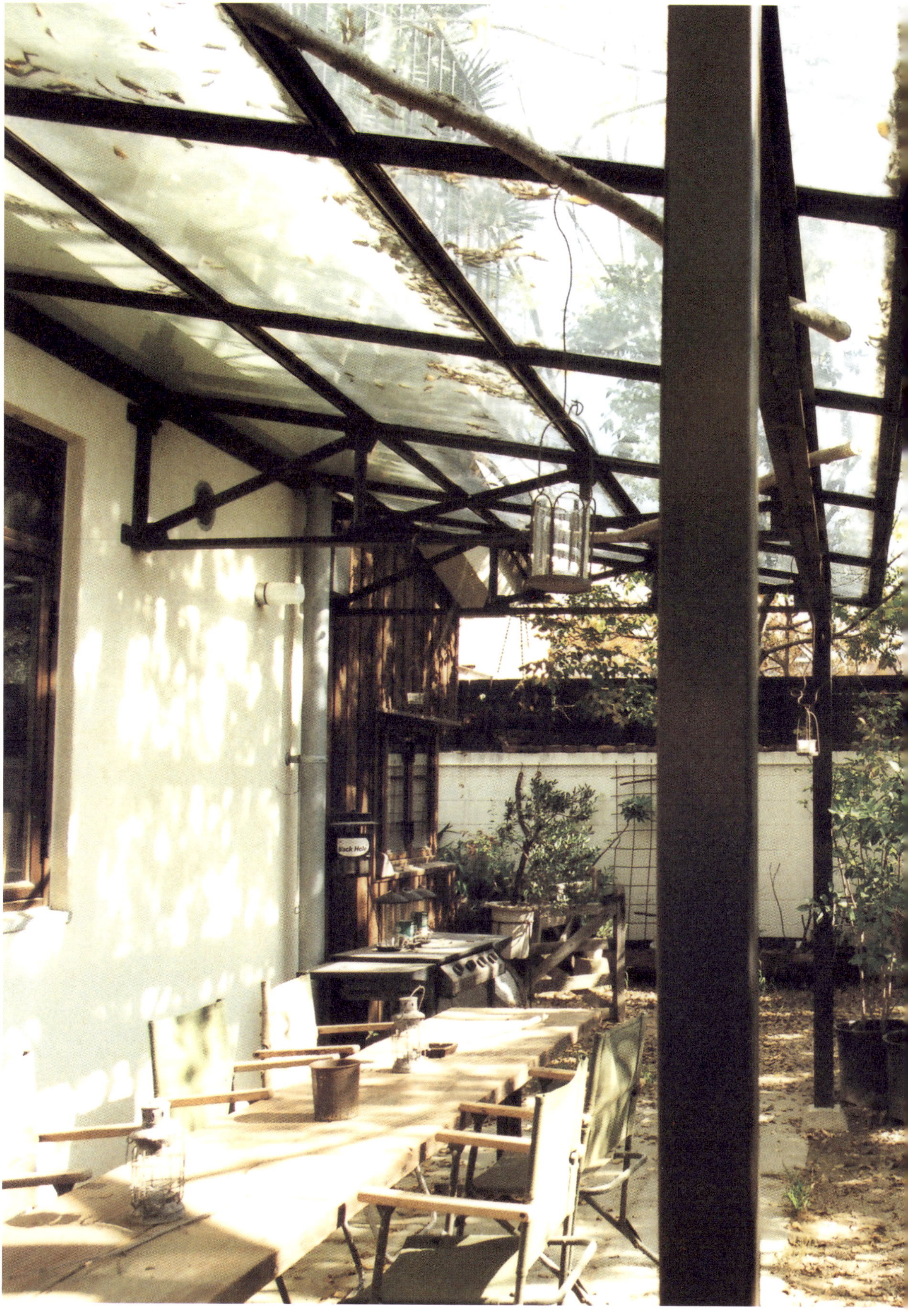

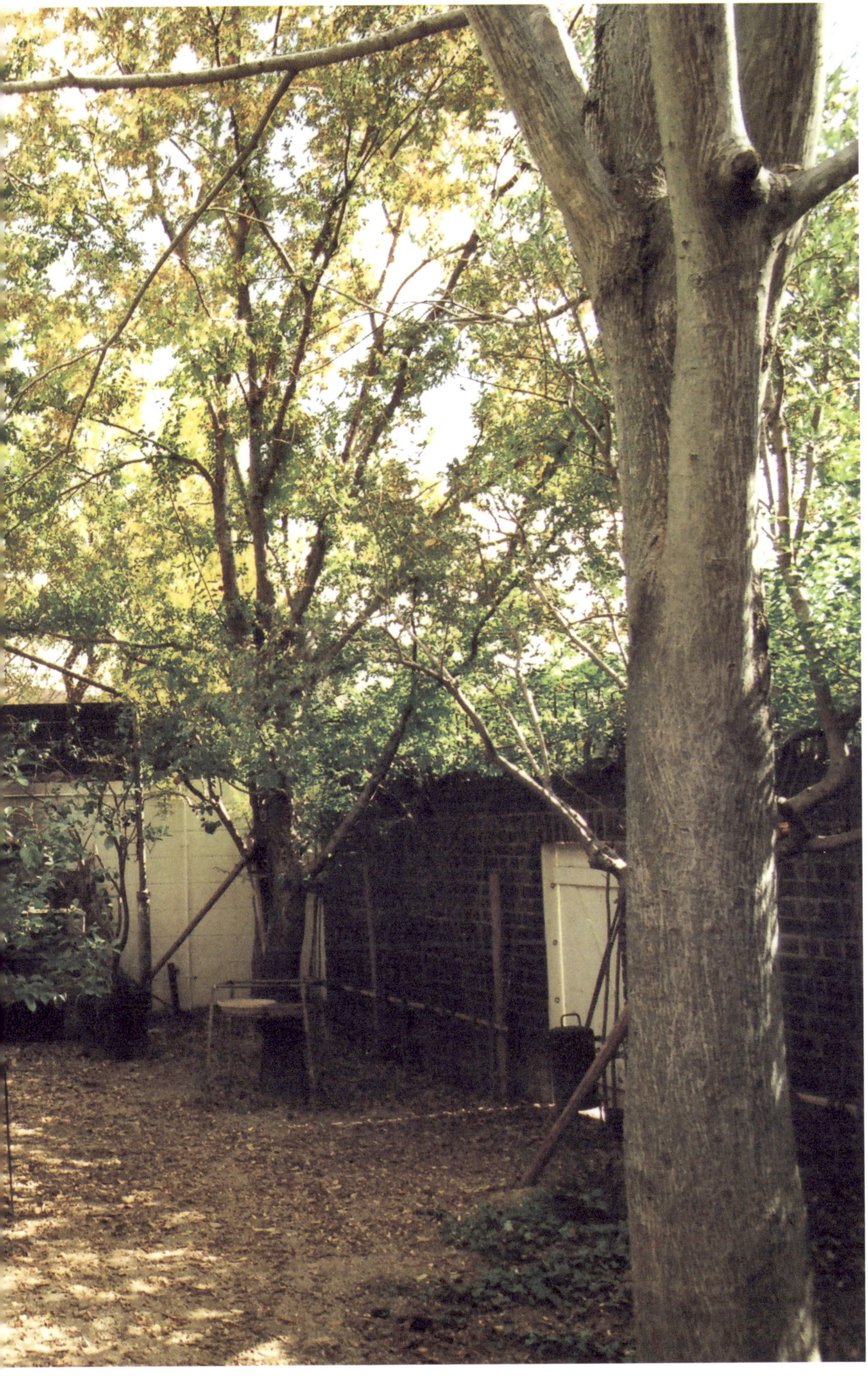

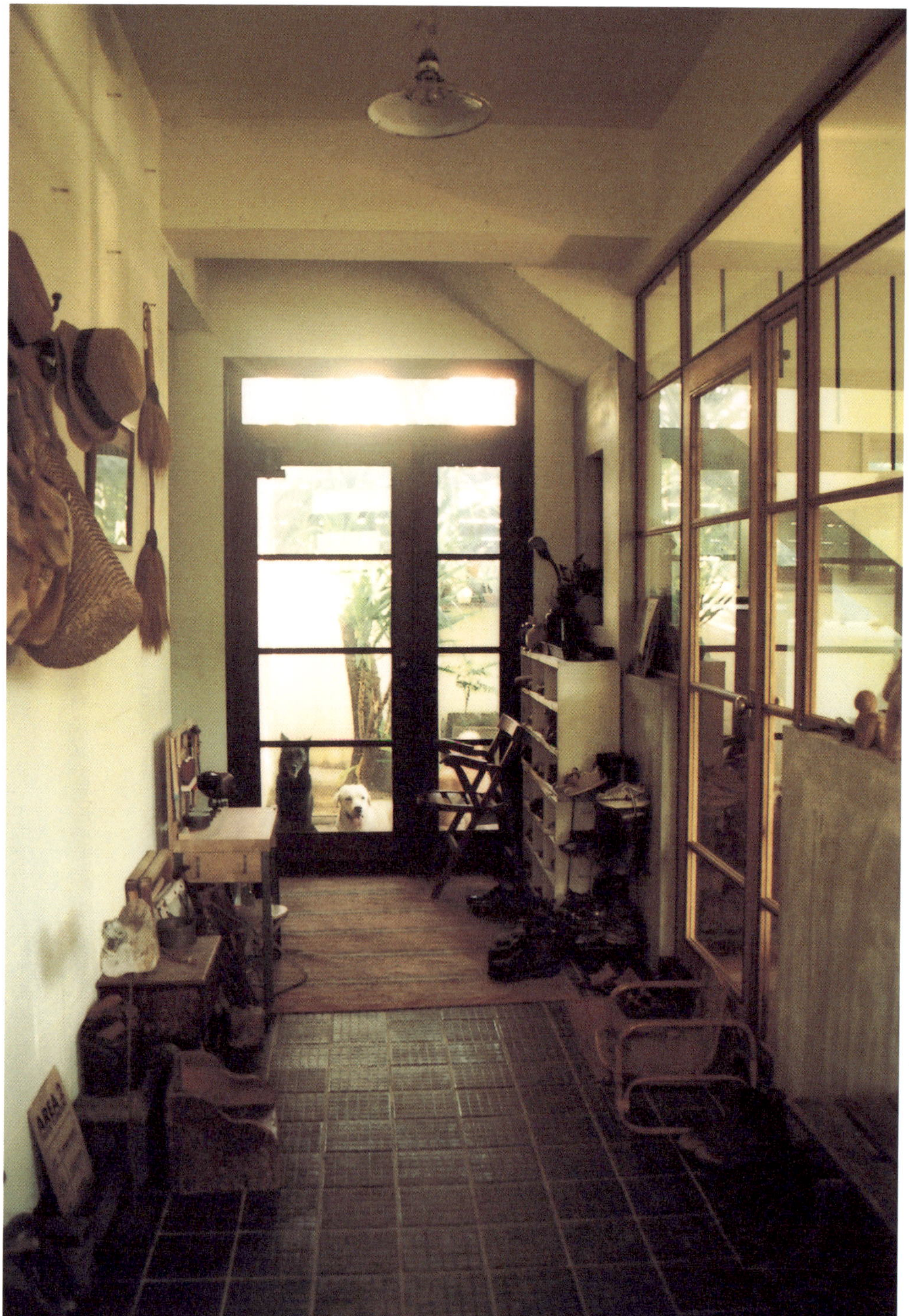

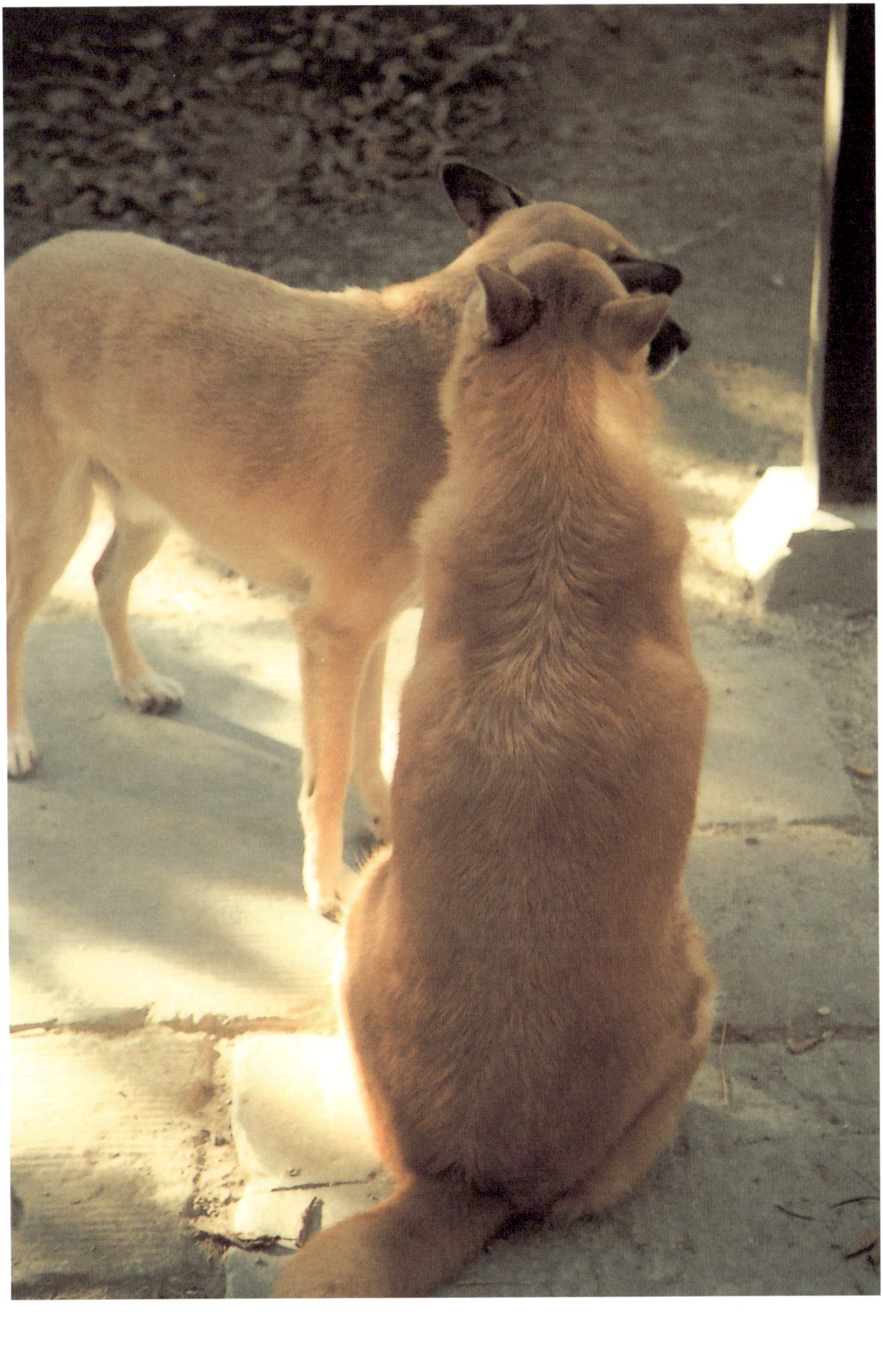

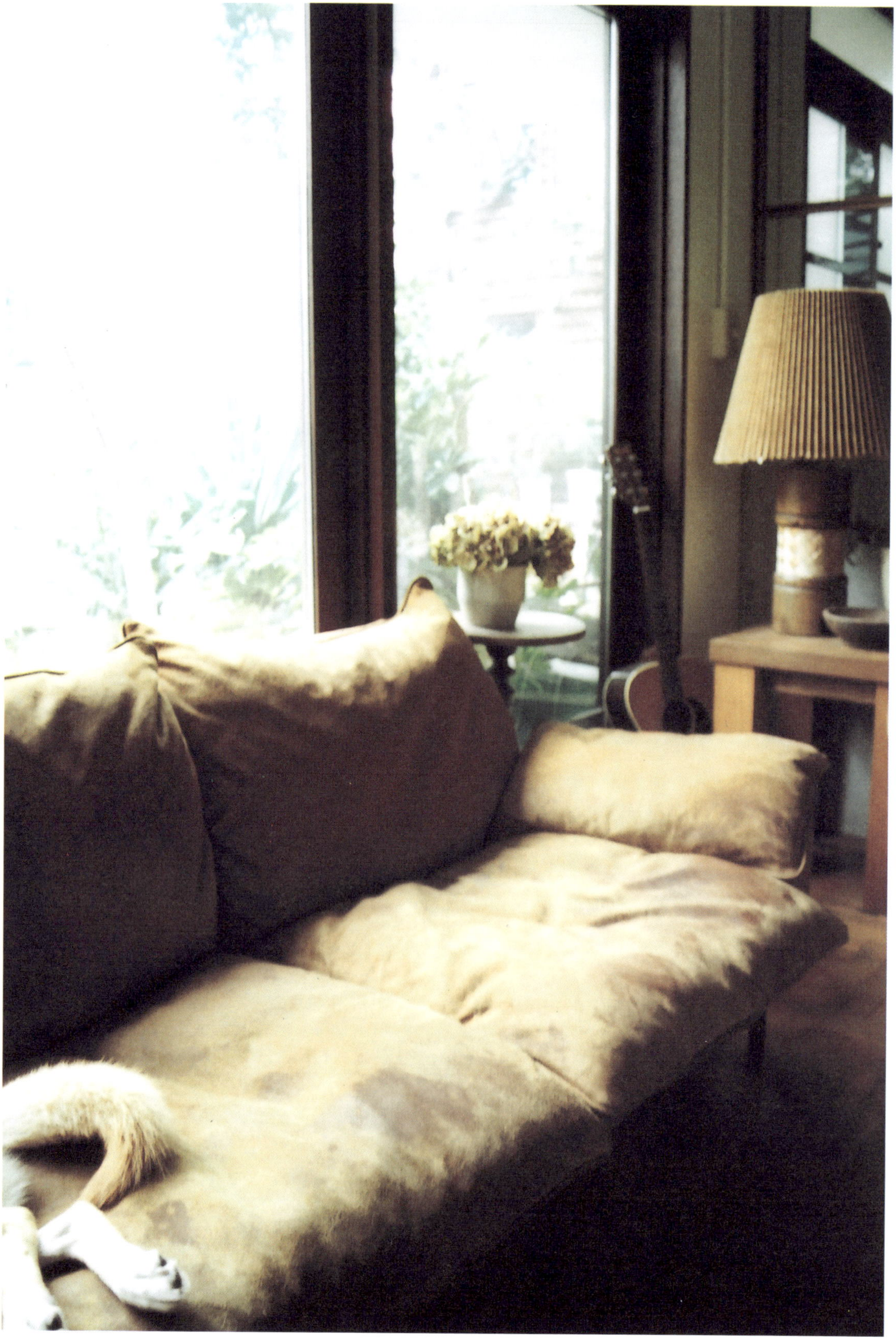

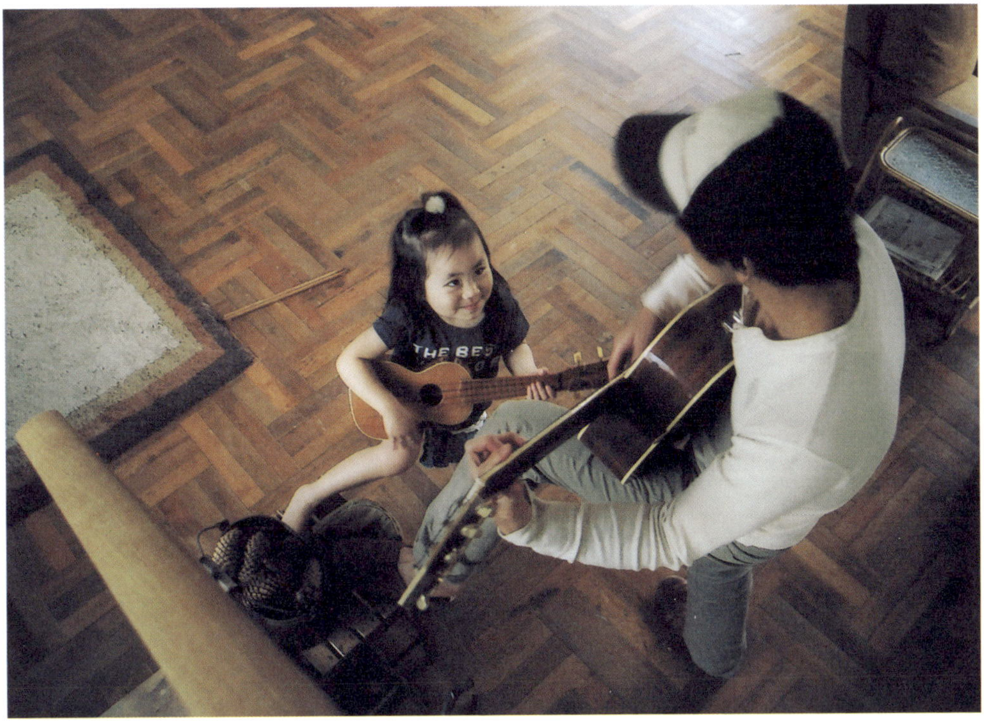

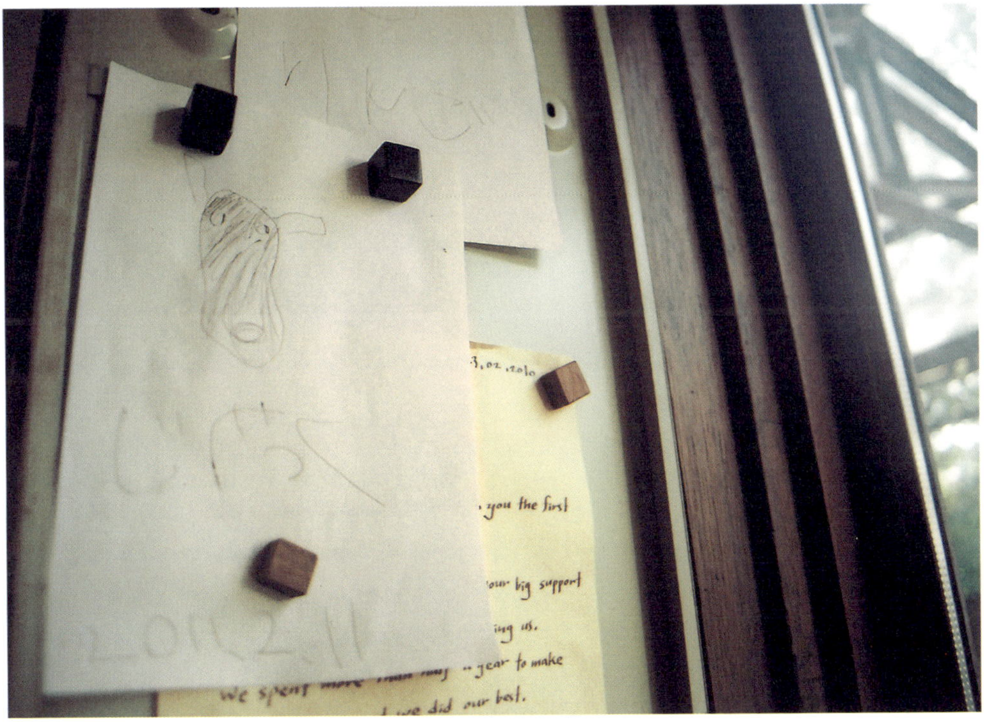

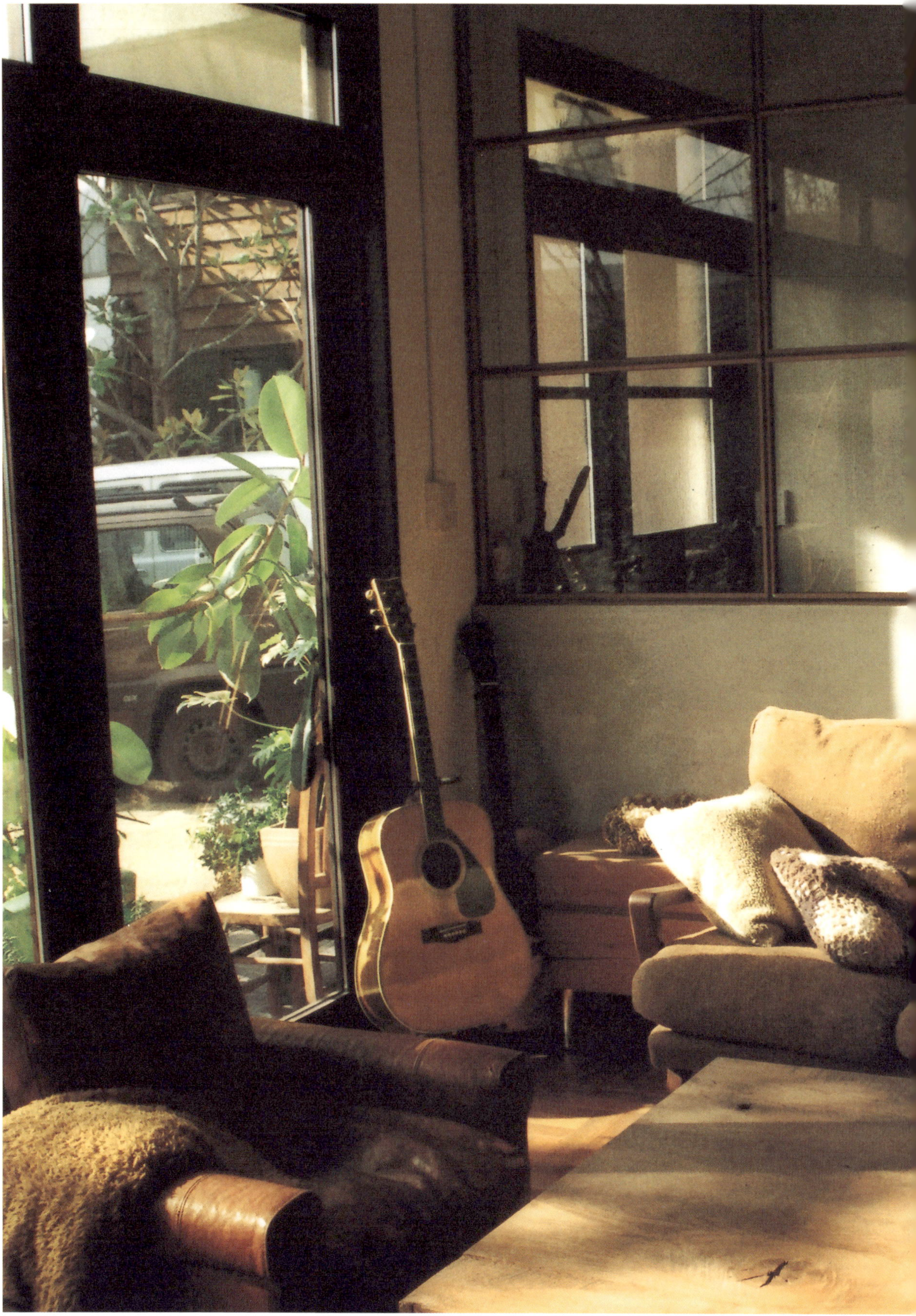

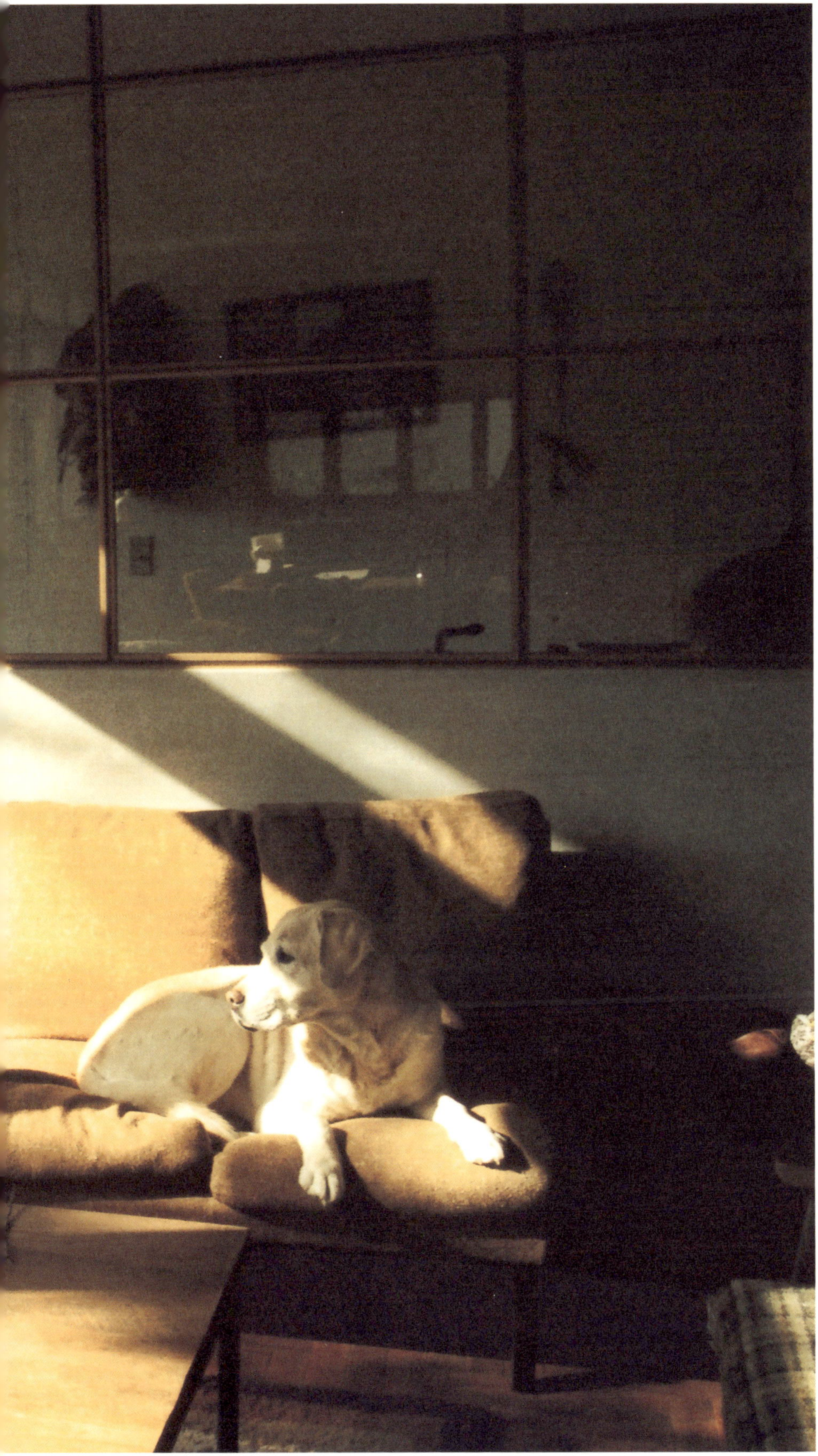

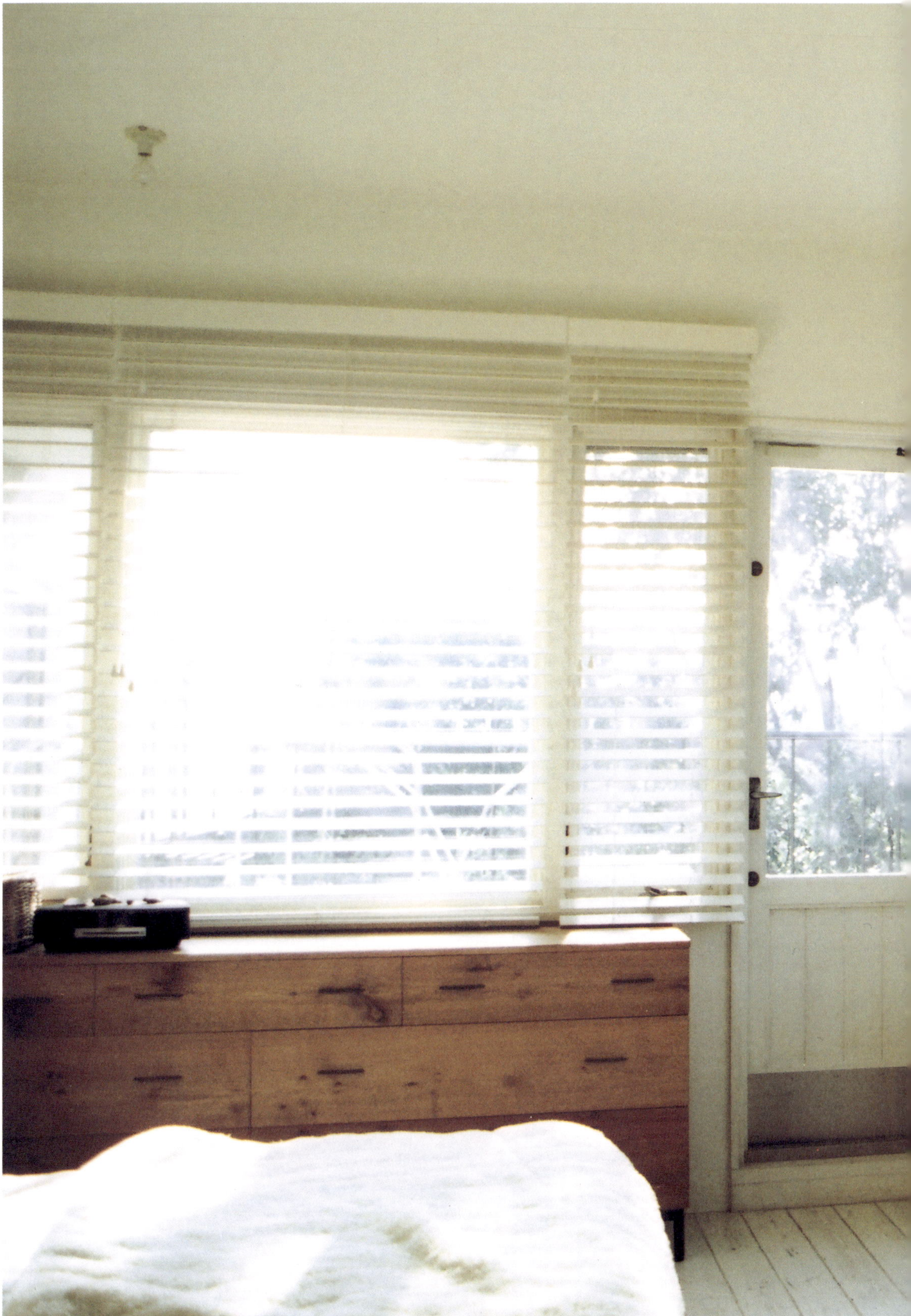

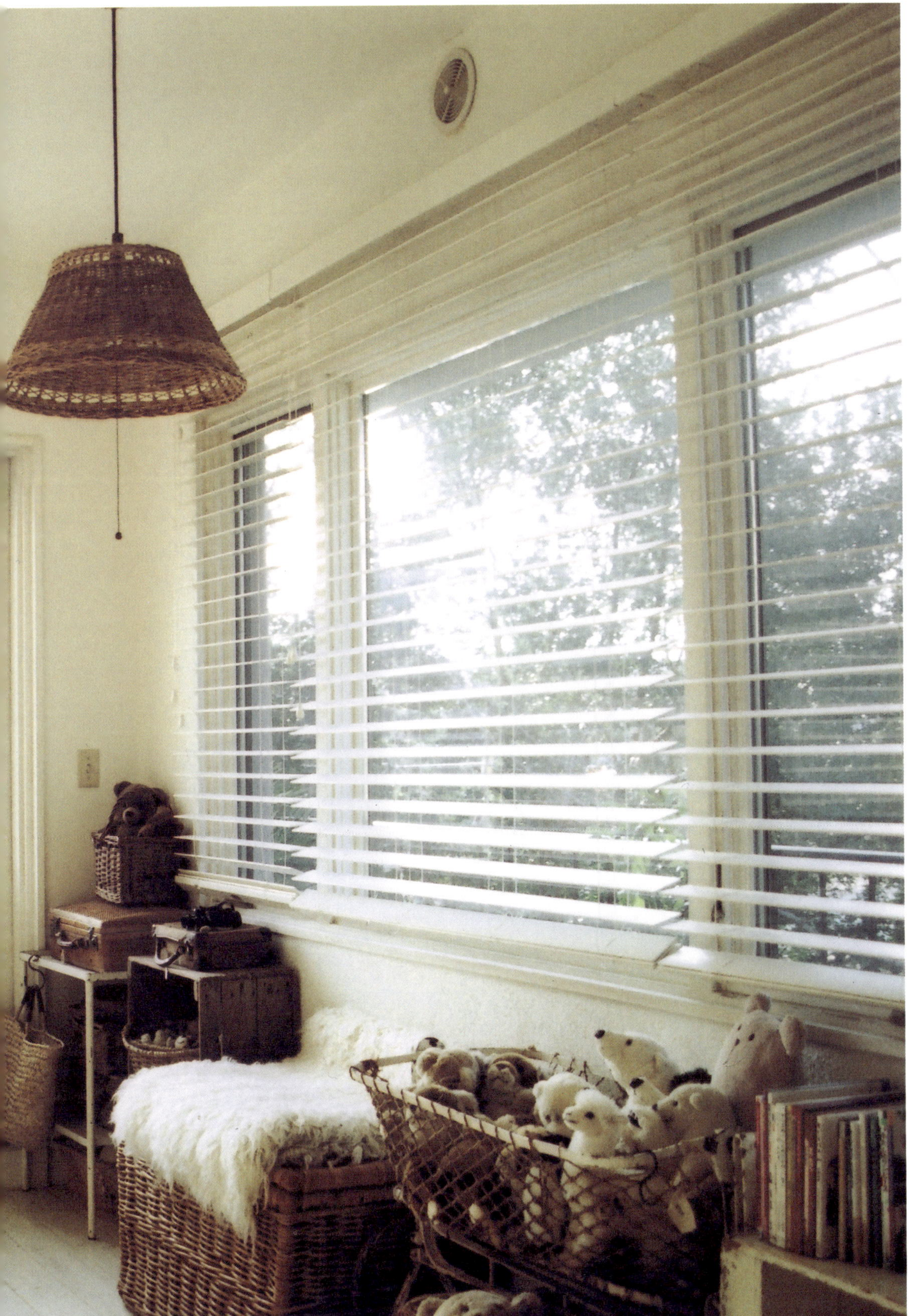

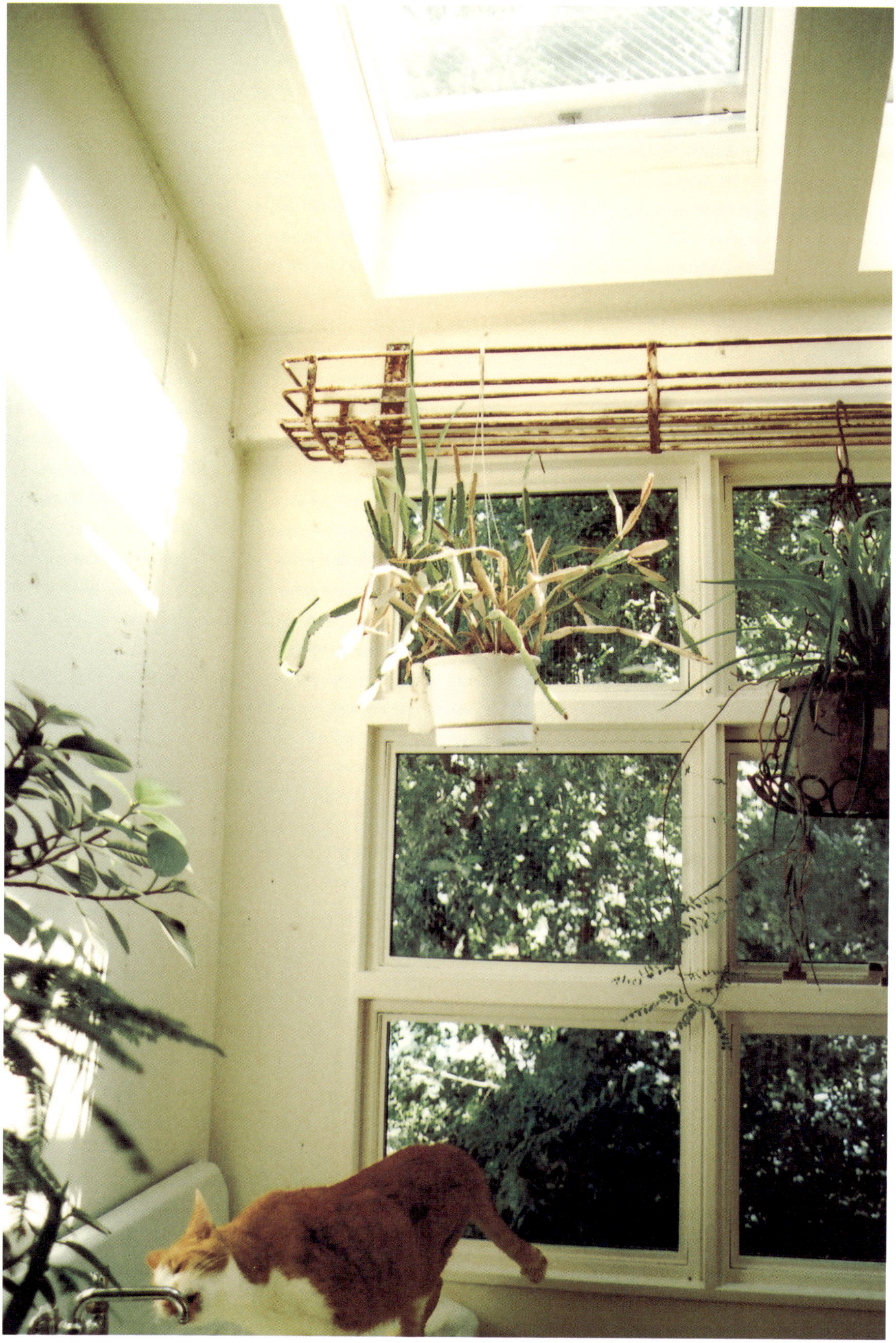

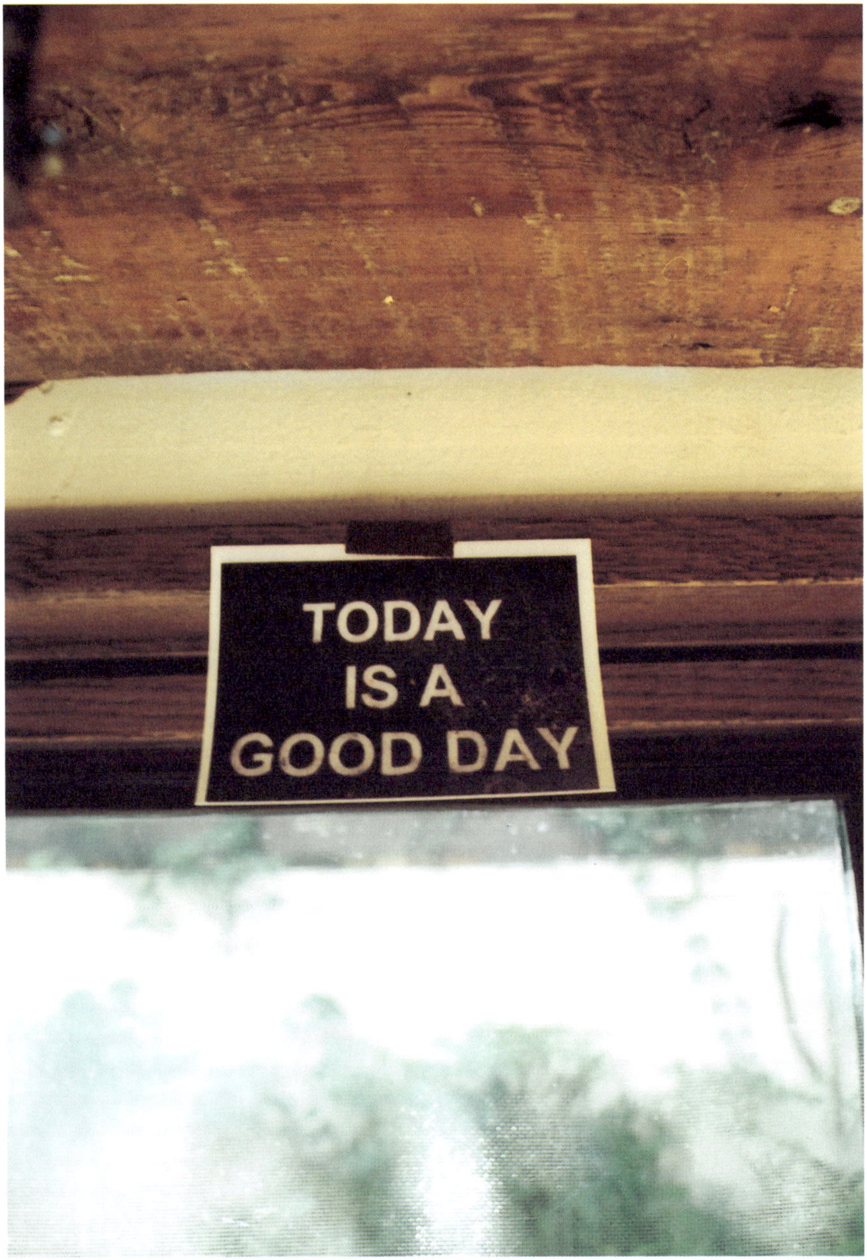
TODAY
IS A
GOOD DAY

Here comes the sun.

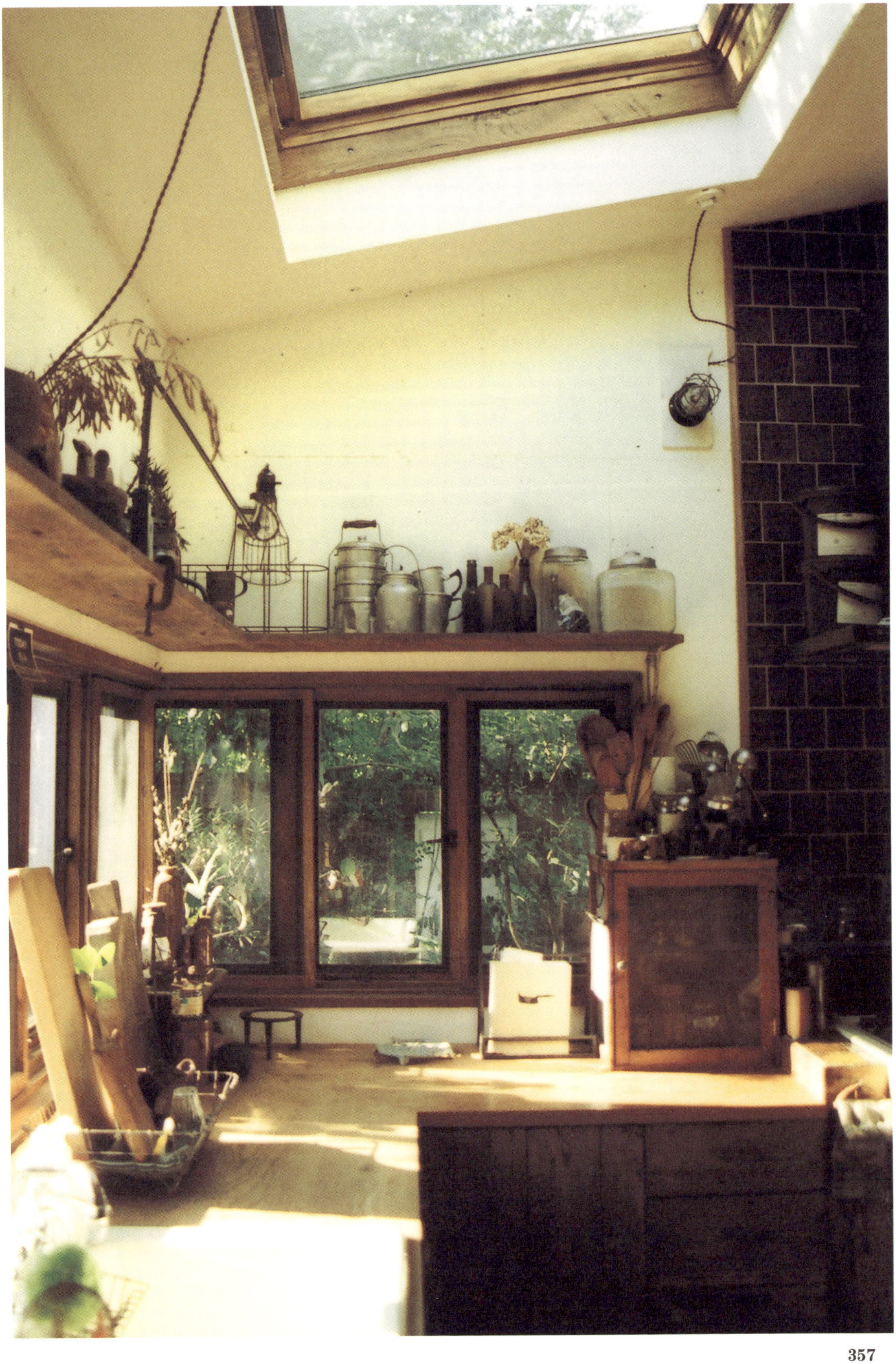

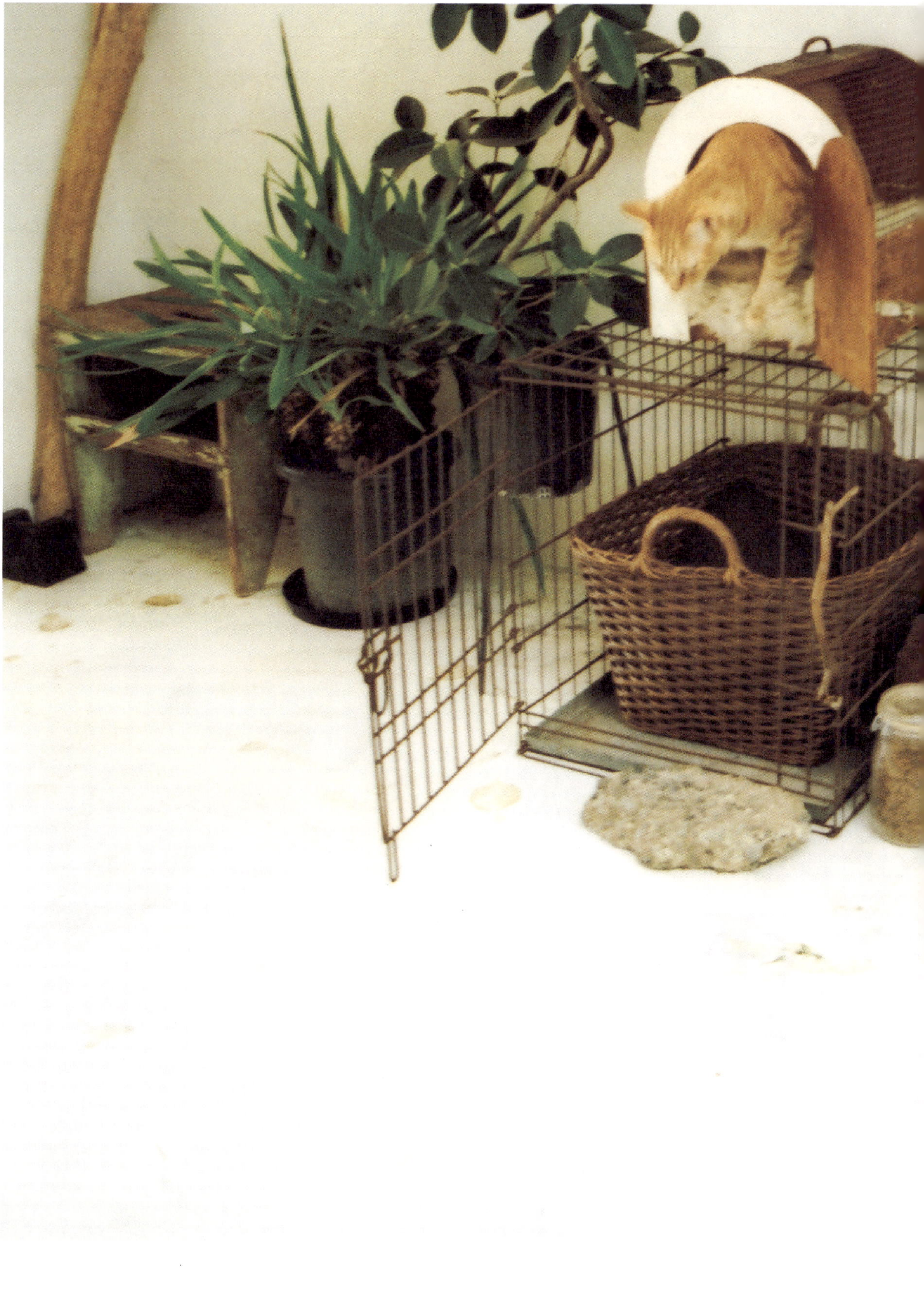

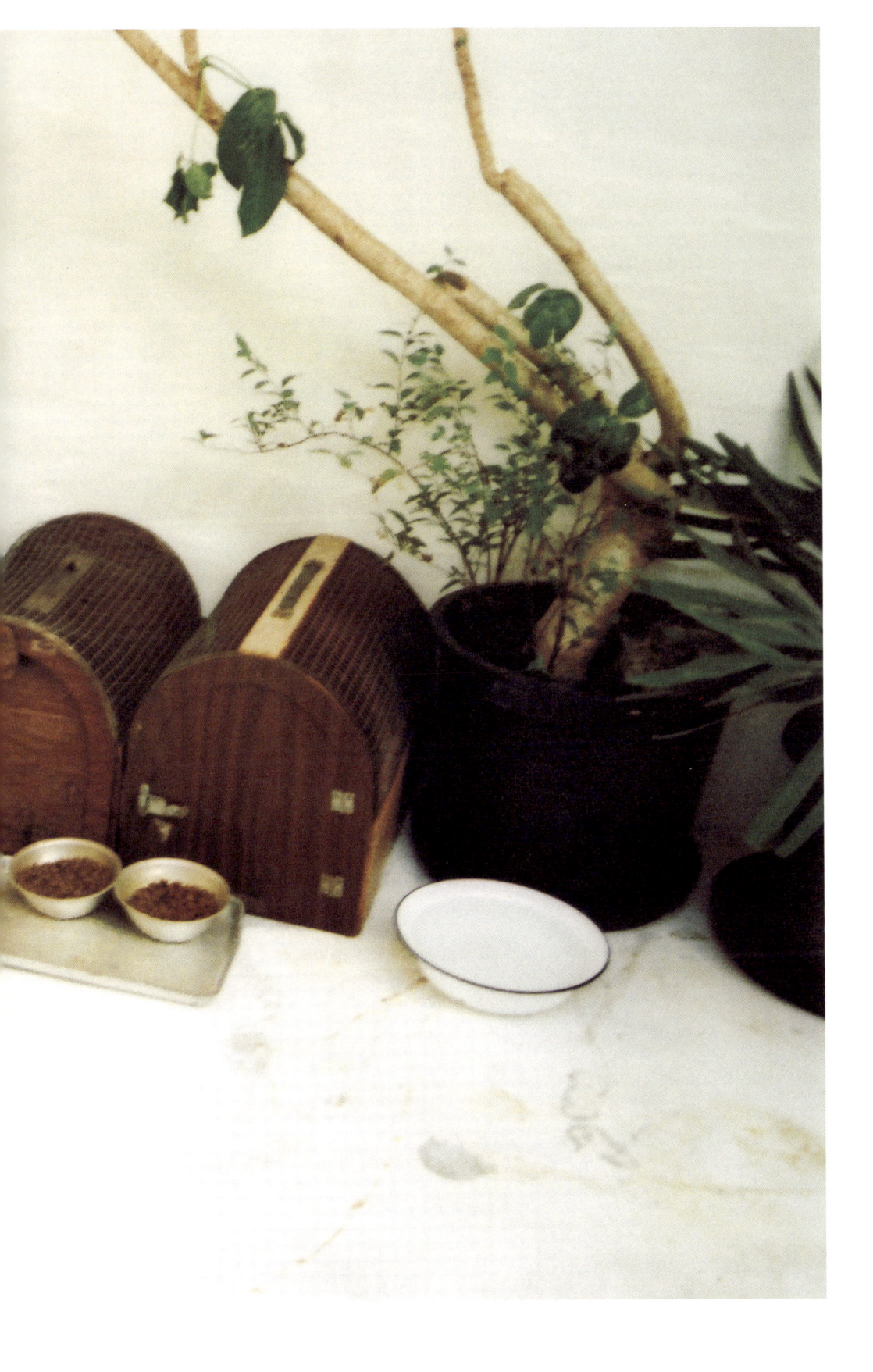

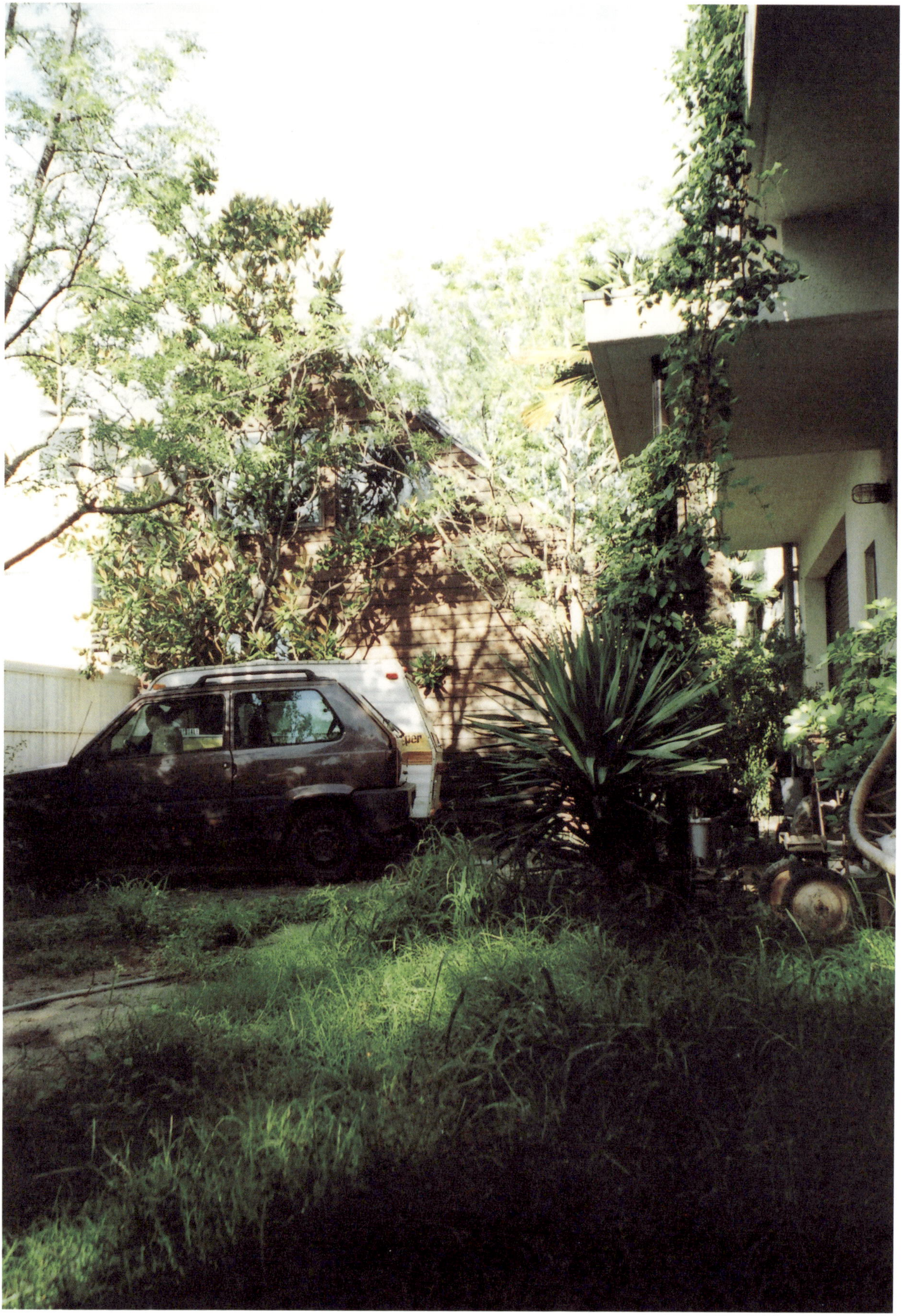

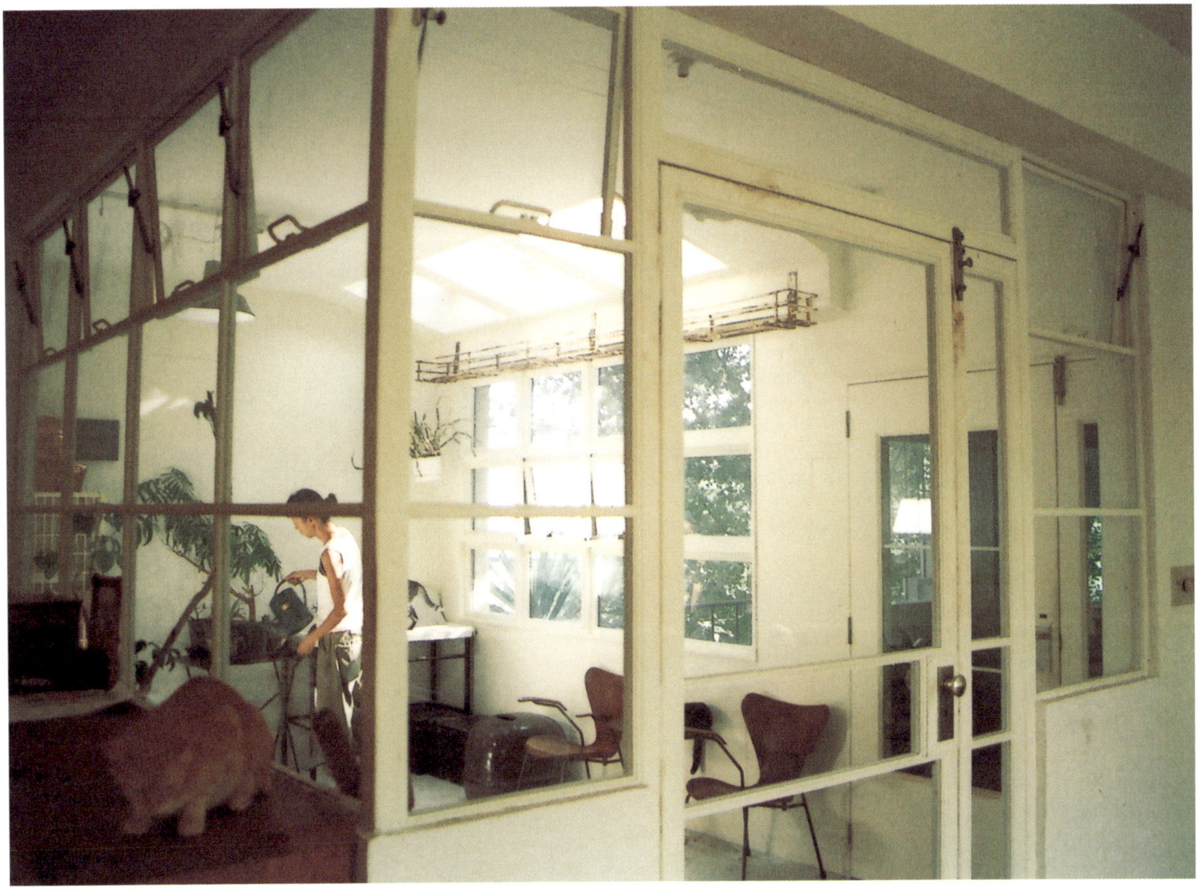

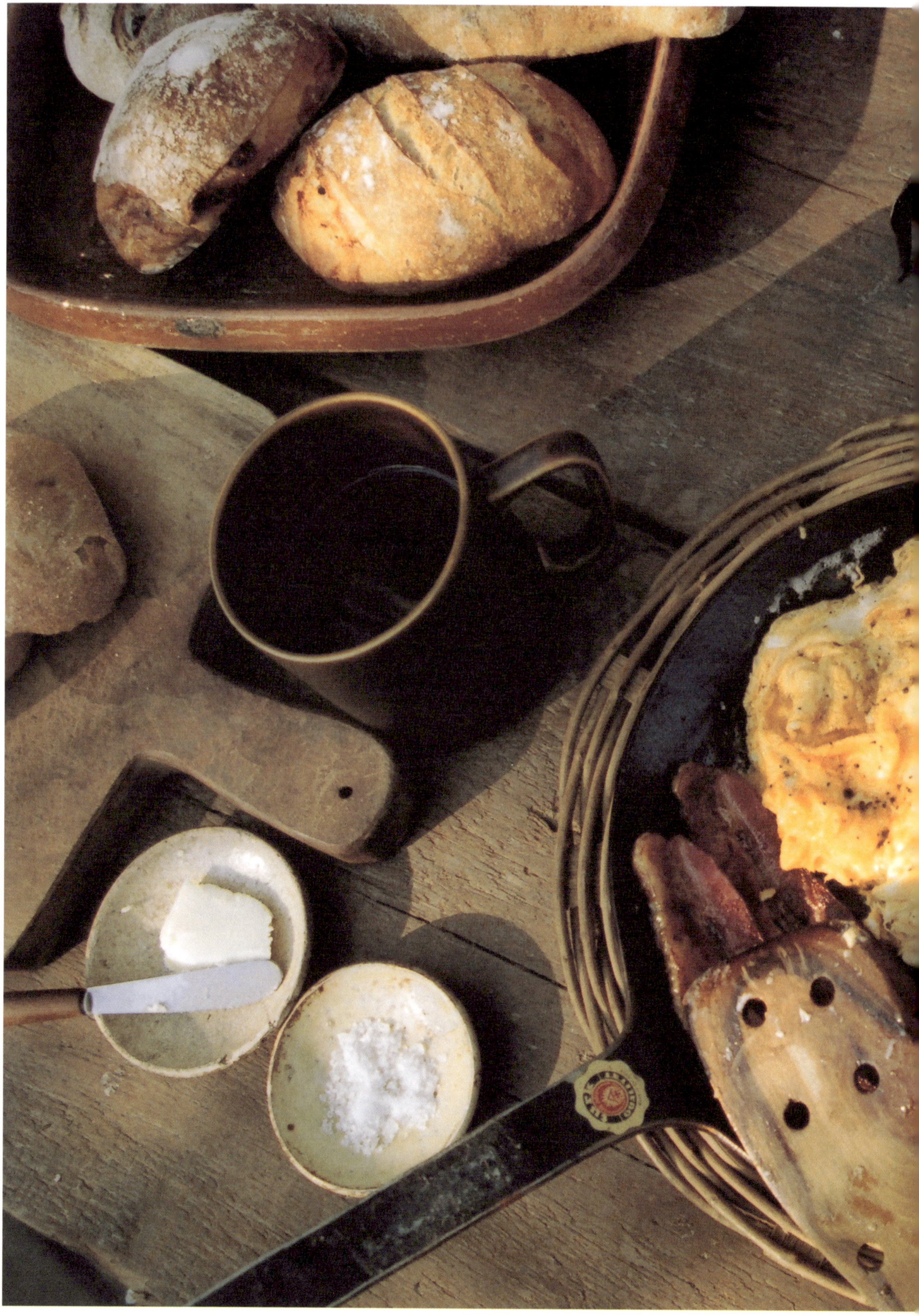

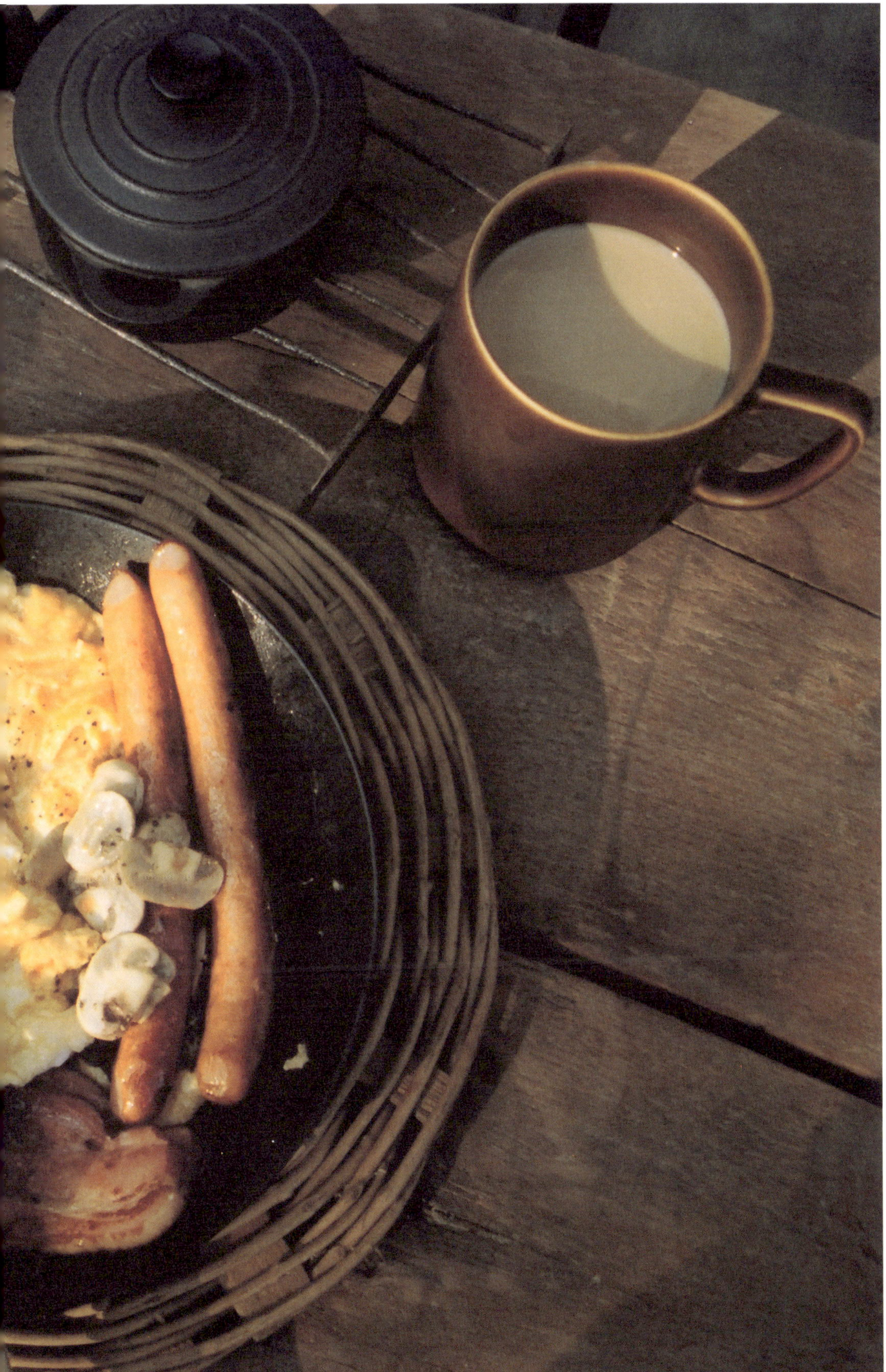

Birds of the Garden

illustration_Hiromi Karatsu

庭の鳥たち

庭に来る鳥たちの話はひりんこが。

前の家のベランダはビルに囲まれた場所だったのに、たくさんのスズメとヤマバトのつがいがエサを食べに来ていた。
ここに引っ越してきて、早速バードテーブルを作った。

近くに大きな鶴見緑地公園があるからか、大阪市内なのにいろんな種類の野鳥が来る。
いつでも観察できるように家の1階、2階それぞれの窓辺には双眼鏡と野鳥図鑑を常備している。
今まで知らなかった鳥たちをたくさん覚えた。

毎朝、スズメは50羽以上やって来る。その軍団に混じってヤマモトさん夫婦が1組。前の家の時から、つがいのヤマバトを
ヤマモトさん夫婦と呼んでいた。もちろん違うヤマモトさんだけど、やっぱりヤマモトさんと呼んでいる。
スズメたちは、朝からアキニレの樹の上のほうで「エサまだか？まだか？」と騒がしい。
私が庭に出ると、シ──ンと静かになる。全員が私に注目している。エサをバードテーブルにたっぷり入れて、「チーチー」
と唇を鳴らすと「よっしゃ！」と軍団が一斉に降りて来る。図体の大きなヤマモトさん夫婦はいつもスズメたちをけちらして
エサを食べる。スズメも負けずにバードテーブルの上を死守している。見ていて面白い。

トネリコの低い位置の枝から「カッ、カッ、カッ」と催促するのはジョウビタキのジョンビー。
生き餌専門なので、生きたミルワームを箸でつまんでジョンビー専用のお皿に入れてあげる。すると、「もう待ちきれません！」
と言わんばかりに急降下で食べに来る。私がそばにいても全然平気。もう少しで頭に乗ってくれるんじゃないかと思うほど
人懐っこい。去年はオスが来ていたが、今年はメスだ。歴代、ジョンビーは必ず1羽で現れる。縄張り意識が強いのか、
車のドアミラーや窓に映った自分の姿を見ると威嚇しているように「ヒッ、ヒッ、ヒッ」と鳴き方が変わる。
秋頃ひょっこり現れ、3月末のある日、パッタリと来なくなる。あんなに懐いていたのに。あっさりと旅立たれ、容器にまだ
残ったミルワームを見るとちょっと寂しくなる。ジョウビタキは海を渡ってチベットへ行くそうだ。
あの小さい体で海を渡るなんてすごい。

同じく渡り鳥のツグミ。去年は数回しか見かけなかったが、今年は群れで庭に来た。
トウネズミモチの紫色をした実をヒヨドリと取り合いっこしている。ツグミの渡り先はシベリア！

オリーブの樹にはカゴをひっかけて半分に切ったミカンを置く。すぐに見つけてメジロがやって来る。リンゴより断然ミカン。
いつもつがいで来て、順番交代でミカンをついばむ。1羽がついばんでる間、もう片方が見張り役。慎重派だ。

シジュウカラにはヒマワリの種。グレーの体に黒いネクタイをしている。
他には、とてもきれいな黄色のマヒワ、元気なヒヨドリ、ムクドリ、センダイムシクイなどなど。
早く、庭の樹に巣を作ってほしいと心待ちにしている。

私の生き物好きは母親の影響。私の師匠である。
未だに鳥の巣を見つける早さは負けるし、アゲハの幼虫をサナギから蝶に羽化させたり、亀のカメ太郎を脱皮、冬眠させ
たり、母の飼育力と観察力には、まだまだ足下にも及ばない。

最近、近所に住む野良猫親子がこのバードテーブルの存在に気づき、時々狙いに庭の中までやって来る。
気をつけないと。でも、ディンゴ親子が猫を発見すると威勢よく走って追い払ってくれる。（家の中では猫と仲よしなのに）
鳥も猫も真剣。犬もシンケン？いや、ただの遊び？

Johnby Bird

The tale of the birds who visit our garden is best left to Hiromi.

Although the verandah in our previous home was surrounded by buildings, many sparrows and turtledoves came to feed there. Soon after we moved to our new place we made a bird table from which they could feed.

I don't know if it's because we are close to Tsurumi Ryokuchi park (one of the few large parks in Osaka City), but many birds come to visit us. We have binoculars and guides to wild birds scattered about the house so that we can watch them at any time. Since moving here, I have learned the names of many birds I never knew before.

Every morning, a flock of about fifty sparrows pays us a visit. Accompanying the sparrows are two turtledoves that we call Mr. and Mrs. Yamamoto. At our previous house there were a pair of turtledoves to whom we gave the same name. (The Japanese word for turtledove is *yamabato* and Yamamoto is a common Japanese name.) This, of course, is a different pair, but we call them Mr. and Mrs. Yamamoto anyway.

In the morning, the birds sit in the Japanese elm tree, chirping away, asking, "Is breakfast ready? Is breakfast ready?" When I step out into the garden, they all go silent and watch me carefully. I pour some birdseed onto the bird table and they descend as a flock. As they begin feeding, Mr. and Mrs. Yamamoto, being larger, dominate the group. The sparrows, though, make sure they get enough to eat, too. It is fun to watch.

In the lower branches of an ash tree, a redstart caws at me repeatedly. It likes live food, so I bought some millworms from a "home center" and use chopsticks to place them on a special eating platform made just for it. It swoops down to eat immediately. Soon, I think, it'll become so friendly that it'll perch on my head.
Last year it was a male that came, this year it's a female. Every year, one redstart is sure to appear. They are very territorial. When they catch a glimpse of themselves reflected in a car mirror or window they caw threateningly at the reflection. They always appear unexpectedly in autumn and disappear in March. Apparently, they fly all the way to Tibet. It's incredible that such a little thing can fly across the sea.

Another migratory bird that visits us is the thrush. Last year we got only a few visits, but this year we got many. They fight with bulbuls for the purple fruit of the Japanese privet tree. They fly all the way to Siberia!

On our olive tree I hung a basket half full of mandarin oranges. A Japanese white-eye discovers it and comes quickly. Mandarin oranges are far more popular than pieces of apple. They always come in pairs, taking turns to peck at the fruit while the other keeps watch. How prudent they are.

Among our other visitors have been great tits, wearing black neckties over their grey bodies, yellow siskins, bulbuls, starlings, and crowned willow warblers.

I'm looking forward to the time when birds start nesting in the trees of our garden. In my love of nature I have been influenced by my mother. If she finds caterpillars on the lemon tree in front of her house she keeps them safe until they create cocoons and become butterflies. Once, she found a turtle on the street and helped it sleep though winter. She finds bird's nests more quickly than me, too.

Recently, some stray cats in the neighborhood have realized the existence of our bird table and sometimes come snooping around. When Dingo and her sons see them, they drive them away with their barks. (The dogs get on well with the house cats, though.) The birds and cats are serious. Are the dogs serious, too? Maybe they're just playing.

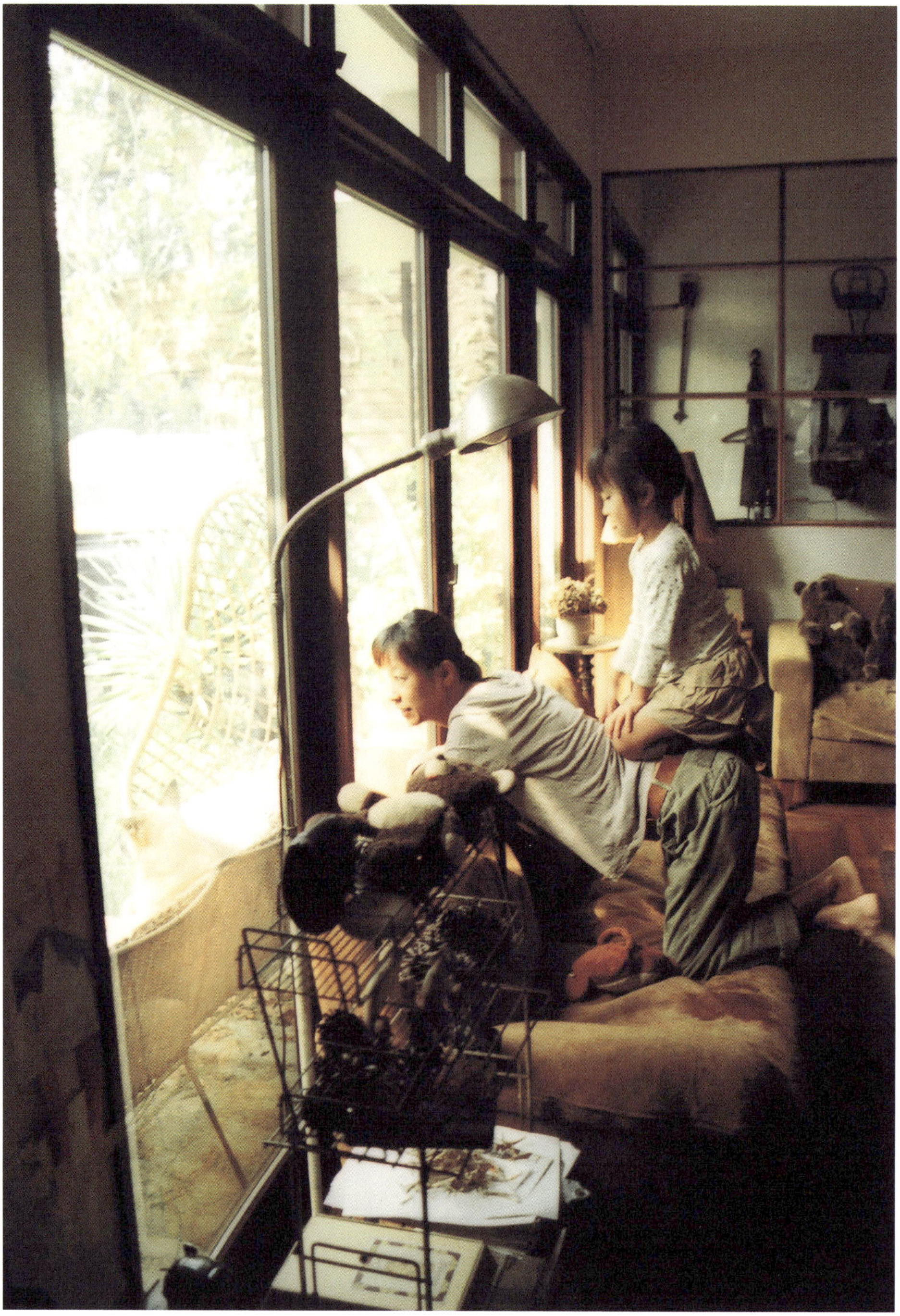

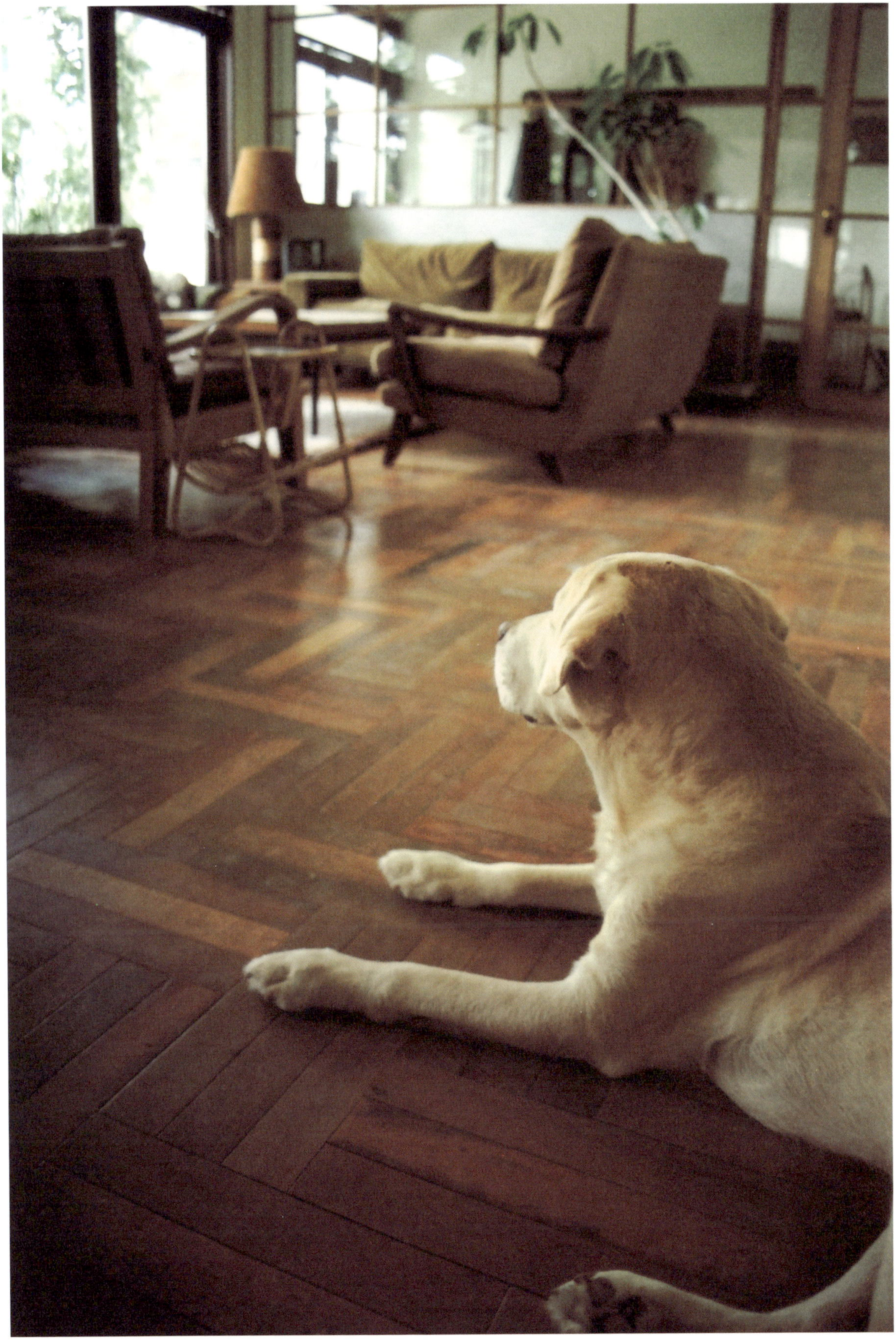

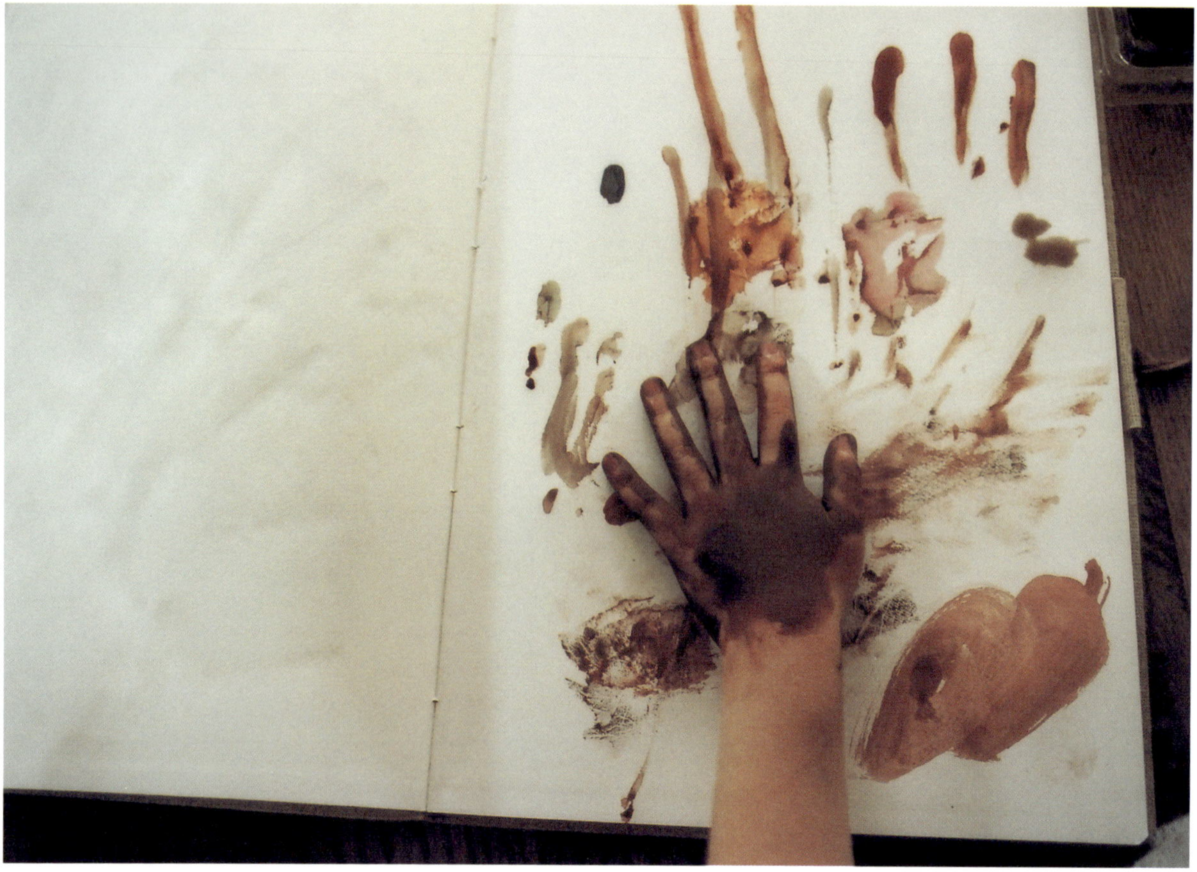

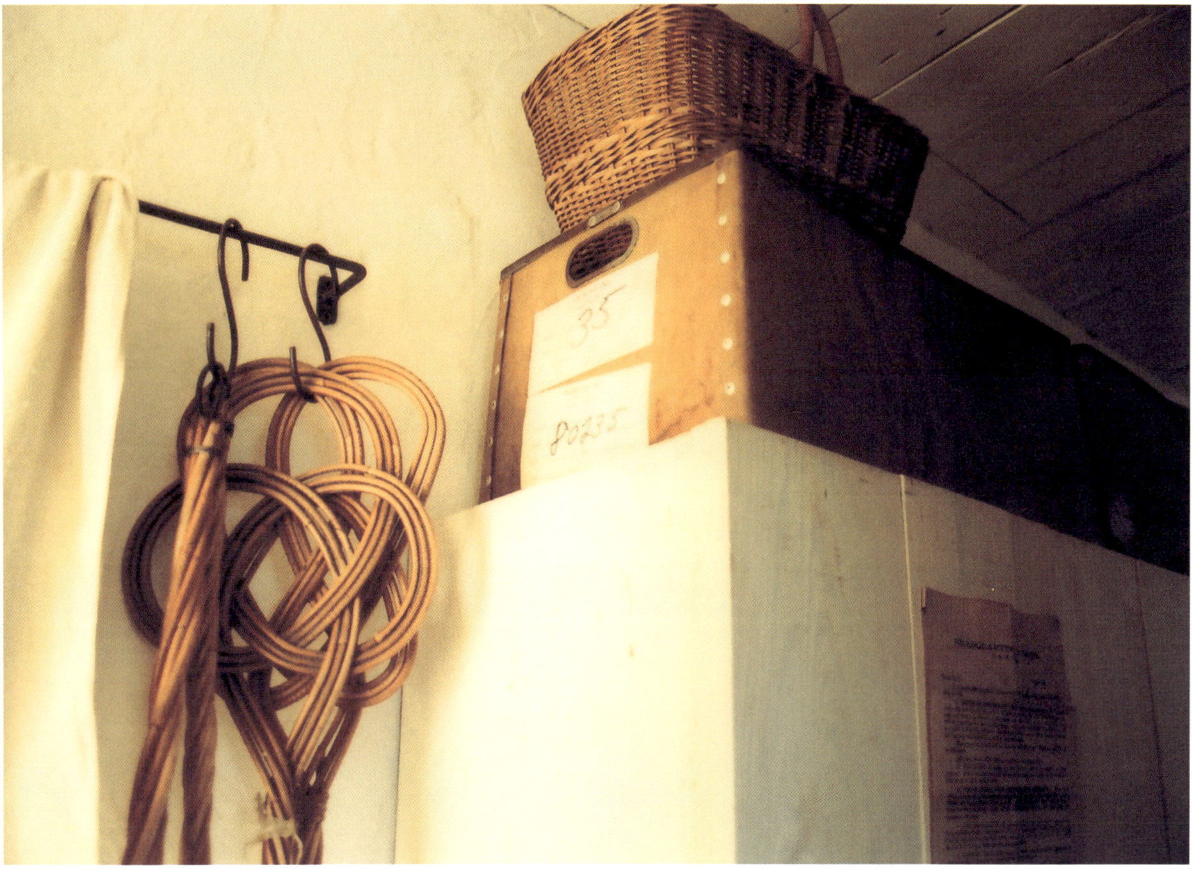
35
80235

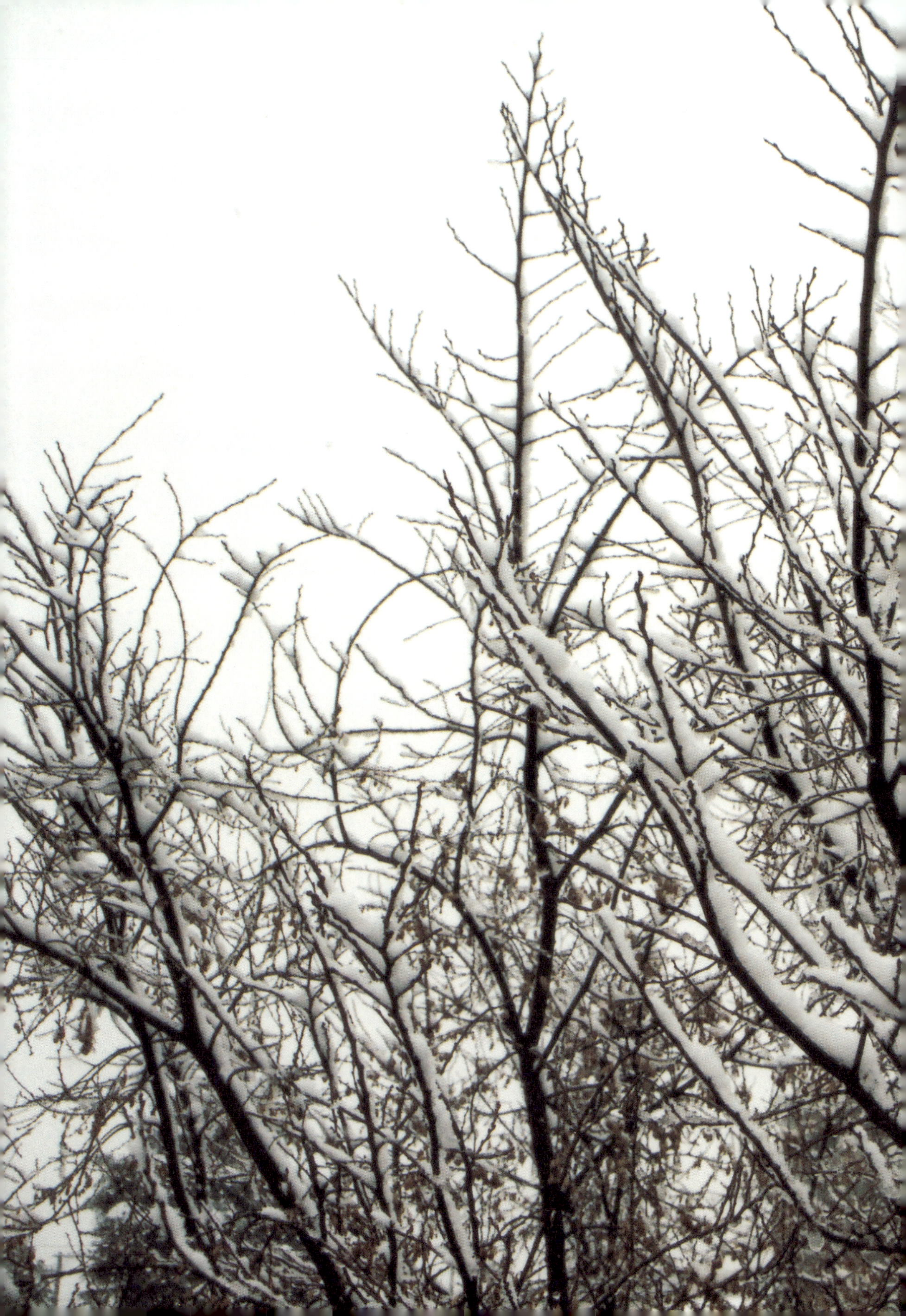

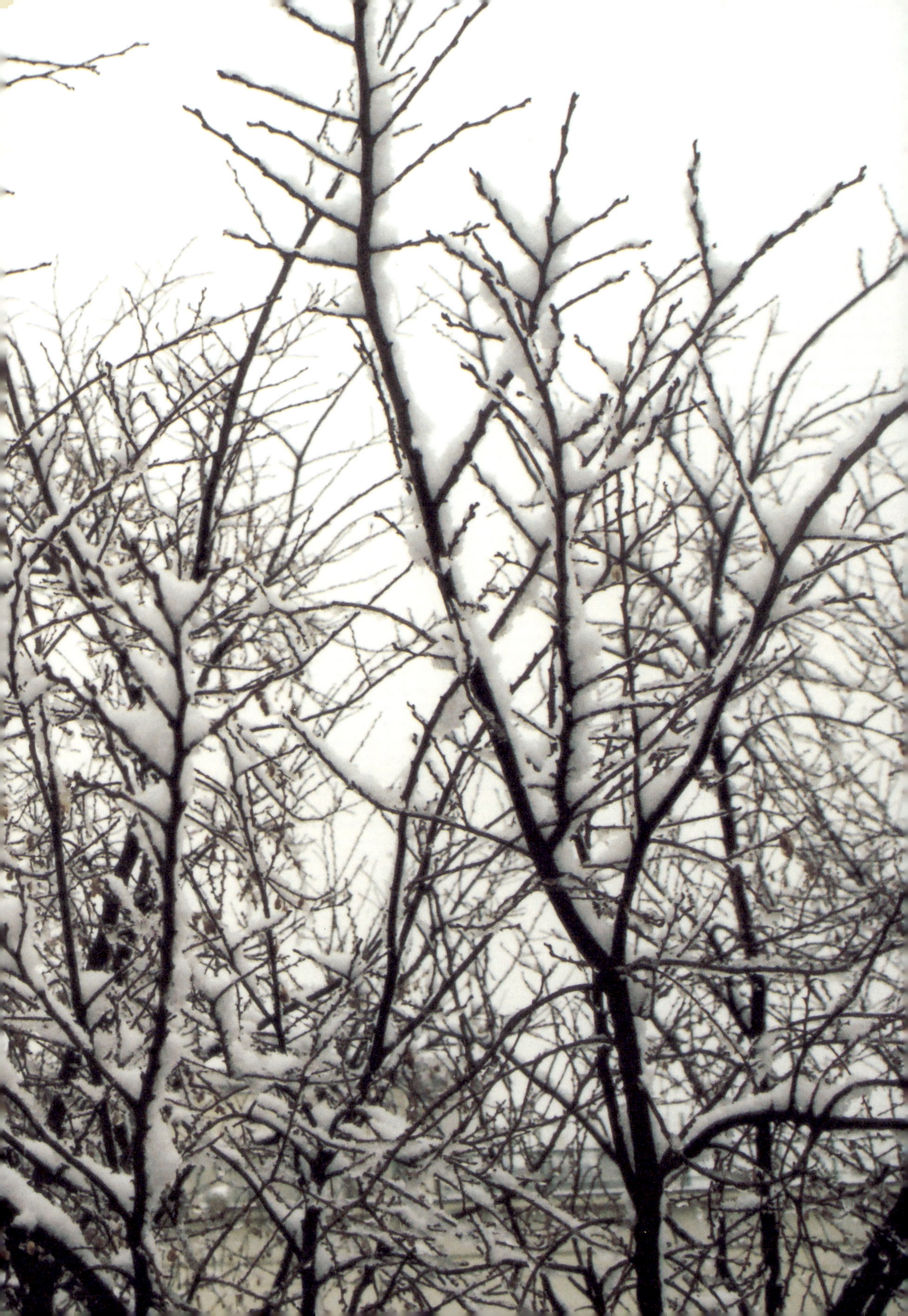

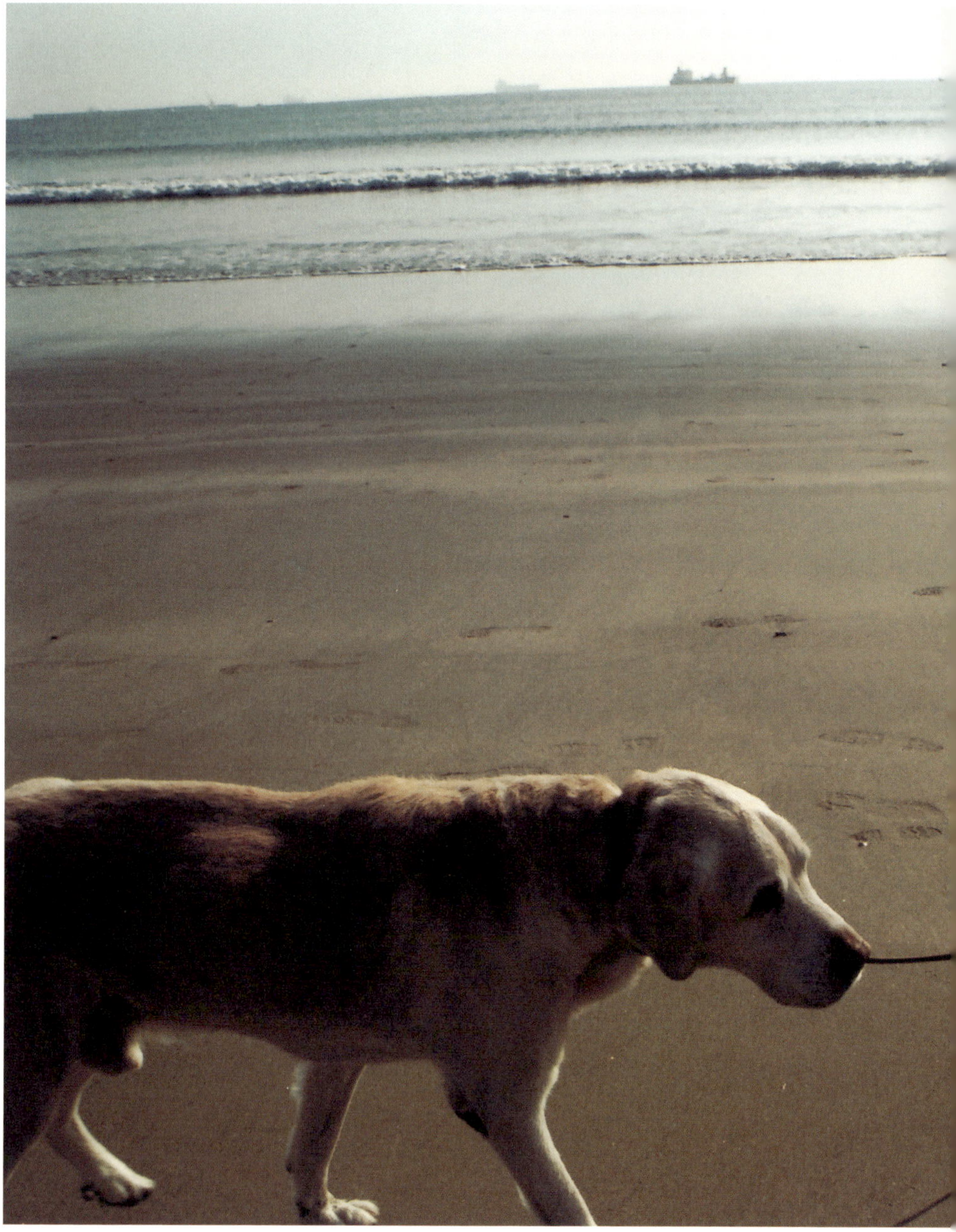

December 6, 2010 Walking with Buddy

Living Here

住んでから

庭のポーチにガラスの屋根をつけて、テーブルも置いた。人が来て、そこにある椅子でコーヒーを飲みながら話す。気がつくと、すでに３時間。風に樹が揺れる。気持ちがいい。コーヒーがワインに変わり、夕方の時間、空の色がゆっくりと移っていく。
これがやりたかったこと。

友達のカナダ人、ブラウンに以前聞いたことがある。
「カナダでは昼ご飯に何を食べる？」
学校から家に帰ってきて冷凍庫(アメリカやカナダでよくある大型の横置き型)をバカッと開けて、知り合いのブッチャーに頼んで作ってもらっているパティを５、６枚鷲掴む。バンズと共にテラスに常設のバーベキューコンロで焼き、お母さん特製ピクルスと一緒に挟んでハンバーガーにして食べる。それが世界で一番おいしいハンバーガーだ。
目を輝かせて彼は言った。その言葉が何年経ってもいつも頭にあった。
食べてみたい。そして、特別なものではないそんな日常感に心惹かれていた。

今、家の冷凍庫にはタケウチさんに焼いてもらったバンズと僕が作ったパティが入っている。
ポーチに置いたバーベキューコンロのスイッチをカチッと回し火をつけバンズとパティを焼く。
玉葱の輪っかを１、２本とチェダーチーズ１枚、塩、胡椒。当たり前に、日常的にささっと作りたいと思いながら、どうもまだ不慣れでバタバタしてしまう。でも、とびきりおいしい。

新しい場所での生活は始まっている。でも、あちこちが未完成。まだまだやりたいことがいっぱいある。
その中のひとつ、キッチンの天窓。
設計が終わりかけた頃に、つけたいと思ったけど間に合わなかった。ちょっと心残りだった。
家の東側につけ足したように平屋で飛び出しているキッチン。
L字に窓があるのに思ったほど明るくなかった。住んでみて分かった。

ある日、決断した。あけよう。天窓をつけよう。
すでに生活が始まっているキッチンのコンクリートの天井に穴をあけるなんて大変そう。
粉塵もすごそう。でも、そこは工夫と作戦。１週間頑張ればいいだけ、その後はずっと明るい毎日が待っている。
そう考えて、友達の工務店のタカシタ君に相談した。作戦が立ち決行。
完成した翌朝、その明るさに驚いた。
下から見上げると、エノキの枝が見える。
その枝に止まっている鳥のおなかも見える。夜にはお月さんもよく見える。
良かった。あけて良かった。

住んでみての実感。性能のことを考えて作った家。断熱や気密、ペアガラスに木製サッシ。驚くほど快適！大正解。
まず、静か。外部の音がほとんど入ってこない。
夏、灼熱とも言える最近の大阪、この家では2階の寝室のエアコン1台を29℃の設定でつけたままにする。
それだけで、1階も涼しい。急激最強の冷たい風で足が冷えるなんてこともない。
冬、ドアを開けて家に入った瞬間、土間からもうすでにじんわりと暖かい。どの部屋も寒くない。
コンクリートに埋め込んだ床暖と性能を高めた家の相乗効果。せっかく設置した薪ストーブの出番がない。
実は、店にある大きな窓。南側に面したずらっと並んだ大きな窓にもペアガラスを入れている。
だからか、暖房、冷房のコストが低い。
僕は死ぬ間際に言うかもしれない。「ガラスだけはいいのにしときや」

家の2階のリビングにしようと思っている部屋、テレビを置いて映画でも見てくつろぐ部屋にしようと作った。
でもそこはまだ空っぽ。猫8匹の部屋と化している。
なぜかというと、こんな時こそ新しく家具を考える時。せっかくだから、どんなものが欲しいか、じっくりと考えて作ろうと思っている。そして作ってみて、実際に自分で使ってみる。それがTRUCKの家具になっていくのだから。とりあえずと定番のものを置いてもしょうがない。そう、今こそ、家具を作る時。

夜には庭に出て、小さな焚き火台でオークの木っ端に火をつけ、それを眺めながらスコッチ（何事も気分！）を飲む。
地面に近い高さに座れる椅子が欲しい。欲しいなら作ろう。ちょっとグラスを置くテーブルも欲しい。それも作ろう。

TRUCKのカタログ。気がついたら、出してから7年も経っている。ヤバい。
最新号が7年前とは。ここのところ、建築のことばっかりだった。
新しいNESTを産み出して、ようやく2人は新しい家具を作りたくてメラメラしている。

家を考えていた頃、ひりんこが出かけていない1人の時。
玉造の部屋のテーブルに座り、まだできていない新しい家で窓の外に見える樹を眺めながら何かを考えている自分の姿を想像していた。そこにはボリュームを絞ったゴンザレスのソロピアノが流れていた。
今、新しい家の2階、まだ猫だけの部屋、窓の近くに小さなデスクを置きこの文章を書いている。同じゴンザレスのピアノが小さく流れ、窓の外では樹の枝が少し揺れている。猫のサビもヒヨドリが木の実を食べているのを眺めている。冬の西日が優しい。そう、こんなことがしたかった。

ワンたちは日中のほとんどをシロクマ舎で過ごす。みんなやーちゃんが大好き。ジョンはやーちゃんの椅子でくつろぎ、仕事椅子をとられたやーちゃんは小さいスツールに座って革を縫っている。時々、休憩？で庭に出て走り回ったり、日向ぼっこをしたりしてる。敷地内を自由にウロウロ。一番喜んでいるのはワンたちかも？

Living Here

日菜も外のテーブルで絵を描いたり、簡単な工作をしたり、シロクマ舎でやーちゃんの仕事を見たり、ひりんこと一緒に店の雑貨を整えたり、伝票を書く真似をしたり、どんぐりを拾ったり、Birdのキッチンを覗いたり。夕方の屋上で走り回ったり。多分、いい経験をしてると思う。まだ5歳やけど。

西日の時間、店の屋上に行くと、ひらけた空、東には生駒山や信貴山、北にも北摂の山並みが見える。
青い空からピンクまでのグラデーション。あまりにもきれいな空の時は、スタッフみんなに「めっちゃきれいな空やで！」と声をかける。みんな上がって来て空を見る。みんなの顔がいい。
ここは大阪、ヌーサではない。でもきれいな空はここにもある。

ペントハウスのように作ったスタッフルーム。簡単なキッチン、洗濯機があり、ドアを開けて裏側に出るとシャワーもある。屋外で屋根もないが、夏に汗と木屑まみれになっても、サクッと流して出かけることができる。テーブルに並んだ椅子に座ると、広くとった窓から視界のほとんどが空と樹と遠くに見える山並み。
ここもペアガラス仕立てなので、冬も天気がいいとぽかぽか暖かい。
玉造では、店の裏の北側で日射しも入らない暗くて寒いスペースしかなくて、着替えや昼ご飯もそこで食べていた。それがとても気になっていた。
今ではこのスタッフルームが一番気持ちいい場所。特等席。

天井高のあるショールーム、大きな窓。
TRUCKを訪れるお客さんのほとんどは、この建物が新築とは思わないようだ。元々あった学校か公民館なんかを改造したのかと聞かれる。レンガの塀、敷石、木造のアトリエ、ここにある大きなアキニレやケヤキも、まるでずっと前からここにあるように馴染んでいる。

Birdでは、1人で本を読みながらコーヒーを飲んでる人、休日のランチにワインを飲んでる人、家族連れでのご飯、ちびっこハンバーグも人気。天気のいいお昼に女子2人がパイントグラスでビールを飲んでいる。カッコいい。
バス停しかなかった頃とは大違い。それぞれの時間を過ごしている人たちの姿を見てBirdを作って良かったと思う。

3月に入り、店から出て階段を降りながら、エノキの枝先に新芽の膨らみを確認する。
間違いなく春がすぐそこに近づいている。

Living Here

トムとマギー、ジョン。
モンテプルチアーノのアグリツーリズモのカリーン。
トスカーナの丘の上、夕方の時間、遥か遠くまで続く景色を見ながら語り合った、たまたまそこで出会ったドイツ人。
アムステルダムのB&Bの元帽子職人のおじいさん、
微かに流れるクラシックを聞きながら、新聞を読みながらの朝ご飯。

それぞれの時間、考え。そんな中の、いいなぁと思う小さな部分、時には大きな部分。それらがいつもずっと記憶としてある。多分、少なからず影響されている。そして、ここ、大阪で作った(完成ではなく、常に進行形だけど)場所。
ここにはここの時間がある。影響を受けた誰かの真似ではない。自分たちの時間が。それでいい。
そしてまたいつか、どこかで、誰かに話そう。自分の話を。
と、ペンを置き、遠くを眺めてみたりして。

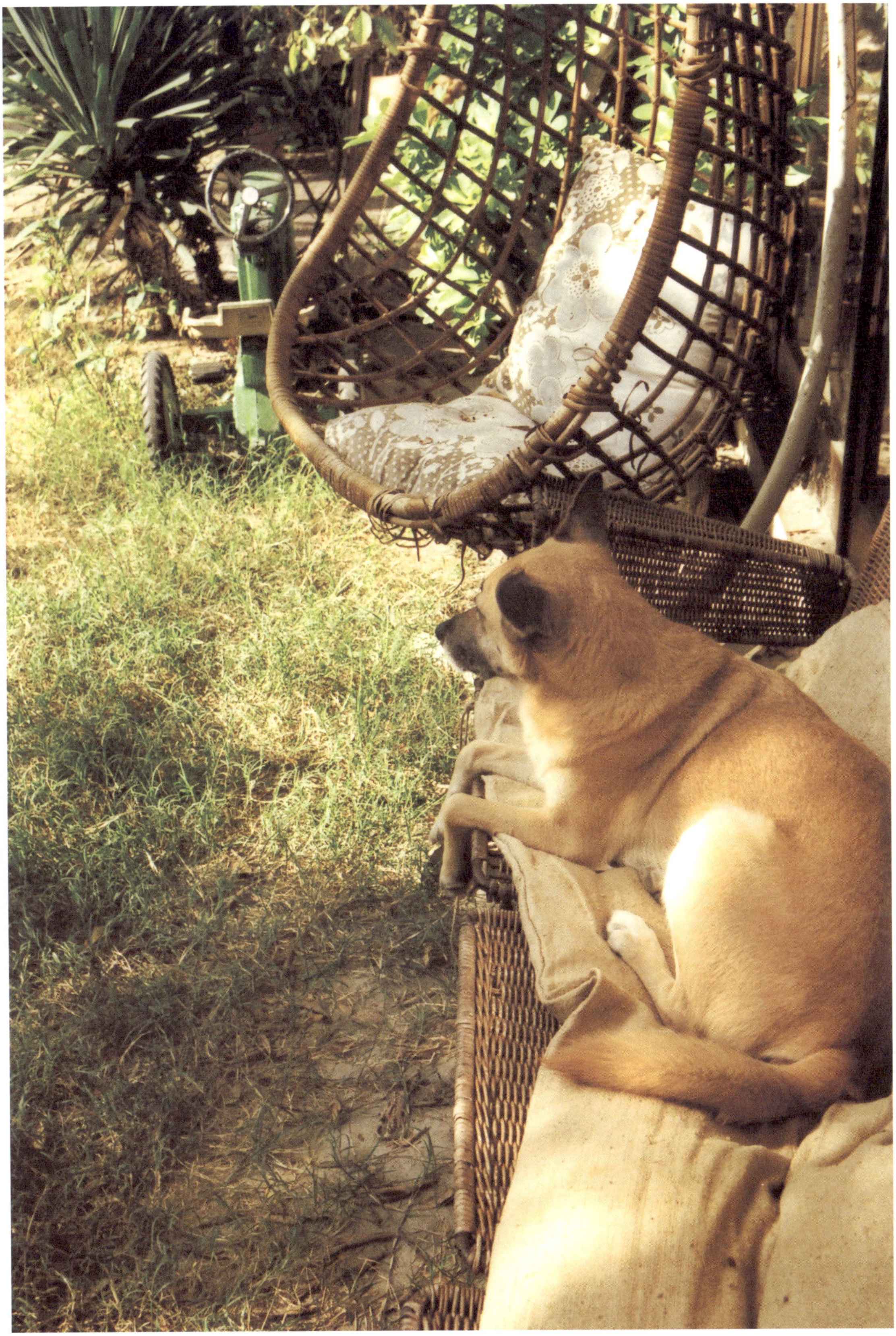

住んでから －ひりんこバージョン－

子供ができたら世界が変わる。作るものまで変わってしまうと、誰かに聞いたりもしたけど、特にTRUCKの家具は何も変わらなかった。急に角が優しいテーブルになるわけでもなく。
ただ、日菜のために作った子供用の椅子と机がラインナップに加わっただけ。

新しい場所に引っ越しても、店も自宅のインテリアも何も変わらない。
好きなものはずっと使い続ける。

古いビルを改造して素人ながら2人で作った前の家。そこで使っていた家具はもちろん、一緒に時間を過ごした床板までめくって持って来た。キッチンの流し台も。余った床板に実験用のシンクをはめ込んだだけの簡単なものだけど、10年以上も使っていると、とてもいい飴色になった。これは現在シロクマ舎の小さなキッチンに収まっている。長いこと使って飽きるどころか、さらに愛着が増したものたち。
新しい場所にもすっと心地よく馴染む。

子供と一緒に暮らす新しい家。
毎朝、一番始めに目に入るのは朝日と窓いっぱいの緑。
とりんこは、家族で一番の早起きさん。早朝からワンニャンのお世話で忙しい。
みんなで朝ご飯を食べる。朝からたくさんおしゃべりする。並んで歯を磨く。2階の洗面所の窓から大好きなアキニレがすぐそばに見える。眉毛の形がとりんこにそっくりな日菜は、いつもご機嫌さんで明るく笑っている。

初めは、ちょっとよそよそしかったキッチン。
特別料理が得意ですってわけではないので、リビングに向かってのオープンキッチンより、好きな景色がいっぱい見える基地みたいにしたかった。そこに立つだけで楽しくなるような。L字型にとった窓からは、庭で走り回るワンたち、植木やバードテーブルの様子がよく見える。天窓をあけ、とりんこに棚をつけてもらって、古い鍋やら集めたカゴやら好きなものをみちっと並べたら、どんどん自分らしくなってきた。

天気のいい日にはベランダに出て布団を干す。これだけでも前の家のことを思うと、嬉しくてニヤけてくる。急に雲行きがあやしくなっても大丈夫。店やシロクマ舎は隣だから、ダッシュで帰って取り込める。

店や家の庭。少し前までは、それぞれ別々の所にあった大きな樹々が、今ではずっと前からそうだったようにここに根をおろし、葉を茂らせる。
芝生やクローバーの種を蒔いたり、山登りに行った時に摘んできたスミレを移植したり、ポーチの柱につる性のハーデンベルギアをからませたり、いっぱいある鉢植えのお世話も結構忙しい。夏の植木の水やりなんか汗だくで1時間以上かかる。

Living Here

庭の北東にちょっとした畑を作る予定だったが、観察していると思ったほど日当たりが良くなかったので、野菜はプランターで南向きのベランダで育てることにした。
そのスペースに、植木用具をしまう小屋を作ろうと考え中。
日菜にも自分用の花壇を作ってやると、見よう見まねで世話をやいている。
いつの間にかどろんこ遊びに変わってるけど。

夕方には仕事をいったん切り上げて、すぐ近くの保育園にママチャリで日菜を迎えに行き、その帰りに一緒に買い物に行く。スーパーもすぐ近くにあって、中央区に住んでいた頃よりも便利。ぎりぎりまで仕事ができるし、毎日のことなので近いのは本当に助かる。そのまま晩ご飯の用意をする時もあれば、また日菜を連れて店に戻り、仕事を続ける時も。忙しい時には無理して作らないで、家族で外に食べに行く。もちろんBirdにもしょっちゅう行く。自分たちの食べたいものと飲みたいビールにワイン。ちびっこハンバーグだってある。そんな最高の店が目の前にあるんだから。

緑がいっぱいあって、スーパーや学校、駅にも歩いて行ける。
カリーンに聞いて羨ましく思ったモンテプルチアーノ。あの景色には及ばないけど。

いい季節には夕方から庭で、とりんこが張り切ってお肉を焼く。
おいしそうな匂いに誘われて、手の空いたスタッフが、次々と仕事の合間に覗きに来る。
石を積んで作った窯に、手際よくとりんこが火をおこし、野菜やソーセージをナイフで削った木の枝にさして焼く。これが思いの他おいしくて大人気。みんな夢中で、マイ木の枝を削る。スーパーで買ってきた普通のソーセージでも、みんなで外で食べるとおいしい。ノッてくると、ギターも登場。調子に乗って歌っても、周りは学校なので夜は誰もいないのだ。
夜のハンモックも人気で、お月さんを見ながらゆ～らゆら。最高。

年末にイベントスペースで開催したTRUCKとBirdのスタッフみんな揃っての"お楽しみ会"。ケンタロウもこのために東京から乱入し、みんなが歌や楽器を披露した。（もちろん黄瀬家も出演。日菜も鈴を持って歌った）
次は、庭で夏フェスやろうと盛り上がったりして。

いいものを作っていくための"NEST"。
これからも、ご機嫌さんでやっていくための大事な場所。

生活のすぐ隣に仕事場がある。このスタイルが私たちには合っている。
暮らすことも、もの作りも、子育てもみんな一緒。

Living Here - Tokuhiko

We put a glass roof over the porch and put a table there. People visit and we sit in the chairs, drink coffee, and talk. Then we realize that three hours have passed. The breeze moves through the trees. It feels good. Wine takes the place of coffee. It's the evening. The color of the sky slowly changes.

This is what I had wanted.

I once asked a Canadian friend what he ate for lunch in Canada. He told me that when he got home from school, he opened up the freezer and took out five or six hamburger patties that had been made by their butcher. He cooked them on the barbecue on the terrace and ate them with home-made pickles. He said it was the best hamburger in the world. His eyes glistened as he spoke.

His words stayed with me for years. I longed to try one of those hamburgers, not because they were special, but because they were so normal.

Now in my freezer there are buns made by my friend Takeuchi and patties that I made myself. I can flick the switch on the barbecue on my porch and cook them whenever I like. I eat them with a slice each of onion and cheddar cheese, and a little salt and pepper. I want to be able to make them as if it were as ordinary as making a cup of coffee. I still haven't gotten the hang of it yet and usually end up fussing about. They really are delicious, though.

Even as our life in the new house began, there were many things that were unfinished. One of those was the kitchen. Our kitchen looks something like an addition. It's just one story, and juts out from the rest of the house. It has a large L-shaped window, but we discovered when we started living there that it was not as bright as we had hoped. I decided that I was going to put in the skylight. I had hoped to include one when we were building, but I didn't think of it until the plans had been finalized.

I knew that make a hole in the ceiling while we were still using the kitchen would be troublesome, but I decided to go ahead anyway. I thought if we could put up with it for a week then it would be nice and bright after that. I contacted my friend Takashita, who runs a construction company, and together we made a plan. It took a week to complete. The morning after we finished I was surprised by the brightness. From below we can see the branches of a Japanese hackberry tree and the stomachs of the birds that perch on its branches. In the evening we have a good view of the moon. It's good that we made it.

When we planned the house we did many things to make it efficient. We used insulation, made it airtight, used double glazed windows, and used wood for the window frames. It's surprisingly comfortable. Our efforts to make it efficient were a complete success. It's very quiet. Hardly any noise comes in from outside.

Even in the scorching heat of summer in Osaka it is easy to cool. We just have one air conditioner upstairs set to 29 degrees and it is enough to cool the whole house. Your feet don't get cold from an air conditioner running full blast, either.

In winter, when you open the door to come inside you can feel the warmth immediately. No rooms are cold. The thermally heated floors and the high efficiency house work together. The wood-burning stove we went out of our way to install has yet to be used. The big shop window and the windows on the south side are also double glazed, so costs from cooling and heating are minimal.

I imagine the words I say with my last breath will be something like, "Use double glazed glass. It's good."

There is a room upstairs that I had intended to be a living room, a place to relax and watch movies on a big TV. Right now, though, it's empty and is only being used as the cats' room.

Why is it empty? Well, I'm thinking about what kind of new furniture I want. When I have an idea, I'll make a prototype, then we'll live with it for a while and maybe eventually it'll go on to become TRUCK furniture. Just using something standard for the time being would be wasting the opportunity. Now is the time for making new furniture.

Sometimes I go to the garden at night and light a small fire of oak chips. I sip scotch while watching it burn. I want a chair that is low to the ground. Perhaps I'll make one. I also want a table to put my glass on. I'll make that, too.

It has been seven years since we released our last catalog. For most of that time my mind was focused on details of construction and building. Having made our new nest, we are beginning to feel a strong urge to design some new furniture.

I remember a time in Tamatsukuri when I was alone and Hiromi had gone out. I sat on one of the tables and tried to imagine what I would think about as I looked out at the trees through our window. Gonzales' *Solo Piano* played quietly in the background. Now, on the second floor of our new home, I have pushed a desk near the window of the room upstairs (that's currently home to the cats) where I'm writing this. Gonzales is playing in the background. The tree outside is swaying gently. One of our cats looks out, staring at a small bird pecking at fruit on the trees. The afternoon sun of winter is gentle.

Yes, this is what I had wanted.

The dogs spend most of their days in Shirokumasha. They love Yasuko. John often sleeps on her chair. Her work chair taken, she perches on a stool while she works the leather. Sometimes the dogs take a break from their busy work of lazing around the atelier and head out to the garden where they run around and lie in the sun. They have freedom to move about wherever they want. I think the dogs are the ones happiest with the move.

Hina often sits and draws at the table outside and does simple craftwork. Otherwise, she spends her time watching Yasuko at work, helping Hiromi arrange stuff in the store (writing order slips in imitation), picking up chestnuts, and watching the chefs at work in the Bird kitchen. Sometimes she runs about on the roof around sunset. She can see many things. I think she's having lots of good experiences. She's still just five years old.

At sunset, I go to the roof of the store, the sky is wide open. To the east sit Mt. Ikoma and Mt. Shigi. To the north there is another range of mountains. The blue sky fades to pink along the horizon. It's extremely beautiful. I call to the staff, "The sky is really beautiful!" They come up and see it. Everyone's face is happy. This is not Noosa, it's Osaka. The sky is beautiful here, too.

The staff room sits like a penthouse above the store. There is a simple kitchen, a washing machine and a shower. In summer, the workers can take a quick shower to wash off the sweat and dust of the day. A long table faces the mountains to the east. Sitting there, they can see the mountains and sky in the distance. We used double glazed glass here, too, so it is comfortable in winter. I was always unhappy about the staff room in Tamatsukuri. It was small, cramped, saw no sun, and was used for changing clothes and eating lunch. This new one is far better.

Very few people who come to TRUCK think that it is a new building. It looks more like an old schoolhouse or city hall that has been remodeled. The brick wall, the paving stones, the wooden atelier, the Chinese elm and zelkova all look like they've been here for a long time.

People enjoy Bird in many different ways. There are people sitting alone, drinking coffee and reading books, people drinking wine with lunch on their day off, people bringing their family for dinner. The special kids *Hamburg steak* is a popular choice. In good weather you might see two women drinking beer from pint glasses. How cool.

It's so much better than the bench at a bus stop in front of our old shop. There are many ways people pass the time at Bird. I'm glad we made it.

In March, as I go down the stairs from the store, I check the Japanese hackberry tree for signs of new buds. Sure enough, spring is on the way.

Tom, Margie, and John.
Karine, who ran the *agritourismo* in Montepulciano.
The German man who I met on a hill in Toscana looking out at the far off scenery.
The old man in the B&B in Amsterdam, listening to quietly playing classical music while he ate breakfast and read the newspaper.
There are things that I like about each of these times. Some small things. Some big things. Each of them has influenced me in some way. I've made a place here in Osaka. It's not perfect, but it's progressing.

This place has its own time. It's not an imitation of something else. It's our time and it's good.
Sometime, somewhere, perhaps I'll tell someone about it. My story.

Trying my best to look like an author, I put down my pen and stare off into the far distance.

Living Here - Hiromi

When you have a child, your world changes. I'd heard it changes even the things you make. But TRUCK furniture has not changed. We made a table and chair for Hina and added them to the TRUCK lineup, but that's about it. Although we moved to a new place the interior of both the house and store have pretty much the same look. When we find something we like we continue to use it.

We brought many things from our old home with us, the floorboards, the furniture, and also the kitchen counter and sink. The counter was a very simple one, made with some leftover floorboards, but we had used it for ten years and it had taken on a lovely amber color. It is now installed, along with the old laboratory style sink, in the small kitchen in Shirokumasha. When we use things for a long time we don't get tired of them. On the contrary, we grow more attached to them. Although it is a new place these things already look like they belong.

The first thing I see when I open my eyes in the morning is the bright morning sun and the green trees outside. Tokuhiko is always the first one up. He sees to the dogs and cats then we all eat breakfast together, talking the whole time. While brushing our teeth we can spy on the birds perched in the Chinese elm outside. Hina, whose eyebrows look like Tokuhiko's, is always in a good mood.

At first, the kitchen did not really feel like mine. I'm not especially fond of cooking, so I wanted something more like a base than an open kitchen facing the living room. Tokuhiko made the skylight and installed some shelves then I got my favorite old pots and things set up. It started to feel more like my place. Through the L-shaped window, I can see the plants, the birds feeding at the bird table, and the dogs running through the garden.

On fine days, I hang our futons out on the veranda to air. Even something as small as this makes me happy about the move. When the sky begins to threaten rain I can just dash over from the store or Shirokumasha and bring them in.

The gardens outside the house and store are full of large trees. Until recently they grew in various places, but they look as if they've always been here, putting down roots and growing thick with leaves. There is also grass, clover, and violets I picked while hiking in the mountains. Taking care of them all is a lot of work. It takes an hour just to water them all in summer. We were planning on making a vegetable patch in the northeast part of the garden, but realized that it wasn't sunny enough. We decided instead to grow some vegetables in a planter on the south facing verandah. We're thinking of building a small shed to keep the gardening equipment. Hina has her own flower bed. She tries to copy me, but before I know it she is just playing with mud.

In the evening, once work is finished, I ride my bicycle to the nearby kindergarten to pick up Hina. On the way home we head to the supermarket. It's very close; much more convenient than our old place in Tamatsukuri. Sometimes I start making dinner when we get home and sometimes I take Hina to the store and continue working. When we are very busy and I don't have time to cook, we eat out. Of course, we often go to Bird. It has many things we like to eat and drink. It's wonderful to have a great restaurant so close.

There's greenery, a supermarket and school nearby, and you can walk to the station. It is similar to Karine's lifestyle in Montepulciano that we had envied. The scenery, though, can't compare.

When the weather is good, we sit in the garden and Tokuhiko cooks on the barbecue, the aroma luring the staff that have a free moment. In the stone oven Tokuhiko cooks sausages that have been skewered on knife-sharpened twigs. They are surprisingly delicious. They are just ordinary sausages from the supermarket, but eating them outside on twigs people have sharpened themselves makes them especially tasty. The school next door is deserted at night, so we don't have to worry about being noisy. We sometimes get out our guitars and, if the mood takes us, even sing. Last year we had an party with the Kentaro and the TRUCK and Bird staff. Everyone had to sing or play an instrument. Of course we took part as well with Hina accompanying us with a bell. We are thinking of having a summer festival this year. We have a hammock from which you can watch the moon while you swaying back and forth. It's wonderful.

This is the "nest" we had intended to build.
It's an important place for us.

Living next door to work.
That's the style that suits us.
Living, working, raising children together.

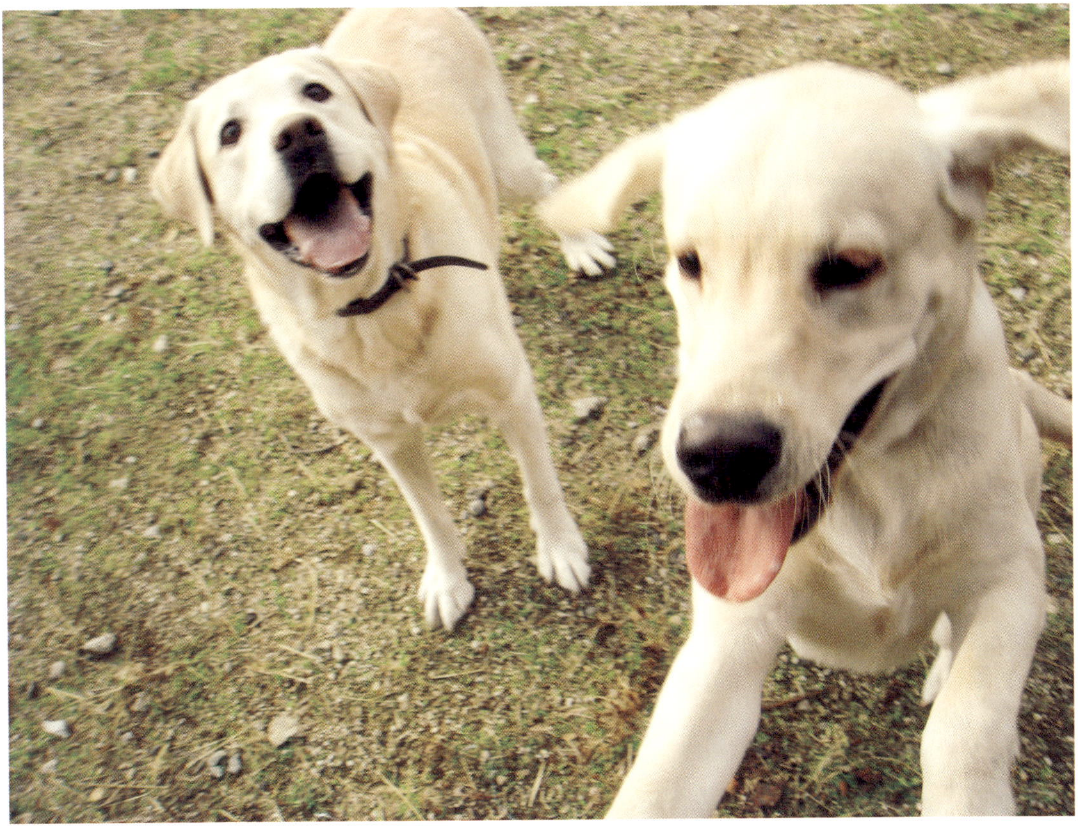

Written by	Tokuhiko Kise, Hiromi Karatsu / TRUCK
Direction	TRUCK
Photos	Hiromi Karatsu, Tokuhiko Kise / TRUCK Keigo Saito (Bird Paper) Kozo Ono (p.272-273)
Translation	Simon Evans
Art direction	Mika Noguchi / miranda co.
Design	Mika Noguchi Yoshiyuki Inoue
Figures	Ayako Miwa
Illustrations	Hiromi Karatsu
Photo collages	Hiromi Karatsu

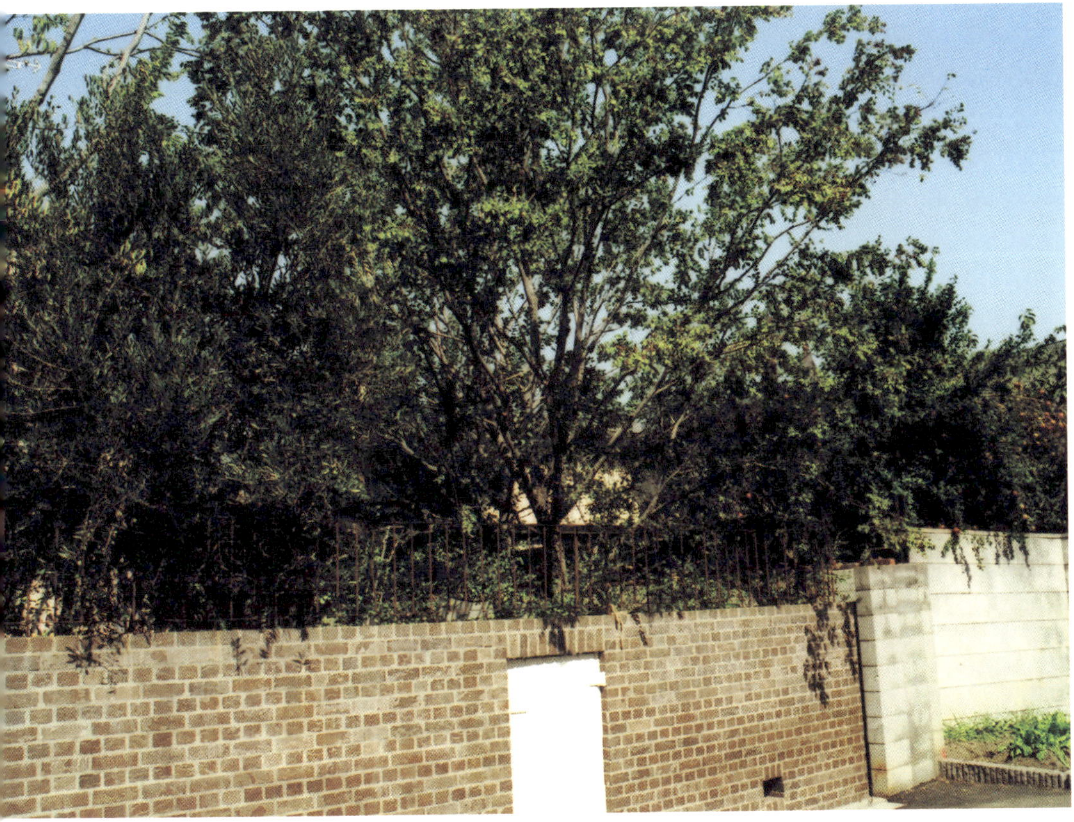

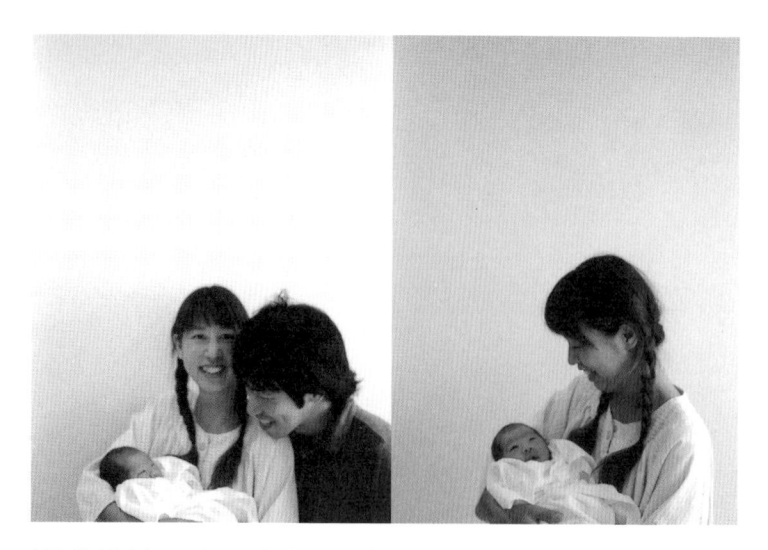

日菜が生まれた次の日。ケンタロウがひりんこに内緒で駆けつけてくれた。
その時に撮ってくれた写真。まるで親戚のおっちゃんのようだった。

The day after Hina was born we got a surprise visit from Kentaro,
who took this picture. He is more like a family member than a mere friend.

黄瀬徳彦　Tokuhiko Kise

1968年 大阪生まれ 高校卒業後、長野県松本技術専門校木工科で家具作りを学ぶ。大阪に戻り、椅子やテーブルを作っている木工所で働く。その後、1991年、23歳で独立。1人で工場を構え家具作りを始める。唐津裕美と出会い1997年1月 TRUCKをオープン。工場と店、そして家が同じ場所という生活が始まる。

Born in Osaka in 1968.
After graduating from high school, he studied furniture construction in the Woodworking faculty of the Matsumoto Technical School in Nagano Prefecture. Upon returning to Osaka, he worked for a woodworking company making tables and chairs. In 1991, at the age of 23, he began working as an independent furniture maker selling to furniture stores. Opened TRUCK in January, 1997, beginning lifestyle with home, workshop and store in the same place.

唐津裕美　Hiromi Karatsu

1967年 大阪生まれ 大阪芸術大学工芸学科テキスタイルデザイン専攻。卒業後、テキスタイルのデザイン企画の会社で働く。その後、フリーのイラストレーターとして活動を始める。2003年7月アトリエシロクマ舎スタート。妹の唐津康子と共に雑貨を作り始める。2006年、39歳で長女を出産。

Born in Osaka in 1967.
Studied Textile Design at the Osaka University of Art. After graduating, she worked at a textile design company. After that she began working as a freelance illustrator. In July 2003, Shirokumasha opened. Began making miscellaneous items with her sister Yasuko Karatsu. In 2006, at the age of 39, she gave birth to her first daughter.

TRUCK PROFILE

1997年 1月	大阪市中央区に TRUCK オープン	
1999年10月	TRUCKの裏に AREA2 オープン	
2003年 7月	アトリエ シロクマ舎設立	
2009年11月	大阪市旭区に TRUCK、AREA2、 工場、シロクマ舎、大移動	
2009年12月	TRUCK、Bird 新しくオープン	

著書にカタログ「TRUCK WORKS 1〜3」、「MAKING TRUCK」がある。

1997	JAN.	TRUCK opened in Osaka's Chuo Ward.
1999	OCT.	AREA2 was opened behind TRUCK.
2003	JUL.	Atelier Shirokumasha opened.
2009	DEC.	TRUCK, AREA2, Shirokumasha, and workshop moved to Osaka's Asahi Ward.

Also produced the catalog "TRUCK WORKS" and "MAKING TRUCK".

Afterword

1998年だったと思う。初めて作ったTRUCKのカタログ。どこか取り扱ってもらえる書店はないかと、数十冊を鞄に詰め込み東京に行商に出かけた。本の流通のことなど何も知らずにいろんな店を自己紹介しながら回った。そして数軒で売ってもらえることになる。
その後、ある日また東京にいた。偶然、代官山の横断歩道でケンタロウを見かけた。ケンタロウの著書「ごくらくの食卓 音楽を聞くように料理する本」がすごく好きだった僕とひりんこはドキドキした。「あっ!ケンタロウや!!」と言い終わる前に僕は走り寄って声をかけた。僕たちの流暢な大阪弁に気を許したのか(ケンタロウのお母さん カツ代さんは大阪千日前育ち)ケンタロウは「大阪では何をしてるんですか?」と聞いた。
「家具屋です」と答えると、
「ひょっとしてTRUCK?」と聞かれた。
行商に出たかいがあって、ケンタロウはすでにTRUCKのカタログを手に入れていた。

"好きなようにもの作りしてるなぁ"と思ったとケンタロウはカタログの感想を後になって聞かせてくれた。自分も本は日々作っている。でも、もちろん出版社やいろんな人と一緒に進めるから、100%自分の好きにはできない。それはそれで楽しいし、やりがいもある。けど、TRUCKのカタログがちょっと羨ましく映ったと。

そんなきっかけで出会ってからというもの、話せば話すほど、気が合う。細かいとこまで通じ合う。ひりんこと3人、会えば夜中遅くまでずっとはしゃぎ合った。些細なことで泣くほど笑った。
そのケンタロウが言った言葉。「好きなようにもの作りしてるなぁ」改めて振り返ると、今も当時も何も変わってない。

純粋に自分たちが「いいやん!」と思えるものを作りたいだけ。その延長で、大きさで言えば家具より遥かに大きな建物を建てたり、樹を植えたりしたけど、根本の気持ちは同じ。いつも1%でも良くしたいと思う。
家具でも、もちろん同じ。まして、それを好きと思って買ってもらえるなんて幸せなこと。だから少しでもいいものにして渡したいと思っている。買ってもらった人の相棒としてずっと使ってもらえたら嬉しいし、使ってもらえるものにしておかないといけない。

そしてその家具が、それぞれの人のNESTを作る仲間になれればすごく幸せ。

(黄瀬徳彦)

In 1998, when we made TRUCK's first catalog, I wondered if bookstores might be interested in selling it. I packed some copies into a suitcase and headed for Tokyo. I knew nothing of how books are distributed so I just went to shops and introduced myself. I was able to get quite a few shops to take it. Sometime later, Hiromi and I were in Tokyo again when we spotted Kentaro at a pedestrian crossing in Daikanyama. He was already quite well known and we were big fans of his cookbooks. I rushed across the road and called out to him. Perhaps he was put at ease by hearing us speak in the Osaka dialect (his mother was from Osaka). He asked us, "What do you do in Osaka?"
"I'm a furniture maker," I answered.
"TRUCK, by any chance?" he asked.
He already had a copy of our catalog. My door to door book selling had paid off.

"They're making things just the way they want." Kentaro later told me he thought when he'd read our catalog.

He was also involved in making books but, because he worked with publishing houses, he couldn't do *exactly* what he wanted. It was fun and rewarding, but he was a little envious of the freedom he'd seen in the catalog.

That was how we met. The more we talked the friendlier we became. Even in small matters we shared the same ideas. Whenever we three met we talked long into the night, laughing over small things.

Kentaro had thought, "They're making things just the way they want."
Looking back, that is still true.

We only make things we genuinely think are good. We extended that same thinking to building a house, and planting trees. We always try to improve things, even if it's by just one percent.

We think of furniture in the same way. It makes us happy when someone likes something we make enough to want to buy it. We want to give them things that are exceptional. We want our furniture to become a partner to our customers. We make sure it can be used for a long time.

We are very happy if people can use our furniture to build their own nests.

Tokuhiko Kise

とりんことと出会ってからというもの、
一緒にいる時間が本当に長い。ずっと一緒。
2人の間には図面も何もない。いつも2人でたくさん話をして、良ければすぐ実行。あとは行動しながら考え足していく。
結構いきあたりばったりで自分たちでも何ができるか分からない。けど、誰のためでもなく、誰に任せるでもなく全部自分たちの手で作っていくので納得のいくものができる。
とりんこと出会ってから、ずっとワクワクすることばかり。
私は家具のことなんて全くの素人だし、2人ともショップを経営するといったことの知識なども全くなかった。建築の勉強だってしていないし経験もない。でも特に知識がなくても、本当に好きなこと、自分のやりたいことにまっすぐ進んで行けば、きっと上手くいくと思う。そうなってきた。そういえばフリーでイラストを始めた時も同じだった。まず、自分が楽しまないと。

たまたまとりんこが家具を作っていたので、TRUCKという家具屋ができた。もし、とりんこがうどんを作ってたら、私は迷わずうどん屋さんになっていた。2人でなら、何をやっても上手くいく自信がある。2人で頑張ると2倍以上の力が出る。とりんこは特別すごい行動力があるので10倍！

そして新しい場所へTRUCKの移転。
2年半かかりっきりの大仕事。確かに、かかった時間と労力はとんでもなく大きかったが、2人で目指しているものには何の不安もなかった。確信していた。いいものができると。

私は子供が苦手で、あまり欲しいとは思ってなかった。
でも、とりんこに出会って考えが変わった。
とりんこにそっくりの子供がいたら絶対楽しいはず!!と。
そうして、大切な家族が増えた。
39歳で初めての妊娠、出産、育児は新しい場所作りにがっつり重なった。その時は大変だった。本当にしんどかった。
でも今になって思えば、小さな日菜を抱えて毎日現場で頑張ったことは、何にも代えがたい貴重な時間だったと思う。
私にとっても、日菜にとっても。

私たちのNESTは暮らしながら、もの作りをしながら、さらに子供の成長に合わせて、これからもまだまだ変化（進化？）していく。
そして、自分たちが好き！と思える魅力ある家具を、
このままずっとご機嫌さんで作り続けていけたら幸せ。

（唐津裕美）

Tokuhiko and I have been together for a long time.

We don't have a detailed plan. We talk to each other all the time and if we have a good idea we start moving quickly. While we are moving we re-think and make adjustments. It's haphazard and we ourselves don't know if we can succeed. But we don't do things for other people and we don't depend on others to do things for us. We do things with our own hands and keep going until we are satisfied. My life since meeting Tokuhiko has been continuously exciting.

I knew nothing about furniture, and neither of us knew anything about running a shop, but I think that if we do something that we really like and keep moving forward, we'll do OK. It was the same when I was a freelance illustrator. You have to enjoy yourself. It was only because Tokuhiko made furniture that we made TRUCK. If he had made something like udon noodles, I would happily have helped start an udon shop. If we are together, I'm confident that whatever we do will work. If we work together, our ability more than doubles. Tokuhiko has ten times the energy of anyone else I've met.

We built a new place and moved TRUCK. It was a big job, lasting over two and a half years, and took a great deal of time, work and money. I never had any doubts about what we were moving towards. I was convinced it would be good.

During this time I became pregnant, gave birth, and raised a child. It was difficult and sometimes I was really tired. We brought Hina to the site and worked hard every day. I think that was a precious experience for both me and her.

Until I had my own child, I was never very good around children. I didn't think much about having one, but when I met Tokuhiko things changed. If I could have a child even a little like him, I thought, it would be fun.

While we live in our nest, making things, as our child grows, I'm sure there will be further changes (or progression).

We will be happy if we can continue like this, making furniture that we want.

Hiromi Karatsu

Timeline （ひりんこの日記から）

年	日付	内容
1967	3/27	ひりんこ誕生
1968	7/8	とりんこ誕生
1991	秋頃	とりんこ独立 23歳
1992	12/18	ひりんこ、フリーのイラストレーターに 25歳
1994	10/12	とりんことひりんこ、初めて出会う
1995	5/7	ひりんこ、カンテGでバイト始める（ブルースバーでチャイを出そうと思っていた）
1996	2/1-11	タイ
	5/16〜	中央区玉造物件契約、改造スタート
	7/13	2人で引っ越し
	9/1	バディが家に来る!! 生後41日
	10/11	DEPTで松田氏と話 店作りに火がつく
1997	1/18	TRUCK オープン!! とりんこ28歳 ひりんこ29歳
	6/28-7/6	友達の結婚式でハワイ
1998	5/19-20	カタログ VOL.1 印刷立ち会い
	5/25	カタログ VOL.1 2000部納品
	6/11-13	カタログ持って東京に行商に出る
	7/1	入籍 仕事の後、家にバディを連れて役所へ 絵に描いたような青シマパジャマ姿の当直のおじさんに書類提出
	10/7-19	パリ、ロンドン
1999	1/18	ニャー 保護 すぐに超大型犬バディと仲よくなる貫禄キャット
	2/8	ホワイトオーク節ありテーブル完成
	3/21	TRUCKの裏の物件契約
	4/15-17	フィリピン
	5/16	東京 代官山でケンタロウに出会う! TRUCKのこと知ってた
	6/20-30	アメリカ
	10/1	AREA2 オープン!!
2000	6/27-7/6	オーストリア ウィーン、ドイツ デュッセルドルフ、オランダ アムステルダム
2001	4/5-9	イタリア ミラノ
	4/18-24	タイ
	5/18-22	ドイツ ケルン
	6/16-17	ケンタロウと四国讃岐うどんツアー
	9/25-11/16	TRUCKリニューアル工事
	10/6-12	カタログ VOL.2 印刷所に泊まり込んで立ち会い
	10/18	カタログ VOL.2 10000部納品
	10/31	山崎まさよしに初めてカタログ渡す! やったー
	11/21-1/16	マルちゃんを里子に迎える
2002	4/7-10	タイ
	5/17	ニコ 保護
	7/1	コロ 保護
	7/4	サビ 保護
	7/28	クマ 保護
	8/3	サンちゃん、オーちゃん 5兄弟 保護 5月から立て続けに子猫を保護する
	10/4	サンちゃん、オーちゃんの姉弟、パンチとチョップが新幹線で東京へ ケンタロウの家族になる 良かった
2003	4/8-16	イタリア モンテプルチアーノ
	4/28	シロクマ舎物件契約
	5/1	シロクマ舎改造スタート やーちゃんとペンキ塗り
	7/16	シロクマ舎アトリエ引っ越し
	11/6-27	オーストラリア ヌーサ 1回目
2004	9/15-24	とりんこイタリア バイク旅行
	9/16	ディンゴ 保護 飼い主見つからず 妊娠発覚
	11/2	ディンゴ出産6匹 4匹里子に出して、息子ジャックとジョンを残す
	11/7-27	ケンタロウとハワイ ひりんこは家でケンタロウの家具イラスト描く
	12/16-21	カタログ VOL.3 印刷所に泊まり込んで立ち会い 今回はバディもこっそり連れて泊まる
	12/29	カタログ VOL.3 15000部納品
2005	3/4-18	オーストラリア ヌーサ 2回目
	6/16	ジョン骨折! ソファから落ちて
	9/13	ティグ 保護
	10/18	陽性反応! 妊娠! やったー! 同時につわり始まる げろー
	12/5-13	とりんこ、ケンタロウとオーストラリア ヌーサ 3回目
2006	1/15	ひりんこ、つわり急に終わる
	1/30	この頃から胎動よく感じる 赤ちゃん、どんどんよく動く
	2/12	平野区タクシー会社物件見に行く
	2/15	もし女の子だったら「日菜」に決まる
	3/27	エコー、多分、女の子かー! おなかに話しかける ひりんこ、誕生日 39歳
	5/22	胎動少ない 日菜を産む夢を見る とりんこベビーベッド作る
	6/8	ベビーベッドもうすぐ完成 PM5:30破水! 入院
	6/10	長女、日菜誕生!!! 2940g 元気な女の子 出産、気持ちよかった!
	6/11	ケンタロウ、まきおさん 東京から駆けつけてくれる
	7/8	とりんこ、誕生日 38歳 この頃サーフィンばっかり
	8/9	日菜、おっぱいよく飲む 3ヶ月健診で6kg超える おっぱいの後もご機嫌でよく笑う 話しかける口元をじーっと見る
	9/11	バディの特技「石ころがし」読売 TV取材
	9/18	日菜、初めての公園お散歩 バディも一緒に
	9/24	「トップランナー」TV収録 楽屋でまきおが日菜のベビーシッターしてくれる
	9/26	馬場俊英シングル「ただ君を待つ」ジャケット撮影 TRUCKにてひりんこが! ニャーとクマも登場
	11/6	この頃、日菜「きぇー!!」って叫び系の発声 おなかにぶーっと息はくとぎゃーって笑う
	12/17-24	とりんこフィンランド
	12/25	堺物件見に行く 他にも土地いろいろ探し回る日々 日菜、寝返り
2007	1/18	日菜、寝返りが余裕で連発できる
	1/27	日菜、下の歯が1本生えてくる
	2/2	堺物件 2月末まで契約待ち DEPT永井氏に「不動産は慎重に」
	2/20-3/4	東京 恵比寿リムアート展示会 おかげさまで大盛況
	3/11-19	オーストラリア ヌーサ 4回目 日菜9ヶ月ファーストディップ
	3/22〜	バディとはなちゃんお見合いチャレンジ
	4/22	旭区の物件初めて見る 2人とも気に入る
	4/26	旭区の物件、契約のなりゆきに、、、大丈夫なのか?
	4/29	TRUCKフリマ会場の前の公園で、向かいの建て売り土地、買い付け証明
	5/10	旭区物件、契約当日にすっぽかされる!
	5/13	旭区物件向かいの建て売り土地契約!!
	5/30	バディの子供たち 5匹誕生! 日菜、グーチーパーできる
	5/31	旭区物件、契約また流れる
	6/5	旭区物件、とうとう契約してしまう!!
	6/10	日菜、誕生日 1歳
	6/14	三田の造園屋に初めて樹を見に行く 平面、立面プラン進める
	6/17-21	ケンタロウ、きぢちゃん一家と那須旅行 SHOZOさんのカフェへ こんな時に限って日菜、突発性発疹で高熱
	7/2〜	旭区、タクシー会社解体開始
	7/15	久しぶりにバディ洗う
	7/16-31	シロクマ舎の展示会
	7/29	バディの子供たちと記念撮影
	8/1	難波宮に樹を見に行く 気になっていた樹種がアキニレと分かる
	8/11	造園屋にアキニレ、ケヤキなど見に行く
	8/12	日菜、やっとつかまり立ち!
	8/15	バディの息子、家に来る! 名前ウィリーに決定
	8/17	"WILLY"は"弱っちい"意味があることが分かって却下 名前ジュニアに変更（そのまんま）
	8/24〜	日菜、この頃夜泣きひどい 新生児の頃はよく寝たのに、、、 ぐずって寝てくれない ほとんど朝方まで眠れない毎日がつづく しんどい 眠い（泣）
	9/5	現場、土壌確認 とりんこショベルカー運転させてもらう この頃建物レイアウト考えまくり
	9/13	造園屋にアキニレ、ケヤキなど紹介してもらう 団地の植物救出に、いろんな所にかけ合ってみる
	10/18〜	ボーリング開始
	10/20	印鑑、サインねつ造事件
	10/25	造園屋で、ひりんこが樹を見る場所を全部覚えててびっくりされる
	10/29〜	植栽、家レイアウト 設備関係詰める
	11/6	日菜、とりんこお手製のカタカタでつかまり歩く! 1歳半（遅）
	12/10	造園屋めぐり 樹種確認、写真撮る
	12/11	ソーラー実験ハウス見学
	12/18	日菜、1歳半健診 80cm 11kg 歩かないので神経科を勧められる（泣）
2008	1/6	ひりんこ左足骨折! 松葉杖して、日菜おんぶって打ち合わせの日々
	1/16	現場電気線工事ライン実験 ひりんこ車椅子 日菜、松葉杖みると「いたた〜」って言う この頃は毎晩夜中までレイアウト ぶっ通しで打ち合わせ あっという間に1日終わる
	2/8〜	日菜、イヤイヤ期 最近お着替えやオムツ替えを嫌がる とりんこのことも嫌がる 「パパイヤッ!」ママの抱っこしかダメ 絶対歩こうとしない 重い（泣）
	2/21	アキニレ根回し見学 トックン、やーちゃんも一緒に
	3/22	元府議会議員から電話があり、団地植物救出できるかも
	3/24	現場 穴掘って土壌チェック 団地で土壌チェックと救出する樹の位置チェック
	3/25	1本目アキニレ植栽! バディもスタッフもみんなで見に行く
	4/12-20	オーストラリア ヌーサ 5回目 日菜、最後の日に1人で歩く 1歳10ヶ月! 良かった!! ひりんこ号泣
	5/3	日菜、オマル特訓
	5/7-9	団地植物救出作戦 そんな日に限って日菜、朝から水疱瘡!! 保育園休み ばーちゃんに助けてもらう
	5/14	地鎮祭 1本目アキニレ、新芽ちゃんと出てた
	5/28〜	杭工事開始
	6/2	クマ病院 開腹手術か?
	6/7-18	クマ入院 膵炎かも
	6/10	日菜、誕生日 2歳 ブランどんどん進める 現場ももっちゅう見に行く ドア、窓の図面、薪ストーブ探し
	6/17	バディ、ジュニアと海
	6/18	日菜、オマルでちっち成功!!
	7/14	現場の異常事態発見!
	7/15	とりんこ、現場鉄筋の歪みデジカメで証拠写真撮る 社長も呼び出し説明求める 設計、工務店は弁解ばかり 態度の悪さ、最悪
	7/16	日菜、夜中高熱 一睡もせず 保育園休まないといけないので、ひりんこ留守番 とりんこだけ現場へ
	7/19	設計事務所社長と話し合い
	7/23	設計事務所会長と話し合い 「プロの説明が分からんのか」と逆ぎれされる とりんことひりんこ、笑顔のない苦しい日々、約1ヶ月
	7/30〜	この頃、クマだけでなくバディもコロも調子悪く、毎日朝から病院で点滴
	8/1	現場証拠写真、追加で撮りに行く
	8/12-14	クマ、また入院 話し合い続く
	8/18〜	現場、とうとう基礎解体開始
	8/23	現場、日菜も何にもなくなった 無惨なガレキの山
	8/28	「ソロモン流」TV打ち合わせ ディレクターの革バッグ、ジャックが食べる!
	9/9	バディ、ジュニアと海
	9/10	とりんこ、玉造物件家主と話し合い
	9/16-18	とりんこ、連日現場 鉄筋監視に行く
	9/26	大雨の中 コンクリート打ち
	10/1	脱型 型枠外したら、手が映るほどの黒い固そうなコンクリート 拍手
	10/20-21	熊本ヘアキニレ見に行く クマ牧場で盛り上がる
	10/22	日菜、ちびごランド運動会
	10/25-27	ケンタロウたちとキャンプ
	11/25	久仁氏に会いに行く コンクリート着々と進む この頃、シンク、カラン、バスタブなど家 外壁塗装 ドア、窓仕様詰める
	12/27	ショップイベントスペース、エレベーターのコンクリート打ちが終わり、上棟!!
	12/30	すぐにスタッフと現場ペンキ塗り
2009	1/5	設計事務所 植栽レイアウト、植物写真整理
	1/10〜	家、ショップのペンキ塗りどんどん進める 金物パーツ探し
	1/22〜	ショップ2階窓取り付け タイル、金物パーツ、外壁塗装 洗い出し検討
	2/10-22	東京 恵比寿リムアート展示会 やーちゃんとばーちゃん、子守り部隊で同行
	2/17	能勢に樹を見に行く 途中吹雪 ムクゲれ根回し ワイエスの絵の中にいるような景色 家床コンクリート 屋上、ベランダ防水 バルコニー柵 植栽と工期の調整

2/23	「ソロモン流」TV放送　リムアート搬出
2/28	植栽　カフェのエノキとネリコ
	そんなに大きいサイズではないエノキが、植えると想像以上にでかくて、この後が不安になる
3/4～	シロクマ舎レイアウト　家外壁汚れ防止吹き付け
3/8	日菜と現場　バケツとスコップ持って、樹を植えるための大穴に入って遊ぶ
3/9	植栽　1.ムクノキ10m、2.エノキ7m　あまりにでかくてビビる　すごいたいそう
	旭区の近所の保育園に行ったら定員いっぱい　待機児童になってしまう！
3/10	植栽　3.アキニレ8m、4.アキニレ株立ち11m（調子悪い）　キッチンレンジフード、タイル
3/11	旭区役所行く　こども待機児童状況　鶴見区で1軒保育園見学に行く
	ドアノブ素材、位置、シャワー、洗面の位置、タイル目地の色
3/12	植栽　5.ホワイトオーク5m、6.エノキ9m　鶴見区で3軒保育園見学に行く
	ドア、窓、外壁サンプル打ち合わせ
3/13	植栽　7.ケヤキ14m、8.熊本アキニレ10m　旭区で4軒保育園見学に行く
3/15	日菜、バディ現場　ハンモック吊ってみたりがんばれぽる
3/16	植栽　9.タイサンボク、10.トキワモチ
3/17	植栽　11.コナラ、12.ザクロ、13.ケヤキ14m、14.モミジ
3/18	植栽　15.トウネズミモチ、16.ネズミモチ、17.イチョウ
	ショップ階段下にシュロ2本入らず　急遽、北西の壁に変更
3/19	植栽　18.プリペット仮植　旭区で2軒保育園見学に行く
	ドアノブ仕込げ、階段、フローリング木材打ち合わせ
3/21	植栽　19.唐津部屋横シュロ、20.玄関シュロ、21.玄関ユッカ、22.ハクチョウゲ、23.ユッカ
3/23	植栽助成金立ち会い確認
3/24～	レンガの堀打ち合わせ　教会を見て回って積み方研究　フランス積みかイギリス積みか？
	ワンたちのサンルームレイアウト、階段木材サンプル、レンガ壁レイアウト、階段左官、
	風呂タイル張り、寝室左官開始、倉庫3階チェック、シロクマ設計打ち合わせ
	薪ストーブ煙突工事、配管ペンキ塗り、リビング、洗面所天井板張り、道路切り崩し
4/10-14	とりんこ、ケンタロウとオーストラリア　6回目　とりんこだけ現場があるので先に帰る
4/15	エノキ、コナラ、ホワイトオーク、ザクロ新芽出てた　アキニレ株立ちは幹から
	2階風呂のタイルはたやり直し！　あほか!!　不具合箇所多すぎて引き渡し延期
4/24	日菜、朝もう一度もぐらずむ寝てくれた！　ひりんこ1年ぶりにAM7:00まで熟睡できた！
5/1	植栽　24.ソテツ
5/2	植栽　25.ユッカ、26.キョウチクトウ　階段2階張り　インナーテラス仕切り窓考える
5/7～	久住チーム、寝室左官開始　ガレージベンキ塗り、廊下床張り、洗面所
5/11	とりんこ、高下君に教えてもらって溶接デビュー　レンガの塀に棚つける　薪ストーブ探す
5/13～	ブロック塀、インナーテラスのペンキ塗り、溶接、お勝手口扉作り、カフェレイアウト、
	ポーチ、工場、玄関前の石畳などもたくさん
5/22	日菜連れ現場　2階リビング漆喰　PM8:00過ぎまで日菜も頑張って塗る
5/29～	シロクマ舎建築打ち合わせ　タイルサンプル、電気配管指図
6/1	日菜、保育園一時保育スタート！　これでちょっと手が離れる　久住チーム洗い出し開始
6/2	ケンタロウ来る　カフェの名前、Birdに決定（NESTは却下される）
6/3	Bird入り口の場所、ドーナツマシン導入か作り話し合い
6/9	タケウチさん1回目ターキッシュブレッド試食　建物やっと引き渡し
6/10	日菜、誕生日　1歳
6/16～	キッチン天板設置、ゲストルーム床張り、イベントスペースペンキ塗り、2階収納
6/19	バディ、ジュニアと海
6/23	タケウチさんターキッシュサンド試食　オーストラリアに行くのか？
	キッチン流し台図考える　Bird内装打ち合わせ　サンルーム工事開始　足場外れる
6/25～	やーちゃんとイベントスペースのバラ張り、ペンキ塗り　寝室収納骨組み
7/1～	シロクマ舎基礎工事　ひりんこ、必死で引っ越し荷造り　200箱以上!!
	日菜と猫たち、ダンボールの山に登って遊んだジャマばかり
7/5	ニャンこちだけ先に引っ越し
7/6	ワンたち5匹と、家引っ越しAM8:30～PM10:00過ぎまで　げーっ
7/7	新しい家で初めての朝　AM5:00日菜泣いて起きる　ヌーサマみたいな朝！最高！
	フローリング材引っ越し　2階リビングにすぐ張る　ひりんこ250箱くらいの段ボールと格闘
	バディ、新しい室内トイレでしっこしてくれない、、、、ショック
7/16-24	ひりんこ原因不明の高熱で入院　その間、シロクマ舎上棟!!
7/20	病室でとりんこ打ち合わせしてでいでだん2人もイライラついてきて点滴が逆流！
	流血してきてびっくり！
	Birdレイアウト、Bird照明、設備、寝室ブラインド、工場ブロック壁立ち上げ、倉庫床
7/24	やっと退院！　ひりんこ、日菜に会えて泣く　日菜、泣がり
	入院中、「ママ」と1言も言わなかったらしい　この頃、シロクマ舎現場
8/9～	ケンタロウ来て打ち合わせ　昼、黄瀬家の冷蔵庫の食材で野菜とライスのプレート作ってくれる
	うまい!!　これを元にBirdライスの原型となる
	コーヒー、ビール選び　Bird厨房打ち合わせ等内装いろいろ、窓枠入る　ロゴ決定
9/5～	シロクマ舎外壁塗装　東、南面　日菜もタオル巻いて参加
9/14	コナラの上のうろう、どんぐりできてる　この頃、ランチは庭で夜はBBQ！
9/23～	スタッフルーム木枠　Birdなかなか料理人決まらず　オリジナル食器型、色　OK
9/27	日菜、卒乳!!　久しぶりにおっぱい吸われたら吸い方忘れてた！　寂しい（泣）
10/1～	Bird足場はずす　ドーナツマシン入る、レジ台、床板、ポーチ、床ペテ、WEB写真撮り
	ムジカティー堀江さん打ち合わせ　TRUCKショップカウンター、照明打ち合わせ
10/15	ドーナツマシン台合う　厨房備品入る
10/19～	TRUCKショップ床板、カウンター回りレイアウト、ディスプレイ棚　シロクマ階段入る
10/21～	植栽　27.オリーブ、28.ザクロ、29.ユーカリ、30.ノウゼンカズラ
	Birdエントランス石畳、工場前、家のガラガラ門できる　TRUCK、Birdの門扉考える
	シロクマ舎移設　日菜保育園願書提出
10/30	あごがれおとりこ入る
11/3～	唐津部屋、シロクマ舎、床板張り、ペンキ塗り　TRUCK照明
11/9	シロクマ引っ越し　タケウチさんとドーナツ試作
11/12	Birdコーヒー最終選考、メニュー試行錯誤続く
11/16	AREA2作業場引っ越し
11/17	倉庫引っ越し
11/20	工場引っ越し　ケンタロウとBirdメニュー打ち合わせ
11/26	シロクマ引っ越し　Birdライス、ハンバーグ、カレー試作続く
11/29	TRUCK、AREA2　玉造での営業最後　記念撮影　涙、、、、
11/30	TRUCK引っ越し　こんなややこしい時に限ってインフルエンザが流行　保育園休み
12/1	AREA2引っ越し　BirdにTRUCKのドア移植
12/2～	新TRUCKレイアウト追い上げ　ショップ、駐車場看板、Birdサイン考える　WEB写真撮り
	押し葉フレーム、カウンター回り、プライスカード、照明等内装仕上げ、スタッフルーム
	この頃、毎日ばーちゃんじーちゃん旭区まで来て日菜の面倒見てくれる
12/8	Birdメニューだいたい完成　これからはさらにサービスが大事である話
	もっと満席を練習しないと、ということでBirdサービス特訓
	夜、とりんこ兄の知り合いで満席にする
12/9	保育園面接！　押し葉フレーム取り付け
	Birdサービス特訓　昼、知り合いで満席にする
12/10	Birdサービス特訓　夜、TRUCKスタッフの知り合いで満席を2回転する
12/12	Birdサービス特訓　昼、黄瀬家一同で満席にする　夜、友達で満席にする
12/13	ケンタロウ、東京から駆けつけてBird仕込み一緒にする
12/14	TRUCKとBird OPEN !!!　やったーーーー!!
	スタッフ集合写真、小野さんに撮ってもらう　バディも一緒に
	おかげさまでBird終日行列　その後もショップを営業しつつ、工事、片付けはまだまだ続く
12/22	倉庫引っ越し
12/24-30	中央区のそれぞれの物件、後片付け、掃除
2010 1/3	金剛山で雪遊びでバディとロープウェイに乗る
1/5	住んでからも家の未完成はまだまだある　ゲストルーム前の収納や庭の片付け、階段手摺、
	洗濯物干バー、洗面所収納、インナーテラス収納棚、2階洗面収納、2階リビング収納扉、
	キッチン棚、シロクマ舎前敷石、とりんこガレージ、黄瀬部屋、農作業小屋などなど
1/13	珍しい雪が積もった　屋上で日菜と雪合戦
1/21	日菜、保育園決定　役所から電話　待ってました！
1/22	日菜、保育園曲談
2/1	日菜、入園!!　やっと
3/13	植栽　ダメになってしまったアキニレをケヤキに植え替える
3/20～	玄関石畳、庭枕木ひく
4/1～	外灯基礎
4/2	ピザ窯、東庭水道立ち上げ　早速タケウチさん指導のもとにピザを焼く！
4/24	ポーチ屋根骨組み完成
6/8	TRUCK中庭に古いコンクリート製のワンコもらう
6/10	日菜、誕生日　4歳
6/22～	「TRUCK NEST」本打ち合わせ始まる　撮りためた写真整理始める
8/15-25	スコットランド　日菜初めて1人で馬に乗る！
9/10-22	とりんこニューヨーク
9/26	バディと海　急な左足引きひったがって帰る　日菜、生まれて初めて前髪切る
10/6～	ガレージ天井板張り
10/11	日菜、運動会
10/25	ひりんこの両親、近所に引っ越ししてくて来ている
10/28	とりんこ、バディの歌作る
11/3-6	とりんこ香港
11/20-21	TRUCKフリーマーケット開催　長蛇の列！
12/4	植栽　唐津実家シュロ、シロクマ前に移植
12/6	バディいつもの海に行く　12月なのにすごくあったかい日　いっぱい写真撮る
12/9	とりんことバディ、公園へ　バディいつまでも忘れないよ、ありがとう
	ジャックとジュニア大ゲンカ　流血事件
12/30-31	植栽　TRUCK入り口に常緑
2011 2/3	造園屋でケヤキの代わりのトネリコ見つける
2/11	雪積もる　日菜と屋上で雪合戦
2/20	DDM料理教室#1　数ヶ月ぶりにBirdにて復活
2/21-26	キッチンに天窓あける　最高！
3/3	キッチンに棚つける
3/10	また熊本にアキニレ見に行く
3/21	とりんこ、初めてのピアノ発表会　子供たちに混じって
3/24	ジョウビタキのジョンビー（オス）旅立ち　寂しい
3/25-26	植栽　ケヤキとトネリコ8m交換　残念　熊本から2本目アキニレ4m
4/24	DDM料理教室#2
5/3	国分太一君のTV番組収録
5/5～	「TRUCK NEST」Bird Paper齋藤君が撮影
6/10	日菜、誕生日　5歳　ムクノキ根上げる　調子悪い
6/12	とりんこと日菜、タケウチさんとパン作り
6/28	北庭に枕木ひく
7/9	ひりんこゴスペル発表会　なかなか歌詞覚えられず
7/14-22	とりんこイギリス
8/4	そろそろ本格的に「TRUCK NEST」ページ打ち合わせ
8/15-16	タケウチ家とタケウチさんとキャンプ場で粉からパン作り！　恐るべし
9/13～	「TRUCK NEST」日記記録まとめ
9/19	DDM料理教室#3
10/1～	「TRUCK NEST」追加撮影、膨大な数の写真整理
10/9	日菜、運動会
10/29-11/8	日菜連れてイギリス　椅子の工場、ニック・アシュレイの家
11/9	去年と違うジョウビタキ（メス）庭に来る　2代目ジョンビー
11/14	この頃、とりんこ、夜の庭での"焚き火BAR"がお気に入り
11/16	ジョン、Bird入り口ドアに座る
11/16～	「TRUCK NEST」プリント写真、ネガ整理
12/3	ひりんこゴスペル発表会
12/22	TRUCK、Bird　お楽しみ会　みんなで大盛り上がり
	黄瀬家発表曲「カントリー・ロード」「根無し草ラプソディー」
	「TRUCK NEST」表紙デザイン決定！
2012 1/4	日菜、自転車乗れるようになる　もちろんコマなし　とりんこカスタマイズの自転車
1/17	「TRUCK NEST」文章キーワードまとめ
1/24	ケンタロウに「TRUCK NEST」の文章は自分たちで書いたほうがいいと熱望される
1/31	とりんこ、クリームにかぶれて顔になる　それ以降少し伸ばす　意外に好評
2/4	ケンタロウ、タケウチさんの自家製バンズとパティでハンバーガー作り　うまい！
2/16～	「TRUCK NEST」文章を自分たちで書くことにする！　けんちゃん、書くで
3/20	とりんこピアノ発表会
4/6	「TRUCK NEST」発売日！　のはずだった
4/9	植栽　TRUCK入り口トネリコ、ローズマリー
4/9	植栽　TRUCK入り口トネリコ、Birdローズマリー
5/9～	「TRUCK NEST」入稿開始　あと、もうひとがんばり！
6/10	日菜、誕生日　6歳

Thanks

この本を作る話が出てからすでに2年以上の時間が経った。
自分たちが納得できるまで諦めないで作っていくのは慣れっこなことだけど、それに根気よくつき合ってくれたミランダの野口さん。本当にありがとう。
「野口さんがいなかったら今のTRUCKはない」と、いつもひりんこと話しています。素人の僕たちが撮った写真を見せた時や、時には僕が庭で作ったハンバーガーにでも、いつも最高のリアクションで受け止めてもらえて嬉しいです。

いつも思ったら即行動、止まったら死ぬ、せからしい僕につき合ってくれる、いつも潔い判断のひりんこ。ちょうどこれを書いている今日はひりんこの誕生日。
ブルーハーツの歌詞をちょっと変えていつも思っていること。
"世界中にさだめられたどんな記念日なんかより あなたが生まれた今日はどんなにすばらしいだろう"
おめでとう！ そしてありがとう!!

Birdのことはもちろん、この本の文章を最後まで「とりんこが書いたのを読みたい。自分で書きや。書くべきやで」と言ってくれたケンタロウ。ほんまにありがとう。自分たちで書いて良かった。これからも一緒にやいのやいの言い合える仲でいたい。僕たちと出会ってからすっかり大阪弁もネイティブになった。もう1回、ありがとう。

いつも突然の投げかけをバシッとキャッチしてくれるタケウチさん。もの作りの探究心の深さ、尊敬しています。ありがとう。

日菜が赤ちゃんの時からベビーシッターとして、たくさんのワンニャンたちのペットシッターとして、それぞれから大人気のやーちゃん。大変な時に日菜を預かってもらって長い時間おままごとにつき合ってくれるひりんこのママとパパ。ありがとう。

BirdにシロクマA、スタッフルームに工場の間仕切り…書き出したらきりがないくらい、何度も"前向きなやり直し"につき合ってくれたタカシタ君。いつもいろんな相談に乗ってもらう、それを優しく受け止めてもらえる、もの作りの大先輩マスザワさん。カッコいい2人。ありがとう！

好き勝手の連続を大きく受け止めて、最後まで、この本が形になるまで導いて下さった、集英社の田中恵さん。ありがとうございました！

翻訳をしてくれたSimon。ただ英語にするだけでなく、いろんな表現を模索してくれた。長い時間向き合って言葉を探してくれた。ありがとう。

ずっと野口さんと一緒に頑張ってくれたイノッチ、デザイナーとしてだけでなく誰よりも文字校が素晴らしかった。ありがとう。

男前揃いの自慢のスタッフ。TRUCKとBirdのみんな、いつもありがとう！

ここに書けてない多くの人々、たくさんの業者さん、職人さん。誰1人欠けてもできなかったと思う。ありがとう。

好き放題やってる末っ子を黙って見てくれている僕のおとんとおかん。おとんからは勉強好きを、おかんからは明るさと馬鹿笑いを受け継いでると思う。ありがとう。

TRUCKができる前から黄瀬家にやって来て、14年と5ヶ月TRUCKを見守り続けてくれたバディ。こうして書いていても、まだ1年そこそこでは思い出として整理がついてないから泣けてくるし鼻もたれる喉の奥が詰まりそうになるけど、頑張って書いておく。バディは最高やった。かっこよかった。ありがとう。

今日も、ニャンたちがそれぞれの場所で気持ちよさそうに日向ぼっこしてる家の2階の部屋、キース・ジャレットの「The Melody At Night, With You」を絞ったボリュームで流し、これを書いてきた。気がつけば長く語ってきたけど、そろそろこの辺で終わりにしようと思う。

いろんなことを書いたけど、どこかでブッと笑ってもらえたなら、それだけで僕たちは大満足です。最後まで読んでもらってありがとう!!

This book has been two years in the making. I am extremely grateful to Ms. Noguchi from miranda. Hiromi and I often say that without Ms. Noguchi there would be no TRUCK. Her wonderful reactions to the pictures we amateurs have taken and even to the hamburgers we make in the garden always give us pleasure.

Thank you Hiromi for being with me and putting up with my restless, nonstop action. Today is her birthday.
To slightly change the lyrics to a song by The Blue Hearts:

"In all the world, could any day match
the day that you were born?"

Congratulations, and thank you.

To Kentaro, for Bird, of course, and for telling me from the start that I should be the one to write this book. Thank you. It was good that we wrote it ourselves. I hope we'll forever be able to talk as friends about even trivial things. Since meeting us, you've come to speak Osaka dialect like a native. Again, thank you.

To Takeuchi, who was always there to catch a ball when I suddenly threw it. We really respect your spirit of enquiry. Thank you.

To Yasuko, who has been a babysitter to Hina since she was a baby, and a sitter to our numerous cats and dogs and is loved by them all. And to Hiromi's mother and father who often looked after Hina. Thank you.

To Takashita, who helped us make Bird and Shirokumasha, the staff room and the workshop and who always looks forward. And to Masuzawa who has always been there to give me advice, who often listened to and guided me. You are two cool people. Thank you.

To Ms. Tanaka from Shueisha who has put up with and accepted my neverending demands and helped us guide this book to completion. Thank you.

To Simon, who did the English translation and spent a long time helping search for the right words and expressions. Thank you.

To Mr. Inoue, who worked with Ms. Noguchi on this book's design. He was not just a designer, he also did a splendid job proofreading. Thank you.

To the excellent staff of Bird and TRUCK. Thank you always.

To the many craftsmen and workers I've dealt with over the years, so many that I cannot write. Thank you.

Thank you to my mother and father, who remained supportive as their youngest child did as he pleased. From my father I got my studiousness. From my mother her brightness and big laugh.

Thank you to Buddy. My dog who watched over me and my family over 14 years as we built TRUCK. It's been a year since he passed away and even as I write this I'm beginning to choke up at his memory. He was the best.

Writing this I am in the cats' room on the second floor. They lounge around me, stretching out in patches of sun. Keith Jarett's *The Melody At Night, With You* is playing softly. This story is getting long. I should set about finishing up.

I wrote about many different things. I hope that there are some places that made you laugh. That by itself would satisfy me. To the readers who made it to the end, thank you.

TRUCK NEST

2012年8月15日　第1刷発行
2023年7月17日　第5刷発行

著者　　　TRUCK

発行人　　萱島　治子
発行所　　株式会社　集英社
　　　　　〒101-8050　東京都千代田区一ツ橋2の5の10
電話　　　(編集部) 03 3230 6250
　　　　　(販売部) 03 3230 6393 (書店専用)
　　　　　(読者係) 03 3230 6080
印刷・製本　凸版印刷株式会社

造本には十分注意しておりますが、印刷・製本など製造上の不備が
ありましたら、お手数ですが小社「読者係」までご連絡ください。
古書店、フリマアプリ、オークションサイト等で入手されたものは
対応いたしかねますのでご了承ください。
なお、本書の一部あるいは全部を無断で複写・複製することは、
法律で認められた場合を除き、著作権の侵害となります。
また、業者など、読者本人以外による本書のデジタル化は、
いかなる場合でも一切認められませんのでご注意ください。

©2012 TRUCK　Printed in Japan　ISBN 978-4-08-333123-7　C0076
©1988 by GINGHAM MUSIC PUBLISHERS INC. JASRAC 出 1207547-203

TRUCK

535-0022 6-8-48 SHINMORI ASAHI, OSAKA JAPAN
+81 (0)6 6958 7055
WWW.TRUCK-FURNITURE.CO.JP

Bird

538-0054 4-1-16 MIDORI TSURUMI, OSAKA JAPAN
+81 (0)6 6958 1616
WWW.BIRD-COFFEE.COM

Copyright © 2012 by TRUCK — Printed in Japan
ISBN 978-4-08-333123-7